# LIBERALISM

# IN CONTEMPORARY AMERICA

DWIGHT D. MURPHEY

*Foreword by*
Otto Scott, Author and Lecturer

*Preface to the 1992 edition by*
Frank O'Connell, Distinguished Member,
The Philadelphia Society

**Council for Social & Economic Studies**
McLean, Virginia

Copyright 1987, 1992 by Dwight D. Murphey

All rights reserved. No part of this book may be reproduced or transmitted in any form or by any means, electronic or mechanical, including photocopying, recording, or by any information storage and retrieval system, without permission in writing from the Publisher.

Council for Social and Economic Studies
6861 Elm Street, Suite 4-H
McLean, Virginia   22101
Tel: (703) 442-8010 Fax: (703) 847-9524

Printed in the United States of America

printing number
1  2  3  4  5  6  7  8  9  10

**Library of Congress Cataloging-in-Publication Data**

Murphey, Dwight D.
    Liberalism in contemporary America / Dwight D. Murphey ; foreword by Otto Scott ; preface to the 1992 edition by Frank O'Connell.
        p.   cm.
    Rev. ed. of: Liberal thought in modern America. c1987
    Includes bibliographical references and index.
    ISBN 0-930690-50-8 : $30.00
    1. Liberalism--United States--History.  I. Murphey, Dwight D. Liberal thought in modern America. II. Title.
JA84.U5M87    1992                                                                92-12389
320.5 ' 1 ' 0973--dc20                                                            CIP

# Acknowledgments

Although I was comfortably settled in a family and university setting, I worked alone during the several years that I spent on my "Understanding the Modern Predicament" series (of which this is the fourth and final volume). I was separated from extreme isolation only by the conviction that my ideas would eventually join the "dialogue over the ages" that links thoughtful writers of all generations. It is because of this that I was especially gratified when two distinguished conservative scholars – Arthur Shenfield and Otto Scott – indicated their readiness to write prefaces for the final two volumes in the series. My thanks accordingly go to the late Arthur Shenfield for his fine contribution to *Socialist Thought* and to Otto Scott for his very generous remarks here. I especially appreciate the tolerance with which he has voiced his reservations about my religious perspective. He is right, I think, in saying that my work has value even to those who feel themselves a cosmos apart from me on religion.

And now, Frank O'Connell has added a sparkling "Preface to the 1992 Edition." It is a delight to have Frank, a fine scholar and a long-time friend, lend his support to this endeavor.

During the five years since the series was finished, I have had time to become more active nationally among conservative scholars. The Philadelphia Society and University Professors for Academic Order (UPAO) have been sources of much intellectual fraternity. An especially rewarding association has been with Dr. Roger Pearson, a former president of UPAO, whose *Conservative Review* and *Journal of Social, Political and Economic Studies* have carried several of my articles. The four volumes of the series were initially published in limited editions by the University Press of America. Dr. Pearson has now caused The Council for Social & Economic Studies to publish this revised, updated version of the final volume, originally titled *Liberal Thought in Modern America*.

As I prepared the notes that underlie this book, I received many hours of help from a sparkling young man of remarkable energy, ability and potential – Dan Walker, my graduate assistant during the 1984-5 academic year. More recently, Greg Beaudoin, Roger Pearson's very capable assistant, has given invaluable and always cheerful help in getting the manuscript ready for this edition.

My thanks go to each of these friends for the wonderful assistance he has given.

# CONTENTS

Foreword: Otto Scott .................................... vi
Preface to the 1992 Edition
    Frank O'Connell ..................................... ix
A Note to the Reader .................................... xii

An Overview:

Chapter 1: Interpretive Essay ............................. 1
Chapter 2: Phases in American Liberalism: 1800-1920 ..... 28
Chapter 3: Phases in American Liberalism: 1920-1953 ..... 45
Chapter 4: Phases in American Liberalism: 1953-1985 ..... 74

Selected Topics:

Chapter 5: The New Republic and The Nation ............. 101
Chapter 6: Dissimulation ............................... 112
Chapter 7: Liberalism and American Culture ............. 119
Chapter 8: Emphasis on Social Change ................... 129
Chapter 9: Legal Philosophy ............................ 146
Chapter 10: Liberalism and the Modern Corporation ...... 164
Chapter 11: The Process of Politicization .............. 178
Chapter 12: The New Left I ............................. 196
Chapter 13: The New Left II ............................ 208
Chapter 14: The New Left III ........................... 227
Chapter 15: Liberalism and International Affairs ....... 238
Chapter 16: Liberalism and a World in Revolution ....... 256
Chapter 17: Liberalism and Anti-Communism .............. 281
Chapter 18: Multiculturalism: Liberalism's Latest
                and Most Threatening Assault ........... 299
Index .................................................. 302

## FOREWORD

This is the final book in a quartet that began with a historical examination of what Dwight Murphey terms man's immaturity – an immaturity that leads him into discontent no matter what his circumstances or position.

The first volume of the quartet takes us through a marvelous sweep of the centuries, and constitutes an overview of the past, concluding with the present. It ends, unforgettably, with an objective description of our society, which has lost the allegiance of our intellectuals, who no longer defend us against totalitarianism.

This is a strong message; almost too strong for a single volume. Therefore Dr. Murphey wisely decided to examine, in depth, the major social and political philosophies that constitute contemporary, contradictory trends. These examinations occupy the remainder of the quartet.

In the course of this great undertaking, Dr. Murphey has persistently quoted from the writings of those he has examined. He has not followed the usual academic fashion of subsuming, or paraphrasing these views into his text and relegating their spokesmen to footnotes or to appendices. He has attached names to views. He has avoided the abstract and stuck to the particular as much as is possible in discussing ideas.

Dr. Murphey has followed this course in examining Socialism, Burkean Conservatism, Classical Liberalism and Modern Liberalism. He has not only traced the development of these philosophies, but their impact on the world through his particulars regarding their spokesmen and leaders.

This is an important approach, though persons caught in the passageways of political structures may not fully appreciate it, because ideas are what rule the world. Men move along the rails of their ideas, however random their movements may appear.

To understand movements, therefore, we must understand ideas. But at the same time, we cannot divorce ideas from the men they motivate. In *Liberalism in Contemporary America*, Dr. Murphey has identified the modern liberal intellectual community as promoting diverse and even contradictory programs in order to create influential power blocs.

In order to accomplish this, Dr. Murphey provides a mountain of evidence indicating that modern liberal leaders have sedulously avoided terming themselves Socialists, failed to create a Socialist Party as such,

## Foreword

but chose instead to conceal their Socialism under the protective coloration of the liberal label. In comparing Socialist programs and principles with those advanced, defended or protected by modern liberals, Dr. Murphey has proven that the difference is almost entirely semantic.

On at least two occasions, Dr. Murphey believes, the American liberal community "has come very close to embracing totalitarian societies. These were," he says, "the early 1930s and the late 1960s...."

There was nothing in the least "liberal" about these slips, any more than there is any evidence of classical liberalism in the modern liberal tendency to shout down opposition, to engage in *ad hominem* methods of argument, or to engage in blacklisting and censorship: all tactics regularly employed by self-styled liberal cadres.

In uncovering the disguises of modern American liberalism, therefore, Dr. Murphey has made a major contribution. He has clarified, in the most scholarly manner, person after person and a stream of events that reveal a consistent pattern of dissimulation.

In the course of this searching examination, such figures as Herbert Croly, Theodore Roosevelt, Christopher Jencks, John Rawls, Robert Heilbroner, Robert Lekachman, Irving Howe and others appear in a new – and not a notably admirable – light.

For dissemblers should not be honored in any society. What Dr. Murphey has done has stripped the masks from many influential dissemblers.

In undertaking this task he has, as we all know, placed himself in a position of peril. It is a notorious fact of American life that anyone who takes issue with our liberal intellectuals can expect to encounter withering silence and private efforts to damage his career, or a torrent of abuse and public efforts to destroy his career.

In such a climate, it requires considerable moral courage to step forward even once. To do so in a major work that spans four volumes is extraordinary. I am proud to contribute a Foreword to such an eminent analysis, although I do not agree with all of Dr. Murphey's positions.

Not too long ago Dr. Robert Nisbet observed that he knew of no society that survived secularization. I tend to agree with that. I believe that the West, by breaking with its Christian heritage, at least on the top reaches of government, by that break began a terrible decline. Its dynamism began to ebb with its spiritual certainty.

Dr. Murphey sees this in part, and has made some very pertinent observations about the loss of a religion for which men are willing to die. On the other hand, we are witnesses to the fact that men will die even for religious substitutes, such as National Socialism, or Communism. Therefore this aspect of our situation may require more thought, more examination, more study.

But no such thought, examination or study will, or in my opinion can, negate or diminish what Dr. Murphey has produced. His analysis of immaturity and alienation carries the observations of Ortega y Gasset, whom he credits with his original inspiration, several steps beyond *The Revolt of the Masses*.

These are steps that needed to be taken; an examination long overdue. All credit, then, to the scholar who has undertaken that task, and published his results.

*Otto Scott, Murphys, California, 15 August 1986*

*Preface*

## PREFACE TO 1992 EDITION

This *ought* to be a book that, in the trite phrase of the toastmaster, "needs no introduction." It *ought* to be familiar to all conservatives – indeed, to all thinking people of whatever political philosophy who are concerned about the state of our civilization as the 20th century speeds to its close. That it is not, is simply one more symptom of the smothering hegemony that characterizes what the author dubs "twentieth century American Liberalism," that label being intended to distinguish that mushy amalgam of trendy Left thinking from *real* (that is, Classical) Liberalism.

Those who lay claim, as do the author and this writer, to the noble title of Classical Liberal need to know this book, because it will tell them all they need to know about why their cause has not prospered, and, perhaps more importantly, what ideas *have* prospered in their stead – and why and how.

This republication (with new material added) of Dwight Murphey's superb historical analysis of American Liberalism comes at a critical juncture, for Classical Liberalism finds itself challenged by two major tasks: (1) The intellectual rehabilitation and education of formerly Communist-dominated peoples, hungry for freedom and eager to erect its institutions, and (2) the need to recapture our own culture and its institutions from the ever more totalitarian grasp of American Liberalism. While Professor Murphey's work undoubtedly will be enormously valuable in the first of those tasks, it will be absolutely indispensable to the second – the recapture of our culture and the repair of the damage done to it from the Left – both the "New Left," born in the '60s (our own version of the Chinese Cultural Revolution) and the "Old Left," whose cultural subversions, Professor Murphey shows us, have been going on for more than a century, beginning with the alienation of American intellectuals early in the nineteenth century.

Professor Murphey's work exhaustively documents the rake's progress by which the Leftwing philosophy fraudulently calling itself "liberal" gradually displaced the Classical Liberalism which was America's birthright. In the course of doing so, he is careful to point out that American liberalism is by no means an evolutionary development or outgrowth of Classical Liberalism (as too many are inclined to accept), but rather a kind of apostasy, totally hostile in every significant respect to the principles of true Liberalism and dedicated, from the outset, to replacing them with the principles of socialism, syndicalism, collectivism, and so on – whatever, from time to time, has constituted the intellectual baggage of what Professor Murphey calls "the World Left." Thus was the way prepared for the New Deal and, in due course, for the so-called "countercultural revolution" of the '60s and '70s.

The emphasis during that era on – indeed, the apotheosizing of – "the young" (those whom Midge Decter so accurately portrayed in "Liberal Parents, Radical Children") takes on an added significance in the light of Professor Murphey's sparkling insights (the book is full of them): We are not, he argues, the advanced civilization we thought we were. In point of fact, mankind is still "immature" and only "partly civilized." Shock gives way to hope as the reader realizes that, if that is true – if we and our institutions are in what he calls a state of "cosmic infancy" – then our flaws and shortcomings ought to be correctable as the flaws and shortcomings of children are correctable. This is not to say that errant children cannot cause grave damage, as the children of the '60s surely did when they ravaged the American cultural fabric. But American Liberalism had been weakening that fabric for decades, as Professor Murphey notes, in a characteristically pungent passage. Speaking of the impact of the '60s on conservatives, he says: "They came to see how tenuous was the hold that the American people of the mid-twentieth century, shallowly rooted and lacking in an intellectual culture appropriate to a free society, had upon fundamental values."

The task and the challenge, then, are to restore to our nation the "intellectual culture appropriate to a free society." Given the staggering array of pulpits commanded by those whom Paul Johnson calls "the enemies of society," Classical Liberals surely have their work cut out for them. That the task of exposing and discrediting those enemies will be less daunting now, we owe to Professor Murphey and his monumental work. He analyzes for us who the intellectual foe of freedom is, where he came from, how he thinks and operates – indispensable intelligence in any combat. The rest is up to us. What is needed now is the resolve!

It would be remiss to end this note without reference to one special illustration of the conspicuous gallantry with which Professor Murphey carried out his mission: In addition to his other research – massive enough – he read every issue (almost 200 volumes) of *The New Republic*, as well as 100 volumes of *The Nation*. That he is able to write coherently at all after exposing himself to stupefaction on so vast a scale speaks volumes for his dedication, as well as his talent!

*Frank O'Connell, Grass Valley, California, September 1991*

# A NOTE TO THE READER

This book concludes a project that I began in 1965. When I started I certainly didn't anticipate that the subject would carry me into four volumes – of which this is the last.

The first volume was *Understanding the Modern Predicament*. Its beginning chapter discussed the nature of what I have called "the modern predicament" and pointed to three factors that I went on to examine in detail.

The first of these had to do with the remarkably insightful analysis made in *The Revolt of the Masses* by the Spanish philosopher Jose Ortega y Gasset. I wanted to extend his analysis and at the same time reflect an uneasiness that I felt about it. Ortega had observed that in advanced civilization the average person has come to occupy all spaces, displacing the earlier aristocracies. Even though he acknowledged that people live at a higher level than ever before, he noted that the spiritual characteristics of this average humanity are mediocre. My own experience has, it seems to me, confirmed Ortega's thesis. The mediocrity profoundly affects both our daily lives and the larger events of our society. Just the same, I felt uneasy. In historical perspective, it was necessary to see this mediocrity not as a decline from a more perfected earlier condition, but as a result of mankind's having come only part of the way on the journey from barbarism. A review of the earlier periods of Western civilization in Greece, Rome and the Middle Ages would show that periods of advanced and humane civilization have been relatively brief. Mankind is in its infancy. The first third of *Understanding the Modern Predicament* was devoted, then, to a review of this immaturity.

This review of history back to the Greeks had an additional advantage: it showed how existentially open-ended the modern age has been. Modern Western society has been heir to a rich heritage – but few, if any, satisfactory solutions. Because of this, it is hardly surprising that modern man has cast about in a crisis of consensus.

The second factor in what I called the "modern predicament" was one of the most striking elements in modern intellectual history: the alienation of the intellectuals, as a subculture, from the predominant "bourgeois" culture. No other fact has been so central to the divisions and neuroses of the modern age. It is impossible to understand the past two centuries without giving full weight to the role of the alienation of the intellectual. This alienation was analyzed in the middle third of *Understanding the Modern Predicament*.

The final third of that book extended the discussion of those first two factors by exploring several episodes of modern history – topics such as the French Revolution, nineteenth century Russian nihilism and the origins of the First World War – in light of both the immaturity and the alienation.

This first book could, of course, only point ahead to the third factor within the modern predicament, which is that the divisions within the modern West have given rise to opposing "systems of interpretation," comprehensive ideologies by which people have understood complex social reality. These ideas have for almost two centuries served as the atmosphere in which we have lived, guiding our understanding of ourselves and of the world. An analysis of each of these ideologies in turn has occasioned the final three volumes.

Despite each ideology's conviction to the contrary, such mental systems are not themselves Truth, directly understood. They are devices that people develop to mediate social reality. The systems are profoundly affected by forces at work in the society; and they are also powerful causal instruments in their own right. People act in the world as they perceive it. This means that their perceptions and those of others are part of the social reality, intermeshed with all other factors.

The second volume discussed two of these interpretive systems: Burkean conservatism and classical liberalism. The third examined socialist thought, and this final volume explores the liberal-Left within the United States. It also discusses the New Left, the ideological variation that emerged in the late 1950's and existed with explosive force in the '60's before withering in the '70's. Residuals of the New Left still strongly affect American life.

At the beginning of each book I have mentioned that the reader can with relatively little difficulty understand the book by itself without studying the others. Needless to say, though, a deeper understanding will be achieved by studying the series as a whole. It is the tension of the ideologies in a setting framed by the immaturity and the alienation that makes a deeper understanding possible.

All four volumes were published in limited editions in the mid-'80's by the University Press of America. I am grateful to Scott-Townsend Publishers for this updated 1992 edition of the final volume. It is my hope, of course, that all volumes will eventually become generally available.

# CHAPTER ONE
# Interpretive Essay

**Use of the term "liberal"**

American conservatives have often objected to the way the word "liberal" has been used in the twentieth century. Those who are today called conservatives have placed quotation marks around "liberal" to indicate their belief that the word has in effect been misappropriated from the liberalism of the nineteenth century, which supported a very different set of values.

Even though I agree with these concerns, since I am a "conservative" myself by holding basically to the tenets of nineteenth century "classical liberalism," I will choose not to use the quotation marks. They would detract from the objective spirit that is important in a book that hopes to make a serious discussion of one of the competing social philosophies.

My agreement with the point that my fellow conservatives make stems from my assessment of the differences between liberalism in its classical sense and the ideology that in twentieth century America has been known as liberalism. As this essay will make apparent, I do not hold to the view that contemporary liberalism arose out of classical liberalism and merely added new dimensions to it. Rather, I see the two as having been enemies from the beginning. The new liberalism was instantly an adversary of the old.

Classical liberalism has been the philosophy of limited government and a free market, has championed middle-class values, and has been adamantly anti-socialist and anti-Communist. Its intellectual content comes largely from the writings of the classical and neo-classical economists, such thinkers as Adam Smith, Frederic Bastiat, Ludwig von Mises and Friedrich Hayek. This sort of liberalism is today a part of what Americans call conservatism, which includes classical liberals, Burkean conservatives, and millions of people who identify with capitalism and traditional American values without perhaps having a distinctly formulated philosophical rationale. (This is the sense in which I will use the word "conservative" unless I explain a temporary deviation from it.)

The body of thought that during my lifetime has been called liberal, however, has been a mixture of diverse tendencies. Perhaps more than anything else, however, it has represented the thinking of the world Left to the extent that American intellectuals who have wanted to stay on speaking terms with the American mainstream have been able to embrace it. It has been the American socialism that has not seen its way clear to call itself socialist.

Most of the time its thinking has coincided with democratic socialists'. At one point this led me to consider defining it as "'social democracy' applied in a politic way to the American context." But on at least two occasions America's liberal-Left has revealed a darker side: in the early 1930's and the late 1960's its thinking has embraced, or has come very close to embracing, totalitarian socialism. This necessarily gives us second thoughts about how precisely to classify it. At other times it has amounted to little more than the watered-down welfare statism and social-market thinking that has been forced upon European socialism by the failures (which many on the Left perceived so acutely several years before the collapse of Communism in Eastern Europe) of the various attempts at socialism.

Readers will understand, then, why I agree with conservatives that the word "liberal," which is the same word that was applied in the nineteenth century to advocates of the free market, is suspect in its twentieth century usage. It is a label taken from one philosophy and applied to another that is fundamentally antagonistic to it. Nevertheless, I shall use it in its currently accepted sense, although frequently adding the adjective "modern" to call to mind the difference from classical liberalism. In this 1991 edition I have also begun to refer to it as "the liberal-Left," which I think is a helpful characterization.

### Relationship to Socialism

It is necessary for me to ask modern liberal readers to hear me out. I realize that what I have just said about the socialist content of this liberalism is anathema to them. While modern liberals have often admitted the relationship to socialism in the writing they have addressed to each other, it has been usual for this liberalism to obscure the connection so far as the American public is concerned. One of the defining characteristics of a liberal in this sense, as distinguished from those on the Left who have declared themselves socialists *per se*, has been that he has been sensitive to the fact that most Americans have not been willing to accept anything directly labelled "socialist."

What I have just said is also anathema to members of the far Left, who in their own frame of reference see this accommodationist-style state activism in either of three ways: as too much of a cop-out to merit the socialist label; as a reformism that runs counter to the things-must-get-worse-before-they-can-get-better school of revolutionary thinking; or as a shoring-up of capitalism by those members of the bourgeoisie who are, from the far Left's point of view, smart enough to see that cooptation is the best defense against a full on-rush of socialism. From the purity of their own position, they are not prepared to acknowledge how much socialist thinking really exists in modern liberal thought.

When I suggest that modern American liberalism has been a product of the socialist worldview, I realize that this is true only in major part. I do not wish to obscure the other dimensions of modern liberalism. A more complete definition will have to reflect the ideology's relation to the main culture, which it has both detested and sought to exist within and to lead. Several factors that are *not* themselves socialist will be considered in the final part of this essay. Some that we should now note at least briefly are:

- That there has at all times, even in the absence of socialist influence, been a movement within American history that has wanted a more active federal government. Much of what we think of as liberal measures would have come about, perhaps in a somewhat more market-oriented form, even if no socialist movement had developed in Europe.
- That a number of longterm tendencies within American life, which have themselves had nothing to do with socialist ideas, have created a demand for a more politicized and centralized life. Local loyalties, once quite strong, have, for example, given way in most people's thinking to a national identification because of mobility and communication.
- That classical liberal thinking, under pressure since the early nineteenth century to defend the main society from unremitting attack, lost its critical and reformist posture. This has long made it deficient in its formulation of the theory of a market economy and, more broadly, of a free society. This weakness has included ignoring the problem of imperfect markets and giving too little attention to the institutional framework that a well-functioning market requires. Some of the concerns voiced by modern liberalism have spoken to issues that a more complete classical liberalism would have addressed.
- That most of the measures that are labelled "liberal" are only a shadow of what liberal thought has called for. They are more the product of interest-group pressures and of the efforts of liberal politicians. (Virtually none of the politicians ever admit to a socialist rationale and, for that reason, almost all of them have been attacked as unworthy by liberal intellectuals.) These interest groups and politicians act within the concrete reality of the American political scene, although they are clearly

influenced by liberal ideology.

Modern liberalism has accordingly been a mixture that has existed, often in varying forms, within a specific and changing historical setting. I doubt whether any ideology (except perhaps Mussolini's) has ever been rooted more relativistically in its own time and place. Few ideologies have been less candid about their aspirations or quite so opportunistic in their quest for approval by blocs that often have not fully sensed or shared those aspirations. Because of this, it would be a mistake to say that everyone who has called himself a modern liberal has been either consciously or subconsciously a socialist. Many no doubt have been socialists; but others have come to the ideology by routes that have had little to do with a socialist worldview. This acknowledges a fact that will become important later when we try to explain the fragmentation and loss of elan that have plagued modern liberalism since the beginning and especially since World War II.

It is worth considering whether I have not overstressed the role of socialist thinking by ignoring the possibility that modern liberalism is a "middle way" between capitalism and socialism, influenced by both, but actually amounting to a separate form.

Such a view seems plausible and has been seriously asserted. But it is contradicted by the facts of liberal history. We need to distinguish between liberal *thought* and the popular version of liberalism that has been preoccupied with the agenda of specific measures that liberal politicians have kept before the country at any given time. The halfway measures that have composed the agenda have made it difficult for conservatives to convince others that there is a socialist content to the liberal program. It has only been in the intellectual dimension that the socialist content has appeared consistently and clearly.

We will review the extent of the liberal intellectual identification with socialist models. This identification includes the enthusiasm for worker-controlled "industrial democracy" during and immediately after World War I; the infatuation with Soviet Russia's centralized planning during the 1920's, '30's and '40's; the great number of openly socialist authors within liberalism prior to World War II; and the fact that even since that war the main liberal thinkers have been men who, sometimes after the fact, have declared themselves socialists. I am thinking especially of Michael Harrington, Gunnar Myrdal, John Kenneth Galbraith, Christopher Jencks, Irving Howe and John Rawls, but secondarily of a great many others.

Liberal thought has never identified itself wholeheartedly with the "mixed society" model. The mixed society has been forced upon its intellectual community by circumstances.

### An historical review:
### The condition of conservatism and liberalism in early America

Later chapters will examine the detail about many of the points I am about to make, but it is important in an overview to understand these points in their historical development and in the relationship that they bear to one another.

The generation of the Founding Fathers in the late eighteenth century was influenced by both streams of social and political thought that struggled for supremacy in that era. One of these was the vibrant classical liberalism that championed the Enlightenment and that was finding expression in the writings of Adam Smith and Jeremy Bentham.

The other was Burkean conservatism. This conservatism gave philosophical form to the value-system of tradition, faith and hierarchy that held sway in various forms in Europe during the Middle Ages and even during the Roman Republic. In *The Conservative Mind*, Russell Kirk told of the extent to which that sort of conservative *ethos* informed early American thinking. Its influence was extensive. That is why it is a mistake to say, as Louis Hartz has, that the United States has been clearly liberal from the beginning. New England in particular, and eventually the South as it felt the pressure to defend slavery, kept a tie with this conservatism.

Nevertheless, the main spirit of the late eighteenth century was formed by the Enlightenment, which for quite a long time had been the onrushing opponent of that conservatism. Tolerant and deistic in religion, republican and constitutionalist in politics, free-market in its economic thinking under the influence of the Physiocrats and (when he became known) of Adam Smith, rationalist and increasingly empiricist in intellect, supportive of the individualism of the rising bourgeoisie, this spirit was liberal in the classical sense.

This liberal conception has formed an underlay that has constituted the American ideal for the two centuries that have followed. Despite the attack it has undergone from so many sides intellectually, this individualistic liberalism has been at the heart of the predominant commercial and middle class culture. The tremendous staying power and force of its view of the world is one of the main facts of American history. It has been against this underlay of ideas and aspirations that all other forces have had to contend, usually with considerable frustration.

Without diminishing that fact, it is important to appreciate that the intellectual foundations of this liberalism had only partly taken form in the eighteenth century. Even though its worldview had been developing for several centuries, it enjoyed no comprehensive philosophical statement. John Locke had expressed some of its elements, the Physiocrats others. Then in 1776 Adam Smith stated a rationale for the market system. He argued that a market system does in fact work. In this, he opposed the Mercantilists, who insisted it does not. The work of the later classical and neo-classical economists, however, remained to be done in the nineteenth and twentieth centuries. But even an economic rationale such as they supplied was not fully adequate, since there are spiritual, ethical, aesthetic, jurisprudential and other dimensions that a complete philosophical system must address.

One of the most damaging intellectual short-comings, at least as we look back on classical liberalism from the twentieth century, was that the eighteenth century's preoccupation with Natural Rights was intellectually related more to a deductive and somewhat fanciful rationalism than to empiricism. This means that it was not fully appropriate to the later development of the social sciences. To say this is not to blame the thinkers of the eighteenth century, but merely to point to something that explains why they have become increasingly irrelevant to modern intellectual culture.

Another problem was that this early liberalism lacked self-consciousness. Classical economics was coming into its own in Europe, but liberals seemed to feel no need to formulate a complete and systematic theory of society and to see it as an integrated philosophy. They were practical men dealing with the specific problems of their day. It is a shame that Franklin, Madison or Jefferson did not lay this sort of intellectual foundation in a form that future generations could look back to as a guiding text for the premises of a liberal society. (This is not surprising for a social system. The medieval value-system was not rationalized by the Burkean intellectual statement until it had existed for many centuries and was so heavily under attack that it was about to expire.)

This remained true even while classical economics did its immensely productive work in the nineteenth century. When classical economics got into full swing with Ricardo, Senior, Say, James Mill and the others, its thinkers did not see themselves as stating a complete theory of society that included a good many value preferences and the reasons for them, but as laying a foundation for a deductive science of economics, which in fact was a much more limited project. I will postpone commenting about John Stuart Mill, since he occupied the stage somewhat later and is important to the next phase of the history I am tracing.

Nor did classical liberalism occupy the stage alone even in its

# Liberalism in Contemporary America

unelaborated and un-self-conscious condition. In the late eighteenth century an articulate cadre of intellectuals rose to support hierarchy, faith, tradition and a hostile critique of the Industrial Revolution and of the rising individualism. Edmund Burke and Samuel Johnson come most immediately to mind. They supplied an intellectual defense of values that had long been implicit in medievalism.

### Revulsion against the Enlightenment

What happened next was one of the more significant occurrences to affect the intellectual development of the modern world. It occurred in Europe but was quickly reflected in the United States, which for most of its history has been an intellectual colony of Europe, as has most of the rest of the world.

I have in mind the revulsion against the Enlightenment that occurred when the French Revolution and the ensuing Napoleonic episode turned sour. The revulsion skewered the Enlightenment on the lance of the Romantic reaction. A major part of European thought turned sharply against rationalism, empiricism, tolerance, individualism, the bourgeoisie, and classical liberalism. In Germany this gave rise to the thinking of Novalis, Schlegel, Schleiermacher, de Maistre – and, mostly importantly, Hegel. In England, Carlyle, Coleridge, Arnold, Ruskin and Southey led a somewhat tamer version. These men nonetheless expressed an intense alienation from the burgeoning bourgeois culture.

This revulsion both manifested and stimulated the "alienation of the intellectual," a force that has been among the most powerful causal agents during the nineteenth and twentieth centuries.

Almost immediately Europe saw the rise of socialist ideology as intellectuals repudiated the bourgeoisie and commercial civilization and sought to gain numerical strength by an ideological alliance with whatever unassimilated and disaffected groups would form common cause with it at any given point in time. By the 1830's and 1840's, socialist thought was coming into its own in Europe.

Outwardly it has seemed that these years were the high point of classical liberalism, which in a sense they were; but there is enormous significance in the fact that the classical liberal economist Frederic Bastiat felt almost totally isolated in France, and hungered for contact with the Manchester School of Cobden and Bright in England for at least some intellectual kinship.

The ideological thrust of a still-incomplete classical liberalism began to fail as the intellectual culture moved sharply to the left. This is best illustrated in the life of John Stuart Mill, a leading classical economist who became disaffected with the commercial middle class's lack of attention to ideas, took an active interest in the conservative thinking of such a Romantic as Coleridge, and finally moved into the socialist camp.

The drying up of classical liberal intellectuality largely deprived American and European middle class culture of the head and heart that it has so vitally needed. The intellectuals who remained behind within classical liberalism during the ensuing century and three-quarters have done valiant work, but they have been far outnumbered and their tone has often been that of doctrinaire apologists rather than of original thinkers and reformers.

In the United States the victory of the Jeffersonians in the election of 1800 should have paved the way for a long period of classical liberal ascendancy. It did play a major role in establishing the "underlay" of classical liberal values that I have mentioned; and the Jeffersonian-Jacksonian liberalism did hold sway politically until 1861. But beginning in the early nineteenth century, its intellectual base was eroding. This was well before it had received a full philosophical exposition.

In his lecture "The New England Reformers" in 1844, Ralph Waldo Emerson looked back upon a quarter of a century of the strangest sort of intellectual dissatisfaction (in which he had shared). There had been "a fertility of projects for the salvation of the world," all expressing "the soul of the soldiery of dissent." At a time when most Americans were developing their reverence for the Constitution and when classical liberal concepts were guiding the majority political party, the literary culture, influenced profoundly by the thinking that was going on in Europe, declared the society sick.

If today we look back at that time with the expectation that a new republic, founded upon the ideals of the Enlightenment, would have been full of enthusiasm and hope, we are bound to be surprised. The intellectual tone was instead one of despair and alienation.

It was still too early for an ideological consensus to have formed around the alienation. Nor was there yet a homogeneous subculture of alienated intellectuality. During the years immediately preceding the Civil War, there were signs of a growing socialist critique, as became evident in the enthusiasm for Fourier that inspired a good many utopian communities; and yet it was taking at least a brief time for socialist philosophy to germinate in Europe and to bridge the Atlantic.

After the death of Jefferson in 1826, the divisions within American society between the North and the South over tariffs and slavery increasingly turned the South away from its earlier classical liberalism and into a defense, largely on Burkean-type grounds, of slavery.

### After the Civil War

The Civil War consolidated the power of the newly-formed Republican Party. This marked the end of the supremacy of the Democratic Party, with its Jeffersonian-Jacksonian commitment to the limitation of the powers of the national government. The Republican Party was heir to the tradition of the Federalists and the Whigs, who had favored a much more active national government.

Classical liberal insights that had once been common ceased to be mentioned in presidential messages to Congress, appearing again only briefly when in the late nineteenth century Grover Cleveland, a Democrat, vetoed aid to drought-stricken Texas farmers. For the most part, the main culture, absorbed in its own expansion and activity, went through a period of lessened philosophical reflection. After the Civil War, classical liberalism found expression mainly in the legal profession, where Constitutional thought was honed into and was seen as a deductive science based on classical liberal desiderata.

In the academic and literary communities, classical liberalism continued to lack a self-conscious ideology. William Graham Sumner was a leading figure, drawing deeply from Herbert Spencer's defense of classical liberalism in England. But the tide was turning. Indeed, there was no movement as such calling itself "liberal" and prepared to fight for even so much as retention of the name.

The decades following the Civil War saw the gradual coalescence of the American academic community into an ideologically homogeneous subculture. I say this advisedly, since anyone who has studied intellectual history knows how much real variety exists within any overall pattern. But there was a yearning for coalescence, as is evidenced by the letter that Henry Adams wrote to his brother Charles in 1862 expressing both alienation and a desire for "a national school of our own generation." And there was the continuing development of a socialist critique in place of the earlier "fertility of projects."

### Influence of the German Historical School

The development of an intellectual community with a common ideology was facilitated enormously by the migration of thousands of American graduate students to German universities, where they studied under the professors of the German Historical School. This migration was heaviest in the final quarter of the nineteenth century. The Historical School repudiated the "scientific pretensions" of classical economics and of the neo-classical Austrian School, and attacked the theoretical foundations of a market economy on relativistic grounds as being no more than an analysis of relationships within a transitory historical period of bourgeois ascendancy. Its opposition to classical economics was part of an overall animus toward a liberalism that was denounced as Philistine by so much of the European intellectual community.

The professors of the Historical School called themselves "socialists of the professorial chair" – *katheder Sozialisten*. They stood in close relationship to the Junker aristocracy as it installed Otto von Bismarck's program of social welfare legislation. There has been considerable debate over whether theirs was a true socialism as distinct from a conservative cooptation of socialism. This same ambiguity has continued with regard to American liberalism itself.

The ambiguity is perhaps best resolved by the life story of Werner Sombart, who in successive steps moved from being a leading member of the fourth generation of the Historical School to being a Marxist and then an enthusiastic follower of Hitler. The thread that tied all of these enthusiasms together was his alienation against the bourgeoisie and his detestation of classical liberalism. His writing contains some of the more lucid explanations of socialist ideas.

The Historical School did not itself adopt the Marxism that was struggling for ascendancy among German socialists. Thus it did not support revolution or class struggle. The fact that it did not is important to its impact on the Americans who studied under it. For the most part, these returned to America as gradualists, not revolutionaries.

Although it is not directly relevant to the ideological history I am relating, it is worthwhile to point out that the Historical School originated the empirical-statistical methodology, with its emphasis on monographs and the piling of fact upon fact often to the exclusion of theoretical connection among the facts, that has been so powerful a force within the American academic community throughout the twentieth century. This methodological sway has formed a powerful intellectual orthodoxy. When combined with the self-absorbed credentialism that it has insisted upon, it has constituted a modern Scholasticism within American university life. I consider myself a friend to an intelligent empiricism, but during my years as a professor I have been in constant revolt against the trivialization and pseudo-scientific pretension that this orthodoxy has worshipped. Needless to say, it carries within it not only its methodology but also a set of ideological suppositions that are far from scientifically neutral. What we know as the "social sciences" came into existence in their current form during this period and have to a very large extent reflected the Historical School.

What is important for us to grasp for the history of liberalism is that the experience with the Historical School represents the phase in which a common intellectual experience resulted in a shared ideology.

### Taking on a style of dissimulation

During this same period, those who came to call themselves "liberal" in the new sense were making a fateful personal decision. Intellectuals who felt the alienation and drank deeply at the well of the European socialist philosophies sometimes chose, at considerable social and professional risk, to declare themselves openly as socialists, and sometimes as revolutionaries. Jack London is a prime example, although he managed to be accepted as one of America's most popular authors. A socialist movement flourished during the opening years of the twentieth century.

But what typified the modern liberal as such, and has been his defining characteristic as distinct from these socialists, was his unwillingness to make so open a break with the main society. For this liberal there was a circumspection born out of a number of ingredients, which almost certainly included a less daring personal psychology and a sharper appreciation for both the individual and ideological benefits of not putting oneself too openly in jeopardy.

The individual who best exemplified the circumspection was Herbert Croly, the leading founder of *The New Republic*. Croly's book *The Promise of American Life* (1909) is one of the monuments of American liberalism. This is so not so much for its content as for the fact that it is a masterpiece of dissimulation. He spoke of the book as "socialistic," but nowhere in it was there a direct endorsement of socialism. Croly continued this circumspection in *Progressive Democracy* (1915) even though its content was in line with the "industrial democracy" that was then so much in vogue among British socialists.

In late 1914 Croly was the leader among the group that founded *The New Republic*. Even though the other founders, Walter Weyl and Walter Lippmann, considered themselves socialists at the time, *The New Republic* was careful not to call itself socialist. This did not change until the early 1930's, when under the influence of the exuberant socialism of the time its editors were moved to throw caution to the winds.

### Liberal orientation in Teens and Twenties

This refusal to make a clear ideological commitment led into the phases that followed. During the late teens and early 1920's, liberal thought centered around "industrial democracy." This represented an infatuation with what was popular at the time among British socialists during the heyday of the Guild Socialist movement. The emphasis was on decentralization, which was consistent with the direction of much of nineteenth century socialist thought. Workers were ultimately to control industry from the bottom up. There was at the same time considerable enthusiasm for cooperatives – either of producers or consumers and, with some thinkers, of both types. The profit-seeking entrepreneur and individual consumer were to be replaced by a grass-roots collectivism.

This, of course, was one of the clearly socialist phases of modern liberal thought, even though *The New Republic* avoided the socialist label.

The decentralist approach of the Guild Socialist movement lost favor among liberal intellectuals in the early 1920's when it was overtaken by enthusiasm for the Bolshevik Revolution and for Soviet Russia's centralized model. The great light that seemed to shine during the 1920's was from Soviet Russia, which was portrayed in idealistic hues by the many liberals who made the pilgrimage.

Apparently, though, Soviet Russia's example was too removed from what seemed possible here to offer much real hope. Liberal thought slipped into a funk. The 1920's was the decade of the "Lost Generation" of literary expatriates and of a counter-culture of Beatnik-like alienates in Greenwich Village. Liberal thought lost focus on social and political issues. Politically, the Progressive movement made a final effort in the 1924 presidential election and then died out.

As editor of *The New Republic*, Herbert Croly continued to personify the liberal mood, this time by turning inward during the 1920's. The journal called upon liberals to devote themselves to inner self-examination. In contrast to the earlier period, its editors and writers saw little value in theorizing about how to reform the existing society, which they considered steeped in Mammon.

This illustrates an important dynamic that has been at work from the beginning as part of the psychology of the liberal-Left and of its associated radicalisms: a cycle passing from a period of despair, fatigue and withdrawal to one of yearning for activity and from that to one of marked militancy and social action, all followed eventually by another period of exhaustion and withdrawal. This alternation reflects the psychology of the alienated intellectual. In Emerson's lecture "The New England Reformers" he spoke of the withdrawal of the "man of tender conscience," followed by that man's reentry into the world with "a ferment of activity 'for the salvation of the world.'"

## The 1930's

After the Depression began in 1929 the mood changed again. The liberal-Left no long felt the dissimulation that had masked the socialist worldview necessary. Overt socialism and enthusiasm toward the "Soviet experiment" filled the liberal journals.

By March 1932 *The New Republic* went so far as to editorialize that "we are not liberals," and added that "the planning we have recommended is not designed to preserve the capitalist system." It will surprise American conservatives to know that liberal intellectuals had little enthusiasm for Franklin Delano Roosevelt during the 1932 campaign. In fact, *The New Republic* urged its readers to vote for Norman Thomas, the Socialist candidate. Under a committee of editors from 1933 to 1936, *The Nation*, the other major liberal journal, was avowedly socialist.

And yet the liberal intellectual community did manage, consistently with its long-standing preference for doing so, to keep at least one foot in the American political context. It warmed to Franklin Roosevelt during his first months in office. Those who favored the "New Nationalist" approach, which involved fashioning corporate capitalism into a wing of government, held out great hopes for the National Recovery Administration; but it wasn't long before the liberal-Left was turned off of the N.R.A.: it's industry-wide codes came to be seen as not reflecting liberal social policy so much as the interests of the corporations themselves.

*The Nation* expressed sympathy for the New Deal, but also was able to say in 1934 that the New Deal amounted to "a half-baked capitalism with so-called liberal trimmings."

The main fact about the intellectual history of the 1930's is that the liberal intellectual culture was far to the left of the New Deal, heavily preoccupied with the Soviet Union's 5-year plan and collectivization of agriculture. It necessarily defended the New Deal against attacks from the Right, but at the same time excoriated the administration bitterly. The New Deal was declared "sadly deficient" so far as a "thorough renovation of our society" was concerned.

This mood continued for *The New Republic* until September 1937. The Soviet Union had by that time stopped denouncing democratic socialists and liberals as "social fascists" and had called for a "United Front" against Hitler. The Communists lavished praise upon Roosevelt and the New Deal in direct opposition to their earlier denunciations. Whether consciously or unconsciously, the American liberal intellectual community, deeply absorbed in the color and texture of the Communist movement and its many front organizations, went along. In a sharp about-face, *The New Republic* praised the New Deal, saying that "we have made more progress toward a socialized economy in the past four and a half years than in the two previous decades."

It is ironic that the New Deal was finally accepted by the intellectual community just shortly before it began to lose whatever impetus Roosevelt's many inconsistencies had allowed it. *The New Republic* had supported F.D.R. in his "court packing plan" in 1937 while still essentially sour toward him, and backed him in 1938 in his effort to purge certain conservative Democratic senators. But this was all quite late, since Republican gains in the congressional elections in 1938 made possible the coalition of conservative Democrats and Republicans that long thereafter possessed a veto in Congress. (Only briefly after the election of 1964 did liberalism again enjoy the combination of a liberal Congress and a liberal president.) In addition, the late 1930's saw the on-rushing international crisis further deflect Roosevelt from domestic reform.

Events in the Soviet Union were at the same time providing major shocks to American liberalism's love affair with Communism.

The liberal intellectual community had been willing to accept the enormities of Soviet brutality so long as what was done was for "a good cause." It had turned a blind eye during Stalin's death-by-starvation holocaust against the kulaks in 1932-33. A variously estimated three to seven million peasants were deliberately starved to overcome their resistance to the collectivization of their land. Fifty years later, in December 1984, *The New Republic*'s editors looked back and admitted that "the scandal in the history of this journal is that in the '30's and '40's it accommodated to the *Zeitgeist* (with occasional and important dissents) by downplaying at best and justifying at worst the crimes of Stalinism."

This acceptance of Communist atrocities started to erode when in 1934 Stalin began his purges of the other leaders among the Bolsheviks – many of them people American liberals knew personally. One thing followed another over a six year span. The two main liberal journals vacillated between justifying the purges and pleading agnosticism about them, but liberals were beginning to see the horror, slowly at first and then in larger numbers, as one atrocity was laid on top of another.

The crowning blow, after years of the United Front against Nazism, was the Hitler-Stalin Pact in August 1939, especially when it was followed so quickly by the invasion of Poland, first by the Nazis and then by the Soviets. The Soviet Union received the larger share of Poland's territory and by the end of 1939 had invaded Finland. In 1940 it attacked Estonia, Latvia and Lithuania, absorbing them into the Soviet Union.

Nor was this all. Bitter divisions were spawned within America's liberal intellectual community by Stalin's purge of Leon Trotsky, second only to Lenin as a leader of the Bolshevik Revolution. Trotsky was sent into exile after Lenin's death and was later charged with crimes against the Soviet Union. The American liberal philosopher John Dewey headed the American subcommission of an international body that inquired, over the objections of the Stalinists, into the facts concerning Trotsky. This was all capped by Stalin's having Trotsky murdered in Mexico in 1940. Each step of the way, liberals (and radicals of all shades on the Left) chose sides, bitterly attacking those on the other.

In the midst of this fragmentation, a cause that seemed to unite them was the Spanish Civil War. Socialists, anarchists and Communists fought together against the forces of General Franco. But this turned out to be a mirage when the Communists became the totalitarian bully on the block, seeking control by executing the others. John Dos Passos left the fold, gravitating eventually into conservatism, after he lost a friend to Communist executioners.

There is reason to expect that these events would have seared an abiding hatred toward Communism into the thinking of American liberals. With some, they did. But the scene shifted again in June 1941 when Hitler broke his Pact with Stalin by invading the Soviet Union. With some exceptions, the mood shifted back to enthusiastic acceptance of the Soviet Union. And when the United States became an ally of the Soviet Union after the attack on Pearl Harbor in December 1941, the long-standing inclination of so many American liberals to favor the Soviet Union even became respectable and patriotic from the general American society's point of view.

It is important for us today to realize how much our perceptions are warped by the legacy of this bias. It continues to affect our view of the world. An example is that we hear so many reminders about the Nazi's Holocaust, which the world should never forget, but almost none about the Gulags of the Soviets or the mass executions under Mao.

### After World War II

After the war, the divisions that had come into being led to the formation of the Americans for Democratic Action (ADA) by liberals who did not want to collaborate with Communists. Those further to the left formed the Progressive Citizens of America (PCA) and in 1948 supported Henry Wallace in his third-party bid for the presidency.

An intensely alienated radicalism remained on the leftward fringe and laid the foundation for the later New Left and for the counter-culture of the 1960's and 1970's. Under the stimulus of the militancy of the civil rights, anti-poverty and anti-Vietnam War movements in the 1960's, much of American liberal intellectuality again flirted with the extremes of the Left and, as in the early 1930's, denounced liberalism *per se*. It is ironic that this undercutting of liberalism was one of the more important causes of the success of American conservatism in the 1980's.

Since World War II, the principal fact about American liberalism has been its loss of thrust toward a comprehensive socialist vision, despite most of its leading thinkers' considering themselves socialists. The coalition of conservative Democrats and Republicans in Congress, combined with the success of the Republican Party in electing a president much of the time, has made it seem remote and naive, as in the 1920's, to propose an overall program for the restructuring of American society. For the most part, liberal intellectuals have given up the attempt, although it would be a mistake to think that their attitudes have not been constantly at work in countless smaller ways within the bureaucracy, the media and academia.

Liberal presidents, when there has been one, have continued to offer the marginal, foot-in-the-door programs that have had to pass for liberal activism in the absence of a constituency for a thorough-going transformation of society. But even here they have mostly been stymied, as Truman was in his domestic program following the outbreak of the Korean War and as Kennedy and Carter were by the lack of a homogeneous and fully supportive liberal foundation. (We know how tenuous Carter's support was; Kennedy's weakness only becomes apparent to an outsider by a week-to-week reading of the liberal journals.)

After the 1964 election, Lyndon Johnson came closest to making a quantum leap, but it wasn't long before his Great Society lost its impetus. This resulted from a combination of factors: the sheer cost of the Vietnam War, along with the absorption of attention that the war entailed; the political and ideological cost of the anti-war movement, with the splitting of his base; and the quickly perceived failure, especially within liberalism, of his War on Poverty programs.

Although for liberalism the 1950's, 1970's and 1980's must be counted as periods of frustration and drift, the second half of the 1950's was typical of that phase of the liberal cycle that consists of an increased yearning for activity. Thus the late 1950's constituted a threshold period that was followed by the feverish activity of the 1960's.

During the 1970's, despite the political windfall that the Watergate scandal provided, the frustration, withdrawal and drift were again present. The Carter presidency was no exception to this. Carter combined qualities of a liberal technocrat with those of a Bible-belt fundamentalist that would have made the literati of the Harold Stearns generation early in the century blanch with horror. His nomination was a demonstration of the impotence of the intellectual elite.

This is an impotence that has always been present, since at no time in the history of liberalism have the literati been able to dictate the Democratic candidate. An awareness of this impotence has been a recurrent theme in liberal thought.

Finally, after the defeat of Walter Mondale by President Reagan in 1984, there was much talk among liberals themselves about the death of liberalism and even of Europe's "social democracy." Whether the obituary notices are premature can only be known with time. The collapse of Communism is bound to be a contributing factor in whatever results.

Much of this is bound to surprise the average American conservative, to whom liberalism has often seemed, at least until the mid-1970's, an irresistible juggernaut. Conservatives in general have not been aware of the fragmentation and self-conscious impotence that have so long been part of both liberal thought and the liberal political movement.

If the inherent weaknesses within liberalism result ultimately in its demise, this will only in small measure have been a result of the strengths of American conservatism. This is so because conservatism has been almost as impotent and fragmented as liberalism itself.

In Chapter 18 I will discuss the intellectual culture's recent emphasis on "multiculturalism." An attempt, supported by long-term demographic trends, to "swamp out" the predominant culture, eventually rendering it a minority itself, offers the alienated intelligentsia a new and potent field of action.

### Causes of the failure

The factors that have been most important to the failure of American liberalism's socialist aspiration have been:

• The constant fact of blockage, imposed by an electorate that has been basically content with the society as it is in the post-New Deal era, giving neither liberal nor conservative an unobstructed mandate. When many years ago Werner Sombart observed that socialism in America would founder on shoals of apple pie and ice cream, he understood the essentially middle class aspirations of the average American.

• The crumbling of the socialist faith in Europe in light of the enormities committed by the Communist regimes, the evident failure of those regimes, and the disillusionment that experience has caused socialists to feel toward their own earlier visions.

• The loss of self-confidence within liberalism as a result of the bitter denunciation of it by the New Left. This criticism in effect amounted to a repudiation of the dissimulation and gradualism that typified liberalism from the beginning. Further, the New Left marked a revival of the decentralist *ethos* of nineteenth century socialist thought, an *ethos* that

saw little worthwhile in the gigantic structure of bureaucratic "state capitalism" and interest-group welfarism that liberalism had been so instrumental in creating.
• The perceived failure of liberal programs in light of the intractability of many of the problems they sought to address. When the *Zeitgeist* no longer accepted the premise that had been at the heart of the liberal political agenda for so long that "all problems can be politicized and then solved by spending government money on them," there seemed nowhere for liberalism to go.
• The inability of a coalition-based ideology and politics to maintain their cohesion. We see how difficult it has been to hold the coalition together when we think of the components of "the Roosevelt coalition": intellectuals (to the extent they chose to be affiliated), the South, racial and ethnic minorities, organized labor, farm laborites and big-city political machines. It is no wonder that there has been a constant call since the late 1960's for "a new coalition." Through most of the post-World War II era the groups have been at odds with one another, coming together mostly on election day, and not always then.
• The movement of several prominent liberals into "neo-conservatism" during the 1970's and 1980's. The New Left brought the alienation to a head, causing many to decide just where their loyalties lay. Some of those who were not primarily motivated by alienation moved to the right and, with Irving Kristol, began to speak in terms of, at least, "two cheers for capitalism." This is potentially one of the most important ideological shifts of our time. If an intellectual base that is both critically intelligent and yet lacking in alienation can come into being, it will tend to reorient the entire direction of modern intellectual culture.

**At first a major diversion: Civil Rights; and then a potent new direction: the "multicultural" attack on the American mainstream**
Despite all that I have said about the condition of liberalism since World War II, a single egalitarian issue has provided it enormous sustenance during those years. At times this issue has swept all else before it on behalf of what the American public has regarded as an unquestionable moral principle. I am referring, of course, to the issue of racial, ethnic and sexual equality.

Liberalism's relation to this form of equality is different than is commonly supposed. The relationship did not arise out of a spontaneous moral conviction in favor of such equality on the part of the liberal-Left. On the world scene, socialists generally have been neither more nor less given to such equality than people holding other ideologies. In fact, Proudhon, one of the leading socialists of the nineteenth century, called for the extermination of the Jews. Collectivists of several types have been rabid in their intolerance. Liberals in the United States did not provide conspicuous leadership to a movement for racial and ethnic equality until the issue came to life during and after World War II. Most Americans will be amazed to hear that it was the Progressives who were most instrumental in establishing the Jim Crow system in the South; they did so after the Populist movement created a fear of the potentially corrupting effects of a movement that would combine blacks and poor whites. Theodore Roosevelt is reputed to have made an embarrassingly bigoted comment about Negroes at the time of the Brownsville Affair. Woodrow Wilson originally wanted to include blacks in his administration, but backed off when this led to criticism from his Southern supporters. Franklin Roosevelt did not make civil rights legislation for blacks a significant part of the New Deal.

During all those years the many liberals connected with the liberal journals as editors and writers, while favorable to Negroes and horrified by lynchings, made no move to make "civil rights" a priority issue. As we look back from the *ethos* of the 1980's and '90's, we tend to think that racial, ethnic and sexual equality have held a place in the pantheon of liberal philosophy from the beginning. But that is just not so.

The migration of Negroes to northern cities and their improving economic condition, among other factors, led blacks to a much-increased activism at the time of World War II. Liberals tagged along. Their ideas did not lead the events; rather, the Negro agitation slowly awakened liberalism to the issue. Among the intellectuals, only the Communists had been active in significant numbers for very long.

Certain elements that make liberalism what it is lend themselves to this issue. Accordingly, modern liberalism, emerging from World War II and searching for a post-war program, had several reasons to consider it appealing. After a slow start, it became the central moral focus.

One reason for this has been that the Left in general, and liberalism as a form of the Left, has been involved from the beginning in a search for coalitions. For a century and a half in Europe the alienated intellectual subculture has sought an alliance with every unassimilated or disaffected group. Political success has depended upon what coalitions have been possible and how well they have been able to stay together. Ideologically, the rationale for any coalition has been readily supplied.

Ideally, of course, all such groups would be brought together in one grand coalition. But selective coalition-making has been forced upon the

Left and liberalism by the fact that the groups have often been at odds with one another and with the intellectual subculture. This is why the experience of liberalism with the various civil rights movements – of blacks, of Chicanos, of women, of homosexuals – as proved so checkered.

Another reason liberalism has been the natural champion of this sort of equality has been that liberalism has been willing to use "direct action" methods that the groups themselves have supported, but that have been unacceptable to conservatives.

To the classical liberal philosophy of individualism that lies at the heart of American conservatism, nothing is more abhorrent than for people to judge each other by the color of their skin rather than by their merits or what they produce. But the classical liberal also (1) wants the police power of the state to remain limited, (2) identifies with the main society without alienation toward it, and (3) sees the processes of change within an open society to be sufficient without techniques of confrontation. The classical liberal believes that the growth of racial tolerance must be accomplished primarily through ethics and education.

The idea of using the police power to command an absence of discrimination among hundreds of millions of people in their daily relationships has, to conservatives, seemed preposterous. Such a state-sponsored assimilation has subordinated the values of freedom of association, freedom of contract and property rights. It has threatened an unprecedented expansion of the police function. That this expansion has not come about has been due to the willingness of contemporary Americans to match their moral sanctimony with an hypocrisy that has kept enforcement to a minimum.

The method of social change through direct-actionist confrontation, even as used by the proponents of "non-violence," seemed offensive and inappropriate to conservatives, who saw a society in which the condition of blacks had been rapidly improving. From the point of view of someone who was not alienated against the main society, it made no sense to engage in a rhetoric of condemnation that could only be consistent with abandoning historical perspective, forgetting all the good and remembering only the bad.

Such concerns did not weigh heavily with the groups themselves or with liberal spokesmen. They dismissed them as excuses for inaction.

So far as ordinary Americans have been concerned, they have been preoccupied, as they normally are, with the day-to-day concerns of their lives. They have not thought deeply about classical liberal values or historical perspective. This lack of interest in ideas makes Americans incredibly receptive to fashionable ideology, at least so long as it does not inconvenience them too severely and seems consistent with their good-hearted natures. Because of this, nothing has seemed more irresistible than the egalitarian moral thrust of the post-World War II era.

Even a near-total intellectual and moral dominance, however, has not been enough to make the egalitarian issue sufficient to assure the political success of liberalism, as events since the mid-1960's have shown. In one national election after another, liberals have sought a "new coalition," each time revealing the extent to which they have been unable to keep the old one together. The process has pushed the Democratic Party to embrace the fringes. But radical feminism, homosexual rights and compensatory preferences for minorities do not constitute a program calculated to engage the majority of the American electorate.

It is especially important to understand that the entire minority-rights emphasis since World War II, regardless of its merits, was a deflection of liberalism from its original impulses, which were heavily socialist. Seen from the point of view of liberalism's intellectual spokesmen, their "creeping socialism" has hardly seemed to creep at all. Their literature has been one of frustration and ennui.

This does not mean, of course, that a program of state activism, perhaps of socialism, may not be revived in America. Nor can the possibility be ruled out that the Left may emerge again in the form of social disintegration and heightened alienation, such as during the 1960's and early '70's. Most recently, it is apparent that the liberal-Left has embraced a multicultural swamping of mainstream society as its long-term weapon. The experiences with the New Left and with multiculturalism must certainly teach us that the Left does not act, as many conservatives think, solely through a growth of governmental functions. Those who make "the growth of government" the sole focus of their concerns will have learned little since the early 1960's.

One of the important facts in the early 1990's is that the predominant culture has not capitalized on the Reagan presidency. Despite Reagan's strongly conservative philosophy, neither presidential election in which he was elected was made a vehicle for a philosophical articulation of conservatism. During his presidency there was no widespread intellectual ferment marking a revival of classical liberalism. The middle class simply kept on doing what it has always done, which is to pursue the daily round without having a strong interest in intellect or aesthetics and without seeing the need to create an intellectual subculture that is appropriate to a free society.

This means not only that "capitalism" continues to lack an ingredient essential to its own sufficiency, but that an ideological void is present which leaves us in a condition of almost total existential indeterminacy. We are in a period of profound drift.

Despite Reagan's personification of conservative values, America to a large extent has lost its memory, which is to say, its meaning. Both the liberal-Left (in terms of its initial socialist impulse) and classical liberalism lie exhausted within a culture that, at least for the present, operates upon the underlay that each has provided.

During the past few years, the liberal-Left has taken what was originally a major diversion from its socialist goal, the Civil Rights issue, and fashioned a new long-term weapon in its century-and-three-quarter struggle against the mainstream American culture. Liberalism has become ever more strident in its assertion of "multiculturalism." The pluralism of unassimilated cultures, not a "melting pot," has become its ideal. One way that this is manifested is that, with totalitarian ferocity, those who feel safely and exclusively ensconced in academia insist on a "politically correct" "sensitivity" to the "feelings" of all minorities. Although the insistence on such "political correctness" has received a great deal of attention, the movement is much broader and all-pervasive than this single issue suggests. The intellectual establishment has been reworking the content of our curricula, our vocabulary, our publishing and our art with a thoroughness that would have seemed familiar to the Soviet cultural commissars of the Stalin era. The elevation of non-Western cultures, and the simultaneous attack upon and diminution of what is now called "white, male-dominated, Eurocentric culture," are rapidly being carried out in all nooks and crannies of our national life. This is not being done by "conspiracy," but by common impulse among the vast majority of those – from school teachers to journalists to high-brow theoreticians – who intuitively identify with the "new class" of the intellectual culture.

Although this is a far cry from the old liberal-Left program of socializing America, it continues to carry out the primary motive-force of the alienated intellectual culture. The alienation persists in seeking allies against the mainstream culture. To this new form of the ideology, the old labor-capital dichotomy has given way to "the Third World against Europe," and the main tool in the new struggle is cultural, intellectual and demographic swamping. The press has reported that by the year 2050 caucasians will become a minority in the United States. The intellectual culture is sponsoring a massive, bloodless demographic invasion that over time will remold the society in a new image.

As with all alliances of the intellectual with erstwhile unassimilated groups, there is no assurance that the alienated intellectual culture will like the results. Who is to say that in the end a non-white America will give the intellectuals the social role they crave? Or that the new immigrants will not value precisely the "bourgeois materialism" that the intellectuals have found so distasteful in American culture for almost two centuries? Most of the intelligentsia's alliances (as with organized labor, say) have gone sour, running afoul of the desire of people just to be people. Indeed, considerable resentment usually arises among the members of any "disaffected group" against the intellectuals themselves. Ultimately, few people like to be led by those who feel superior to them.

### Indigenous factors in American history that have reenforced liberalism while adding other dimensions to it.

This overview of modern liberalism would be incomplete if I did not give attention to several other factors in American history. These factors have mostly augmented the call for a more powerful federal government, but without emanating from a radical alienation. Their presence has given liberalism a diversity that makes it unsound to define liberalism in terms of any one component. Liberalism has been historically complex.

When the United States was founded, the situation was ideal from the classical liberal point of view. (An enormous exception was the presence of slavery within an otherwise liberal republic.) Free institutions had been established on the principles of the Enlightenment, and the thirteen states were so heterogeneous that they had little inclination to surrender their power to the central government.

By the beginning of the twentieth century, however, many tendencies existed that would have lent themselves to state activism and centralization even if the intellectual community had not veered sharply to the left.

1. There was a continuing erosion of the intense loyalty that had originally been given to state and local units. A more national perspective came into being.

In part this was due to the transiency created by the frontier's movement westward. It was also caused by the constant improvements in transportation and communication. The victory of the national government in the Nullification Crisis and the Civil War put an end to centripetal tendencies. Thereafter, it was clear both politically and psychologically that the states were simply parts of a whole.

2. A Hamiltonian neo-Mercantilism inspired first the Federalists and then the Whigs. At all times, at least one of the major parties favored a federal government that would play an active role in the economy. The

Republican Party continued this tradition after the Civil War with the high protective tariff, which was seen throughout the nineteenth century as the primary form of governmental intervention. Toward the end of the nineteenth century, *The Nation*, at that time still strongly classical liberal, commented that the tariff had accustomed people to look to the government for economic intervention on their behalf.

3. The Jeffersonian tradition, even though it was articulately classical liberal, contributed two ingredients to the mix that was to be important at the end of the century. They were:
• Support for participation by more and more people in a broader democratic base.
• An opposition to corruption and governmental favoritism.

These were both compatible with classical liberalism, but they were also important to the Populist and Progressive movements, which had other ingredients that were incompatible with it.

4. During the nineteenth century the standard of living rose in the most successful economic expansion, democratically distributed, the world has ever known. It is ironic that this relates to the later welfare liberalism, but the connection becomes clear when we consider that the average person had always been so close to poverty that he had never been able to think seriously about insurance, doing away with child labor, and a steadily assured income. Only affluence made that possible.

The twentieth century's "safety net" could have been attained with less anti-capitalist rhetoric and more reliance upon market mechanisms within a classical liberal context. The fact that it was not, and that it came in upon the wave of a very different ideology, should not keep us from realizing that the essential preconditions were laid by science, the Industrial Revolution, abundant resources and a remarkably productive capitalism. Marxism has long been aware of this when it has held that capitalism is a precondition to socialism.

5. Despite this affluence, the continuing existence of poverty has brought about a number of governmental measures.

This poverty has largely been the result of a world-wide phenomenon that I call "peasant pressure." In England during the early Industrial Revolution the factory towns teemed with the poor who came from the countryside and from Ireland seeking the wages that the factories could pay. In Russia at the end of the nineteenth century, the textile mills of the beginning industrialization were flooded with serfs who swarmed into the cities.

One of the very real perversities of socialist thought has been to blame the squalor of the factory towns on the factories themselves and on their owners. In fact the presence of rural millions, mired in poverty but eager to move to jobs in the cities, has been both the creator and the constant replenisher of urban slums.

In the United States, the rural population has steadily declined, with migration to the cities; immigrants from all over the world have come first to hardship and then to a more complete enjoyment of our higher standard of living; Negroes have migrated from the rural South into the cities of the north and the west, and then partially back again. The sociologist Edward Banfield has pointed out that successive waves of poverty have been overcome, with new poverty taking their place.

The "peasant pressure" continues to this day. It comes in part from our still-shrinking agricultural population, but mostly from the immigration of the poor from Mexico, Latin America, Asia and the Middle East. (We also obtain many of their best minds.) Our affluence and freedom have continued to call into existence the very "problem" that has in turn provided the discontent and the votes to serve as the base for anti-capitalistic rhetoric and remedial governmental programs.

6. War and the need to remain prepared for war have played an important role in the long decline of classical liberal values.

Jacksonian classical liberalism understood the dangers, and therefore opposed a standing army. But the Civil War brought centralization and a shattering of the Jacksonian ideology. The great wars and threat of totalitarian expansionism in the twentieth century have made governmental powers necessary that would otherwise have stayed dormant. Just as significantly, they have contributed to the erosion of the social, moral and aesthetic base of middle-class culture, an erosion that has led to some of the most visible characteristics of our national life in the late twentieth century.

Ronald Reagan, the president with the most articulately classical liberal values in our history, was handicapped from the beginning of his administration by the need for vast defense expenditures to match the Soviet build-up. It was largely because to this that he was unable to implement his desire simultaneously to reduce taxation, the federal deficit, and the size of the federal government.

At the same time, this factor has produced a counter-effect. War and the heavy cost of national defense have done much to frustrate the goals of modern liberal presidents. The New Deal effectively ended when

Franklin Roosevelt turned his attention to international issues. The North Korean attack in June 1950 put an end to President Harry Truman's domestic program. And the Vietnam War overshadowed Lyndon Johnson's Great Society program.

7. Immigration has played a major role in the "peasant pressure." It has also contributed to the shift in the country's ideological orientation. We have undergone successive waves of immigration since the middle of the nineteenth century from parts of the world that have known little about classical liberalism. An example of this appears in Nathan Glazer's account of the all-absorbing socialist presuppositions of the Jews who immigrated to this country from eastern Europe.

Much of the liberalism since World War II has been an "interest-group liberalism." The teeming multiplicity of the new ethnic culture has no doubt been a major contributor. The groups have come with ideologically conditioned expectations about the role of government. They have constituted voting blocs, and this voting power has lent itself to the coalition-seeking imperative within liberal politics and ideology.

8. The booms and busts of the trade cycle have several times undermined important preconditions of a market system. Classical liberalism calls upon individuals and families to rely upon their own active role within a market system. This presupposes an adequately functioning market.

As we have seen, however, classical liberalism has long been on the defensive and drained of intellectual manpower. This has caused it to give too little attention to the institutional framework essential to a market. Its thinking has, of course, been relegated to the sidelines in any case. While technically the solutions making possible an acceptably stable market system have been known, there has been no coordinated thrust toward their implementation. An example is provided by the policies followed after the Crash in 1929, when the money supply was allowed to deflate by a third and the Smoot-Hawley Tariff and other protectionist measures strangled the revival of international trade.

9. There is a less tangible but still quite real factor that has long seemed to me to be essential to an understanding of contemporary life. It is a fact that I discussed at length in *Understanding the Modern Predicament*: the fundamental immaturity of mankind, even in advanced civilization, at our current level of development. Emerson was on the mark when he said that humanity is only at the cockcrowing and the morning star.

As a classical liberal, I see the Enlightenment as having been humanity's most significant advance toward a liberal and humane civilization. It is impossible, however, for someone with my values to look back upon the past two centuries without profound regret. Even in Europe and America people have been mentally and spiritually unable and unwilling to grasp and then to meet those aspirations. The important exceptions have reflected the extent to which the cultural capital of the Enlightenment, which we are still consuming, has remained present.

All of the factors I have discussed have been important, but the failure has also been due to the nature of people themselves. If we ask why we are plagued by mediocrity in personal and ethical relations, why performance is often so shoddy, why our public is the vehicle for so many thoughtless ideological fancies, why the aesthetic atmosphere is so poor and often so shrill, why so few genuinely well-founded ideas are brought forward, why the participation in our political process is so meager, why massive educational facilities accomplish so little by way of true literacy and learning, why our families cannot stay together, why there is even a loss of the ethic of family obligation, we can see many parts of the answer in the intellectual and social factors I am analyzing. But ultimate responsibility lies with the average person. It remains true, as it has from the beginning of history, that the ordinary person is too preoccupied, as Thoreau said, with "the factitious cares and superfluously coarse labors of life" to be very much concerned about qualitative issues.

The disappointment that this engenders in idealists has shaken socialists since the mid-1930's and has sapped the elan of modern liberalism. But it is also true that many of the characteristics of this weakness form the substance of what is considered liberalism in contemporary America. The average person's intellectual and spiritual mediocrity complements the intellectual culture's long-standing attack upon personal responsibility, the "bourgeois ethic," and the institutions and acculturations of a classical liberal society.

## Conclusion

This chapter has had both the advantages and disadvantages of an interpretive overview. The reader is aware, of course, that I have not sought to footnote anything I have said. The remaining chapters will examine the specifics in much greater detail and will, I think, provide ample documentation. They will also examine a number of additional aspects of liberalism.

## CHAPTER TWO
## Phases in American Liberalism: 1800-1920

In *Rendezvous With Destiny,* Eric Goldman began his history of liberalism with the end of the Civil War. This was appropriate to his own purposes, since he considered liberalism essentially a movement of "modern American reform" that has responded to the needs created by the urban, industrial, corporate environment that came into existence in the second half of the nineteenth century.

My own analysis differs significantly. I believe that by starting as late as he did Goldman missed three factors that were crucial in the United States before the Civil War and that have been central to modern liberalism: the growing alienation of the intellectual against middle class culture; the resulting drain of intellectual resources away from classical liberal thought; and the continuing role of traditionalist conservative forces that stood at odds with the secular, rationalist, open society that had come into being. If these earlier developments are missed, the role of alienation is deemphasized and the historian is unable to see the continuity that has existed within the intellectual culture both in this country and in its relation to European thought.

The developments we will trace before the Civil War are important for still another reason. Their presence at the earlier time, a time that was agrarian and given only to small-shop capitalism, shows how the core impulse behind liberalism was *not* a reaction to industrialization, urbanization, or the rise of the large corporation, as Goldman believed it was. The alienation *preceded* rather than *followed* the advent of large-scale capitalism

### Before the Civil War: Romantic reaction
### and alienation, but without coalescence

From Jefferson's election in 1800 to the beginning of the Civil War in 1861, most Americans shared the *ethos* of the Jeffersonian-Jacksonian party – an *ethos* that was articulately classical liberal. On the main economic question of the nineteenth century, it strongly favored free trade, wanting a tariff for revenue only, not for "protection." In a running debate that lasted over the entire 60-year period, it opposed the construction of internal improvements by the national government.

Consistently with its focus on liberty, it saw dangers in Henry Clay's call for a standing army. And it was firmly democratic, in keeping with the contemporaneous views of John Bright of the Manchester School in England. It saw value in democratic simplicity and strongly opposed aristocratic privilege. Andrew Jackson's fight against the rechartering of the second United States Bank must be understood in this light, since it reflected a belief that the Bank enjoyed a privileged position resulting from a marriage of government and finance. The Jacksonian opposition to privilege resulted from the premises of classical liberal individualism rather than from an animus against capitalism.

When the anti-slavery agitation began, the Jacksonians urged moderation. In his Farewell Address in 1837, Jackson criticized incendiaries on both sides. This reflected the priorities of the Jacksonian *ethos*, since to it the newly created republic was the thing of paramount importance. Because the Jacksonian majority felt no alienation, most of its adherents saw enormous value in the main society. It was during those years that the Constitution took on the reverential glow that it has possessed within the American myth.

It was a time of extraordinary expansion. A country that a few years before had hugged the eastern seashore soon extended to the Pacific. In one of the greatest migrations of all time, its exploding population spread across thousands of miles. The telegraph, railroad and steam engine were typical of the many developments in science, technology and capital.

Oddly, these achievements contrasted sharply with the profoundly pessimistic mood of the intellectual minority. The intellectual culture saw little value in the achievements of the main society (which were, however, revolutionary in the truest sense).

Beginning in the early nineteenth century, the Romantic movement in Europe reacted violently against the Enlightenment, changing the direction of the world intellectual community. This caused a drain of intellectual resources away from classical liberalism, which thereafter received relatively little work outside of economics. It is of the utmost significance that there was no major classical liberal philosopher in the United States after Jefferson. Ralph Waldo Emerson might, in a different climate, have been that thinker, but he felt no calling to serve as a philosopher for individualistic liberalism. Instead, his great talent, as well as that of Henry David Thoreau, turned to the other-worldliness of Transcendentalism, a philosophy that Alice Felt Tyler says included a theory of an oversoul in "mystical union with God."[1]

It is possible that John Calhoun would have filled the role if the sectional differences developing in the country had not taken command of his life. However, it is a mistake to think mainly in terms of the failure of any given thinker. There is a larger responsibility for the philosophical void, which is shared. It lies with the intellectual culture in its faithlessness to the Enlightenment. It also lies with the "bourgeoisie" (the commercial mainstream), which throughout history has rarely given enough attention to general ideas to germinate an intellectual culture appropriate to the free society in which it thrives.

All sorts of streams then fed a current that flowed into the void created by the intellectual movement away from classical liberalism. One of them was aristocratic, neo-Mercantilist conservatism in New England. Another was the Burkean-style Southern conservatism that sprang up after 1830 in defense of slavery. In George Fitzhugh's eyes the South came to represent a cultured, hierarchical civilization superior to the Northern society that he perceived as money-grubbing and vulgar.

A third stream was resurgent Protestant religion. In the "Second Great Awakening" which began shortly after 1800, the evangelical spirit reached a fever pitch. It possessed a puritanical temper that had a lot to do with myopic self-righteousness and very little to do with how to build a truly liberal society. Protestantism no doubt played an historic role in establishing the foundations for individual freedom, but much of its worldview has also been at odds with precisely such a society. This provides one of the themes of modern history, since there has been a direct connection between other-worldly religious values and a loss of balance by the nihilist and by many reformers. Both nineteenth century Russia and pre-Civil War America experienced this connection.

Yet another element was a naive sentimentality, formed out of a combination of good intentions and foreshortened perspective. This was a mentality that emoted over all perceived abuses while ignoring the enormous progress that had been made. In England during the same period, the historian Thomas Babington Macaulay lamented how much this contributed to a generalized dissatisfaction. Despite conditions having improved at an historically unprecedented rate over the conditions of earlier periods, the existing society was denounced over and over again as depraved. This lack of perspective, characteristic of the entire modern period, is a product of both the shallowness of a semi-educated public and the predispositions ideologically of the intellectual culture. Much of the neurotic tone of modern life is established by it.

Of greatest significance was the Romantic movement itself. Most of the other factors had existed before. The Romantic revulsion against the Enlightenment brought them to a head, stifled the development of classical liberalism, and led to the alienation of the literary culture. In

Europe, mystical, anti-rational, anti-bourgeois, anti-liberal thought became predominant. It was the spirit of a resurgent medievalism.

Those who absorbed this atmosphere began to consider the main society diseased. Abuses were seen everywhere, remedies of all kinds suggested. Emerson spoke of "a fertility of projects for the salvation of the world." C. S. Griffin writes of movements that together "attacked every American institution, every idea, every conceivable sin, evil, or burden of suffering." Intellectually, the United States passed through a period similar to the Muckraker era of the early twentieth century and to the intense alienation of the late 1960's and early 1970's. Such periods have involved a generalized disgust, in which everyone other than the speaker and his immediate audience is blamed, and only the vaguest rationale is presented for what is wrong.[2]

We know, of course, that the abolitionist movement was building to a white heat against slavery. Although it was on the Enlightenment's side with regard to an extremely important moral issue, abolitionism reflected the hierarchy of values that is inherent in alienation. It subordinated the very existence of the United States, with all that that meant, to the slavery question. The Northern victory in the Civil War, both keeping the Union together and abolishing slavery, necessarily obscures this fact for us today. But before the Civil War there could have been no certainty that a drumbeat of hatred toward the South would produce anything but a fracturing of the Union, the assured continuation of slavery in one section, and incessant warfare between the two resulting countries (especially over westward expansion, which was such a bone of contention even while they were together). Slavery was an anachronism in the modern age. All that was needed for its eventual disappearance was a modicum of patience and the general society's continued adherence to classical liberal values. (It is no coincidence that serfdom was abolished in Russia in 1861 without a civil war.)

Abolitionism was, however, just one of several movements. Some reformers threw themselves into Prohibition, seeing alcohol as the principal evil; there was a crusade against prostitution; pacifism was the focus for others. The religious revival called for a return to the Bible and to an emphasis on the Sabbath. There was an active anti-Catholic movement, since the vast immigration of Catholics, many of them the poor of Ireland and other places, was seen as a cause of the other problems. There were fads of phrenology, diet, free love, spiritualism, mesmerism, and hydropathy. The feminist movement got underway with the first Women's Rights Convention, organized by Lucretia Mott, in 1848. In his 1844 lecture "The New England Reformers," after speaking of the "fertility of projects for the salvation of the world," Emerson said that "one apostle thought all men should go to farming, and another that no man should buy or sell, that the use of money was the cardinal evil." He said that "others attacked the system of agriculture, the use of animal manures in farming," while "others attacked the institution of marriage as the fountain of social evils."[3]

One of the more significant movements had to do with the creation of utopian socialist communities. The Oneida community was established by John Humphrey Noyes, and embraced "Bible Communism" and "complex marriage." It was one of the more successful, continuing into the 1880's. Most of them were short-lived, and in historical perspective all have been considered failures. Robert Owen, a leader of early British socialism, set up New Harmony, which failed within two years. The Hopedale Community was created in 1841 to attempt a Christian socialism. Brook Farm began with Transcendentalism and shifted to the communism of the French socialist Charles Fourier. Fourier's thinking received attention in the 1840's under the sponsorship of Horace Greeley and Albert Brisbane, when dozens of Fourierist communities were started. Anarchism was the basis for Modern Times, a community established by Stephen Pearl Andrews and Josiah Warren in 1851. Speaking generally, Walter Hugins says that "European socialists ... formed only a small part of the European migration to the United States after 1815, but they contributed immeasurably to the reform agitation."[4]

The "fertility of projects" did not reflect a consensus favoring a socialist critique (just as it did not during the Progressive period almost a century later). As the different movements indicate, there were widely divergent diagnoses of the disease that they all claimed to see in society. Some of the movements in fact represented the antipathy of the middle class itself to deviations from its values. It is noteworthy that the writings of both Emerson and Thoreau contain many comments that differ sharply from attitudes taken later by the Left. This reflects the fact that the intellectual culture had not yet begun to seek alliances with the have-nots. Nevertheless, socialist thinking was important to the coalescence of ideology that came later in the century.

### After the Civil War: alienation, yearning and coalescence

The ferment was largely stilled during the first few years after the Civil War. We know from *The Education of Henry Adams* that there was a rush of excitement among intellectuals when Ulysses S. Grant was elected president, but that disillusionment set in quickly when his administration failed to meet their expectations.

A letter that Adams sent to his brother Charles in 1862 is significant. It shows that this period remained within the cyclical paradigm of the psychology of the alienated intellectual. There had been years of intense activity, capped by the exhausting experience of the Civil War. Now there was a period of quiescence, during which the alienation continued and nurtured a yearning for the renewal of activity. Adams showed the yearning when he wrote that "what we want is a school ... a national set of young men like ourselves or better, to start new influences ... throughout the whole social organism of the country...." He then illustrated both his alienation and the historic failure of the bourgeoisie when he said that "that is what America has no power to create... It's all random, insulated work, for special and temporary and personal purposes."[5]

The reform movements after the Civil War were of two types. One involved reform from the top, led by such liberals (in the classical sense) as Edwin Lawrence Godkin and Samuel Tilden. These movements included the Liberal Republicans in 1872, a similar movement in the Democratic Party in 1876, and the Mugwumps in the 1880's. Tilden, raised in the Jacksonian school, has been called the father of the modern anti-boss reform spirit. Although these movements sought reform, primarily through Civil Service, they did not embody cultural alienation.

The other type of reform movement was agrarian. The agrarian crusades voiced the dissatisfaction of farmers with what they perceived as exploitation by lenders, railroads and storage elevators. Accordingly, they lent themselves to the growing rhetoric of anti-capitalism. They were especially susceptible to crank-money schemes. As a debtor class, the farmers of that time saw advantages in easy credit and inflation.

Depressions, the rise of labor, and the influx of immigrants (many influenced by the socialist movement growing in Europe after the revolutionary fervor in 1848) contributed to a rising turbulence. Labor-management relations became violent. The Molly Maguires, dynamiting and murdering in the Pennsylvania coal mines, were put down only when ten of their members were hanged. Anarchism, an import from southern Europe, flourished until public opinion turned sharply against it after the Haymarket Square bombing in 1886. (Later terrorist acts attest to the fact that it didn't disappear totally.)

Later in the century, books began appearing with a socialist critique. The most popular was Edward Bellamy's *Looking Backward* (1888). It soon sold 10,000 copies a week. In part, it was a novel, telling the story of a man who sleeps until the year 2,000 and then wakes up in a socialist utopia; in the main, however, it was a bitingly alienated description of capitalism and a glowing description of a model socialist society.

During the 1880's and 1890's Lester Ward published a series of books and articles advocating what he called "Sociocracy," and looking forward to the day when "all the important public operations of society shall come more or less directly under the power of State regulation." His writing is characteristic of much twentieth century liberal thought.

Most important, however, is the fact that the alienation finally coalesced into an ideology. Thereafter, there would still be "a fertility of projects," but the intellectual culture would at least share a common worldview, which it did not in the pre-Civil War period. It is probable that this coalescence would have occurred in any case, since European thought had arrived at that point, but the specific influence that most directly brought it about was the migration of several thousand American graduate students to German universities, mostly in the last quarter of the nineteenth century, where they studied under the German Historical School. I described this in Chapter 10 of *Understanding the Modern Predicament*. The details I gave there are of the greatest significance to the development of American liberal ideology. Rather than repeat them here, though, it will suffice to highlight the following influences:

- The Historical School stood in close relation to the Junker aristocracy and to Bismarck's government, which was putting into place the first welfare state program in Europe.
- In common with so much European thought during the nineteenth century, the members of the School were intensely anti-bourgeois, and liberalism in its individualistic sense was anathema.
- Its "historical method" stressed empirical scholarship, surveys, specialization, publication of monographs, and the like. It thus created the paradigm to which American higher education adheres to this day.
- At the same time, the historical method adopted a relativism that attacked the scientific pretensions of classical and neo-classical economics. The School argued that that economic theory generalized from patterns that exist only in a bourgeois phase of history, and that therefore its conclusions have no permanent validity. This attack on classical and neo-classical economics was important both for the methodological point it was making and because of its assault on the main body of work within classical liberalism; it was also important because such a relativism has been one of the main weapons used by the Left and by modern liberalism to undercut the foundations of bourgeois society.

In its stress on relativism, the Historical School reflected two very different aspects of modern intellectuality. One was its anti-middle class, anti-capitalist, anti-classical liberal ideology. The other was the emphasis that secular intellectuals have put on empirical science. The ideology stemmed from the phenomenon of the alienation of the intellectual, based on several causes. One of these causes was the Romantic movement's restimulation of Medieval values (which of course have never been fully defeated), with their stress on hierarchy, religion, subordination of the individual, and a strong state. At the same time, the empirical aspect was in line with the thoroughly secular nature of modern science.

• The members of the School were gradualists, not revolutionaries. This was important to the decision by modern liberals, distinct from that made by avowed socialists, to stay within their culture, not putting themselves beyond its pale. In the United States, a gradualistic program based on a socialistic worldview would require dissimulation. This need led directly to "liberalism" as we have known it.

• It is relevant to the later Progressive movement and to modern liberalism in general that the members of the German Historical School believed in leadership from the top through a statesman who would embody the aspirations of the whole people. They also wanted the intellectual culture to stand in close relation to that leader.

The influence was not simply a direct one. The British Left, which had a major impact in the United States, had itself been under the sway of the German thinking. In 1915, Randolph Bourne wrote that "British thought for forty years has come straight from German sources. What is the new social politics of liberalism," he asked, "but a German collectivism, half-heartedly grafted on a raw stock of individualist 'liberty'?"[6]

The direct influence came through a number of American thinkers and universities. Simon Patten observed in 1914 that the "Wisconsin Idea," under which the University of Wisconsin became the intellectual center for state activism, was based on the German example. Lincoln Steffens was educated in Germany; W. E. B. DuBois graduated from both Harvard and Heidelberg; Edward Alsworth Ross attended the University of Berlin. Richard T. Ely studied under the Historical School and later became a teacher to both Thorstein Veblen and John R. Commons. Ely was an important member of the faculty at both Johns Hopkins and the University of Wisconsin. John Bates Clark studied in Germany, came to advocate Christian socialism, and was one of Veblen's teachers at Carleton College. George S. Morris became an Hegelian while studying in Germany, and later taught John Dewey. Louis Brandeis studied at Dresden in 1873-5. Eric Goldman says that five American universities became the principal repositories of these ideas: Johns

Hopkins, Columbia, Chicago, Wisconsin and Washington. Newly forming academic associations reflected the rise of modern American social science. Lewis Gould tells us that "in 1885, a group of young men just back from German universities founded the American Economic Association." He refers specifically to Ely, Commons, Clark and Edward W. Bemis.[7]

### The Populist Episode

Twentieth century historical literature has fiercely debated the nature of Populism. (The same is true of Progressivism.) Because of the diverse nature of their subject, historians of each period have been akin to the blind men feeling the different parts of an elephant and thus arriving at very different descriptions.

Lawrence Goodwyn has emphasized a particular component. He argues that the central fact about Populism is that a "movement culture" arose among farmers, primarily in the South, reflecting first their discontent over the "crop-lien system" and then the efforts of the Farmers' Alliance. To Goodwyn, Populism's other factions were appendages. He accordingly considers the Free Silver component a "shadow movement." Fusion with the other factions, and especially with Free Silver, led to dissimulation and to an acceptance by reformers of the "hierarchical culture" that he says has dominated America ever since. Accordingly, he considers the election of 1896 the fateful turning point in modern American history, since it was to him the last desperate effort for real democracy. He criticizes John Hicks, Richard Hofstadter and Norman Pollack as historians who have not understood that the Alliance movement was the "core experience" of Populism.[8]

In addition to the agrarian movement that is central to Goodwyn's analysis, Populism included:

- The economic radicalism that had shown itself earlier in Kelloggism and the Greenback movement. This called for monetary inflation, divided the economic world conceptually into producers and non-producers, and advocated extensive governmental intervention.
- The socialist followers of Bellamy, who formed the "Eastern wing" of Populism. Compared to some of the other components, however, this wing was not a major contributor either of votes or of leadership.
- The enthusiasts for Henry George's "Single Tax." Despite the radical sweep of George's proposal to tax away the unearned increment in land values, his overall views were not socialistic.
- Labor, to the limited extent it chose to become affiliated. Major efforts were made to bring labor into the movement in Wisconsin, Illinois

and Ohio after the panic of 1893. The Populists were split, however, over "Plank 10" of the American Federation of Labor program. This called for socialism, advocating the collective ownership of the means of production and distribution. Samuel Gompers favored a go-it-alone policy for labor, and opposed an alliance with Populism.

• The Free Silver movement, headed by William Jennings Bryan. To advocates of the gold standard, this represented a call away from "hard money" and toward inflation; to enthusiasts for fiat money, though, it was insufficient, since to them it appeared simply to add another metal to what was essentially a hard-money policy.

Formed of these elements, the Populist coalition necessarily had a difficult time staying together. We have seen that Populists split over Plank 10 and that Gompers opposed labor's affiliation. Henry George opposed governmental intervention, which was at the heart of what most Populists wanted. Poor whites in the South were hostile toward participation by blacks. Socialists wanted a more radical program. As a result, the movement flew apart, fading away after the defeat of William Jennings Bryan in the presidential election of 1896 and with the improvement of farm prices. The difficulty of cementing a coalition, in light of the diverse interests and theoretical rationales, has continued in the twentieth century as one of liberalism's central problems.

The Omaha platform in 1892 summed up Populism's positions: There was a call for the federal ownership and operation of the railroads, telegraph and telephone; for Free Silver; for the eight-hour work day; for government to regulate all corporations and to break up monopolies. Democratizing measures were favored such as the secret ballot, the direct election of Senators, initiative and referendum. At the same time, unrestricted immigration was condemned as injurious to the workers and farmers who were already here. Little interest was shown in Civil Service or in the reduction of the tariff.

## The Progressive episode

Another surge of reformist energy occurred in the Progressive movement in the early twentieth century. Although historians of the epoch generally say it ended with the advent of World War I, there was political activity under the Progressive label until LaFollette was defeated as a third party presidential candidate in 1924.

"Progressivism," too, is subject to varied interpretations as a product of a loose coalition of divergent streams. But its coalition was not identical to Populism's, and the issues it stressed were somewhat, though by no means entirely, different.

So diverse were its factions that *The New Republic* could say in 1924 that "American progressivism is nourished almost exclusively by the grievances and the demands of special regions and groups. There is no one idea, program or leader." John D. Buenker observed that "there is no single progressive movement at work during the period, but rather many separate groups interacting and coalescing."[9]

Progressivism's emphasis was urban, replacing Populism's agrarian focus. Farmers had receded from their radicalism at the same time the new urban middle class of business and the professions in America's rapidly developing cities was coming into its own. This middle class, urban base was reflected in many of the issues that Progressivism championed, such as the opposition to corruption, the promotion of the city-manager system of city administration, and the control of franchise monopolies. It is significant that a study by L. Otis Graham, Jr., found that a clear majority of Progressives who lived into the 1930's were sufficiently conservative that they opposed the New Deal as too radical. This sheds light on the ideological complexion of Progressivism. Since we will see that there was a substantial socialist influence within the intellectual culture of Progressivism, the presence of middle class "conservatives" shows once again how diverse the movements were that we are reviewing. Much of what Progressivism crusaded for would easily have been the platform of a classical liberal reformist party if developments within the preceding century had not deflected that possibility.[10]

A second element was evangelical Protestant reformism. Robert M. Crunden has said that this "provided the chief thrust ... of the original progressive *ethos*." We see again the continuing role played by what has been called "pietistic Protestantism." This time it threw itself into the Prohibition movement, obtaining the eventual passage of the Eighteenth Amendment to the Constitution, while an influential portion expounded the "Social Gospel." Ralph Henry Gabriel says the work of Sheldon, Grinnell, Munger and Gladden had "borne fruit in an increased social consciousness on the part of the churches." The Social Gospel led to the publication in 1907 of Walter Rauschenbusch's *Christianity and the Social Crisis* and the formation in 1908 of the Federal Council of Churches. In this and two later books, Rauschenbusch argued that "God is against capitalism" and called for socialism.[11]

Two historians of the period, J. Joseph Huthmacher and his student John D. Buenker, have stressed the role of "urban new stock Democrats." They point to the millions of immigrants who crowded the cities, coming first from Ireland and, in the New Immigration after 1880, from southern and eastern Europe. These millions provided the base for the city political machines, which catered to their needs. Buenker says that the legislation that was enacted in the industrial states during the Progressive era with the active assistance of the city machines laid the foundation for the New Deal and the welfare state. Thus, there were two "urban liberalisms": one of middle class reformers, and another on behalf of the millions of first and second generation Americans.

In an analysis of liberal thought, we should never overlook, however, the role of the intellectual culture. Malcolm Cowley later wrote of "the bustle and hopefulness that filled the early years from 1911 to 1916. Everywhere new writers were...marching forward arm in arm against the old standards of life and culture." Joseph Featherstone has added that "between 1913 and 1922,...anybody who was anybody wrote for *Masses*." The counter-culture of bohemian radicalism was at its height in Greenwich Village. According to Lewis Coser, "the young men and women who began flocking to Greenwich Village about 1910 were in revolt against small-town philistinism ... For a few years the Village embodied the full flowering of an intellectual, artistic, political, and emotional counterculture." As with all such phenomena since the early nineteenth century, a central theme was alienation from the middle class. The counter-culture was enthusiastically socialist. Although *The Masses* under the editorship of Max Eastman was most influential, this was the period of the "little magazines" that appeared in great profusion, vibrant with the intellectual, artistic vitality of that period.[12]

Although the deeper origins of the Greenwich Village counterculture lay in the Romantic movement and in European intellectual developments during the preceding century, the counterculture was more immediately stimulated by the sensationalist condemnation of a great many facets of American life during the Muckraker movement between 1902 and 1911. Louis Filler says that Henry Demarest Lloyd's *Wealth Against Commonwealth* in 1894 had been "the first Muckraking book," but that Muckraking did not become a movement as such until *McClure's* publication in October 1902 of Lincoln Steffen's "Tweed Days in St. Louis." The serialization of Ida Tarbell's *The History of the Standard Oil Company* began in the following month's issue. For the next nine years, exposes appeared in rapid succession not just in the popular magazines, but in books and in newspapers noted for their "yellow journalism."

The ice, sugar, coal, patent-medicine, beef and other trusts were attacked. The stockyards and meat packing industry were investigated, and this led in 1906 to Upton Sinclair's famous book *The Jungle*. There was a Post Office scandal. Senators were identified as part of land frauds. Bribery was exposed in state legislatures. Organized finance was challenged, becoming the focus of Louis Brandeis' early career and of his book *Other People's Money*. A crusade was begun against railroad accidents. Life insurance frauds were brought to light. Child labor was bitterly assailed. Political bossism was attacked and a movement for municipal reform begun. There was a campaign against the power of the Speaker in the House of Representatives (and ironically this resulted in the power of committee chairmen under the seniority system, which in turn became an issue a half-century later). It is no wonder, then, that Theodore Roosevelt, although essentially friendly toward the Muckraker movement, made his reference to "the man with a muckrake" in Bunyon's *Pilgrim's Progress*, thereby giving the epoch its name.

Within the intellectual culture, certain issues were of course more important than others. The one that stands out most prominently, and that divided the intellectuals themselves, both during the Progressive movement and at all times since, had to do with big business.

Herbert Croly's book *The Promise of American Life* made him the intellectual mentor of the "New Nationalism." Edward Bellamy's utopian socialism had been known as "Nationalism." Bellamy had predicted that socialism would come through corporations' growing ever larger and merging together until finally there would be one giant trust, which would then blend with government to undertake all social and economic functions. Croly likewise envisioned corporations' becoming larger, and favored their coming more and more under the wing of government. In contrast to Bellamy, however, Croly masked his socialist content with a fog of dissimulation. There was hence a "new" Nationalism. It welcomed bigness as industrially efficient and wanted government to make that bigness an instrument of national policy.

Despite his reputation as a "trust buster," Theodore Roosevelt became the political champion of the New Nationalism. (It is worth noticing, however, that liberal authors have mainly remembered him as opportunistic and inconsistent, as they have with virtually all liberal politicians.) There is an interesting, although minor, dispute in the literature about who influenced whom. Learned Hand sent Croly's book to Theodore Roosevelt in Africa. According to John Chamberlain, Roosevelt read it with "a leaping brain." Roosevelt thereupon had Croly to lunch at Oyster Bay. But Arthur Schlesinger, Jr., argues that Croly's "influence on Roosevelt has been considerably exaggerated" and says that "it was certainly less than Roosevelt's upon him." He points out that much of the programmatic content of Croly's book seemed based on Roosevelt's January 31, 1908, message to Congress.[13]

At the same time, Louis Brandeis was the intellectual mentor of an opposing view called "the New Freedom," which was championed by Woodrow Wilson in the campaign of 1912. This advocated a "regulated competition" in which government would be the guarantor of a truly competitive market. Instead of encouraging the growth of business and then absorbing it into government, the New Freedom envisioned what Charles Beard, one of its critics, called "a democracy of small business."[14]

Again, however, the political leader fell short of the aspiration. Even during the campaign of 1912, Wilson couched his advocacy in platitudes. There was little follow-through by him as president, except to the extent that lowering the tariff helped remove one of the major causes of bigness. His other pre-World War I measures, such as the creation of the Federal Reserve System and the passage of the Clayton and Federal Trade Commission Acts, did not involve breaking up big business. After 1916 the war in Europe deflected Wilson from domestic reform, and in fact augmented quite significantly the forces leading toward concentration. Years later, Max Lerner looked back and said that Wilson "never made any efforts to smash the trusts."[15]

The difference between the New Nationalism and the New Freedom paralleled the argument that was going on within socialist thought, both in the United States and England, about the relative advantages of a centralized or a decentralized collectivism. The Guild Socialist movement, strong in England until it was eclipsed by the allure of the Soviet system that followed the Bolshevik Revolution, opposed "state socialism" and wanted a decentralized socialism based on worker control.

In the United States, the intellectuals among the New Nationalists wanted an absorption of large-scale corporate capitalism by the federal government – really a state socialism, masked by dissimulation. So far as the New Freedomites in general were concerned, they cannot be said to have wanted a decentralized socialism, since on the whole they were not socialists. Certainly Woodrow Wilson was no socialist. But in this book we are concerned about liberal *thought*, and it is of no small significance that Louis Brandeis, the New Freedom's principal intellectual mentor, embraced the Guild Socialist model in his private letters when he said that he looked forward to an ultimate worker control. In a letter in 1922 he spoke of workers' "participation in, and eventual control of, industry." So far as liberal thought in either school was concerned, the socialist models were never very far out of mind.[16]

I have brought up the Guild Socialist influence in connection with the New Freedom. This influence was much more pronounced, however, in the intellectual vogue, during the 'teens and early 1920's, of what was called "industrial democracy." Herbert Croly's book *Progressive Demo-*

*cracy* in 1915 reflected this vogue, and looked forward to eventual worker control, speaking of the need for "the deliberate education of the wage-earners for the position, which they must eventually assume, of being responsible as a group of self-governing communities for the proper organization and execution of the productive work of society." (He didn't foresake his habitual elitism, however; he saw the need for "a body of expert administrative officials" to carry out the public will, which, in common with Rousseau, he perceived as not being the same thing as the wishes of any given electorate.)[17]

When *The New Republic* began publication under Herbert Croly, Walter Weyl and Walter Lippmann in November 1914, it repeatedly called for the two sides of industrial democracy: worker control and the extensive organization of consumer cooperatives. British socialist authors were for several years prominent in its pages. This continued as the journal's emphasis until the early 1920's and is one of the threads that has reappeared from time to time. In the 1980's the idea of worker control was again popular within the American Left.

The broad themes that I have discussed were important to the theory. In the politics of Progressivism, however, a number of specific proposals, each backed by its own special constituency, provided the momentum for the movement. Many of the proposals were democratizing, notwithstanding Croly's elitism: the campaigns for the short ballot, the city-manager system of city governance combined with proportional representation, the abolition of the electoral college, a uniform system of presidential primaries, the direct election of Senators, initiative, referendum, recall, the recall of judicial decisions, and women's suffrage. In significant contrast to the post-World War II emphasis on ethnic rights, however, there was little interest in enhancing the position of Negroes. The democratizing measures related closely to the fierce opposition to corruption (except that recent authors have shown that the city political machines, catering to the votes of immigrants, also played a major role, even though this runs counter to the anti-corruption theme of the middle class supporters of Progressivism).

Social measures such as support for minimum wage laws, social insurance, the Settlement House movement to aid the poor, and the income tax amendment gave substance to the program. One of the more important issues, Prohibition, reflected a moral emphasis.

Historians, looking back, have identified certain concepts that they consider typical of Progressivism. (These are often belittled in the literature as naive.) One was the thrust toward openness in politics (a thrust that reached its culmination a half a century later after the

Watergate episode). Another was the focus on national politics. This related to a third, the faith in a strong popular leader. Together, these shifted power to the presidency. They also reflected the influence of German attitudes, which emphasized the "leadership-principle" long before Hitler came onto the scene. Associated with this was the faith in management by experts.

A fifth concept had to do with the mixture of reform and moralism. (Liberals later criticized the moralism as inconsistent with a "scientific" attitude toward social control. Progressivism was ambivalent, as liberalism has continued to be, in its combination of moralism and expertise.)

The combination of all these things has led historians into a running debate over just what Progressivism really was. The debate is largely an argument over what social groups should be considered most representative of it. It has been common to think of Progressivism as a middle-class movement, but Huthmacher and Buenker have shown the importance of the city political machines and the ethnic-immigrant vote. The reader is aware, too, that I would never have us lose sight of what was happening in the intellectual culture. Most certainly the Progressive period was an age of ferment. In light of the diversity within the movement, however, I see some merit in the conclusion by Peter G. Filene, as paraphrased by Link and McCormick, that "what has been called the progressive movement never existed as a historical phenomenon."[18]

Progressivism is said to have gone into eclipse by the time the United States became involved in World War I, but major activity actually continued until the defeat of Robert LaFollette as a third-party presidential candidate under a Progressive Party label in 1924.

Why did the ferment die away? A *New Republic* article in 1926 said that "the 'new freedom' was buried during the War in the same grave with the 'new nationalism,'" thus ascribing the demise to the war, which absorbed national attention. Otis Graham, Jr., speaks of the disheartening effect of both the war and the disappointing peace that followed it; of the frustration that idealists felt in light of public apathy and the perseverance of special interests; of the "high personal costs of attention to public affairs"; of "the persistent leadership crisis"; and of the "minimal effect" of Progressive measures "upon the visible ills of America." We must add the fragmentation that inevitably occurs among the various groups within so diverse a movement and the fatigue that follows a period of high ferment.[19]

# NOTES

[1] Alice Felt Tyler, *Freedom's Ferment* (New York: Harper Torchbooks, 1944), p. 48.

[2] C. S. Griffin, *The Ferment of Reform, 1830-1860* (New York: Thomas Y. Crowell Company, 1967), p. 2.

[3] For books dealing with the movements during the half-century before the Civil War, see Tyler, *Freedom's Ferment*; Griffin, *Ferment of Reform*; and Walter Hugins (ed.), *The Reform Impulse, 1825-1850* (New York: Harper Paperbacks, 1972).

[4] Hugins, *Reform Impulse*, p. 6.

[5] Henry Adams' letter is quoted in Henry May, *The Discontent of the Intellectuals: A Problem of the Twenties* (Chicago: Rand McNally & Company, 1963), p. 42.

[6] New Republic, September 4, 1915, p. 117.

[7] New Republic, November 14, 1914, p. 22; see also Charles McCarthy, *Wisconsin Idea*, published in 1912; Eric F. Goldman, *Rendezvous With Destiny* (New York: Vintage Books, 1977), pp. 80-1; Lewis L. Gould, *The Progressive Era* (Syracuse: Syracuse University Press, 1974), p. 16.

[8] Lawrence Goodwyn, *The Populist Movement* (New York: Oxford University Press, 1978).

[9] New Republic, May 14, 1924, p. 297, editorial; John D. Buenker, *Liberalism and Progressive Reform* (New York: Charles Scribner's Sons, 1973), p. 40.

[10] L. Otis Graham, Jr., *An Encore for Reform: The Old Progressives and the New Deal* (New York: Oxford University Press, 1967), p. 50.

[11] New Republic, March 7, 1983, p. 36; Ralph Henry Gabriel, *The Course of American Democratic Thought* (New York: Ronald Press Company, 2nd Ed., 1956), pp. 274, 276-7.

[12] New Republic, March 3, 1937, p. 102; New Republic, January 16, 1965, p. 19; Lewis A. Coser, *Men of Ideas, A Sociologist's View* (New York: The Free Press, 1965), pp. 111, 118.

[13] New Republic, November 8, 1939, p. 34; New Republic, May 8, 1965, p. 17; New Republic, April 8, 1972, p. 22.

[14] New Republic, November 14, 1914, p. 18.

[15] New Republic, October 11, 1933, p. 251.

[16] The Brandeis letter referred to is quoted at length in Alpheus Thomas Mason, *Brandeis: A Free Man's Life* (New York: The Viking Press, 1946), p. 585.

[17] Herbert Croly, *Progressive Democracy* (New York: The Macmillan Company, 1915), pp. 390, 356, 227.

[18] Arthur S. Link and Richard L. McCormick, *Progressivism* (Arlington Heights, Ill.: Harlan Davidson, Inc., 1983), p. 2.

[19] New Republic, June 9, 1926, p. 73; Graham, *Encore for Reform*, pp. 162-3.

# CHAPTER THREE
## Phases in American Liberalism: 1920-1953

### The 1920's: a period of drift and yearning

Several themes were important to liberalism during the 1920's, but the overriding tone was one of disillusionment and withdrawal.

This corresponds to the psychology of the intellectual. As an individual, an intellectual passes through a series of alternations. He is acutely sensitive to the imperfections of the world, which run counter to what he sees as possible. The weight of these things causes him to withdraw. But eventually he reenters the world, led by his fervent concerns and by his tendency, after a period of withdrawal, to forget the reasons for it. He then throws himself into passionate activity, believing that people can be brought to see things as he does and to reform themselves accordingly. But it is not long before he sees through to their essential apathy and self-interest, and before they themselves react hostilely to the inconveniences of his idealism. This sends him flying back into withdrawal, partly of his own accord, partly because that is where the world wants him.

This is the pattern described by Emerson; it is the pattern shown by the withdrawals of the 1920's, of the late 1940's, of the 1970's. The intellectual culture as a whole reflects the cycle (not because I think there is any automatic transference of individual characteristics to a group, but as a matter of empirical observation). At the same time, a counterculture of withdrawal seems, at least at a certain level, to be a permanent institution. There were the Beatniks in the 1950's and the Hippies in the 1960's before the mass movement into mysticism in the 1970's.

As always, Herbert Croly was paradigmatic of the liberal mood. Beginning in 1922, *The New Republic* under his editorship began to urge an inner cultivation in place of politics. Arthur Schlesinger, Jr., says that "Croly himself lost faith in political solutions after the First World War and grew increasingly absorbed in psychology and mysticism." Eric Goldman reports how Croly "began bringing to *New Republic* luncheons a bearded Englishman named Orage, who explained that what the world needed was the self-discipline of yoga."[1]

This found its counterpart in the broader literary world. Gertrude

Stein had Ernest Hemingway in mind when she spoke of "the Lost Generation," and it was a label that stuck for the entire literary generation. Malcolm Cowley's book *Exile's Return* tells of the "flight" of "American writers ... from hometown to Greenwich Village – from the Village to Paris – from Paris to New England farms." The period of withdrawal lasted roughly until 1930. Cowley told his readers in 1935 that "it was during the second year of the depression that everyone began talking about a new phenomenon. The intelligentsia was 'going left'; it was becoming friendly with the Communists; it was discussing the need for a new American revolution." The withdrawal was over and a new period of ferment had begun.

One of the manifestations of the withdrawal had been the student counterculture of the early 1920's. "The students of the early twenties," William Harlan Hale wrote in 1931, "were the last word in radicalism and smart progressivism ... Everyone remembers ... the baggy trousers, the collegiate semi-bohemianism." In 1923, H. M. Kallen wrote of "rebellious youth," whose hero was Randolph Bourne. The youth culture's "spirit," he said, "is discontent; its cry: There is no good in the institutions of modern life." George Soule reported in 1931 that "the more intelligent escaped to Europe, to sexual experiment, to egocentric psychological fads, to religion, to esoteric literary and esthetic expression or to an irresponsible Menckenian cynicism."[2]

Alienation burned intensely within the intellectual culture. Its focus came to rest primarily in two *cause celebre's*: the Mooney-Billings case and the more famous Sacco-Vanzetti case.

The Mooney-Billings case stemmed from a bomb explosion at the Preparedness Day parade in San Francisco on July 22, 1916. Thomas J. Mooney and Warren K. Billings were convicted of complicity in the explosion and sentenced to life imprisonment. For many years *The New Republic* crusaded for their release, arguing that they had been given an unfair trial because they were "radicals."

The case that brought liberal fury to a white heat, however, was the conviction and execution of Nicola Sacco and Bartolomeo Vanzetti for the murder of a paymaster and a guard during a robbery in South Braintree, Massachusetts, on April 15, 1920. Each anniversary of their execution on August 23, 1927, was for several years commemorated bitterly by *The New Republic*, which at first claimed only that they had not received a fair trial (again because they were radicals) but later that they were innocent. The years prior to their execution were filled with rising alienation – the proclamations of defense committees, demonstrations, fund-raising appeals, seemingly endless editorials. Sacco and

Vanzetti became martyred folk heroes of the Left. (During the revolutionary fervor of the late 1960's a folk song by Joan Baez recalled their memory.)

I have not been able to make a detailed study of the case to comment upon its merits, but it is worth pointing out that there were many such episodes, including labor violence and terrorist attacks, each with its aftermath of prosecution and punishment, during the late nineteenth century and the first half of the twentieth. During that period the Left rarely, if ever, admitted the guilt of anyone who was prosecuted. It was always as though the wrong men had been apprehended, and frequently the Left pointed to the possibility of *agent provocateurs* to explain the violence. The main society was always painted as venal in its response to the crimes. Because of that pattern, the protests of the Left carry little *prima facie* credibility. It is worth noting that the Sacco-Vanzetti convictions underwent years of review by the courts and by the governor of Massachusetts before the executions were carried out.

During these years of withdrawal and alienation, the primary intellectual focus was on Soviet Russia, newly emerged after the October Revolution in 1917. We will later discuss the 1930's as "the Red Decade," which is a label often attached to it; but even though that label is appropriate, we should not lose sight of the fact that the infatuation of the intellectual culture with the Soviets began much earlier, and that it continued through much of the 1940's.

The following items that I noted from *The New Republic* are representative of a phenomenon that went far beyond that single magazine, since they are typical of the liberal literature of the period: In 1923, Robert Dunn wrote an article "Seven Lies About Russia." In 1924, the first advertisement for the *Daily Worker* appeared, initiating what was to become the texture of the journal for the next fifteen years, during which advertisements for trips to the Soviet Union, for Communist books and journals, and for front-group meetings and proclamations were liberally distributed through its pages. In 1926, an article by Jerome Davis called "Russia Today" justified the secret police: "...every country has its G.P.U., especially in a period of war and revolution." In 1927, H. N. Brailsford wrote that "society in Russia is spontaneously evolving its own appropriate organs of democracy." Albert Rhys Williams added an article making a Pioneer (young Communist) meeting seem like a Boy Scout outing (can we imagine such an article about the Hitler Youth?). Also in 1927, H. M. Kallen wrote in an article about religion in Soviet Russia that "dictatorship though it be, [the Soviet regime] has liberated their energies, animated them with an altogether unprecedented sense of personal dignity and inward worth."[3]

In 1928, the premier liberal philosopher John Dewey contributed a series of six articles about his trip to Russia. His tone: "In spite of secret police, inquisitions, arrests and deportations of Nepmen and Kulaks...life for the masses goes on with regularity ... There is an enormous constructive effort taking place in the creation of a new collective mentality." The American Federation of Labor thereupon voted to expunge a tribute to Dewey because he had "aligned himself with Bolshevist propaganda," to which *The New Republic* editorially responded that the A.F. of L.'s action was a "stupid thing."[4]

Domestically, liberalism suffered "the blahs." Leaders were scarce; there was little interest, even by *The New Republic*, in formulating a program. In 1925 a *New Republic* editorial said that "liberalism is at present paralyzed politically by its lack of a program." Senator Nye's "Platform for Progressives" in 1927 set forth twelve remarkably mundane planks. In 1929, TRB (*The New Republic*'s unnamed columnist) surveyed the existing leaders – and found each lacking. At the end of the period, in 1930, John Dewey wrote that "liberalism today is hardly more than a temper of mind, vaguely called forward-looking, but quite uncertain as to where to look and what to look forward to...."[5]

The result was, as John Buenker has written, that "until the publication of Arthur Link's article in 1959, the prevailing view had always been that the 1920's was a decade of unrelieved reaction, an arid valley between two peaks of social progress." But Link and Buenker argue that something *was* going on, that the focus had simply shifted back to the states. "Despite the decade's reputation for reaction," Buenker writes, "it saw great advances in most states in the realm of welfare legislation." He cites "rent controls, public housing, regulation of the milk industry, expanded public health facilities," and the like.[6]

### The 1930's: the New Deal

There are two sides to the intellectual history that I wish to relate about the 1930's. The first will pertain to the intellectuals' response to the New Deal of Franklin Delano Roosevelt. The second will have to do with the extreme leftwing infatuation of the intellectual culture that has caused the period to be labelled "The Red Decade." I shall leave this second aspect to the next section.

It will be worthwhile to review a number of the New Deal's specific programs, noticing the continuity that links them with the liberal thinking that preceded and has followed them. We will leave some of the main issues, however, for more detailed discussion later in this section.

1. The Tennessee Valley Authority reflected an aspiration for large federal reclamation projects that had been voiced in *The New Republic* in 1915.[7] In the socialist thinking that surfaced repeatedly in liberal writing, regional "valley authorities" were seen as one of the alternative routes to socialism, especially when combined with the nationalization of natural resources, transportation, communication and banking that was so often proposed. This was the original thinking behind the T.V.A., as *The New Republic*'s readers were told by Jonathan Mitchell in October 1933. He said that "the Tennessee Valley Authority was designed consciously to be the first large-scale experiment in economic and social planning ever undertaken outside Soviet Russia. It was expected to produce, as rapidly as possible, a sort of baby Gosplan which later, perhaps, might serve as a model for the nation."[8]

An article by John T. Moutoux in January 1934 described the extent of intended governmental activity: "The town of Norris, Tennessee,...will be the first example in the United States of what genuine, coordinated planning can accomplish ... The sole landlord, the sole builder, will be the T.V.A. itself ... The land and buildings at Norris will be for rent only...At one end of the common will be the town center, which will include ... a hotel, a restaurant, a drug store, a barber shop and beauty parlor, a general store and a post office. All these will be built and owned by the T.V.A. It has not yet been decided whether the T.V.A. will operate them itself or lease them...."[9]

Perhaps most significantly, the aspiration among liberal theorists was eventually to establish such an authority in every feasible river valley in the United States. In 1936, *The New Republic* "warmly approved" when Senator George Norris proposed a valley authority for the entire Mississippi Valley except for the Ohio River area. Rexford Tugwell was reported by TRB to have "had great plans" in 1933-4, "such things as rehousing industrial workers in greenbelt cities and organizing farmers in collective farms." I cite this not because it related to a valley authority, but because it was in the same spirit as the Town of Norris conception. In 1943, the members of President Roosevelt's National Resources Planning Board had, according to a *New Republic* special section, "the vision and courage to demand that there should be a similar enterprise [to T.V.A.] wherever in America the geographical conditions make it possible." In 1949, President Harry Truman's program included a Columbia Valley Authority. It is part of the ultimate disillusionment of liberalism that very few of these objectives were met.[10]

2. The Securities Act of 1933 and Securities Exchange Act of 1934 established a national framework for the full disclosure of information

in securities transactions. This was consistent with the article by Professor William Z. Ripley in *Atlantic Monthly* in 1926 that urged the Federal Trade Commission to become the vehicle for such a disclosure system.

In terms of intellectual history, however, it is significant that in 1934 Bruce Bliven, the leading editor of *The New Republic* after Croly's death, was critical of the "truth-in-securities" approach. He wanted much more – a determination by government of the allocation of capital. His preference was consistent with *The New Republic*'s advocacy in 1933 of complete government ownership and operation of banking.[11]

3. England had created an unemployment insurance system in 1911. Germany patterned its system after England's in 1927.

In the United States in 1910, New York established the first unemployment compensation system. Forty-four states had such laws by the time the federal government came into the picture in 1935. Liberals debated among themselves about the most desirable sort of system. Wisconsin created one in 1932 that placed substantial financial incentives on employers to stabilize their own hiring. But in an article in *The New Republic* in 1934 Abraham Epstein opposed such a system based on individual company reserves, arguing that help for the unemployed was more important than the prevention of unemployment.[12]

The unemployment insurance system established by the Social Security Act in 1935 has, in common with the Social Security system in general, been criticized by liberals for having made a meager beginning. Paul Conkin says it "delegated most responsibility to the states and invited chaotic variations in always inadequate payments." During the ensuing half-century the system's scope and benefits have been substantially enlarged.[13]

4. Conkin says that "the Social Security Act of 1935 became the supreme symbol of a welfare state." But he adds that "it hardly deserved the honor or opprobrium," since it covered only half the population, included a tax upon the workers themselves, did not cover accident and illness during the working years, had no medical insurance feature, and "paid benefits on the basis of past earnings instead of present needs."

It, too, has been expanded over the years, but it has frustrated liberals that the United States has never adopted a system of national health insurance. Almost a half-century after the Social Security system was established, it ran into deep financial trouble. Despite the impression it creates of being an insurance system, it is not based on a fund that is actuarially determined. Essentially it is a system of benefits paid for by taxes. The tax has risen to an astonishing level that for many taxpayers exceeds that of the income tax. With the increasing number of elderly

Americans, more and more of the burden is placed on the correspondingly few who are currently employed.[14]

5. The New Deal is closely associated in the public mind with large public works projects to provide employment. For the intellectual history of such programs, we know what H. N. Brailsford told readers of *The New Republic* in 1929: "The broad idea – that public works should be used as a regulator to counteract the vagaries of the trade cycle... – is as old as the famous minority report on the Poor Law which the Webbs drafted twenty years ago ... It has always been a Fabian doctrine." Most classical liberal opponents of expanded government have been unfavorable to such programs, since they believe that the trade cycle is preventable through sound monetary policy. Herbert Hoover, however, had supported the concept since at least 1922.[15]

The actual spending on public works during the New Deal was spotty. Roosevelt was, until his conversion to Keynesianism became complete in 1938, ambivalent between the opposing philosophies of budget-balancing and contracyclical spending.

6. With Section 7(a) of the National Industrial Recovery Act and the Wagner Act of 1935, the federal government placed its imprimatur on collective bargaining. The union movement grew enormously during the 1930's. This would be a major fact within liberal history if the union movement had not flagged and if the "New Deal coalition" had stayed together better than it has since World War II. Since the New Deal, the labor movement has been, as it was before the 1930's, one of the anchors that has rooted liberalism in the actualities of American life. Its increasing weakness relative to other forces was well illustrated in 1976, when neither organized labor nor the intellectual culture was able to determine the Democratic presidential candidate.

7. There were many programs that I will not be able to discuss, but a final one that I will mention because of its prominence as a liberal concept after World War II is the idea of "yardstick industries." This involved having government corporations compete in private industries, thus establishing a "yardstick" to evaluate capitalism's performance. In 1974, Melville Ulmer said the idea was "one of the seminal ideas introduced in the New Deal, though its initial formulation appeared in an article by Walter Durand in *The New Republic* ... [in] 1926." (The idea of using governmental enterprises as a way to measure the performance of privately owned ones seems strange as we look back from the perspective of the early 1990's, now that the world has seen the collapse of Communist economic systems.)[16]

I have left other issues for more extended discussion. The first of these is the split that occurred within the New Deal over the New Nationalist and New Freedom approaches to the regulation of business (thus continuing the liberal debate of 1912).

The New Nationalist policy suffered from a multiple personality. Three things are worth noting: First, its business supporters wanted a legal and institutional framework for a "more rational" conduct of industry that would avoid the rigors of competition. This was intended to be consistent with the profit motive and the businessmen's own control of their industries. Second, the intellectuals who supported it saw it as perhaps the best vehicle for a centralist socialism, albeit one that integrated businessmen into its administrative structure. And third, similar integrations of business and government had for several years been popular within the totalitarian ideologies.

A business proposal for the "stabilization of industry" through trade associations under federal supervision that could "stabilize prices" came from Gerard Swope, president of the General Electric Company, in 1931. In the same year, the United States Chamber of Commerce wanted the antitrust laws amended to allow competitors to allocate production with government oversight.[17]

Those liberal intellectuals who were inclined toward a centralized socialism wanted industry organized under government with an eye primarily to social goals. In May 1933, TRB reported Franklin Roosevelt's call for a "partnership" of government and business. "Actually, I think, control is a more accurate word," TRB said. "That this trend is distinctly towards socialization of industry is not denied. Private operation and ownership will be retained, but there will be federal planning and control." The next week, *The New Republic*'s editors responded to the bill to establish the National Recovery Administration by saying that "conceivably, it may mark the beginning not merely of recovery but of a collectivization of the economic system ... We are now about to be committed to national economic planning and control."[18]

A proposal that Lenin had made shortly before the Bolshevik Revolution was actually preferred by the editors of *The New Republic*. "Lenin's proposal went much further than Mr. Roosevelt's does in two significant directions – control by organized labor and organization of consumers," the editors said. "Unless the partnership is extended to these important functions, monopolistic capital will almost certainly attempt to sequester too large a share."[19] In Italy, Mussolini had in 1925 announced a plan for a similar organization of the economy, but he did not actually institute it until he established his 22 "corporazioni" in 1934. In 1936, an article by Paul H. Douglas said that "these are roughly comparable to the code authorities under the N.R.A., except that the workers' syndicates have nominally equal representation with the employers." A *New Republic* editorial had commented on the Swope plan by saying that "this type of control is exactly what Mussolini means by 'the corporate state' – though with a considerably larger formal place both for labor and for the government...."[20]

In Germany, according to Malcolm Cowley in 1941, "Hermann Rauschning and his conservative friends were planning to use the Nazis for their own ends ... They believed that in each industry or trade, the employers, the salaried employees and the workers should together form a corporation legally authorized to fix prices and wages and to limit production; it would be a permanent N.R.A." Nor was this simply a futile dream by Rauschning. Hitler placed industry under centralized direction, integrating its constituent elements. He, too, included a substantial ingredient of ideological cohesion.[21]

The New Nationalism was instituted in the United States through the National Industrial Recovery Act's establishment of the National Recovery Administration (the N.R.A.). There was a corresponding program for agriculture through the Agricultural Adjustment Act (the A.A.A.).

Under the N.R.A., industry-wide codes were drawn up in virtually every field. These codes put limits on production, raised prices, forbade "unfair competition," and set out wage-and-hour provisions, collective bargaining rights, and stipulations against child labor. Under the A.A.A., farmers were induced to cut production in exchange for government payments.

The personalities whose names are associated with one or another of the variants of the New Nationalist phase of the New Deal are Raymond Moley, Hugh Johnson, Adolf Berle, Gardiner Means, Donald Richberg, Rexford Tugwell, Jerome Frank and Charles Beard.

Almost immediately after N.R.A. was established, liberal intellectuals who were predisposed in its favor became soured. A *New Republic* editorial in August 1933 referred to "a heart-breaking record two and a half months after the Recovery Act came into effect" and said that "the nation's great fundamental industries...are fighting the government." In early September another editorial said that "the industrial aspect..., as it stands today, is a failure." By December, John T. Flynn, then quite prominent among *The New Republic*'s writers, made what was to become the standard liberal complaint against the N.R.A.: that both the content and the enforcement of the codes served the purposes of business itself and not of governmentally-established social policy.[22]

In April 1935, TRB said that the N.R.A. "and to a less degree the A.A.A." were "in a state of collapse." An editorial two weeks earlier urged new legislation for the direct regulation of business in place of the "partnership" represented by N.R.A., although the editors said dolefully that "the whole effort is likely to fail unless industry is socialized." Within a short time thereafter, the United States Supreme Court declared the N.R.A. and parts of the A.A.A. unconstitutional. Liberal intellectuals weren't all that sorry.[23]

This marked the demise of the New Nationalist phase of the New Deal, and led into what is considered the New Freedom phase. The phasing should, however, be considered mainly a classification for convenience. It should be taken with caution and reservations. After the passing of the N.R.A. the administration had no clear commitment to the breaking up of big business; nor did Franklin Roosevelt forsake entirely the effort to adopt an integrationist approach.

The new phase, such as it was, was backed by Felix Frankfurter, Thomas Corcoran, Benjamin Cohen, James Landis, Marriner Eccles, William O. Douglas, Leon Henderson and Lauchlin Curry, among others.[24]

The phase included President Roosevelt's call in 1935 for a "tax on bigness" that would place high progressive tax rates on corporations and would eventually use taxation to eliminate holding companies. (*The New Republic*, still preferring the New Nationalist approach if properly applied from its point of view, ran an article by Jonathan Mitchell attacking "the primitive economic system of the so-called 'Brandeis group'... which was illustrated by the 'tax on bigness'....")[25]

In 1936, Roosevelt made his famous attack on "economic royalists" in his speech accepting the Democratic nomination; and in 1937 he strongly trumpeted the antitrust laws. Thurman Arnold was put in charge of the antitrust division of the Justice Department in 1938 and began vigorous enforcement. This was muted, however, by the onrush of World War II and by inconsistency within the administration, so that Barton Bernstein has concluded that "there was no effort to atomize business, no real threat to concentration." The administration's version of the Public Utilities Holding Company Act would have empowered the S.E.C. to give a "death sentence" to any utility holding company that it found to be without economic justification, but this was softened by Congress.[26]

Notwithstanding these measures, Roosevelt made no clear philosophical commitment. Even after the "New Freedom phase" was supposedly underway, the administration obtained passage of the Guffey Act, which *The New Republic* said "created "a 'little N.R.A.' for coal." The Federal

Trade Commission established N.R.A.-type rules for the wholesale tobacco industry. In February 1937, TRB reported that Roosevelt wanted to revamp the Supreme Court so that he could recreate the N.R.A. and the A.A.A. Donald Richberg had proposed a new N.R.A. to be run by the Federal Trade Commission.[27]

Roosevelt was a master politician and philosophically indeterminate. These combined to create an almost legendary inconsistency. He played all sides and made frequent use of deception, especially before elections. During the 1932 campaign, *The New Republic* reported "the philosophical opportunism at the base of the candidate's thought." In January 1934, the journal said that the New Deal was going partly right, partly left, following the line of least resistance. That October, Lewis Mumford spoke disparagingly of the New Deal's "pragmatism," which he called "aimless experiment, sporadic patchwork."[28]

Although this pragmatism was praised after the Left, including the Communist Party, shifted its support dramatically behind Roosevelt as a result of the United Front that was called for by Stalin, the ultimate verdict by the intellectual culture was expressed by Paul Conkin when he wrote that "the story of the New Deal is a sad story, the ever recurring story of what might have been." He said that "the New Deal failed to fulfill even the minimal dream of most reformers."[29]

This inconsistency causes some difficulty for those who have broken the period into a "First" and a "Second" New Deal (a classification that differs somewhat from the distinction, also foggy, between the New Nationalist and New Freedom phases).

Basil Rauch's *The History of the New Deal* in 1944 is said to have been the first commentary to speak in terms of two New Deals. The first phase was that of the N.R.A.; the second was from 1935 to 1938, consisting of "reforms intended to raise mass purchasing power and security." Walter Lippmann later spoke of the first New Deal as continuing until Roosevelt's court-packing debacle in 1937, followed by a second New Deal consisting of "the compensated economy."[30]

Arthur Schlesinger, Jr., has distinguished between a first New Deal of 1933-4 and a second New Deal, starting in 1935-6, that mixed the New Freedomite tendencies of Brandeis and the countercyclical spending theories of Keynes. Needless to say, all such classifications have had their critics because of the complexity of the subject-matter and the ambivalence of the administration. Huthmacher represents a sizeable body of thought when he writes that "the attempt to define a Second New Deal may be as misleading as the attempt to depict the so-called First New Deal of 1933 in terms of a coherent, prearranged plan of action." He says that "the Brandeis-Frankfurter faction failed to win a clear-cut victory during the Second Hundred Days." The New Deal in general, he says, was characterized by a "bewildering pattern of conflicts."[31]

In the preceding discussion, the reader will have noticed the references to Keynes and to the theory of countercyclical spending. The victory of the Keynesians in 1938 established one of the main features of liberalism as it emerged into the post-World War II period.

We have already seen that in 1929 H. N. Brailsford referred to the idea of government spending to counteract the trade cycle as "as old as the famous minority report on the Poor Law which the Webbs drafted twenty years ago," and that he added that "it has always been a Fabian doctrine." In 1931, Gordon Hayes wrote that "for more than a hundred years, socialists have been fond of attributing depressions to the inability of the masses to buy the products...However, it is only recently that the idea has been accepted in...respectable circles."[32]

John Maynard Keynes, then, did not originate the idea. He was, however, its chief twentieth century theoretician and popularizer, especially through his *General Theory of Employment, Interest and Money*, published in February 1936. He also played an important role in the dissimulative dynamic of American liberalism, since he provided a more current source for the ideas, which since that time have not had to be attributed to socialist thought. A similar role has been played by Berle and Means with regard to the Marxist concept of the separation between ownership and control in corporations.

According to Dean May, the concepts of the "multiplier," of the "propensity to consume" and of "liquidity preference" which are at the heart of the Keynesian system all existed independently of Keynes.[33]

*The New Republic's* George Soule gave what he called a "brief and oversimplified" summary of "the essentials of the theory of a compensatory fiscal policy." These include the idea that "there is a tendency for people to save money faster than money is invested in new production. This means that there occurs, from time to time, a net reduction in... purchasing power...The result is depression...The government can compensate for this shrinkage by spending more than it collects in taxes."[34]

Before he became converted to Keynesianism in 1938, Franklin Roosevelt was torn between balancing the budget and countercyclical spending. The administration spent freely in late 1933, but curtailed spending in early 1934. TRB said later that Keynes' influence was "enormous" among New Dealers in 1934-5. In 1935, there was the $4.8 billion work-relief program, but the P.W.A. was dismantled in the same year and Henry F. Morgenthau, Jr., a staunch advocate of a balanced budget, came to the fore. In December 1937, Roosevelt vowed to veto any new spending. But then in April 1938 he responded to the downturn of 1937-8 by embracing the Keynesian system.[35] *The New Republic* said that Leon Henderson had been "one of the first and sternest evangelists of the consumer-purchasing- power theory." But it was Marriner Eccles, with the assistance of Harry Hopkins, who won both Morgenthau and Roosevelt over to the Keynesian view in early 1938.[36]

Keynesian-type fiscal policy has played a central role since World War II, although not without increasing difficulty due to the dilemma of "stagflation" (which, contrary to the Keynesian expectation, combines inflation and unemployment). Liberal thinkers have often urged going beyond it, seeing social goals beyond mere stabilization. Dean May is correct, though, when he says that "the eventual widespread diffusion of the idea that budgetary policy is really social policy was one of the significant consequences of the New Deal response to the events of 1937-38."[37]

This is not to say, however, that the New Deal ever really solved the problem of the depression. There is much to support the conclusion that Herbert Hoover stated in his memoirs that the New Deal strung the depression out. In March 1935 – two years after Roosevelt was inaugurated – 22 million people were on relief. The downturn in 1937-8 was as sharp as in 1929-30. As late as 1940, eight million people were unemployed, constituting 14.6 percent of the workforce.[38]

The New Deal's political support arose in large part, of course, from Franklin Roosevelt's popularity and from the Depression, but political theorists speak also of what has become known as the "New Deal coalition." This was a diverse combination: organized labor, ethnic and religious minorities, the Solid South, the big-city political machines, farm laborites, liberal Republicans and the intellectuals (when, especially after the United Front began, they chose to lend support).

The coalition had been a long time in coming. Woodrow Wilson had tried to put it together in 1912, hoping to combine Catholics, Jews, labor, immigrants and the South. The Al Smith candidacy in 1928 had, according to TRB in 1968, "opened the doors" to millions of newcomers; there had been 20 million immigrants between 1880 and 1910. Smith's candidacy "made it possible for FDR to put together his 1932 coalition."[39]

The coalition has provided the political base for liberalism, but also committed it to the "interest group politics" that came under such fire from the New Left purists in the 1960's. Perhaps, too, the most remarkable thing about the coalition has been its diversity and fragility. It is no wonder that liberals have been searching for a "new coalition" since at least 1968.

As I read *The New Republic* for the New Deal period, I was surprised by the extent of the intellectuals' hostility toward various parts of the coalition. In 1935, an editorial referred to "reactionaries of the South" and to "sordid political machines." The next year, the editors criticized James Farley and "machine politics." In 1939, Bruce Bliven was talking about the "ladling out of federal patronage to crooked politicians." In 1943, Bliven said that Southern Democrats and corrupt city machines "never were convinced in their hearts that the New Deal was a good thing." And in 1947, James Loeb, Jr., lamented that "there never existed an authentic liberal coalition which could survive the loss of Roosevelt." Henry Wallace looked back and said that even during the New Deal Roosevelt had "no unified labor movement and no coherent liberal movement with which to work."[40]

The deadlock that has existed in American politics became evident in about 1937. According to Leon Keyserling, "FDR lost his power to put through domestic legislation circa 1937, when the Southerners in Congress withdrew their support." Since then, with the exception of the brief period following the election of 1964, there has been no time when there has been both a liberal president and a clearly liberal Congress. Roosevelt lost momentum in the late 1930's as a result of the fight over his court-packing proposal, his effort to purge certain conservative Democratic senators, and the Republican victory in the 1938 congressional elections. He sought no significant legislation after 1938.[41]

So far as the intellectual culture was concerned, it remained far to the left of the New Deal until, as I have said, the United Front, seeking a unified opposition to Hitler, caused it to become much more favorable. *The New Republic* repeatedly called for a new labor party in 1931 and 1932; it urged its readers to vote for Norman Thomas, the Socialist candidate, and not for Roosevelt, in 1932. Despite its brief interest in the N.R.A., it set down a drumbeat of criticism of Roosevelt: as he came in as president it said that he did not understand "the fundamental malady" and was offering a patch-up job; after he had been in office a year, the editors spoke of his "dismal" record; after another year, John T. Flynn opined that the New Deal was "crumbling" and was "a grand bust"; in June 1936 the editors said the New Deal was "sadly deficient" compared to their socialist aspirations.[42]

But then in late 1937 the journal's mood changed dramatically. The editors exulted that "we have made more progress toward a socialized economy in the past four and a half years than in the two previous decades." And the next June an article by John Chamberlain was able to make the change appear a thing of the distant past: "Only a few short years ago (sic.) it was a favorite ideological sport of radicals, whether Communist, Socialist, Brandeisian or free-lance, to pour scorn upon Franklin Delano Roosevelt's 'confused' [efforts]...to make the American economic system work." "I must," he said, "plead guilty with the rest." Granville Hicks, long on the extreme Left, was even able to write a book entitled *I Like America*. It was a time when the Communist Party was declaring Communism the very pillar of free enterprise.[43]

I will close this discussion of the New Deal by telling of an issue that throughout the 1930's was one of the intellectual culture's major themes: the call for "planning." In January 1931, *The New Republic* editorialized for a national structure to "allot new capital according to plan, regulate prices, profits and incomes." Rexford Tugwell said in 1932 that "...the interest of the liberals among us in the institutions of the new Russia of the Soviets...has created wide popular interest in 'planning'...."[44]

Oddly, in light of the fact that there was so much open support for socialism, "planning" served as a euphemism that perpetuated a certain amount of dissimulation. Many liberals, however, were at that time willing to be as forthright as Edmund Wilson was when he wrote that "we have always talked about the desirability of a planned society...But if this means anything, does it not mean socialism? And should we not do well to make this perfectly plain?"

Beginning in March 1931, George Soule became one of the leading advocates of planning: "We shall have to have a textile plan, a coal plan, a housing plan. Indeed, there ought to be a general staff for every industrial group, heading into the General Staff...Private investment will have to be planned...." This remained his theme for several years. His book *A Planned Society* appeared in 1932; in 1939 he set out details for "scientific planning." That same year, W. Jett Lauck called for a "National Planning Board," with "Industry Councils" consisting of "equal representation of industry, labor and the public." There would be a "Capital Issues Banking Board" to determine the direction of investment.[45]

An interesting twist is that John T. Flynn, who had written prolifically for *The New Republic* during the '30's, eventually became a crusader against the dissimulative introduction of socialism through "planning." In *The Road Ahead* he warned that "planning" was a euphemism for socialism and that, although George Soule and Stuart Chase had supported it for several years, it became "respectable" as the program of a broad movement in about 1938. His warnings came after his falling out with *The New Republic*. By that time, he had moved toward conservatism.

He had earlier associated himself with the journal during years in which it was far to the left.

### The 1930's: the Red Decade

Although the intellectual culture kept one foot in the domestic political scene, the other was squarely planted in far-Left ideology. We have already seen the infatuation with Soviet Russia in the 1920's. By the late '20's, this had become a passionate theme. In my earlier discussion of the 1920's, I cited examples of the intense interest in Soviet Russia that appeared in *The New Republic*.

This continued at even higher intensity during the 1930's. The excitement was reflected in *The New Republic* by advertisements for Communist causes, manifestoes of front organizations, enthusiastic letters from readers, all combined with innumerable editorials, articles and book reviews. Although there is no substitute for reading the actual journals of that period, I hope that a few examples from *The New Republic* will give some idea of the tone:

Bruce Bliven, who spent many years with the journal and was the leading editor after Croly, wrote in 1931 that "even with all proper cautions..., I still find this graphic picture of Russia's material progress tremendously exciting." M. R. Werner said that Stalin emerged from a book he was reviewing "as a person for whose character one has a tremendous respect." The next year, Edmund Wilson wrote that "Communism...has for the first time brought humanity out into the great world of creative thought and work." In 1935, Waldo Frank, a frequent contributor, sent in a letter saying that "I wish to stress...my entire loyalty to the Soviet cause and my strict partisanship with its government in its struggles against a hostile world...The U.S.S.R. is the 'fatherland' of all true revolutionaries, the world over."[46]

In 1937 Andre Gide asked in *The New Republic* "Who shall say what the Soviet Union has been to us? More than a chosen land – an example, a guide. What we have dreamt of, what we have hardly dared to hope, but towards which we were straining all our will and all our strength, was coming into being over there."[47]

*The Nation* was just as far left. Its editor Oswald Garrison Villard wrote after a trip to Soviet Russia in 1929 that "it is all so new, so genuinely thrilling." In 1934, *The Nation* editorialized that the New Deal was just "a half-baked capitalism with so-called liberal trimmings"; and in 1937 that "the Soviet government...[is] the leadership of the anti-fascist forces in the world...the chief element of hope."[48]

So engrossing was this ideological partisanship that it led to what future generations will almost certainly consider an intellectual scandal of unspeakable proportions. A major fact about the 1930's is that the world intellectual culture condoned and even justified the mass slaughter within the Soviet Union, just as it has been a major fact since World War II that Hitler's Holocaust has been made the justifiable subject of absolute moral condemnation while the Gulags under Stalin, the execution of many millions under Mao, the genocide in Cambodia, and countless other atrocities under Communist regimes have in the main been ignored by the intellectual culture when they have occurred and then have been given only passing attention.

We have seen that in 1926 Jerome Davis wrote a justification for the Soviet secret police in *The New Republic* when he said that "...every country has its G.P.U., especially in a period of war and revolution." In 1927, an article told of the execution of twenty-two counter-revolutionaries in Russia, and attributed it to Soviet fears caused by the West and by the assassination of the Soviet ambassador to Poland. In 1930, there was an article justifying the "rooting out" of the kulaks (the prosperous and not-so-prosperous peasants). On the same page, Vera Micheles Dean was the author of a strangely non-judgmental article about the Soviet drive to "liquidate" the kulaks. Later that year, after the *New York Times* reported the execution of "scores of men" for shortcomings in carrying out the Soviet Five-Year Plan, the *New Republic*'s editors wrote: "Well, in America we execute people for murder and for holding unorthodox political opinions; in Russia they execute people for abusing positions of high responsibility."[49]

In 1931, William Henry Chamberlain informed *The New Republic*'s readers (and, if they didn't know already, its editors) of the "ruthless smashing of the kulaks...[who are] banished to concentration camps and places of remote exile." But later that year Herman Simpson reviewed Anna Louise Strong's book *The Soviets Conquer Wheat* and argued that "the violence which has marked the agrarian revolution seems...to be an inevitable accompaniment of so profound and far-reaching a transformation...." In the issue of October 11, 1933, Maxwell S. Stewart spoke of "the bountiful harvest of 1933," and said that "in view of the truly remarkable advance made during the past year, it is difficult to explain the large number of reports in the American press depicting famine conditions in Russia...."[50]

In 1934, Joshua Kunitz reported that "with the exception of a relatively few kulaks and anti-Bolshevik die-hards, the Soviet population stands solidly behind the government." In 1935, *The New Republic* ran an article by Anna Louise Strong (with an equivocating editorial note introducing it) which said that "there are 'labor camps' in many parts of the country, as part of the Soviet method of reclaiming anti-social elements by useful, collective work...Men in the labor camps draw wages, have vacations...."[51]

In 1937, a book review by Corliss Lamont praised the Soviet Union for building production with "less suffering than capitalism at any time." That same year, Maurice Hindus looked back and praised the collectivization of agriculture and "...the brilliance with which this leadership has converted the most disastrous calamity, which collectivization was in its early years, into the most consummate triumph of the Revolution, if not of all history."[52]

But slowly the terrible truth began to seep through. Eugene Lyons wrote a letter to *The New Republic* in 1937 saying that "Mr. Josephson is egregiously in error in asserting that in 1932 American intellectuals were 'misinformed' about Soviet blunders of that period. Not *mis*informed, but *un*informed. The 1932 equivalent of today's Josephson's prevented knowledge from reaching their breathren by shouting down every unpleasant truth...." In 1939, John Chamberlain wrote of "...the great 1932-33 famine, in which three or four million peasants died as a result of the inept handling of the drive for agrarian collectivization." [Notice that even then he attributed the famine to "ineptness," and that he went on to blame the famine primarily on the West's refusal to give Russia capital.][53]

Two months later, Vincent Sheean wrote that "a program of collectivization in agriculture was enforced from 1931 onwards by means of the most ghastly sacrifices, in which six or seven million peasants are believed to have died of starvation in the Ukraine alone." The intellectual tragedy of the period is encapsulated in his admission that "this is the first criticism I have ever made of the Soviet Union."[54]

Eugene Lyons, whom I quoted above, became staunchly anti-Communist after serving as editor of the *Soviet Russia Pictorial* and working for four years for Tass, the Soviet news agency. After he broke with Communism, he wrote *The Red Decade*, in which he revealed that "in the winter of 1932-33 a famine greater than any in Russia's history devastated...the Ukraine, North Caucasis and Central Asia. What made it unspeakably sadistic was that it was...a planned famine...." He said that "we all saw it coming. We all knew that the government could head it off by spending a few million dollars for Canadian or South American grain. But these little men in the Kremlin....decided to 'punish' a population of forty or fifty million for their sullen passive resistance against the state's seizure of their land, tools and livestock...How many millions died?

Maurice Hindus, while still among the leading apologists for Soviet horrors, 'admitted' three million corpses. Soviet officials and journalists in private conversation put it at seven millions – mentioning the figure, sometimes, even a little boastfully."[55]

Adam B. Ulam has cited a figure of "four or five million." He mentions that during the famine "the state exported a million and a half tons of grain to secure foreign currency for industrialization."[56]

From what we have seen, it is little wonder that in December 1984 a later generation of the *New Republic*'s editors would look back and say that "the scandal in the history of this journal is that in the '30's and '40's it accommodated to the *Zeitgeist* (with occasional and important dissents...) by downplaying at best and justifying at worst the crimes of Stalinism."[57]

The intellectual scandal was, however, much broader than simply within *The New Republic*. In 1963, Malcolm Muggeridge wrote about "the monstrous cruelties which accompanied the collectivization of agriculture" that had occurred while he had been a correspondent in Moscow, and how both "the flower of the English intelligentsia" and prominent Englishmen had ignored the horror. Frank A. Warren III has told how in the United States Louis Fischer, Maurice Hindus and Walter Duranty (each of them a prolific liberal author) had all justified the slaughter on the basis that "the end justifies the means."[58]

Although the largest part of the intellectual culture turned a blind eye to the starvation of the kulaks (and additionally to the imprisonment of many millions in the Gulags over more than a thirty-year span), it watched Stalin's purges with intense interest. The purges bitterly divided the Left as the 1930's went on and as the slaughter, often of Bolshevik leaders whom the liberals who had travelled to Soviet Russia knew personally, mounted. The purges were one of several "shocks" that eventually led many intellectuals to oppose Communism.

Again, it is a history that can be illustrated graphically through the pages of *The New Republic*:

There was an ironic optimism in a 1933 editorial which forecast that "there will be a new 'purging' of the [Soviet] Communist party...to weed out incompetents, traitors and the indolent." Then its reports of the actual purges began. Its issue of December 19, 1934, reported that "since the assassination of Sergei Kirov, member of the all-powerful Political Committee..., 127 men and women have been arrested. Of these,...sixty-six were executed within twenty-four hours." The editors were non-judgmental. A month later they argued that "fairness demands a suspension of judgment until all the facts are available."[59]

The issue of August 26, 1936, spoke of the trial of Zinoviev and Kamenev, and reported that they and 14 others had been executed for allegedly participating in a plot in which Trotsky collaborated with the Nazis. "The evidence points," the editors said, "to the genuineness of the plot."[60]

In January 1937, Edmund Wilson and Malcolm Cowley wrote opposing articles about Stalinism. Wilson attacked, Cowley defended. In February, the editors professed their agnosticism toward the treason trials. In April, they reported that John Dewey had become chairman of the American subcommission of the "commission of inquiry into the guilt or innocence of Trotsky." By June, they expressed bewilderment: "The world was puzzled and disturbed by news from the Soviet Union of further convictions and executions for treason, including eight prominent generals." Finally, they shed their neutrality, at least temporarily, saying that "the events...carry their own implications."[61]

*The New Republic* did not, however, swing decisively to the anti-Stalinist camp. It continued to reflect the competing views. In July it carried an article by Walter Duranty defending Stalin. Duranty said of "the Kremlin's enemies" that "their Trojan horse is broken and its occupants destroyed." In October, an article by John Stevens upheld Stalin: "The trials and arrests definitely strengthened the Soviet Union."[62]

On the other side, the editors reported in December that "Dr. Dewey said the members of the committee 'are appalled by the utterly discreditable character of the whole Moscow trial proceedings, at once flimsy and vicious.'" The editors wrote in January 1938 that "nearly every member of the group that made the Russian Revolution is gone"--and called it "a major disaster." Nevertheless, they reiterated their inability to make a judgment. This was followed by a long interval during which the purges were hardly mentioned. Then in June 1939 the editors said that "we have seen no evidence conclusive to us that the political trials were 'frame-ups'....."[63]

A startling accumulation of events, which included the purge trials, laid the foundation for a reevaluation of Communism and the Soviet Union. The purges had created doubt and bitter division. Then the brutality of Communist power-seeking against the other leftist factions during the Spanish Civil War precipitated the breaking away of others, most notably John Dos Passos. Finally, the Hitler-Stalin Pact, followed almost immediately by the invasion and partition of Poland by Germany and the Soviet Union, and then within a short time by the Soviet invasion of Finland and of Latvia, Lithuania and Estonia, shook the intellectual culture to its core.

Unfortunately much of the old affinity was reestablished after Hitler invaded the Soviet Union in June 1941 and after England and the United States became allies of the Soviet Union in World War II. But things were never totally the same, and the "shocks" that rocked the Communist world after World War II (such things as the Lysenko affair, the Hungarian Revolution, Krushchev's revelations about Stalin, the "Polish October," and the crushing of the Dubcek regime in Czechoslovakia) continued to erode the position of the Soviets within the world intellectual community. The announcement of the Hitler-Stalin Pact on August 23, 1939, stunned the intellectual culture. *The New Republic* called it "paralyzing." *The Nation* said "the disillusion which will follow among the left forces here and abroad will be bitter."[64]

The shock was compounded by embarrassment. On August 10, less than two weeks before the Pact was declared, a group of America's most prominent liberal writers, calling itself "the Committee of 400," had issued its famous letter stating their collective faith that political dictatorship was only a transitional phase in the Soviet Union and that "the Soviet Union continues as always to be a bulwark against war and aggression." The signers included many of the names best known to readers of the liberal journals: Waldo Frank, Granville Hicks, Matthew Josephson, Max Lerner, Robert Morss Lovett, Frederick L. Schuman, Vincent Sheean, Maxwell Stewart, I. F. Stone, and James Thurber.

The shock was not enough, however, to keep a tenacious *New Republic* from rationalizing the Pact: "The Russian explanation of why the treaty was signed seems to make good sense...it frees her from having to fight on two fronts at once in case of a major conflict with Japan."[65]

In late September the journal reported the Soviet armistice with Japan and invasion of Poland. The next week, a letter from Granville Hicks told why he was resigning from the Communist Party, but pledged to continue to defend the party and not to denounce the Soviet Union. Then in early November Vincent Sheean's description of the Soviet Union as a "fascist state" appeared. In mid-December the editors finally came forward: "There never has been a clearer case of...aggression...than the invasion of Finland by the Soviet Union."[66]

This eventual candor was followed by surprisingly little comment in *The New Republic* during the next year and a half. There was no introspection into the role it had played. Even after reporting the assassination of Trotsky in Mexico in 1940, the journal chose not to mention it again for several months.

This insouciance lasted until Hitler attacked the U.S.S.R. on June 22, 1941. *The New Republic* immediately urged aid to the Soviet Union (a policy favored, as well, by Winston Churchill). In November, Roger Baldwin wrote hopefully that there would now be a way to influence the Soviets toward "socialist democracy." In the same issue, A. Jugow glowingly praised the social justice within the Soviet Union, and Maurice Hindus argued that Stalin's ruthlessness had had the advantage of hardening the Soviet Union for its contest with Germany. The new mood, which for many was a renewal of the old, was captured by Vice President Henry Wallace in a speech in early 1942: "Russia...was changed from an illiterate to a literate nation within one generation and, in the process, Russia's appreciation of freedom was enormously enhanced."[67]

## During World War II

Everyone knows, of course, that the Allies won militarily in World War II, defeating Germany, Japan and Italy. But it is equally significant that the non-Communist world lost the peace. Within slightly more than four years after the war ended, the Soviet Union took the eastern half of Europe and the Communists under Mao conquered China. This set the stage for the Cold War and for the Korean and Vietnam wars.

I will leave a more complete discussion of this to my chapter on liberalism's international worldview and policies. For the present, it will be sufficient to refer ahead to the subject and to observe that the major cause of the disastrous aftermath of the war lay in the illusions that the Left and liberalism fostered about Communism.

The tone of the intellectual culture during the war is well illustrated by *The Nation*'s having run a number of articles by Anna Louise Strong, for many years prior to her own fall from grace one of the most unquestioning apologists for the Soviet Union. One of these was her 1944 article "With the Red Army."[68]

While Winston Churchill saw the war in realistic geopolitical terms and sought a strategy that would minimize the post-war position of the Soviet Union, Roosevelt overrode him. This was due to a blindness born out of the illusion spawned by the ideological context that I have been tracing. In vitally important ways, although not entirely, Harry Truman continued to act under this illusion after he became president. Although liberalism has been ambivalent, the illusion remained for decades as a vitally important part of the liberal worldview. An understanding of its presence and of the consequences that have flowed from it is essential to a comprehension of the second half of the twentieth century.

On the domestic front, Roosevelt in 1943 proposed his "American Charter" for the post-war period. This included his "Economic Bill of Rights," with its explicit politicization of the problem of individual economic well-being, and a number of interventionist measures. A T.V.A.-type project was proposed for all feasible river valleys. Roosevelt's 1944 State of the Union address expounded on his "Second Bill of Rights."[69]

The issue of racial segregation began to appear in liberal writing. In April 1943, *The New Republic* declared that "segregation has made possible the greatest injuries to the Negro people."[70]

In May 1944, *The New Republic* published "A Platform for Progressives" that corresponded to Roosevelt's proposals. Although it wanted "more T.V.A.'s," it did not otherwise call for socialism. Rather, there was to be a strengthening of what the journal referred to as "the social service state." The editors included a forceful call for a fight against racial discrimination.[71]

A conservative coalition controlled both houses of Congress. There was, in addition, dissension among the factions of the "New Deal coalition." It infuriated the intellectual culture, for example, when William Green, the president of the American Federation of Labor, endorsed Martin Dies, the chairman of the House Committee on Un-American Activities, for reelection. In another matter, *The New Republic* denounced "corrupt big-city machines" and "Southern Tories" for having forced Henry Wallace out as Roosevelt's running mate in 1944.[72]

### Truman's "Fair Deal"

Domestically, the years of the Truman administration between 1945 and 1953 were marked by the scaling down of liberal aspirations from those of socialism to those of a "welfare state," which Michael Straight, by then the editor of *The New Republic*, described in 1949 as "a cooperative, state-aided capitalism dedicated to human welfare."[73]

Throughout the post-World War II period, the most prominent liberal authors retained their aspiration for socialism, but this was relegated to the background because there seemed no route to attain it. At the same time, a number of historic factors brought European socialism to embrace a combination of the market economy and the welfare state. The British socialist G. D. H. Cole wrote in *The New Republic* in 1952 that the social democratic variant of Marxism in Western Europe "has accepted the idea of using the parliamentary instrument for advancing in the direction of the Welfare State." Ben Seligman said, in commenting on a book by Harry K. Girvetz, that "the positive program for today's liberals that he offers is a compound of Beveridge, Keynes and Hansen, with Britain and Scandinavia set up as suitable models."[74]

This was the beginning of the type of liberalism that we have known since World War II, a liberalism that has consisted of a "liberal agenda" before the Congress for measures leading to a piecemeal expansion of federal power.

Since many of the proposals were of the "foot-in-the-door" variety, with liberals intending further growth of the function once government began to exercise it, conservatives labelled it – correctly, I think – "creeping socialism."

In early 1946, *The New Republic* praised Truman's State of the Union message, which Henry Wallace later said "contained a magnificent New Deal program." The speech proposed federal aid to education, a national public works program, a federal health system, a permanent Fair Employment Practices Commission, an increased minimum wage and a federal scientific research agency.[75]

Keynesian economics was institutionalized by the Employment Act of 1946. After his conversion to conservatism, one of *The New Republic's* writers, Garet Garrett, described the Act as "a law of revolutionary purport" that "delivered into the hands of government ultimate control of the American economy." The Act committed the federal government to maintain full employment.[76]

In the 1948 presidential election campaign, Truman went to the country with what TRB described as "the most radical platform in presidential history." Among other things, the platform, he said, "advocates government ownership and operation of transmission lines from government dams right up to the consumers' electric stoves." A *New Republic* editorial reported that Truman "has chosen to fight on principles of militant liberalism."[77]

Then in his 1949 State of the Union message in which he set forth his "Fair Deal," Truman proposed what TRB called "a social-welfare state [that] amounts to the most leftward-leaning program ever sent by an American president to Congress." Truman urged creation of a Columbia Valley Authority for the Northwest. To TRB, the Brannan Plan for agriculture was "breath-taking." He wrote that "the basic theory's simple and revolutionary: We give a particular class economic security in return for quite heavy regimentation." The administration called for public housing, the extension of Social Security, and more progressive rates for the income tax.[78]

From all of this it may seem that those were exuberant years for a liberalism willing to content itself at least temporarily with the incremental techniques of a welfare state. But such an impression would seriously miss the mark.

Although Truman's program and rhetoric were applauded by liberal intellectuals, the actual direction of his administration was not to their liking. In 1946, a *New Republic* editorial reported that progressives no longer had a major spokesman within the administration. In 1948, Henry Wallace wrote that "no significant part" of the "magnificent New Deal program" that Truman had submitted two years before had been enacted. In May of that year, the editors complained that Truman's actions had been quite different from his speeches, and that the New Dealers in the administration had been replaced by men from the military and from Wall Street.[79]

*The New Republic* endorsed Truman for election later that fall after he stepped up his militant rhetoric and after Henry Wallace (who was editor for a very short time) was replaced by Michael Straight as editor. But in 1949 TRB observed again that there was "a basic paradox" in "the difference between the President's almost radical words and the men advising him." James Wechsler's verdict years later was that Truman "was something less than a resolute, adventurous liberal crusader... [He] could gruffly pay his rhetorical respects to progressive legislation but he was neither creative nor original in this realm."[80]

Even if Truman had had the qualities that a man like Wechsler would have wanted, there were three obstacles standing in the way of the Fair Deal program: the presence of the Republican 80th Congress in 1947 and 1948, the Republican-Southern Democrat coalition in Congress the rest of the time, and the Korean War that began in June 1950 and drained away the possibility of domestic innovation.

During all of this, there was a struggle within the liberal intellectual culture over the movement's relation to Communism. The far-left Progressive Citizens of America (P.C.A.) was formed in December 1946. This stimulated the formation of the Americans for Democratic Action (A.D.A.) in early 1947, which Chilton Williamson, Jr., says "adamantly opposed...working with Communists and fellow-travelers." According to Wechsler, the A.D.A. became "a leading factor in the rout of the U.S. Communist movement in the 1948 campaign" when the Communist-run Progressive Party failed to attract widespread liberal support.[81]

Thus, the main body of American liberals had broken with the Communist Left. Instead, in Wechsler's words, "the A.D.A. has provided the stimulus of a sort of American Fabian Society." It is interesting how this was seen by the differing points of view: to the Left it meant a major movement of American liberalism to the right; to conservatives the Fabian tactic of piecemeal socialism seemed just as threatening as before.[82]

It will be best for me to leave my discussion of liberalism's relationship to international affairs during this period to my later chapter on that subject, since it deserves detailed attention. The capsule summary that follows is necessarily oversimplified:

American liberals slowly struggled toward the doctrine of containment *vis a vis* Communist expansion, proposed by George Kennan in 1947. Nevertheless, American policy was disastrously influenced by the continuing illusion about Communism, which unfortunately was not fully dispelled by the split between the P.C.A. and the A.D.A.

Over Churchill's objections, Eastern Europe was allowed to fall into the hands of the Red Army and to become consolidated as part of the Soviet empire; the Soviet Union was encouraged to come into the war against Japan despite the United States' possession of the atom bomb, and this gave the Communists great strategic advantages in their fight to conquer China; illusions were vigorously advanced about the nature of the Maoist movement in China, and the anti-Communist government of Chiang Kai-shek was vilified unmercifully, leading to policies that resulted in the Communist victory in late 1949; and policies were pursued and declarations made that encouraged the North Korean Communists to invade South Korea, which they did on June 25, 1950.

On the other side of the ledger, Western Europe was maintained and strengthened as part of the non-Communist world. Once the idea of inviting the Soviet Union to join in the Marshall Plan was out of the way, the Marshall Plan became a major instrument on behalf of the free world. In Greece, the Truman Doctrine successfully defeated the Communist insurgency. This prevented a shift in the balance of power to the Soviet Union in the eastern Mediterranean. It is worth observing, however, that the Truman Doctrine was strenuously opposed editorially by both *The New Republic* and *The Nation*.[83]

## NOTES

[1] New Republic, June 7, 1922, p. 34; New Republic, April 8, 1972, p. 23; Eric F. Goldman, *Rendezvous With Destiny* (New York: Vintage Books, 1977), p. 223.

[2] New Republic, May 13, 1931, p. 348; New Republic, January 10, 1923, p. 168; New Republic, January 31, 1931.

[3] New Republic, June 6, 1923, p. 42; New Republic, April 9, 1924, p. 187-III; New Republic, October 13, 1926, p. 211; New Republic, June 1, 1927, p. 36; New Republic, September 21, 1927, p. 112; New Republic, November 2, 1927, p. 279.

[4] New Republic, November 21, 1928, p. 12; New Republic, December 12, 1928, p. 79.

[5] New Republic, December 23, 1925, p. 123; New Republic, September 28, 1927, p. 133; New Republic, February 20, 1929, p. 15; New Republic, February 5, 1930, p. 295.

[6] John D. Buenker, *Liberalism and Progressive Reform* (New York: Charles Scribner's Sons, 1973), pp. 230, 231, 51.

[7] New Republic, April 10, 1915, p. 250.

[8] New Republic, October 18, 1933, p. 272.

[9] New Republic, January 31, 1934, p. 330.

[10] New Republic, April 22, 1936, p. 302; New Republic, March 1, 1939, p. 100; New Republic, April 11, 1949, p. 14; New Republic, April 19, 1943, p. 536.

[11] New Republic, May 16, 1934, p. 13; New Republic, March 15, 1933, p. 118.

[12] New Republic, November 30, 1927, p. 42; New Republic, November 21, 1934, p. 38.

[13] Paul K. Conkin, *The New Deal* (New York: Thomas Y. Crowell Company, 1967), p. 61.

[14] Conkin, *The New Deal*, p. 61.

[15] New Republic, May 15, 1929, p. 355; New Republic, Nov. 28, 1928, p. 27.

[16] New Republic, January 5, 1974, p. 14.

[17] New Republic, September 23, 1931, p. 137; New Republic, October 14, 1931, p. 217

[18] New Republic, May 24, 1933, p. 44; New Republic, May 31, 1933, p. 57.

[19] New Republic, May 17, 1933, p. 4.

[20] New Republic, March 4, 1936, p. 105; New Republic, Nov. 15, 1933, p. 4.

[21] New Republic, August 25, 1941, p. 260.

[22] New Republic, August 23, 1933, p. 33; New Republic, September 6, 1933, p. 87; New Republic, December 6, 1933, p. 100.

[23] New Republic, April 3, 1935, p. 21; New Republic, March 20, 1935, p. 146.

[24] Arthur M. Schlesinger, Jr., *The Age of Roosevelt: The Politics of Upheaval* (Boston: Houghton Mifflin Company, 1960), p. 387.

[25] New Republic, July 3, 1935, p. 205.

[26] New Republic, January 29, 1936, p. 334; Richard S. Kirkendall (ed.), *The New Deal: The Historical Debate* (New York: John Wiley & Sons, Inc., 1973), p. 131; Conkin, *The New Deal*, p. 66.

[27] New Republic, September 4, 1935, p. 87; New Republic, February 24, 1937, p. 72.

[28] New Republic, September 28, 1932, p. 164; New Republic, January 17, 1934, p. 263; New Republic, October 3, 1934, p. 223.

[29] Conkin, *The New Deal*, p. 73.

[30] Bernard Sternsher, *Rexford Tugwell and the New Deal* (New Brunswick: Rutgers University Press, 1964), p. 122; New Republic, December 25, 1944, p. 877; New Republic, July 25, 1960, p. 21.

[31] New Republic, September 26, 1960, p. 23.

[32] New Republic, June 3, 1931, p. 67.

[33] Dean L. May, *From New Deal to New Economics* (New York: Garland Publishing, Inc., 1981), p. 59.

[34] New Republic, January 28, 1944, p. 268.
[35] New Republic, July 5, 1939, p. 250.
[36] New Republic, May 10, 1939, p. 3; May, *From New Deal*, p. x.
[37] May, *From New Deal*, p. 26.
[38] Sternsher, *Rexford Tugwell*, p. 76 (re Hoover); New Republic, March 20, 1935, p. 141; May, *From New Deal*, p. 4; Louis A. Zurcher, Jr., and Charles M. Bonjean (ed.s), *Planned Social Intervention* (London: Chandler Publishing Company, 1970), p. 213.
[39] Lewis L. Gould, *The Progressive Era* (New York: Syracuse University Press, 1974), p. 97; New Republic, September 7, 1968, p. 6.
[40] New Republic, May 22, 1935, p. 33; New Republic, January 1, 1936, p. 211; New Republic, February 8, 1939, p. 12; New Republic, May 17, 1943, p. 660; New Republic, January 27, 1947, p. 3; New Republic, December 16, 1946, p. 785.
[41] New Republic, October 27, 1958, p. 13.
[42] New Republic, March 8, 1933, p. 89; New Republic, March 14, 1934, p. 116; New Republic, January 9, 1935, p. 245; New Republic, January 30, 1935, p. 332; New Republic, June 10, 1936, p. 157.
[43] New Republic, Sept. 29, 1937, p. 201; New Republic, June 15, 1938, p. 163.
[44] New Republic, January 21, 1931, p. 259; Howard Zinn (ed.), *New Deal Thought* (Indianapolis: Bobbs-Merrill Company, 1966), p. 14.
[45] New Republic, Jan. 14, 1931, p. 234; New Republic, March 11, 1931, p. 89; New Republic, Nov. 8, 1939, p. 29; New Republic, July 5, 1939, pp. 244, 245.
[46] New Republic, May 27, 1931, p. 42; New Republic, June 10, 1931, p. 102; New Republic, May 11, 1932, p. 349; New Republic, February 27, 1935, p. 77.
[47] New Republic, March 31, 1937, p. 231.
[48] The Nation, Vol. 129, p. 515; The Nation, October 31, 1934, p. 498; The Nation, Vol. 145, p. 521.
[49] New Republic, October 13, 1926, p. 211; New Republic, June 29, 1927, p. 137; New Republic, March 5, 1930, p. 59; New Republic, Dec. 3, 1930, p. 57.
[50] New Republic, February 25, 1931, p. 42; New Republic, December 16, 1931, p. 142; New Republic, October 11, 1933, p. 230.
[51] New Republic, Jan. 17, 1934, p. 277; New Republic, Aug. 7, 1935, p. 358.
[52] New Republic, Jan. 20, 1937, p. 363; New Republic, Aug. 18, 1937, p. 35.
[53] New Republic, Dec. 29, 1937, p. 229; New Republic, Sept. 6, 1939, p. 112.
[54] New Republic, November 8, 1939, p. 7.
[55] Eugene Lyons, *The Red Decade* (Indianapolis: Bobbs-Merrill Company, 1941), p. 97.
[56] New Republic, March 27, 1976, p. 13.
[57] New Republic, December 10, 1984, p. 10.
[58] New Republic, November 9, 1963, p. 47; Frank A. Warren III, *Liberals and Communism: The 'Red Decade' Revisited* (Bloomington: Indiana University Press, 1966), pp. 71, 72.
[59] New Republic, January 4, 1933, p. 198; New Republic, December 19, 1934, p. 151; New Republic, January 23, 1935, p. 293.
[60] New Republic, August 26, 1936, pp. 58, 88.

[61] New Republic, January 20, 1937, pp. 345, 348; New Republic, February 10, 1937, p. 33; New Republic, April 28, 1937, p. 343; New Republic, June 23, 1937, pp. 169, 174.

[62] New Republic, July 14, 1937, p. 272; New Republic, Oct. 20, 1937, p. 296.

[63] New Republic, December 22, 1937, p. 182; New Republic, January 5, 1938, p. 240; New Republic, June 28, 1939, p. 202.

[64] New Republic, Aug. 30, 1939, p. 85; The Nation, Aug. 26, 1939, pp. 212, 228.

[65] New Republic, September 6, 1939, p. 118.

[66] New Republic, October 4, 1939, p. 244; New Republic, November 8, 1939, p. 7; New Republic, December 13, 1939, p. 219.

[67] New Republic, June 30, 1941, p. 871; New Republic, November 17, 1941, pp. 651, 654, 665; New Republic, May 25, 1942, p. 725.

[68] The Nation, Vol. 159, p. 121.

[69] New Republic, April 19, 1943, p. 523.

[70] New Republic, April 19, 1943, p. 492.

[71] New Republic, May 8, 1944, p. 644; New Republic, Oct. 22, 1945, p. 515.

[72] New Republic, March 6, 1944, p. 301; New Republic, July 31, 1944, p. 115.

[73] New Republic, August 15, 1949, p. 2.

[74] New Republic, March 24, 1952, p. 10; New Republic, March 12, 1951, p.20.

[75] New Republic, January 28, 1946, p. 108; New Republic, Jan. 5, 1948, p. 9.

[76] Garet Garrett, *The American Story* (Chicago: Henry Regnery Company, 1955), p. 387.

[77] New Republic, November 15, 1948, p. 3; New Republic, September 27, 1948, p. 32.

[78] New Republic, January 31, 1949, p. 3; New Republic, May 9, 1949, p. 3.

[79] New Republic, September 30, 1946, p. 396; New Republic, January 5, 1948, p. 9; New Republic, May 17, 1948, pp. 14, 18.

[80] New Republic, August 8, 1949, p. 3; James A. Wechsler, *The Crucial Decade: America, 1945-1955* (New York: Alfred A. Knopf, Inc., 1956), p. 47.

[81] New Republic, Feb. 9, 1974, p. 23; Wechsler, *The Crucial Decade*, p. 55.

[82] Wechsler, *The Crucial Decade*, p. 56.

[83] New Republic, March 24, 1947, p. 6; The Nation, Vol. 166, p. 342.

# CHAPTER FOUR
# Phases in American Liberalism: 1953-1985

### Four postwar decades: all one period

The analysis I am about to make of the phases of liberalism since the Truman administration is a different analysis than I would have made before I read as extensively as I did in the liberal literature of the period. My impression had been that there were distinct phases – the 1950's, the tumultuous '60's, and the uncertainties and drift of the 1970's and '80's. I am persuaded now that the entire span (in which we could just as well include the eight years under Truman) has involved a continuous trend. If we do not treat it as the same period, we are likely to lose sight of that continuity. Surprisingly enough, the 1960's are best thought of as an interlude of frenetic activity in what has otherwise been a steady liberal decline (at least in terms of its original socialist impulse; most recently, the alienation of the intellectual culture that lies at the heart of the modern liberal-Left has found a major long-term strategy in "multiculturalism," and this can pose an even greater challenge to the main society than was posed by the drive toward socialism).

### A capsule summary

Variations will appear as we look into the detail, but a summary of the trends within liberalism since World War II will include the following characteristics that have been common to the period as a whole:

• Even though most of the principal liberal authors retained their allegiance to socialism, they did so in a world in which many socialists, especially in Europe, had long been at loose ends. Within both European "social democracy" and American liberalism there has for many years been a more or less constant feeling of drift, of loss of vision, of futility.

• This has been accompanied by a general puncturing, within the public at large and the intellectual culture, of the liberal myths that were powerful for so long. This includes a loss of faith in the ability of government, given an application of reason and enough money, to solve every problem. This deflation was only in small measure a result of conservative efforts. It came more from the Left's own acceptance of the biting attacks upon "interest group liberalism" and "the Establishment" made by the New Left in the 1960's. It has also come from the seeming intractability of certain realities for a Keynesian-social service society: of inflation; of unemployment even during inflation; of the infinite expandability of social spending without seeming effect; of the decline of productivity; and of the continuance for many years of the Cold War.

- Even into the 1990s, American voters have continued the deadlock between liberals and conservatives, giving neither of them enough power to carry out initiatives. Although there is some tinkering and much fidgeting, the country has long-since settled into a post-New Deal consensus following what was in effect the consolidation of the New Deal under Eisenhower. Even the Reagan administration had little power to carry out a conservative agenda.

- The New Deal coalition has had some staying power – or else liberalism would have passed out of existence long ago; but the members of the coalition have also been engaged in a constant process of bickering and division. This has led to a long and thusfar futile search for a "new coalition."

- The Civil Rights movement, on the cutting edge of liberalism during the 1950's and the first half of the '60's, eventually lost much of its moral force. With the stress on compensatory programs, known to the general public as reverse discrimination, much of the moral appeal has shifted to the other side, since the programs smack of special privilege. Pathetically, the Civil Rights movement deteriorated into a collection of narrowly self-interested groups, some of which – especially radical feminists and militant homosexuals – are on a politically unappealing fringe of American society.

- New movements have struggled for vision and may (or may not) point the way to the future: neo-conservatism, with its dispelling of illusion, its anti-Communism and its "two cheers for capitalism"; neo-liberalism, thusfar calling uncertainly for a new Mercantilism that will place government activism behind selected forces within the market; and academic Marxism, which for fifteen years has kept an anti-capitalist critique and the emotions of radicalism simmering within an intellectual culture that has otherwise made its peace, more than ever before, with the society at large.

- It is a fact of the greatest significance that I cannot include in this list an emergent neo-classical liberalism. On the Right, Ronald Reagan's popularity should by all reasonable expectation have stimulated a great intellectual resurgence. Nevertheless, his administration did not see the importance of being midwife to a new intellectual culture, and one did not develop spontaneously among the country's young people (or otherwise). This suggests that the Reagan years were only be interregnum. By this failure, the predominant middle class culture exemplified the flaw that has plagued civilization in virtually all periods of history. This includes the same void that has dominated Western society since the Enlightenment. Such a vacuum, if it continues, will make future ideological neuroses inescapable.

• During all this, both American society and the world have been undergoing changes at an unprecedented rate that will produce existential effects that even the best futurist cannot foretell: American cultural and moral standards have continued their long decline. The "space age" and "cybernetic age" offer hopeful new worlds. Women have left home for business and the professions. Our society has become increasingly heterogeneous ethnically and racially, for whatever revitalization or division that may produce. Europe after the world wars shrank from its preeminence, although European unification may raise it up again. Its hegemony has been replaced in the "Third World" by a tragic contradiction in which the potential for emergence into modernity is pitted against an insistent tendency on the part of powerful prehistoric forces to pull whole peoples back down into poverty and degradation. Islamic fundamentalism haunts the world with its militant medievalism. We see how fast things are changing: In the 1986 edition of this book, I wrote: "The Soviets hold fast to their totalitarian state, but the Chinese now want more of Athens, less of Sparta." This has become reversed by 1991, and in each country the situation is subject to rapid change.

In all, it's a world "at sea with lots of sail and little anchor."

### A socialist intellectual core

We have seen that American liberal intellectuality was an eclectic hodge-podge of leftist fashions prior to 1945. As I describe the "decline" of its socialist vision after World War II, I don't wish to suggest that it was ever very solid or sure of itself. But it did at least know what it liked and what it disliked, and this knowledge kept it consistently identified with the various fashions of the Left.

Since World War II, liberal thought's socialist core has been apparent to anyone who has read the literature extensively. Many of post-World War II liberalism's most prominent writers have been socialists. Michael Harrington and Gunnar Myrdal, both socialists, laid the foundation for the War on Poverty that John F. Kennedy was about to launch when he was assassinated and that became central to Lyndon Johnson's "Great Society." Harrington and Myrdal were, in addition, prolific authors of books and contributors to the liberal journals.

John Kenneth Galbraith, after many years as a leading liberal spokesman, finally declared himself a socialist – and added that he had been one for many years. This revelation was, of course, no particular surprise; what was surprising was his willingness to breach the usual dissimulation on the subject. Readers of his books had known their actual content for years. It is significant that similar content appeared in the writings of many others who did not discover such candor.[1]

Others who wrote prominently within post-World War II liberalism and who at the same time identified themselves with socialism included Christopher Jencks, John Rawls, Robert Heilbroner, Robert Lekachman, Irving Howe, Sidney Hook and Christopher Lasch. Irving Kristol was among them until he moved into neo-conservatism. In 1991, under the impact of the collapse of Communism in Eastern Europe and its apparently impending demise in the Soviet Union, Heilbroner wrote a grudging admission that the supporters of a market economy had been right all along.

There were other authors, of course, who did not make the identification with socialism, or who even denied that liberalism had such a connection.

One of the more prominent of these was Eric Goldman, whose book *Rendezvous With Destiny* is an immensely readable history of "modern American reform." Goldman argues that liberalism is distinct from socialism, even though it has been influenced by it and has adopted some of its measures. But his argument is puzzling unless we limit it to liberal politics and exclude liberal thought. During my reading of *The New Republic*, the first article I noticed by Goldman was in November 1944. Thus, he began writing for that journal just shortly after it participated so effulgently in the excesses of the Red Decade. In 1944 the editors were still actively justifying the Soviet system, and had launched a major campaign in favor of the Communists in China.

Goldman presented his interpretation of liberalism in a *New Republic* article co-authored with Mary Paull in July 1946. I remember how incongruous it seemed among the other articles. (As if deliberately to defrock Goldman's argument, for example, the next week's issue contained a book review by Heinz Eulau entitled "Liberal Manifesto" about a book by a "liberal socialist" that contained "a good deal of Marxist thinking.") Goldman's thesis would seem more plausible today, but made no sense at the time.[2]

### Liberalism's loss of vision

Despite the continuation of a generalized socialist faith, liberal intellectuals since World War II have had a problem that didn't exist during the preceding half-century. No longer has it been so easy for them to base their enthusiasms on up-and-coming European movements. The role models have dissolved in the disrepute of the Soviet Union, in the quandary of European social democracy, and most recently in the collapse of Communism in Eastern Europe.

As early as 1948 George Mayberry was writing in *The New Republic* that "the hope for international socialism seems more remote today than in many generations." During the 1950's reports repeatedly came in of disillusionment with British socialism. By 1958, Carl Kaysen wrote that "we are all Jeffersonians, now that belief in socialism is dead." In 1960, Daniel Friedenberg wrote that the "failure of American Fabianism" was due to the watering down of German and English socialism. Friedenberg himself was critical of that dilution, concluding that "whores cannot be Fabians." As part of the soul-searching after Walter Mondale's defeat in 1984, *The New Republic* ran an article speculating on "the death of social democracy" in Europe. Clearly, European socialism since World War II has not seemed the wave of the future. Without a model to go by, only vague aspirations remained.[3]

During the entire span since 1945, subject to less of a respite in the 1960's than may be imagined, liberal writing bemoaned the loss of clear vision, of a long-term aspiration.

In 1946, *The New Republic's* editors wrote that "there is no clear way beyond the New Deal." Two years later, the Americans for Democratic Action tried to draft Eisenhower to run for president. Since they had no hint of his philosophy or positions on issues, they were as opportunistic and ideologically bankrupt in that attempt as Eisenhower's pre-convention Republican supporters were four years later.[4]

In 1953, John Kenneth Galbraith wrote that "it would be hard at the moment to say what the Democratic Party is for...We are still trading on the imagination and intellectual vigor of the Roosevelt era and that capital is running thin." The columnist TRB in 1956 saw no improvement: "The Democrats' chief obstacle is...their own bankruptcy. [They lack] any clear-cut issue of principle...." In a book in 1960, James Wechsler said that "liberalism admittedly seems defensive, sluggish, apologetic...."[5]

It would be reasonable to think that this ennui was soon replaced by excitement during the Kennedy years and the feverish first two years under Johnson. But to think so is again to confuse the liberal intellectual culture with the effusions of liberal pop and media culture. In the issue of *The New Republic* that was written immediately before John F.

Kennedy's assassination, Victor Lange spoke of the prevailing sense of futility. He wrote of "the dilemma in which the contemporary intellectual finds himself: unable to accept the reality of his time but being far from any prospect of changing it by a social revolution, he has made up his mind that he must acquiesce in it."[6]

This emptiness at a time when the liberal media were enthusiastically mythologizing the Camelot-like qualities of the Kennedy presidency shows us something that we have not previously had occasion to notice – that Lange's "contemporary intellectual" was someone quite different from the popular image of a liberal. The great orthodoxy of the liberal media, which had by that time become such an aggressive national institution, has actively projected what we might appropriately call a "pop liberalism." This is a simplistic liberalism that is fashioned at almost a comic-book level. Emotional and non-introspective, it reflects the media's manipulation of the general public's extreme shallowness. Accordingly, the public sees very little of the self-doubt and fragmentation that has been so characteristic of the liberal intellectual culture.

As Richard Nixon's fortunes went to smash in mid-1974, *The New Republic* observed that "the Democratic party is rich in possible presidential candidates," but that rank-and-file Democrats "are not sure where they wish to be led." In 1975, at a time when the prospects for electing a Democratic president the next year were excellent because of the Watergate scandal, Kalman Silver wrote that "ideas about how to achieve social change and the good society are in disarray almost everywhere." Curtis Gans at the same time reported that "when 125 liberal Democrats gathered...to plot 1976 presidential campaign strategy...they departed without a candidate, a program or a strategy." He surmised that "perhaps underlying the lack of agreement was the feeling that the people gathered here shared in common only the past but not a common vision of the future...[One participant said] 'Some of us are populists; others of us are socialists.'"[7]

A month after Jimmy Carter was inaugurated in 1977, Alan Tonelson wrote that "there is no constituency for reform in this country" and that "Jimmy Carter has stepped into the moral vacuum left by Democratic liberals." In late 1982, a year and a half after Carter left office, a *New Republic* book review said that Robert Lekachman was observing that "New Deal and Great Society liberalism" had "run out not only of policy ideas, but of inspiring symbols." Lekachman was said to be calling for "a new and more comprehensive 'agenda for the left,' which would fill the intellectual void." Then after Walter Mondale's landslide loss to Ronald Reagan in 1984, *The New Republic* editorialized that

"American liberalism is in crisis...The old liberal confidences...now lie shattered...."[8]

This review since 1945 shows that the loss of vision, the shattering of confidence, has been a continuing theme within American liberalism since World War II, not just a reaction to a particular electoral defeat. Its roots lie in the diminished vitality of the world Left.

This general disillusionment has had certain specific counterparts. One of these has been a perception by liberals that their own programs haven't worked. In 1969, Norman S. Care reported "the rethinking of liberalism prompted by the failure of organized political attempts to realize liberal aims." TRB said in 1972 that there was "an undercurrent of disassociation, a feeling almost of despair," consisting of a "terrifying...lack of confidence in the capacity of government to solve problems...." In early 1980 Henry Fairlie wrote that "there seems at last to be an end to the belief in the ability of quick if not deep or penetrating minds – seducible or purchasable or both – to identify real problems and their possible political resolution."[9]

A century ago, Herbert Spencer wrote that in England until the middle of the nineteenth century it was considered progressive to remove governmental interventions into people's lives, but that the tone had then shifted to a clamor for more and more political solutions. The latter mood, reflecting the influence of the Left, lasted in the United States until recently. During most of my lifetime, the call for the politicization of all identifiable problems, followed by the formation of interest-group constituencies around each issue and by programs of governmental expenditure to solve the problems has seemed irresistible. The move away from that fixation, if it proves more than a temporary fashion, will be of the utmost significance.

This has been accompanied by and has reflected a diminished trust in government and the presidency. In October 1967, Hans J. Morgenthau spoke of "this withering away of the public's trust in the government." A year later James MacGregor Burns said that "for the first time in decades the power of the Presidency is undergoing critical reevaluation by American liberals." In 1976, a *New Republic* review spoke of "the hundreds of books and monographs assessing Great Society undertakings [that are] mostly expressive of a 'new realism' mood – a perspective sobered by the short-comings of positive government in its encounters with social complexity."[10]

Liberals also have for many years been becoming more sceptical about governmental regulation. The old Progressive faith in the rationality and objectivity of independent experts has given way to a "realistic" awareness that the agencies become the captives of the very processes they regulate.

This awareness was not a new insight to the period we are discussing, since there were various references to it earlier. In 1934, for example, a *New Republic* editorial said that "the effort of the speculative community, knowing that it was to be regulated" by the Securities Act of 1933, "has been to control the regulators." But it is a view that has grown within liberalism since World War II. In 1949, the editors referred to the I.C.C., F.T.C., C.A.B., S.E.C., F.C.C. and F.P.C., and said that "the regulatory agencies created during reform waves soon pass into industry's hands." The skepticism gained momentum later when consumer advocate Ralph Nader levelled his criticisms. By the mid-1970's, Irving Kristol was able to say that "everyone suddenly seems to be in favor of 'deregulation.'" Many liberals and conservatives came to share the view that in a number of areas a return to the market would be preferable to regulation. This "odd coalition," as Kristol called it, ironically came about during an enormous expansion of regulatory activity in the 1970's, in which "vertical agencies" regulating a particular industry were complemented by vast "horizontal agencies" addressing a certain problem wherever it may exist in the country.[11]

From what I said earlier, it would have been surprising if psychologically the alienated intellectual culture had ceased during this long period of disillusionment to go through the cycle in which yearning-for-action led to energetic activity and then to frustration, fatigue and withdrawal. Such a cycle has, in fact, been an important part of the history of the decades following World War II. In my chapters on the New Left I will discuss in detail how the yearning became apparent in the late 1950's, led into the passions of the '60's, and finally eventuated in withdrawal and religious faddism in the '70's.

## Presidents and programs

As a result of the New Deal, there had been a vast shift of Constitutional jurisdiction and of activity to the federal government. The shift seemed meager to those who wanted socialism, but to conservatives it amounted to a revolutionary break from the Constitutional limitations of the past.

The Eisenhower presidency resolved the question of whether the Republican Party, once it regained power, would seek to undo the New Deal. The issue was fought out inside the Republican Party at each national convention. When eventually the conservatives have been able to nominate the presidential candidate, their own initiatives have been blocked, first by the defeat of Barry Goldwater and later by the many constraints under which Ronald Reagan has found it necessary to work.

The consolidation of the New Deal under Eisenhower was commented upon by Reinhold Niebuhr in 1956 when he wrote that Eisenhower "reconciled the American business community to the social revolution, initiated by Roosevelt and resisted by the business community until Eisenhower swallowed the whole revolution with a minimum of polemics and no explicit recognition of the volte face." I would add, though, that the consolidation was fought over quite bitterly within the Republican Party. It certainly didn't creep up on the Republicans who chose Eisenhower over Taft in 1952.[12]

The consolidation continued under Presidents Nixon and Ford. Melville J. Ulmer commented, for example, that Nixon's wage and price controls in 1971 "went farther to the left than the proposals of most Democrats." The Ford administration stayed within the flow. Lyndon Johnson's "Great Society" had expanded the concept of "entitlements," by which all citizens were considered to have a legal right to the benefits provided by a broad substratum of governmental action, and Theodore H. White says that "no succeeding Congresses, from Nixon, through Ford, through Carter, dared deviate from the path of the Great Society." Social spending and horizontal regulation continued their upward spiral until the public's thinking began to shift in the late 1970's.[13]

This growth of entitlements and regulation had been consistent with the main programmatic thrust of post-World War II liberalism, which was always to have a "liberal agenda" of incremental increases before the country. It was clearly a Fabian program of "blowing air into the balloon." In 1950, J. Roland Pennock wrote in his book *Liberal Democracy* that "there is not the slightest suggestion of any point beyond which this process may not go if its indefinite continuation proves acceptable to the majority of Americans."[14]

This process was accelerated from 1961 through 1965 under Presidents Kennedy and Johnson. John Kenneth Galbraith's book *The Affluent Society* was highly popular among liberals in the late 1950's. It argued that the public sector is starved while the private sector is surfeited. (Leon Keyserling soon interjected, however, that growth should be the source of increased public spending, so that a liberal program should emphasize economic growth as well as the usual "change in 'priorities.'") In 1959 TRB reported that "the demand for activist government is arising" and added that "the country (is) waiting for an FDR." Galbraith called for, among other things, a "final attack on poverty," even though he acknowledged that "there has been much progress in the reduction of privation and want." This stress on poverty was something new. It was soon augmented by Michael Harrington's book *The Other America*. Post World War II liberalism had found a constituency and a cause.[15]

In the late '50's, there were two types of yearnings within liberalism: one was for governmental activism, a "new New Deal"; the other, composed of those further to the left, was for more "movement-type" activism, as we shall see in the chapters on the New Left.

Liberal intellectuals began to express disappointment, however, almost immediately after John F. Kennedy took office. In September 1961, TRB complained that "Kennedy has been a disappointment as a teacher...No rousing 'cause' has forced Kennedy to appeal to the nation over the heads of Congress." Kennedy moved to the center as Congress balked at his proposals. As it turned out, Kennedy did not fully accept Galbraith's position; with his tax cut proposal, Kennedy sought to bolster private purchasing power rather than to increase government spending. The long-standing liberal-conservative deadlock was continued, too, when the 1962 Congressional elections again left Kennedy without a majority that would enact his program.[16]

After Kennedy was assassinated on November 22, 1963, Lyndon Johnson took massive advantage of one of the rare occasions when a liberal president has had full Congressional support. He benefitted from the national mood following the assassination. He was also able to capitalize on his landslide victory in the 1964 election. Then, under pressure from a number of factors, things began to fall apart.

Johnson declared his "War on Poverty," in which the poor were engaged in the planning process within "Community Action" programs. He put through the tax cut and came forward with a rent subsidy program that TRB called "one of the boldest ever sent to Congress." When he secured passage of the Civil Rights Act of 1964, he signed into law one of the most comprehensive enactments in our history. The Voting Rights Act of 1965 laid the foundation for greatly expanded Negro participation in Southern politics. In July 1965, TRB exulted that "Johnson's...domestic record in this Congress will be historic."[17]

It is valuable to understand the relationship of all this to liberal theory. I have already commented on the influence of the Galbraith and Harrington books. Galbraith's *The Affluent Society* had stressed essentially the same theme that had been raised early in the century by Simon Patten and Walter Weyl (a socialist and one of the three founding editors of *The New Republic*) when they talked about a "social surplus." Charles Forcey says that "by social surplus Weyl meant the increment of wealth the United States had produced over basic human needs. The surplus was social because it was the product of all society and not of particular individuals. Being surplus...it could easily be directed toward social ends." He points out that "Weyl borrowed his notion of the social surplus largely from Simon Patten."[18]

Gunnar Myrdal contributed what Leon Keyserling called "a great book," *Challenge to Affluence*, in 1962, in which he argued that growth and social priorities must be bound together.[19]

The War on Poverty's stress on decentralization and on "maximum feasible participation" by the poor themselves on Community Action boards is discussed in the literature as having arisen more or less accidentally. It has a long history, though, in leftist thought. During the same period, the New Left talked about "participatory democracy," which was much the same thing. Nathan Glazer has written that "participatory democracy...is a concept derived from the Paris Commune (of 1870) in which, according to Marx's account, the people, permanently politicized, permanently in arms, met every day to settle their fate."[20]

Despite the rush of activity in 1964 and 1965, all was not well. The Civil Rights movement became more fragmented; in its militancy it took on an "anti-white-liberal" tone. The movement opposing the war in Vietnam was heating up, and led to a bitter split among liberals and to Johnson's eventual withdrawal from the presidential race in 1968. The New Left was damning liberalism as the voice of an "establishment" that combined the military, big business, and politics. Inflation became rampant as the administration sought simultaneously to sustain the war and social spending. The congressional elections in 1966, in which the Democrats lost 47 seats, again gave conservatives a veto. And the War on Poverty programs were soon perceived by many liberals to be failures, eaten alive by the tussle of interest groups, the poor's own lack of interest, and the beginning of some realistic thinking about the poor.

The dissatisfaction with the War on Poverty was apparent as early as December 1965 when James G. Patton, the President of the National Farmers Union, wrote that "sleazy politicians and self-serving private groups conduct a tug-of-war for poverty money." He said that "it appears that the poor are not to be served but to be perpetuated." Two months later, Andrew Kopkind wrote that "the War on Poverty...is more attentive to the politicians, the businessmen and the social workers than it is to the poor." Paul Marx reported in 1968 that "everyone is dissatisfied" with the Community Action programs.[21]

Heresy sprang up within liberalism questioning the whole theory of the civil rights movement. Ronald Berman has written that "the great event of the Sixties was, I think, the publication of the Moynihan Report [on the Negro family]." Daniel Moynihan, Nathan Glazer, Edward Banfield and others began to question whether the condition of the Negro was entirely the fault of white society and to suggest that such things as the matriarchal family structure and the lack of an adequate time-perspective were contributing factors. "*The Negro Family*, with its description of social pathology," Berman said, "was particularly demoralizing to those who gave their faith to political action."[22]

Even Keynesianism, which not long before had seemed to offer the ultimate solution to the trade cycle, was in trouble. As early as 1958, Leon Keyserling had recognized what later became known as "stagflation." This was the problem that unemployment and a sluggish economy, instead of disappearing in the face of inflation, would often co-exist with it. Prices were rising despite the 1958 recession. By the late 1970's and early '80's, experience had caused a major reevaluation of Keynesianism. In 1977, *The New York Times* complained of "the bankruptcy of modern theory." In 1980, Gar Alperovitz and Jeff Fox were speaking in *The New Republic* of "the bankruptcy of the basic assumption of American Keynesianism: that the upward trends of the immediate postwar period could be maintained by the simple manipulation of fiscal and monetary policy, and that the resulting economic growth would allow the nation to avoid politically sticky questions of income and wealth distribution."[23]

The poor performance of Keynesianism was attributed to rigidities in the economy. Thomas Balogh voiced a common theme in 1980 when he faulted the increased concentration of business and labor. He said that "the combination of oligopoly in the goods markets and bilateral monopoly in the labor market destroyed the basis of conventional economic analysis." What this translates to, in part, is an admission that various deviations that liberalism itself has encouraged from a competitive market were the cause of the economic dilemma. Keynesianism had sought to use inflation to out-strip the structural unemployment caused by collective bargaining, minimum wage laws and a fixation against downward adjustments in wages. But even that wasn't working. In addition, the inflation, which became rampant in the late 1970's, was among the factors destroying the basis for liberal social policy. Theodore H. White summed it up in 1982 when he wrote that "inflation is the...leukemia of planning and hope."[24]

### Important, but tangential, issues

The absence of an overriding liberal mission was compensated for during the 1970's by other issues. In long-term perspective these must be understood as at best only tangential to liberalism's socialist aspiration.

The moral imperative of equality, in the sense of everyone's participating without differentiation, provided the most burning issue, which was feminism. But while the more radical feminists drew upon a century-and-a-half of socialist denunciations of marriage to give feminism a socialist meaning, the movement has hardly meant that for the great majority of American women. To this majority, it has meant the meeting of the practical needs posed by their assumption of careers.

A career orientation for women within a market economy is no doubt damaging to certain important social values that classical liberalism considers important to a free society, but the career orientation does not itself move the society closer to socialism. The movement into careers mainly results from a number of underlying economic and social causes that are not essentially ideological. Rather than causing those factors, the feminist movement has reflected them, at least so far as its mass support has been concerned.

The homosexual-rights movement has not had nearly the drawing-power for public acceptance, but has occupied much the same role. It, too, has been related to the thrust toward equality in the participative sense, and has thus been tangential to what liberals before World War II would have considered their main aspiration. This is not to say that certain aspects of leftist ideology do not play a part; it is no doubt much easier for the liberal-Left to support the homosexual-rights movement than for conservatism to do so: liberal ideology, in common with the Left in general, has long been alienated from many middle-class values, has stressed relativism as a cutting tool, and has depended upon alliances with unassimilated groups.

Consumer protection was another issue identified with liberalism in the 1970's. This reflected a combination of factors. One was the continuing imperfections within the market system and its legal framework. These are imperfections that a vigorous classical liberalism would be just as inclined to root out. Another factor was the tendency of modern liberalism to fall back upon Muckraking espouses at times when liberalism is not occupied with a more systematic program. (I don't mean to suggest that the exposes, to the extent they are not exaggerated, are off the mark in pointing to abuses. But it is significant that liberals themselves have denigrated the Muckraking tendency when they have felt that they have had better things to do.) The criticism of abuses within the market system may reflect alienation, but is peripheral to a socialist program unless it can be made part of a general assault on capitalism.

An issue of the 1970's that received less public awareness was the call for "the social responsibility of business." This phrase is so ambiguous that it could mean almost anything, and indeed it has been used by most ideologies, including the Nazis'; but to liberals it has meant making the large corporation a vehicle for a wide range of social policies, largely through exhortation and without systematic governmental oversight.

It should be apparent, in light of all that we have covered, how desperately this is a "fall-back" position for the liberal-Left. Although it is in the tradition of New Nationalism, it is a pale substitute for what liberals have traditionally wanted. To most earlier liberals it would have seemed ludicrous to make an unsupervised corporate capitalism the executor of liberal policies.

The closest that contemporary liberals have been able to come to an ideological justification for the "social responsibility" emphasis has been the argument, which has time-honored origins in Marx and Bellamy and several others, that large corporations are composed of the members of a new technocratic professional class that it has become more and more divorced from the traditional values of capitalism. Galbraith's next generation of writings after *The Affluent Society* was based on this theme. But at a time when liberal confidence is as low as it is, such a rationale, once a powerful tool in the effort to pull corporate capitalism into a collectivist orbit, seems too much like wishful thinking.

Still another peripheral issue was the post-Watergate call for "openness in government." This is reminiscent of the Progressive movement's early twentieth century drive for "good government." In part it reflected the generalized distrust for all institutions that was fostered by the New Left.

There was a time when "environmentalism" was an incendiary issue. The New Left made it a vehicle for alienation in the late 1960's, giving it an hysterical revolutionary quality. But the issue was soon "coopted," as the Left would say, when federal and state legislation was enacted to deal with it. It has remained an issue on two levels: as a practical concern for the solution of remaining problems; and, on a very different plane, as part of the anti-industrial Romanticism of some groups that continue on the left.

The main product of domestic liberalism during these years was the vast increase in social spending. In 1980, Morton Kondracke spoke of "what actually has been accomplished in the United States in the past 20 years: a total reversal of federal priorities from defense spending to domestic concerns. In 1958 the U.S. budget allocated $43.7 billion to defense and $38.9 billion to non-defense programs. In 1980, non-defense outlays were more than three times the Pentagon budget." His comparison, of course, includes the '60's, but the process remained underway in the '70's. The shift provided the background for the Reagan administration's push in the '80's to hold the line on social spending and revitalize military forces that had been allowed to deteriorate badly while the Soviet Union had been engaged in a rapid build-up.[25]

## The Carter presidency

The end of the 1970's witnessed, of course, the presidency of Jimmy Carter. For liberalism, this meant another opportunity under a Democratic president; but above all it was a telling sign of liberalism's fragmentation and weakness. After one term as governor of Georgia, Carter was able to win the Democratic nomination by defeating the established Democratic leaders. The liberal intellectual component wasn't able to secure the victory of one of its own; and neither was organized labor able to make up its mind and impose its will. A *New Republic* editorial pointed out that Carter was able to win the presidency "without establishing any strong base within his own party and often without committing himself on the party's main issues."[26]

The Carter presidency then proved a debacle from nearly everyone's perspective. Its story from a liberal point of view can be traced through the reports in *The New Republic*: In the issue that appeared two days after Carter's inauguration on January 20, 1977, Doris Kearns Goodwin reported "the widespread disappointment with the establishment nature of the Cabinet he has chosen." Michael Harrington said that "Mr. Carter rushed to the center ground as he prepared to assume power. It has turned into a swamp. Unless he finds some new place to stand, he will be sunk before 1980." A month later E. N. Luttwak asked whether the administration had a foreign policy. "All we have heard from it so far has been an unsorted collection of single-issue declarations, often contradictory." In October, an editorial said that "at just about the time a new administration should begin hitting its stride, Jimmy Carter's is slumping badly." It complained that "the Carter legislative programs amount to unrestrained activism, grounded in no ideology beyond the 111-page loose-leaf book of campaign promises...."[27]

In July 1978, the editors spoke of Carter's "stern words...followed by weak deeds." The next month, they reported that his legislative program had bogged down; "the list of wrecks is impressive." In March of the next year they said that "Carter's poll rankings are nearly new lows, cartoonists are making him a laughing stock."

A year later, they declared the administration "incompetent and reckless in the conduct of foreign policy." Later that year they endorsed John Anderson, an independent, for president over Carter. Mark Green has written that after "beginning with enormous good will and popularity, Jimmy Carter managed to leave office with no close associates on Capitol Hill and no Democratic constituency he could call his own – for by November 1980, Jewish, Catholic, and labor voters were unhappy with him." If I were quoting conservative commentaries, that would be one thing; but these were observations by liberals about the only Democratic president between 1969 and the updating of this book in 1991.[28]

### Liberal thought's disdain for all of liberalism's political leaders

The Carter presidency deserved much of the opprobrium it received, but it is significant to the history of liberalism that the intellectual culture has been to the left of working liberal politicians generally and has been unenthused about virtually all of them. Certainly that was true of Theodore Roosevelt, Woodrow Wilson, Franklin Roosevelt and Harry Truman.

Adlai Stevenson was an urbane, articulate standard-bearer for the Democratic Party in two presidential campaigns in the 1950's. He would seem to have been, in the language of the day, an "egghead's delight." But in fact the enthusiasm for him was mitigated by considerable reservations within the liberal journals. Edwin A. Lahey said that Stevenson's nomination meant a defeat for the left wing of the Democratic Party and a victory for organized labor. Stevenson, he wrote, was "a middle-of-the- road candidate who is probably the most conservative man to head the ticket since John W. Davis." For its part, *The Nation* endorsed Stevenson, since it considered Eisenhower "a captive of big business," but its editors criticized Stevenson as "exaggerating both the dangers of Communism and the measures required to deal with it."[29]

There was little enthusiasm in 1956. Michael Straight complained of Stevenson's vagueness on issues, and in March 1956 TRB spoke of the Democrats' overall "bankruptcy," which he said made a victory that fall unlikely. *The New Republic* took little interest in the fall campaign.[30]

The most withering denigration of Stevenson occurred later. According to Gilbert Harrison, Stevenson was an object of ridicule within the Kennedy group. In 1968, reflecting the atmosphere of the late '60's, Anthony Howard in *The New Republic* called Stevenson "a puzzling pouchy little figure who brought out the throngs of students and the middle-aged hosts." Howard spoke of Stevenson's "servile performance" as ambassador to the United Nations under Kennedy.[31]

For his part, John F. Kennedy received faint praise in *The Nation* in 1960 in an editorial entitled "Two Cheers for Kennedy." *The New*

*Republic* greeted his candidacy more favorably. Right before his election in 1960, James MacGregor Burns wrote that "I believe that Kennedy in his campaign has deliberately prepared the way for the most consistently and comprehensively liberal Administration in the history of the country." A year later, though, TRB was complaining, as we saw earlier, that "Kennedy has been a disappointment as a teacher." And in early 1962 TRB complained again to the effect that "the electrifying 'let's get going' slogan is almost forgotten." Later that year he reported "considerable irritation toward Kennedy from a lot of liberals."[32]

In 1971, Gerald Clarke wrote in *The New Republic* that "only lately have I put it all together and realized that the Administration of John F. Kennedy was a failure, by his standard as well as mine." He asked, "how could we have been thrilled by that pompous Inaugural Address?"[33]

This perspective has survived the New Left period. In 1978, the mood was summed up by Henry Fairlie when he said that "the disaster wrought by the Kennedy's is that they did so little but in a way that we cannot forget them." A *New Republic* editorial referred to the Kennedy's as "that cohort of monomaniacal ideologues and whiz-kid technocrats" and spoke of "the haughty style...often mistaken for ability." In 1980, Wilfrid Sheed wrote in a book review that "by the time they're through digging and peering under skirts, it may turn out that none of the Kennedy's was fit for the presidency." All of this contrasts starkly with the adulation the liberal press gave Kennedy. Inside the intellectual culture, there have been few, if any, heroes.[34]

Hubert Humphrey was a favorite until his association with the Johnson administration and the Vietnam War tainted him in liberals' eyes. In August 1964, TRB said "Mr. Humphrey is about our favorite man in Washington." This is to be compared with a *New Republic* editorial's observation in early 1968 that "Humphrey can count on the backing of George Meany and his allies in the labor movement," but that Humphrey had been "fatally compromised by his dutiful performance as number-one salesman for Johnson's Asian policy."[35]

Lyndon Johnson was looked upon with suspicion while he was Senate majority leader and then Vice President under Kennedy. There was enthusiasm for him in 1964 and early 1965 during the rush of Great Society legislation. But his period as a liberal hero was brief. In May 1965, James Deakin wrote that "Mr. Johnson's alienation from the academic and intellectual communities over Vietnam and the Dominican Republic is now almost complete." His support having evaporated, Johnson took himself out of the race for reelection in 1968.[36]

Neither Eugene McCarthy nor Robert Kennedy, the two competing leaders of the stop-Johnson movement in 1968, have gone unscathed in liberal literature. Each comes across as flawed.

There was then a time when it seemed that Teddy Kennedy would be the natural heir to liberal leadership, but this was one of the casualties at Chappaquiddick in 1969. He made a bid for the presidency in late 1979, but was cut up unmercifully by liberals themselves. Theodore White says that when Kennedy was interviewed by Roger Mudd on television on November 4, "Mudd dissected Kennedy on the tube and left him shredded, as a man without any real purpose in his pursuit of the presidency." A *New Republic* editorial in 1980 said Kennedy's "elevated talk about national purpose masks a peculiarly impoverished and fragmented vision...He sees the country primarily as a patchwork of interests...."[37]

### Splits in the coalition

This negative critique of all of their leaders has been symptomatic, of course, of liberalism's own fragmentation and loss of vision. The fragmentation has been most evident, however, in the splits within the "coalition" – and in the inability of liberals, despite constant effort since 1968, to put together a "new coalition."

We have already seen that Southern congressmen began in 1937 to combine with conservative Republicans in a coalition that held a veto during much of the ensuing half century. The Solid South's participation in the liberal coalition so far as presidential politics was concerned also began to crumble immediately after World War II. Indications of Republican presidential vitality in the South were already apparent in 1924 when Calvin Coolidge garnered a large vote. The 1948 Dixiecrat split from the Democratic Party marked a significant break. Frances Fox Piven and Richard A. Cloward have said that "the first overt signs that the North-South partnership was in danger of dissolving appeared during the presidential campaign of 1948." They added that "the South has not been 'solid' since."[38]

These authors foresaw an eventual liberal resurgence in the South through a coalition of the newly-enfranchised Negroes with white liberals. Although black voting has increased enormously in the South since the Voting Rights Act of 1965 and a large number of Negroes have been elected to office, Republican presidential candidates have continued to receive the bulk of the electoral votes, with the exception of 1976 when the South went for Carter as a native son.

The labor movement would in most countries have been considered the traditional rock upon which the politics of the Left would be based.

But to the American intellectual culture, the labor movement has long been a disappointment. Until 1906, Samuel Gompers, distrusting the state, kept labor out of electoral politics. It entered politics only sporadically until 1933. Since then, of course, organized labor has given enormous support to Democratic and liberal candidates. But the main body of the labor movement has always been to the right of the intellectual culture. (We remember how *The New Republic* in 1928 considered it "stupid" for the A.F. of L. to expunge a tribute to John Dewey because of his articles praising Soviet Russia.) After World War II, liberal literature showed a growing split between organized labor, which has itself often been divided, and the intellectual culture.

Despite the merger of the A.F. of L. and the C.I.O., Tom Brooks reported in 1959 that "lethargy and constant bickering within the federation has paralyzed the will to act." In 1965, TRB complained that "the American labor movement is a disappointment ... Its membership seems stuck on dead center. So far from being radical, it is to the right of the Chamber of Commerce in international affairs." Then in the bitterness of 1968, a *New Republic* editorial spoke of "the ossified trade union executives – men like George Meany, who have transformed the labor movement from an inspiring force for social justice into a baronial club."[39]

In 1972, George McGovern won the Democratic nomination despite the opposition of most unions. Labor's impotence in 1976 was apparent when it formed a coalition that supported almost all Democratic candidates successively, hoping for no more than to "back a winner." The declining numerical strength of unions was commented upon in 1980 by James Ring Adams: "American unionism peaked in the 1950's, when it included some 35 percent of the country's non-farm work force. But...its share has fallen steadily to under 25 percent." Municipal unions had "grown explosively," but the change in the economy toward high-tech industry has continued to erode the base for unionism.[40]

Big-city political machines were once a powerful part of the coalition. We have seen how Huthmacher and Buenker emphasize the role they played in the Progressive movement. The intellectual culture has from the beginning, however, felt liberalism's hands soiled by their presence. A *New Republic* editorial in 1930 praised Franklin Roosevelt as governor of New York, but said that "he can hold office only with the approval of Tammany Hall, an organization which...stands for corruption." In 1932, TRB criticized F.D.R. severely for not repudiating his Tammany support. In 1938, an editorial said Mayor Frank Hague of Jersey City had "one of the most brazenly corrupt political machines ever brought into existence."[41]

The machine system began to crumble after World War II. In 1948, *The New Republic* reported that "the basic supports of the machine system are rotting away," in part because the welfare state had done away with the machines' role in giving "doles and baskets." Despite this erosion, however, an editorial in early 1952 was able to say that the machine leaders had been "the powers in the last four Democratic conventions." Amid a bitter chorus of ridicule from the New Left, the liberal media and the intellectual culture, Mayor Daley of Chicago was a leading figure in securing the nomination for Hubert Humphrey at the 1968 Democratic convention.[42]

Religious and ethnic minorities were important parts of the New Deal coalition, and have continued to give major support since World War II. Bloc voting, little commented upon in the media, has been a prominent feature. In 1964, the vote of Southern Negroes was more than 95 percent Democratic; in 1976, "Carter received over 90 percent of the black vote nationwide, and blacks provided his margin in at least 13 states," according to *The New Republic*. Catholic participation in the coalition stemmed in part from Al Smith's candidacy in 1928. Smith was not only the first Catholic candidate; he also gave impetus to the process of bringing the heavily Catholic "immigrant" vote into the coalition. The Jewish vote, consisting largely of immigrants from eastern Europe, was related to this. The socialist orientation of these eastern European Jews is described in detail by Nathan Glazer in *Remembering the Answers*, where he concludes that "the Jews are people of the left." In 1980, Morton Kondracke said that "normally, Jews vote heavily Democratic...In 1968, Hubert Humphrey received close to 80 percent...."[43]

Although they remain important, the religious and ethnic components of the coalition have been eroding. Many blacks demonstrated their independence of the Democratic party in 1984 when they supported Jesse Jackson's third-party candidacy. Over the years there has been, for a number of reasons, considerable friction between blacks and organized labor, the Jews and liberal intellectuals: with labor over the discrimination it has so often perpetuated; with Jews over "affirmative action" quotas, which many Jews have considered a threat to the rationale for an achievement-oriented equality within American life; and with intellectuals because of the widespread denunciation of "white liberals" within militant black groups starting in the early 1960's.

The Jews have declined in numbers and in devotion to the Democratic cause. Theodore White says that "they are a diminishing population group in the United States," and that "politically, they are still

Democratic property, but much less so than formerly." The neo-conservative movement that began in the late 1960's has been primarily Jewish.[44]

Liberals at one time considered the media conservative, but since World War II it has been a highly partisan center for popular liberalism. The media have had a collective elan amounting to a herd quality that permeates the culture. This is created in large part by the imperative that every newspaper feature-story writer, every television special reporter, every free lance author, and every social science teacher assigning a project apparently feels to produce something that will fit in snugly with the prevailing enthusiasm. The swings of liberal bathos give the media an overwhelmingly propagandistic quality.

I have written elsewhere that even a classical liberal society needs myths, in the sense of commonly-held beliefs that mold values together with selected facts, as an essential social cement. All social systems are reenforced by them. We should notice that myth-making is precisely what the pop-liberalism has been doing, and that ironically the effect is at least in part conservative.

On a trip to Nashville, I attended a stageshow at Opryland that fashioned a patriotic review of twentieth century American history out of such figures as Franklin Roosevelt and Elvis Presley. During the writing of this chapter, I witnessed the torrent of media images that have attended the first national observance of the Martin Luther King, Jr., holiday. The far Left would say that this absorption merely proves that these personalities were part of the bourgeois society in the first place. The New Left would have called the process "cooptation." We should see, though, that it is the molding of popular myths. The figures are folded into the culture. This is "conservative" in its down-playing of the discordance that actually marked these men's lives and in its demand that everyone accept the same sanitized images.

I have already commented on the difference between the liberal intellectual culture, with its long-standing despair, and the pop-liberalism of the media, which reflects little of the self-doubt and fragmentation. This means that liberalism has one face for itself, another for the culture at large.

Liberal domination of the media continues in 1991, but I indicated earlier that we have seen an important change since the early 1960's. The media no longer stand solidly behind liberal leaders. Since 1968, they have been about as willing to cannibalize these leaders as they have to devour conservatives. This has lessened the propagandistic effect and has both reflected, and contributed immeasurably to, the fragmentation.

Perhaps the most telling development in recent years has been the deterioration of the Civil Rights and welfarist movements into a collection of narrowly self-interested groups. Theodore White summed it up by saying that "one movement in the grand transformation slowly developed, year by year, into a monster...: the division of Americans by race and national origin into groups, each entitled to special privileges." This divides the country, but the division focuses most obviously within the Democratic party. It enhances the image of contemporary liberalism as lacking a high moral aspiration.[45]

There are several components of the liberal coalition that I have not discussed. These include the farm-laborites, consumer groups, a significant part of big business, the radical and liberal clergy, the Hispanics, and the welfare constituency, among others. Each is a subject in itself, with its own complexity. No group is ever totally cohesive or passively a member of the coalition.

### The search for a new coalition

There has been much talk since 1968 of a search for a "new coalition," which has sometimes also been referred to as a "new politics."

Strangely, the term "new politics" seems to have originated in the wildly chaotic effort in 1967 to create a Popular Front among the various groups on the far left. A tumultuous convention of the "National Conference of New Politics" was attended, according to James Ridgeway's report in *The New Republic*, by black nationalists, members of the W.E.B. DuBois Clubs, members of the Communist Party (who "were out in the open for the first time in years" and "were the most conservative element present"), peace advocates, some labor leaders, members of Students for a Democratic Society (SDS), a large group from the Vietnam Summer Project, and others. Martin Luther King, Jr., was the keynote speaker.[46]

In 1968, Senator Eugene McCarthy challenged Lyndon Johnson in the primaries and labelled his movement "the New Politics." A *New Republic* editorial spoke of a proposed coalition of "the students, the clergy, professional workers, teachers, suburbanites (many of them women)." In December 1968, Paul R. Wieck said that "the most visible organization of the new politics is the New Democratic Coalition (NDC)...put together by leaders of the McCarthy-McGovern-Kennedy forces at Chicago." But fourteen months later Wieck reported that "NDC's national operation has been meager...No sturdy new politics has been built. Why? Perhaps exhaustion...A lot of people left Chicago drained, disillusioned."[47]

Within what would have to be called (in the context of the times) the right wing of the Democratic party, two associates of Hubert Humphrey, Richard C. Scammon and Ben J. Wattenberg, called in 1970 for a different sort of effort. Leonard Ross summarized their book *The Real Majority* by saying that their "prescription is extremely simple...The real majority is neither young nor black nor poor. Rather it is middle-aged and middle-class, increasingly liberal on economic questions but ever more conservative on social issues such as race, crime and drugs." This sort of coalition was pursued in 1971 by Senator Henry Jackson, who Wieck said was seeking "a broad centrist national coalition" which would "isolate the Democratic left."[48]

Senator Fred Harris countered from the left with a call for a "New Populism." Then in 1972, Senator George McGovern tried unsuccessfully to draw a vast constituency from blacks, students, women, minorities and workers. Four years later, Jimmy Carter was able to call upon enough of the old New Deal coalition to defeat Gerald Ford in a close election. His status as a Southerner, combined with a special effort to appeal to blacks, gave him both the South and the black vote; and, consistently with the Democratic patterns of the past, he was able to win enough of the large industrial states to put him over the top. Nevertheless, a *New Republic* editorial after the election warned that "it would be misleading to conclude that Carter has actually revived FDR's New Deal coalition." The mercurial nature of Carter's support became apparent during the four years of his presidency. By 1981, Michael Kinsley could write that "good people everywhere view the future of the Democratic party with growing indifference...It represents a dwindling collection of special interest groups whose interests are less and less those of either the general populace or the tired and poor."[49]

In 1984, Thomas Ferguson and Joel Rogers said in *The Nation* that during Walter Mondale's campaign "almost every group in the party came to recognize how violently its interests clashed with those of the others." Nevertheless, the journal's editors again called for a new coalition – of the very same groups that have been proposed so many times since 1968. *The New Republic*, however, saw deeper: "The Democratic Party must find a way to represent a national interest that transcends the mere sum of these perfectly legitimate but still compara- tively narrow group interests."[50]

### Developments pointing to the future
Prominent members of the Left have been converting to one form or another of conservatism since the mid-'30's. Former Communists, for example, made up the bulk of the intellectual circle that founded the

Burkean-conservative *National Review*.

The movement by various intellectuals, primarily Jewish, from the Left into "neo-conservatism" that began in the mid-'60's did not lead into Burkean thought. Generally speaking, neo-conservatives have not renounced liberalism as such, or even the welfare state, but still believe that there is much for government to do. Their thinking is touched, however, by a realism about the poor and about blacks; they no longer accept the ideas that have arisen from the Left's ideological, political coalition-seeking with such groups, ideas that have found it easy to lay exclusive blame on the predominant society and to command solutions by decree. The neo-conservatives also abandoned liberalism's continuing illusions about Communism. No longer alienated from the main society, they unabashedly support America's role as the leader of the free world.

Although neo-conservatives are quick to point out how loosely defined a category it is, some of those whose names are most often associated with it are Irving Kristol, Norman Podhoretz, Nathan Glazer, Jeane Kirkpatrick, Daniel Patrick Moynihan and Edward Banfield.

"Neo-liberalism" also received attention in the early 1980's. Only vaguely defined, and with no real consensus about specifics, it stemmed from the efforts of Democratic congressmen and presidential candidates to develop a revitalized program in light of an increasingly competitive world market and the shift from heavy industry to "high tech."

Although he was not the first to speak in these terms, Senator Paul Tsongas called for a "new liberalism" in a speech delivered to the Americans for Democratic Action (ADA) in June 1980. He wanted a liberal attitude on social issues such as homosexual rights, abortion, school busing to overcome de facto racial segregation, affirmative action programs to encourage the hiring of minorities, and opposition to capital punishment. On economic issues, Tsongas wanted what Robert M. Kaus in *The New Republic* later called "a modified 'Japan, Inc.' strategy...a broader labor role in management...government investment in research and education...export subsidies" and other governmental measures to stimulate keener American competition for world markets and to provide "shock absorbers" to alleviate any displacements caused.[51]

Along the same lines, Morton Kondracke reported in October 1982 that Democrats were working out a program that would consist of several elements. One was "large-scale expenditures to restore America's 'infrastructure' – its decaying roads, bridges, sewers, and waterways." Another was "increased federal spending on 'human capital' programs" to develop skills. There would be an "industrial policy" involving government spending on research and on the sponsorship of "technological 'winners'." These things would be paid for out of a cut-back in the arms build-up.

Japan's success produced many other calls for a neo-Mercantilist imitation. In March 1983, Bob Kuttner in *The New Republic* referred to "Japan's brilliantly successful mercantilism" that "doesn't try to pick winners blindfolded," but "creates them." Kuttner called for a system of "managed trade."

Mondale's defeat in 1984 and Dukakis's in 1988 left open the debate over future liberal policy. If the neo-liberals had their way, liberalism would become energetically state-capitalist, with a welfare state floor and an increasing role for labor in the ownership and management of industry. The similarity of such a liberalism to the "industrial democracy" so popular among British socialists and liberals in the 'teens and early 1920's is apparent.

Despite this similarity, liberalism is not quite coming full circle. In late 1984, *The New Republic* found it both possible and necessary to say many things that earlier would have been unthinkable. The editors mixed a call for worker ownership and control, which is clearly socialist, with calls for more deregulation and lower tax rates. They made the earth-shaking admission that "there may be some problems that can't be solved, even with ... a hefty bit of cash." The editors urged that the United Nations be replaced by a "United Nations of the democracies" and David Bell added that the pull-out from UNESCO was justified. Glenn C. Loury wanted black leaders to "have the courage to reexamine their ideas" and then to support more market-oriented solutions in the ghettos. Such ideas are fundamentally at odds with the liberal worldview as we have known it.[52]

*The Nation*, however, continued to speak in traditional leftist categories. Sidney Lens praised Austria's socialism, but said it couldn't work in the United States because the bourgeoisie would simply make it a vehicle "for the suppression of the class struggle." David Gordon urged, what? – "broader and stronger coalitions."[53]

# NOTES

[1] Irving Kristol, *Two Cheers for Capitalism* (New York: Mentor Book, 1978), p. 11.
[2] New Republic, July 22, 1946, p. 70; New Republic, July 29, 1946, p. 106.
[3] New Republic, November 1, 1948, p. 24; New Republic, March 17, 1958, p. 20; New Republic, February 29, 1960, pp. 17, 18.
[4] New Republic, October 21, 1946, p. 500.

## Liberalism in Contemporary America 99

⁵ Mr. Galbraith is quoted in Mark Green, *Winning Back America* (Toronto: Bantam Books, 1982), p. 7; New Republic, March 12, 1956, p. 2; James A. Wechsler, *Reflections of an Angry Middle-Aged Editor* (New York: Random House, 1960), p. 33.

⁶ New Republic, November 23, 1963, p. 23.

⁷ New Republic, June 29, 1974, p. 5; New Republic, March 22, 1975, p. 19; New Republic, April 5, 1975, p. 9.

⁸ New Republic, February 26, 1977, pp. 18, 19; New Republic, September 20, 1982, p. 32; New Republic, December 10, 1984, pp. 9, 12.

⁹ New Republic, November 11, 1969, p. 26; New Republic, January 1, 1972, p. 6; New Republic, May 31, 1980, p. 19.

¹⁰ New Republic, October 28, 1967, p. 20; New Republic, March 16, 1968, p. 25; New Republic, August 7, 1976, p. 29.

¹¹ New Republic, June 6, 1934, p. 84; New Republic, October 17, 1949, p. 5; Kristol, *Two Cheers*, p. 100; for a discussion of the expansion of regulatory activity in the 1970's, see Theodore H. White, *America in Search of Itself* (New York: Harper & Row, 1982), pp. 128, 129.

¹² New Republic, October 29, 1956, p. 11.

¹³ New Republic, December 11, 1971, p. 19; White, *America in Search*, p. 126.

¹⁴ J. Roland Pennock, *Liberal Democracy* (New York: Rinehart and Company, Inc., 1950), p. 267.

¹⁵ New Republic, October 27, 1958, p. 15; New Republic, January 5, 1959, p. 2; New Republic, February 9, 1959, p. 7.

¹⁶ New Republic, September 11, 1961, p. 2.

¹⁷ New Republic, July 3, 1965, p. 4; New Republic, July 10, 1965, p. 4.

¹⁸ Charles Forcey, *The Crossroads of Liberalism* (New York: Oxford University Press, 1961), pp. 80, 81.

¹⁹ New Republic, April 4, 1970, p. 35.

²⁰ Nathan Glazer, *Remembering the Answers: Essays on the American Student Revolt* (New York: Basic Books, Inc., 1970), p. 182.

²¹ New Republic, December 11, 1965, p. 38; New Republic, February 5, 1966, p. 15; New Republic, July 6, 1968, p. 31.

²² Ronald Berman, *America in the Sixties: An Intellectual History* (New York: The Free Press, 1968), p. 73.

²³ New Republic, October 27, 1958, p. 17; the New York Times is quoted in Green, *Winning Back America*, p. 38; New Republic, May 10, 1980, p. 28.

²⁴ New Republic, June 7, 1980, p. 16; White, *America in Search*, p. 137.

²⁵ New Republic, July 19, 1980, p. 11.

²⁶ New Republic, January 29, 1977, p. 8.

²⁷ New Republic, January 22, 1977, p. 34; New Republic, January 22, 1977, p. 60; New Republic, February 26, 1977, p. 13; New Republic, October 22, 1977, p. 5.

²⁸ New Republic, July 29, 1978, p. 5; New Republic, August 5, 1978, p. 5; New Republic, March 3, 1979, p. 5; New Republic, March 15, 1980, p. 5; Green,

*Winning Back America*, p. 4.

[29] New Republic, August 25, 1952, p. 8; The Nation, Vol. 175, p. 341.

[30] New Republic, November 21, 1955, p. 12; New Republic, March 12, 1956, p. 2.

[31] New Republic, December 15, 1962, p. 8; New Republic, December 21, 1968, p. 35.

[32] The Nation, Vol. 191, p. 237; New Republic, October 31, 1960, p. 14; New Republic, September 11, 1961, p. 2; New Republic, January 8, 1962, p. 2; New Republic, September 10, 1962, p. 2.

[33] New Republic, January 15, 1971, p. 13.

[34] New Republic, September 9, 1978, p. 34; New Republic, September 23, 1978, p. 5; New Republic, June 7, 1980, p. 28.

[35] New Republic, September 5, 1964, p. 2; New Republic, April 13, 1968, p. 5.

[36] New Republic, May 29, 1965, p. 11.

[37] White, *America in Search*, p. 13; New Republic, January 19, 1980, p. 7.

[38] New Republic, April 20, 1968, pp. 20, 22.

[39] New Republic, September 7, 1959, p. 19; New Republic, May 15, 1965, p. 4; New Republic, July 27, 1968, p. 5.

[40] New Republic, May 10, 1980, p. 19.

[41] New Republic, October 15, 1930, p. 220; New Republic, May 4, 1932, p. 324; New Republic, February 2, 1938, p. 352.

[42] New Republic, July 12, 1948, p. 15; New Republic, May 19, 1959, p. 5.

[43] New Republic, November 28, 1964, p. 7; New Republic, September 17, 1977, p. 5; Glazer, *Remembering the Answers*, pp. 222, 231, 236, 242; New Republic, September 6, 1980, p. 10.

[44] White, *America in Search*, p. 371.

[45] White, *America in Search*, p. 129.

[46] New Republic, September 16, 1967, pp. 9, 10.

[47] New Republic, September 7, 1968, p. 8; New Republic, December 14, 1968, p. 21; New Republic, February 28, 1970, p. 12.

[48] New Republic, October 24, 1970, p. 26; New Republic, September 18, 1971, p. 17.

[49] New Republic, November 13, 1976, p. 7; New Republic, July 25, 1981, p. 14.

[50] The Nation, October 6, 1984, p. 315; The Nation, November 17, 1984, p. 501; New Republic, November 26, 1984, p. 8.

[51] New Republic, November 25, 1981, pp. 29, 30.

[52] New Republic, December 3, 1984, p. 6; New Republic, November 26, 1984, p. 8; New Republic, December 31, 1984, p. 9.

[53] The Nation, November 17, 1984, p. 301; The Nation, January 12, 1985, p. 15; The Nation, February 9, 1985.

# CHAPTER FIVE
## *The Nation* and *The New Republic*

*The Nation* and *The New Republic* have been preeminent among the liberal journals of opinion. Their pages have conveyed the views of such a wide variety of authors over such a long period of time that anyone who wants to be familiar with the development of liberal thought will need to be conversant with the history of these journals.

*The Nation* existed as a classical liberal journal for almost a half-century before *The New Republic* was founded in 1914. Because it was first in chronological order, it is natural to discuss it first.

### The Nation

Edwin Lawrence Godkin was the commanding figure on *The Nation* from its founding in 1865 until shortly before his death in 1902. Born in Ireland to English parents, he served as a correspondent in the Crimean War before coming to the United States from England in 1856. He was considered a follower of John Stuart Mill, although he possessed none of Mill's eventual affinity for socialism. *The Nation* itself contains conflicting information about who, as between Godkin and Wendell Phillips Garrison, was formally the first editor. It is clear, though, that Godkin was at least the *de facto* editor until as late as 1899. Godkin's name is thus synonymous with the early *Nation*.[1]

Wendell Phillips Garrison worked closely with Godkin from the beginning, and after Godkin stepped down in 1899 continued the journal until his own death in 1907. He was the son of William Lloyd Garrison, whose *The Liberator* had been a fiery Abolitionist weekly in Boston for the thirty years preceding the Civil War.

Under both Godkin and Garrison, *The Nation* was independent, reformist – and steadfastly classical liberal. (It is, however, significant that its pages do not reflect the existence at that time of a coherent, self-conscious classical liberal movement.) The journal was at first associated with liberal Republicanism, but threw its support to Grover Cleveland in 1884. It broke with Cleveland a year later, considering him too jingoistic. As it looked back later, however, it gave him high praise.

*The Nation*'s classical liberalism was apparent in the many positions it took on the issues of the late nineteenth and early twentieth centuries:

It was strongly for free trade and against the protectionism that the Republican Party had imposed since the Civil War. It believed that free trade could solve the problem of business concentration, and so it did not favor anti-trust legislation against bigness. It did, however, favor legislation against specific abuses such as price discrimination.

*The Nation's* free trade, freedom-of-contract rationale caused it to oppose not only the protectionist tariff, but also such interventions as were proposed for the 8-hour-day, minimum wages, the nationalization of coal (which Bellamy demanded), the municipal ownership of utilities, and usury laws. It favored collective bargaining, but not the closed shop. On the money question, it stood for the gold standard against bimetallism and the various inflationary schemes that were so much in the air.

Under Godkin and Garrison, *The Nation* supported the trend toward greater democracy and the struggle for cleaner government. They accordingly favored the proposal for the direct election of senators, encouraged the revolt against political bossism, opposed the spoils system, and urged every city to have a league for good government.

Although they blamed the tariff most especially for the "venality of politics," they were acutely aware of a serious erosion of American values and classical liberal perspectives during the decades following the Civil War. They commented upon how "money-making eminence" had superseded "intellectual eminence," and how a "belief in paternalism" had grown out of the activities of government during and after the Civil War. They saw "the eclipse of Liberalism" both in the United States and Europe. In the United States, they said, "nationalism in the sense of national greed has supplanted Liberalism."[2]

During those years, *The Nation* was strongly opposed to socialism. "Human nature," an editorial thundered in 1890, "will never agree to pass its life in a hugh boarding house with a lot of ranting orators regulating the diet and hours of sleep of the inmates." It gave respectful but critical attention to the writings of such socialists as Rodbertus and the Webbs, and concluded that "real Liberalism can never be socialistic."[3]

In foreign affairs, it favored a non-belligerent policy. When the Spanish-American War was about to break out, it condemned the hysteria over the sinking of the *Maine*, arguing perceptively that it was not known whether Spain had done the sinking. It opposed an American colonialism, and urged the government to set up a self-governing system in Cuba and then to get out. The editors protested the brutality of the subjugation of the Phillipines, and opposed any effort to "raise the Phillipines to a higher level of civilization." They compared Theodore Roosevelt to French militarists for what they considered his glorification of the army. And they called upon other nations to join with the United States in a confederation for the prevention of war.

*The Nation* was always interested in the well-being of blacks, although it is not surprising that the editors, consistently with their overall classical liberal orientation, agreed with Booker T. Washington's position that the situation of blacks would best improve if they devoted themselves to gaining education and property. An editorial in 1890 criticized the notion that laws can correct the effects of discrimination. The editors continually drew attention to the barbarity of lynching, and argued that in part the lynching came from an exaggeration of the number of black rapes of white women. They pointed out that the best way to stop a lynch mob would be for the authorities to shoot the first person to act. And they opposed the South's move into segregation, such as when a proposed statute in Kentucky threatened to abolish Berea College by prohibiting the coeducation of whites and negroes.[4]

When the Muckraking movement began, *The Nation* welcomed the illumination of actual abuses, but opposed a nihilistic exaggeration. In 1894 the editors called Henry Demarest Lloyd's *Wealth Against Commonwealth* "the wildest rant," but in 1905 they were sympathetic to the early Muckraking articles and joined in a call for an investigation of the Equitable Life Assurance Society's affairs. By 1906, however, they were fed up, and said that Muckraking "runs unceasingly through the daily and periodical press, spreading dark suspicion abroad without suggesting remedies." They pointed out that "the idea of reforming is quite subordinate to...creating a hatred."[5]

Their comments on an income tax were perceptive. They reasoned that such a tax is just, but that because its collection would depend upon a self-reporting system "its burden [would] fall chiefly on those who are too honest to shirk it."[6]

And finally, the editors took a dim view of the "scientific pretensions" of the German-trained academics pouring in from the Historical School. Of the new sociologists, they said that "the great thing is to get their work called scientific, no matter whether it is useful or reasonable." "Scholarship," they added later, "suffers from an overproduction of monographs...stretching a thin substance to the cracking point."[7]

It was a fascinating period. Article after article presaged the issues of the twentieth century, which were by that time far more than negligible clouds on the horizon. *The Nation* under Godkin and Garrison met those issues head on, speaking for classical liberal values that even then were sinking into the status of a gigantic underlay. There was no broad classical liberal movement it could champion, and intellectually the journal left much untouched that is vital to a sound classical liberalism. Just the same, the dust-covered volumes of *The Nation* for that period stand as monuments to American values.

Within eleven years after Garrison's death, *The Nation* passed through the hands of three editors, Hammond Lamont, Paul Elmer More and Harold deWolf Fuller. All three were described in the 100-year-centennary issue in 1965 as "conservatives." Both More and Fuller were said to have been breaking away from the laissez-faire liberalism of Godkin and Garrison. Despite these descriptions, my own reading shows *The Nation*'s content to have remained remarkably consistent with the earlier views until at least 1913. Only then do we begin to see legislation favored, and rationales expressed, that were at odds with the earlier philosophy. Just the same, no sharp break occurred. In 1914 and 1915, criticisms appeared of socialism and of Croly's book on industrial democracy.

All that I have traced so far has been looked upon later as "the 'pre-modern' *Nation*." The ideological watershed was in 1918 when Oswald Garrison Villard, a nephew of Wendell Phillips Garrison, became owner and editor. Villard remained editor until 1933, and then stayed with the journal as a columnist until 1940 when he broke with it over his conviction that the United States should stay out war in Europe.

Under Villard, *The Nation* during the late 'teens and 1920's was virtually a twin of *The New Republic*, except for a few specifics. Garrison had considered closing down *The Nation* for want of an appropriate successor as editor, but had been persuaded to allow it to continue under Hammond Lamont. No doubt he would have let it die if he had foreseen the editorial in 1919 that said that "out of the soviet experiment, and out of the ideas of the Guild Socialists in England, is evolving what some sanguine optimists hope will prove to be the State-norm of the immediate future." The editorial spoke of "the freedom to prey upon others, which was really the essence of the old individualism...."[8]

The "modern" *Nation* threw itself wholeheartedly behind "industrial democracy," which it said "courageously undertakes to substitute service for profits as the motive force in industry." It published a speech by the French socialist Anatole France in which he said that "I wish with all my heart that a delegation of the teachers of all nations might soon join the Workers' Internationale...We shall see fulfilled the great socialist prophecy: 'The union of the workers will be the peace of the world.'" Louis Fischer was the journal's main correspondent in Soviet Russia – and sent glowing reports. Villard himself made a trip to Russia in 1929 and told the readers that "it is all so new, so genuinely thrilling."[9]

Villard did not parallel Croly's mystical withdrawal in the '20's, but much else was the same. There were calls for the extensive organization of cooperatives, for the public ownership of power, for the nationalization of the mines. *The Nation* joined in the impassioned defense of Sacco and Vanzetti. In 1932, it endorsed Norman Thomas, the Socialist candidate, for president.

Editorial control was under a board of editors between 1933 and 1936, with Freda Kirchwey a major figure. Under this leadership, *The Nation* considered the N.R.A. insufficient and called for "a socialist approach to the economic crisis," according to Richard Clark Sterne in the centennary issue. It published an article by Norman Thomas calling for the nationalization of banking. The editors showed some sympathy for Franklin Delano Roosevelt, but they considered the New Deal itself "a half-baked capitalism with so-called liberal trimmings."[10]

Between 1936 and 1938, Kirchwey and Max Lerner shared the editorship. Kirchwey then served as the editor for the long period between 1938 and 1955. *The Nation* enthusiastically supported the Left in the Spanish Civil War, again sending Louis Fischer as its correspondent. In 1937, there was lavish praise for the Soviet Union on the twentieth anniversary of the Bolshevik Revolution, and elaborate justifications were made for Stalin's purges. The collectivization of agriculture was praised – with no mention of the mass starvation.

During this period there was at least one major difference between *The Nation* and *The New Republic*. Over Villard's objections, *The Nation* supported the idea of collective security against Hitler. *The New Republic* took a pacifist position until 1940.

*The Nation* softened its attitude toward the New Deal somewhat earlier than *The New Republic*. It was basically favorable to Roosevelt in 1936, while still being careful to maintain its connections with the far Left. (Villard, however, used his column to endorse Norman Thomas in 1936.) *The Nation* endorsed Roosevelt for third and fourth terms in 1940 and 1944.

The Hitler-Stalin Pact and the aggressions that followed it were shocks to those associated with *The Nation* just as they were to those connected with *The New Republic*, but after Hitler attacked the Soviet Union it wasn't long before *The Nation* was filled with adulatory articles about the Soviet Union by Anna Louise Strong. *The Nation* joined, too, in the growing drumbeat of criticism of Chiang Kai-shek and of praise for Mao.

As Europe faced the post-war period, *The Nation* under Kirchwey called for the creation of a socialist "third force" in Britain and on the continent. She criticized the Marshall Plan, thinking it bad that it was being used to stop Communism in Western Europe rather than to create such a third force. She considered the Truman Doctrine in Greece a "failure" for having defeated the Communist insurgency by keeping a "cruel, corrupt oligarchy" in power. In the meantime, Alexander Werth, the journal's Moscow correspondent, wrote still more glowing reports about the Soviet Union. (We should remember that this was the period during which the Gulags described by Solzhenitsyn were at their worst.) The attacks on Chiang Kai-shek were continued until mainland China fell to the Communists in 1949. Mao had no sooner won than *The Nation* began urging the United States to recognize his government.[11]

A 1948 editorial held back from endorsing Henry Wallace's Progressive Party candidacy. It argued that the Progressive Party could not become a viable labor party without organized labor's support, which it did not have, and that a large third-party vote would elect the Republicans. *The Nation* thus adopted a stance very similar to that taken by *The New Republic* after Wallace ceased being its editor. In 1952, *The Nation* endorsed Adlai Stevenson despite its criticism of him as "exaggerating the dangers of Communism."

Carey McWilliams became editor in 1955 and by continuing in that capacity until 1976 established most of the post-World War II posture of *The Nation*. During his tenure, *The Nation* shared *The New Republic*'s malaise about domestic policy. Its position was nondescript, with one foot placed tenuously in domestic liberal politics, the other in socialist yearnings. These yearnings did not take form as a detailed program; they were evidenced primarily by the presence within *The Nation*'s pages of such socialist authors as Christopher Lasch, Theodore Roszak, Erich Fromm, Theodore Lowi and Michael Harrington. The journal was never in close privity with either the New Frontier or the Great Society.

The clearest direction was on foreign policy. Under McWilliams, *The Nation* continued to criticize the United States for a "Cold War" posture based on an "anti-Communist obsession" toward the Soviet Union. Alexander Werth travelled to the Soviet Union again in 1960 to write still another favorable report. Castro's bloodbath after gaining power was justified as unfortunate but necessary. The American role in the Vietnam War was denounced as "a dirty, shameful war in which we are trying to put down an indigenous revolutionary movement whose aim is to free the country from foreign domination."[12]

As the New Left heated up in the second half of the 1960's, *The Nation* reported its activities and, with scatter-gun ambivalence, served as something of a platform for it. Mainly, though, it held to a more orthodox line on the "moderate Left." Examples of this would include Richard F. Hamilton's call in 1965 for the formation of "a socialist or labor party in this country" and Michael Harrington's 1972 "Call to American Socialists." In 1972, there were many editorials mildly favoring George McGovern's candidacy against Richard Nixon, but there was no ringing endorsement.[13]

Blair Clark was editor for the brief period between 1976 and 1978, and then Victor Navasky held the position through the end of my reading in early 1985. *The Nation* remained to the left of the Democratic Party. It was severely critical of Walter Mondale as the candidate in 1984, and did not associate itself with the mercantilist "neo-liberalism" that was receiving so much attention. In an article in February 1985, entitled "Up From the Ashes: Getting Our Act Together," David Gordon called for long, patient work to create "permanent networks" that would link labor, women, minorities, small farmers, church activists, homosexuals, environmentalists, middle class liberals, and senior citizens in a "broader and stronger coalition."[14]

### The New Republic

It would be redundant for me to give a detailed chronological history of *The New Republic*, since my many references to that journal in the chapters on "the phases of liberalism" have in effect already done that. It will be enough to add any significant details that have not already been covered.

Off and on during my reading of the almost-200 volumes of *The New Republic* for the period between 1914 and 1985, I have been surprised when liberal associates in the academic community have asked me querulously, "Why *The New Republic*?" They have not considered it sufficiently to the left to be truly representative of liberalism. When I have asked them to explain, they have made it clear that this is their impression based on the last few years rather than on the first sixty or so years of the journal's history. It is interesting that even though *The New Republic* made no sharp swing to the right prior to 1985, they consider themselves sufficiently to the left of it that it is no longer representative of their thinking.

Their observation obscures the main truth that *The New Republic* has since 1914 served as a vast sounding-board for quite literally hundreds upon hundreds of authors, many of them famous as the intellectual and literary leaders of liberalism.

I have already quoted many of these authors, seeking to give the feel and texture of the thinking they represented. The reader should be aware, of course, that it would be possible to distort a history by such a process; the ocean of material is so vast that differing emphases can easily be supported by quotation. The author of such a history as this must immerse himself so deeply in the reading that he can know what is representative and what is not. As I have selected my quotations, I have sought to be representative.

Nevertheless, the attempt to describe accurately the main thrust of liberal thought has had a certain distorting effect, since the main thrust is not the only thing that has appeared in *The New Republic*. I have been impressed from the beginning by the diversity of authors and views. The journal has served a broad literary and intellectual purpose and has at no time been narrowly sectarian, even during the Red Decade. The views have been within the range of the American Left, of course, and there has been no recognition of a conservative intellectual position of any respectability, but the views have not been restricted generally to any given slice of the Left. It is valid to say this even though there have no doubt been many instances in which some exclusion has been exercised.

I have already commented upon the distinction that I have come to feel between the intellectualized liberalism of *The New Republic* and the "pop-liberalism" of current fads generated primarily by the media.

The identity of the chief editor of *The New Republic* was not made entirely clear from the masthead of the journal until the mid-1940's. Herbert Croly was simply listed among several editors, but liberal literature is unanimous in designating him the first editor. He served as such from the opening issue of November 7, 1914, until his death in 1930. For the next several years, a committee of editors was listed without differentiation. The literature does not point nearly so strongly to one individual as dominant. It seems justifiable to say, though, that Bruce Bliven, who joined *The New Republic* as one of its editors in 1923 and remained as chairman of the editorial board even during the 1950's while Michael Straight was editor, can be considered to have been "first among equals" on the editorial staff during those years.

Henry Wallace was made editor with much fanfare on December 16, 1946. Michael Straight commented years later, however, that Wallace was so preoccupied with other things that he paid little attention to his editorial duties. Certainly Wallace's tenure as editor was brief. He served only until January 12, 1948, although he retained a column for a short time thereafter. He was the Progressive Party candidate for president that year, but did not receive the indorsement of *The New Republic* under its new editor, Michael Straight, despite Straight's continued liking for him personally. In part, Wallace's leaving reflected the division that was becoming bitter within the American Left. The split between those, such as Wallace, who were "willing to work with Communists" and those, such as the A.D.A., who were not was being fought out in 1948.

Michael Straight was editor from 1948 until May 1956. It was a period marked by the deepest hypocrisy. The public face of *The New Republic* was one thing; the secret harbored through all those years by its editor was something very different.

By far the most heated national issue during his editorship had to do with Communism. Although Straight liked Herbert Philbrick's book *I Led Three Lives* about Philbrick's years as an undercover agent within the Communist Party and there was a review critical of a book defending Alger Hiss, the main emphasis of *The New Republic* during these years was one of vehement denunciation of virtually all efforts by anti-Communists.

Congressman Thomas, the chairman of the House Committee on Un-American Activities, was denounced by Daniel Gillmor as "a master of loading a phrase, at ripping a quotation out of context and at implying guilt without leveling an outright accusation." An editorial argued that Attorney General Tom Clark was arbitrary in listing certain organizations as "subversive." Jack Winocour wrote that the French were "obsessed with anti-Communist hysteria." An editorial denounced the New York City Board of Education as bigoted and hysterical for "attempting to bar from the teaching profession known Communists or suspected Communists." TRB wrote that Harry Dexter White was being "smeared by Miss Bentley." An editorial defended Owen Lattimore against the McCarran Committee's charge that he had been "a conscious articulate instrument" of Communism in his writing about China. Another editorial acknowledged the guilt of the Rosenbergs, but called for a reduction of their sentence to life imprisonment. And, most emphatically, the journal joined in liberalism's scathing denunciations of Senator Joseph McCarthy's crusade against suspected Communists in government.[15]

Many years later, in 1981, it became publicly known that Straight had joined a Communist cell at Cambridge in 1935 and had for several years been a part of the espionage ring that included Guy Burgess and Anthony Blunt. Straight has told the story of those years in his 1983 book *After Long Silence*. His book tells of his Communist activities and meetings with both Burgess and a Soviet agent acting under the pseudonym "Michael Green." One meeting with Burgess was as late as 1949. This was four years before Burgess and another agent, Donald Maclean, of whom Straight says he had no knowledge, fled to the Soviet Union. If Straight's book can be taken at face value, he was always a reluctant, peripheral member of the espionage cell, and never sought or conveyed information other than his own impressions of the American political scene. He says that he faked a break with Communism when he became part of the espionage cell, but held mixed feelings and was for several years plagued with fear and guilt.

These years included a time when he had easy access to President and Mrs. Roosevelt. He even worked with Eleanor Roosevelt "as she struggled to maintain the ties between the administration and the radicals in America." They included all of the years he was editor of *The New Republic*. He finally went to the F.B.I. and then to British intelligence in 1963 when President Kennedy's offer to appoint him chairman of the National Endowment for the Arts made an F.B.I. check of his background imminent. The public did not know the story until the London *Daily Mail* broke it in 1981.

The hypocrisy has been summarized by Straight himself: "My fear and sense of guilt were secret, shared by no one. At the same time, as editor of *The New Republic*, I had to share my thoughts and my feelings week after week on the allegations of espionage that were surfacing and on the larger issues that they raised."[16]

Debts incurred during the effort to build *The New Republic*'s circulation at the time of the Wallace editorship finally forced Straight to sell the journal in 1956. This ended many years of financial association by the Straight family with *The New Republic*. Michael Straight's parents, Willard and Dorothy Straight, had been the first owners and financial benefactors, establishing the journal in 1914 with Herbert Croly as editor after they read his book *The Promise of American Life*. Willard Straight died of influenza at the end of World War I. It tells us a lot about Mrs. Straight, and provides some explanation of her son Michael's role, that she continued her financial support throughout the journal's most radical phase in the 1930's.

Gilbert A. Harrison became the editor after Michael Straight, serving during the tempestuous years from 1956 to early 1975. Martin Peretz purchased *The New Republic* in 1974 and took Harrison's place as editor the next year. This remained the situation when I completed my reading in preparation for this book in early 1985.

During most of *The New Republic*'s existence, the column by "T.R.B." has been something of an institution. It was begun in 1925 with Frank Kent as the first of several anonymous authors. Kenneth Crawford and Jonathan Mitchell have also been mentioned as having contributed to it before Richard Strout began his 40-odd year tenure in March 1943.

*The New Republic* has itself given varying explanations of what the initials mean. In 1946, an editorial broke silence, saying that "the idea of 'T.R.B.' was born during a ride on the old Brooklyn Rapid Transit subway...." The initials were simply reversed, and thus came to stand for "Transit R. Brooklyn." The explanation was disputed, however, by an editorial in 1983, which said that "there's no such line as the BRT." The editorial told of competing explanations. One was that the initials stand for the typeface Times Roman Bold. Another, offered by John Midgley of the *Economist*, "is a variation of the subway theory: the editor took the initials IRT (for Interboro Rapid Transit) and BMT (for Brooklyn Manhattan Transit), and crunched them together."[17]

Fortunately, we can say about the T.R.B. mystery that it is as harmless as it is amusing.

# NOTES

[1] During the "pre-modern" era, *The Nation*'s editorial masthead did not indicate who the editors were. The conflicting commentary about the editorship appears in the issues of July 13, 1905, p. 30, where Garrison is said to have been editor since the beginning, and of July 8, 1915, p. 68, where Godkin is referred to as "the founder and first editor." The 100-year-anniversary article by Richard Clark Sterne on September 20, 1965, is obscure on the point.

[2] The Nation, August 9, 1900, p. 105.

[3] The Nation, May 8, 1890, p. 367; The Nation, December 5, 1897, p. 442.

[4] The Nation, January 23, 1890, p. 61.

[5] The Nation, November 8, 1894, p. 348; The Nation, March 22, 1906, p. 234.

[6] The Nation, November 30, 1893, p. 404.

[7] The Nation, May 24, 1894, p. 382; The Nation, October 11, 1894, p. 264; The Nation, April 25, 1901, p. 332.

[8] The Nation, August 2, 1919, p. 137.

[9] The Nation, September 16, 1919, pp. 327, 353; The Nation, Vol. 129, p. 515.

[10] The Nation, October 31, 1934, p. 493.

[11] The Nation, Vol. 166, pp. 117, 341.

[12] The Nation, Vol. 190, p. 63; The Nation, Vol. 201, pp. 149, 317.

[13] The Nation, Vol. 201, p. 384.

[14] The Nation, February 9, 1985.

[15] New Republic, May 31, 1948, p. 17; New Republic, June 7, 1948, p. 13; New Republic, June 28, 1948, p. 13; New Republic, July 12, 1948, p. 7; New Republic, December 6, 1948, p. 3; New Republic, July 14, 1952, p. 7; New Republic, January 19, 1953, p. 7.

[16] Michael Straight, *After Long Silence* (New York: W. W. Norton Company, 1983), p. 231.

[17] New Republic, March 18, 1946, p. 390; New Republic, April 18, 1983, p. 11.

# CHAPTER SIX
## Dissimulation

In various of its aspects, liberalism cannot be identified precisely with either socialism or alienation. The coalition that has made up the modern Democratic Party has been broader than liberalism and has included groups and individuals who have been neither socialist nor alienated. This is even true of a more narrowly defined "liberal coalition" and of liberalism in its popular expression as a mass phenomenon. It is important to realize this if we are to avoid thinking of liberalism as more homogeneous than it actually is.

If, however, we inquire into the nature of liberal *thought,* we are involved with a body of ideas that has been intimately related to the intellectual culture. A completely honest analysis then requires a recognition that this thought has been fundamentally socialist. Liberalism in its aspect as an ideology has been one of the consequences of the alienation of the intellectual and of the intellectuals' search for alliances.

This is not to say that liberal and socialist thought have been identical. They have not. The difference has been in the willingness of socialists to accept the socialist label – indeed, to proclaim it loudly – and to stand up openly for their objectives. Subject to brief periods of overt radicalism, American liberal thinkers have generally done everything they can to avoid the socialist label and to obscure their ultimate objectives. This has been especially true with regard to the face they have presented to the American public. This face has differed substantially from what they have said in the writing they have addressed to each other.

Beginning in the late nineteenth century, the thinkers who have been designated "liberal" have been those who for reasons of personality and tactics have chosen not to divorce themselves from the American mainstream. To embrace the socialist values of the West's intellectual culture (of which they have wanted very much to be a part) without seeming to do so, such men as Herbert Croly, Thorstein Veblen, John Dewey and John Kenneth Galbraith have woven into their ideology an elaborate fabric of dissimulation.

The other ideologies I have discussed in my series of books on the theme of understanding the modern predicament – Burkean conservatism, classical liberalism and the various forms of socialist thought – have all been straight-forward. They have said what they mean, directly and forcefully. But this has not been true with modern American liberalism. Much of its expression has been masked by euphemism and dissimulation.

This subject irritates liberals. They detest any suggestion of dissimulation when it is mentioned by conservatives. It is worth noting, though, that the dissimulation has been discussed at length within liberal literature. That discussion is what I will be review in this chapter.

1. Liberal literature has often admitted the existence of the dissimulation quite candidly.

Thus, Max Lerner wrote about Thorstein Veblen that "the Veblenian irony is a way of saying things and yet not saying them, the Veblenian mystification is a form of protective coloration." Lerner argued in 1935 that Veblen "no longer needed to hide his meaning" after he finally tore away the veil by publishing *The Engineer and the Price System*. In that book, Veblen had called for a seizure of power and the creation of a "technical soviet."[1]

In 1931, John Dewey called for a new political party. Here is his discussion of the dissimulation he thought necessary for it: "I think a new party will have to adopt many measures which are now labelled socialistic...But while support for such measures in the concrete, when they are adapted to actual situations, will win support from the American people, I cannot imagine the American people supporting them on the ground of Socialism...The prejudice against the name may be a regrettable prejudice, but its influence is so powerful."[2]

In 1970, Michael Harrington wrote of "a mass social democracy in the United States." He said that it "is invisible because, in typically American fashion, its socialistic aims are phrased in capitalistic rhetoric."[3]

Irving Kristol has spoken of the "paradoxical" use of labels in the United States, and has said about liberals that "it would certainly help to clarify matters if they were called, with greater propriety and accuracy, 'socialists' or 'neo-socialists.' And yet we are reluctant to be so candid. In part, this lack of candor is simply the consequence of a great many 'liberals' being demagogic or hypocritical about their political intentions." He went on to say that "I find it striking that the media...should consistently refer to John Kenneth Galbraith as a 'liberal' when he has actually taken the pains to write a book explaining why he is a socialist."[4]

In 1939, Bernard Smith wrote a review of Parrington's *Main Currents in American Thought*. Of Parrington, Smith said that "his radicalism wasn't altogether obvious. He was certainly not so foolish as to flaunt it...I can state quite dogmatically that he had some acquaintance with Marxism, had been influenced by it, and knew that his method was related to it. I have seen a letter by him in which he said as much."[5]

Dissimulation has not only been acknowledged generally, but also in connection with specific liberal undertakings. In 1936, for example, the British socialist Harold Laski, writing in *The New Republic*, wrote that "under the auspices of the American Historical Association a commission sat for the five years from 1929 to survey the educational position in the United States with special reference to social studies." He said that "stripped of its carefully neutral phrases, the report is an educational program for a socialist America."[6]

In 1939, a *New Republic* editorial reported that "Mr. Thomas R. Amlie, nominated to be Interstate Commerce Commissioner, admitted to a great skepticism about the future of capitalism. His senatorial listeners watched him with shocked faces. As experienced men, they themselves had precisely the same skepticism; what shocked them was the fact that Mr. Amlie had the courage and candor to say what was in him."[7]

Christopher Jencks said that the Elementary and Secondary Education Act of 1965 was "like all Johnson proposals, ... being promoted with a highly traditional rhetoric." He added candidly that "nevertheless, anyone who looks carefully at the bill will see that it...proposes" what Jencks described as a major centralization of educational decision-making.[8]

Liberal literature has often referred to the compromise and opportunism inherent in the Fabian method. In 1914 in one of its first editorials, *The New Republic* said that "anything so vast as a reconstruction of society can only be accomplished by an immense amount of little steps, a constant readjustment of theory, and a depressing amount of compromise." It called for people "who are loyal to their end and opportunist about their means." In 1930, an article by William Orton about England urged progressives to "avoid everything doctrinaire" and "to leave the particular means to be developed pragmatically." He added that "this is, no doubt, a plea for opportunism." In 1939, Bruce Bliven called for a Fabian emphasis on incremental steps: "New Dealers...need to stop talking in cliches which unnecessarily frighten the average citizen, and to appeal instead to the concrete opportunities for a nation."[9]

Liberals have often spoken among themselves of their "foot-in-the-door" strategy – or, as Senator Robert Wagner referred to it, of their tactic of "getting the camel's nose under the tent." In the context of Lyndon Johnson's Great Society agenda in 1965, TRB wrote that "many of these are toe-in-the-door programs for future amplification." A year later, he spoke of "the government's foot in the door with the rent subsidy program."[10]

2. Liberal literature has also commented extensively on the reasons for the dissimulation.

In 1931, Matthew Josephson spoke of the personal motives that often lie behind it. He told about "how in adolescence those of us who received their education more or less consciously became socialist at heart," but that "then, as prospective men of letters or of the professions, we foresaw the most meager stake for ourselves under the heedless capitalist arrangement; so that our interests, quite deterministically, lay behind our indifference and made us secretly or waitingly Marxian...Not all of us wished as yet to be uninvited 'martyrs': or, as successful, practising agitators, to pass a life resembling that of Jesuits."[11]

A fear of the adverse impact of candor on the political acceptability of liberalism has, of course, long been a major concern among liberal politicians. Charles Beard said that "Theodore Roosevelt praised [Croly's *The Promise of American Life*] but looked upon Mr. Croly as too radical for practical purposes." In a 1912 editorial about Robert LaFollette, *The Nation* observed that "radical public men...when they seek support for high office...minimize their radicalism." In 1936, Thurman Arnold, later Franklin Roosevelt's chief trust-buster, wrote that "I decline to support the Socialists until they become less perfectionist...and show signs of becoming an effective political group with ability to use political techniques." In 1968, David Riesman revealed that "a senator from one of the Mountain States once said to me, if my constituents knew what I was really like (which in fact the right wing keeps telling them) they would throw me out."[12]

Not surprisingly, though, liberalism has been recognized as an advantage for a faculty member's success in the academic world. Morton Cronin wrote in 1957 that "the adoption of a liberal orientation is an important method for getting on in the academic world." Personal motivations for success in a career are important in sustaining an ideology. Cronin added that "the world of academic liberals, in short, is saturated with careerism."[13]

3. Liberalism's dissimulation has been the counterpart of American conservatism's success in causing the American public to reject socialism and anything that the public understands to be socialist.

Benjamin Ginsburg was angry but accurate when he pointed to the practical underpinning of liberalism in *The New Republic* in 1931. He paraphrased liberals as saying: "One must never mention the word socialism, inasmuch as the American people will not hear of socialism...."[14]

4. Euphemism, used extensively, has been a stylistic by-product of the dissimulation.

One of the earliest, best and most influential examples of this was Herbert Croly's book *The Promise of American Life* (1909). The closest he came in hundreds of pages to announcing his socialist goals was a sentence such as: "...the organization of labor like the organization of capital may gradually be fitted into a nationalized economic system." No one could quarrel with a suggestion that something *may* happen; nor could anyone say absolutely that he had advocated it. Croly's style of suggestion rather than advocacy has remained typical of much liberal writing. Thus, we have become accustomed to seeing such statements as that made by Dow Votaw in his book *Modern Corporations*: "The great corporation may ultimately itself become a political or electoral unit in a vastly different governmental structure than we know today."[15]

After John T. Flynn broke with *The New Republic*, Flynn attacked the term "planned economy" as a euphemistic substitute for socialism. In 1949, he wrote in *The Road Ahead* that socialism "is being promoted in America by organizations that never pronounce in public the word socialism. They call their system the Planned Economy." He added that "that is a fraudulent brand name. It is used to sell socialism to an unsuspecting population." (Flynn was guilty of considerable dissimulation himself in that book, in which he did not tell his conservative readers of his own earlier endorsement of the "planning" concept. He had been a leading columnist for *The New Republic* during most of the 1930's. In 1936, he declared he would vote for Norman Thomas, and found it "disconcerting" that many on the Left were coming out for Roosevelt. "The great choice which confronts the peoples of every country today is – who is to control their economic societies? By control I mean conscious, deliberate, planned control.")[16]

5. Those further to the left, of course, have always looked upon the dissimulation with contempt; and during the brief periods when the liberal intellectual culture has itself been willing to endorse socialism more overtly, many have expressed disgust with the cravenness of the less forthright approach. On other occasions, individual liberals have from time to time become willing to declare their socialist affinity – and then have looked back scornfully.

*The New Republic* had no sooner started publication than Amos Pinchot wrote it complaining that "*The New Republic*... concentrates attention on symptoms and incidentals, and maintains silence in regard to the foundations upon which the whole fabric of social injustice rests."[17]

In 1931, Edmund Wilson argued passionately for liberals to give up Croly's "gradual and natural approximation to socialism" and to embrace socialism openly. "They must take Communism away from the Communists, and take it without ambiguities or reservations...." A letter from Lewis Mumford in 1935 congratulated *The New Republic* for "leaving behind the stale liberalism of capitalist compromise," and called for liberals to create a non-totalitarian communism.[18]

In 1956, Paul Goodman, one of those who laid the foundation for the New Left, made the same radical critique: "Throughout the nineteenth and twentieth centuries, the radical-liberal program was continually compromised, curtailed, sometimes realized in form without content." In 1957, Harvey Goldberg and William Appleman Williams wrote that "'radical' defines a nature different in quality from the temporizing 'liberal' spirit, so expert in weighing principle against expediency." They said that Heywood Broun had "made the point with characteristic directness: 'In the final count of reckoning I believe the angels will indulge in few long cheers for any liberal. With minor exceptions he's a trimmer.'"[19]

6. It is this tension between temporizing and radical assertiveness that explains the phenomenon of "liberal 'guilt'" that is so often commented upon. Thus, Ronald Berman has spoken of "the guilt of liberalism – a guilt which exists because liberalism refuses to make the leap between what it is and what, given its doctrine, it might become."[20]

A pathetic passage in Arthur Schlesinger, Jr.'s, *The Politics of Upheaval* speaks to this: "Measured against the Bolshevik, with his infinite courage and his terrible calm, the American bourgeois [liberal] could only feel a sense of his own unworthiness." Referring to the time in 1934 when Lincoln Steffens had declined an offer to join the Communist Party, Schlesinger quoted him as having said: "I think I am not to be trusted in the party or in the front ranks of the struggle...We liberals must not have power, not ever; we must not be leaders, we must not be allowed to be parties in the leadership...We, who have fitted successfully into the old culture, are to the very degree of our education and adjustment, – we are corrupted and unfit for, – the kingdom of heaven.'" Schlesinger spoke of this as "liberal self-abasement."[21]

# NOTES

[1] New Republic, May 15, 1935, pp. 8, 9.

[2] New Republic, April 1, 1931, p. 178.

[3] Michael Harrington, *Socialism* (New York: Saturday Review Press, 1970), p. 133.

[4] Irving Kristol, *Two Cheers for Capitalism* (New York: Mentor Books, 1978), p. 127.
[5] New Republic, February 15, 1939, p. 42.
[6] New Republic, July 29, 1936, p. 342.
[7] New Republic, March 1, 1939, p. 86.
[8] New Republic, February 6, 1965, p. 17.
[9] New Republic, December 26, 1914, p. 6; New Republic, January 29, 1930, p. 266; New Republic, June 21, 1939, p. 184.
[10] Senator Wagner's tactic is discussed by J. Joseph Huthmacher in his *Senator Robert F. Wagner and the Rise of Urban Liberalism* (New York: Atheneum, 1968), at p. 113 and again at p. 214; New Republic July 10, 1965, p. 4; New Republic, May 14, 1966, p. 4.
[11] New Republic, February 18, 1931.
[12] New Republic, November 8, 1939, p. 78; The Nation, January 4, 1912, p. 4; New Republic, September 30, 1936, p. 223; New Republic, April 13, 1968, p. 21.
[13] New Republic, January 7, 1957, p. 11.
[14] New Republic, February 18, 1931, p. 17.
[15] Herbert Croly, *The Promise of American Life* (New York: The Macmillan Company, 1914), p. 390; Dow Votaw, *Modern Corporations* (Englewood Cliffs, N. J.: Prentice-Hall, 1965), p. 96.
[16] New Republic, November 4, 1936, pp. 17, 18.
[17] New Republic, May 29, 1915, p. 96.
[18] New Republic, January 14, 1931, p. 234; New Republic, February 6, 1935, p. 361.
[19] Paul Goodman, *Growing Up Absurd* (New York: Random House, 1956), p. 15; Harvey Goldberg (ed.), *American Radicals* (New York: Modern Reader Paperbacks, 1957), p. 1.
[20] Ronald Berman, *America in the Sixties: An Intellectual History* (New York: The Free Press, 1968), p. 108.
[21] Arthur M. Schlesinger, Jr., *The Politics of Upheaval* (Boston: Houghton Mifflin Company, 1960), p. 185.

## CHAPTER SEVEN
## Liberalism and American Culture

A vastly important dimension of American liberalism comes from the liberal intellectual culture's having for the most part joined in the Left's century-and-a-half old assault upon the values and culture of the middle class (often referred to as the "bourgeoisie"). This is an assault that continues in many forms in the 1990s, though most prominently in the form of a projected multicultural swamping of the mainstream culture.

Before the Civil War, as we have seen, the intellectual culture began quite early to see American life as sick. Henry David Thoreau spoke of "lives of quiet desperation" in which effluvia took the place of serious values. He complained that he could find no one in Concord who could discuss a good English classic with him. "Our reading, our conversation and thinking are all on a very low level, worthy only of pygmies and manikins," he said. "We are a race of tit-men, and soar but little higher in our intellectual flights than the columns of the daily paper."[1]

A comparable period of social criticism occurred in the early twentieth century. Liberals of Randolph Bourne and Harold Stearns' generation found fault with almost every facet of our national life. In the present chapter we will examine the main contours of that critique.

1. The social critics have often complained of the middle class's traditional commitment to the work ethic and to moral constraints. As Morris Cohen wrote under the pseudonym "Philonous" in 1919, "it is the Puritanic feeling of responsibility which has blighted our art and philosophy and has made us as a people unskilled in the art of enjoying life." Alfred Kuttner wrote in 1914 that "so long as we frown upon leisure as a yielding to the devil and an invitation to our competitor to overreach us, the finer issues of life must remain in abeyance."[2]

Randolph Bourne objected to the redemptive theme within American novels which sought "the moral transformation" of the characters. Bourne praised Theodore Dreiser and urged all literature to "follow the pattern of life, sincere, wistful and unredeemed." An article in *The New Republic* in 1930 by another author spoke of "a country stifled by generations of Puritanism," and in the area of sexuality called for a "breaking down of the secrecy and hypocrisy."[3]

To classical liberalism, the culture's internalizing of moral values and discipline within its individuals is a vitally important part of the social cements that allow a free society to exist. This is precisely something that the Left, including such modern liberals as Cohen and Bourne, has attacked as part of its assault on individualistic liberalism.

Perhaps the most incredible statement of the Left's view has come from Jerry Rubin in his book *Growing (Up) at 37*. Using the typical Dadaistic shock method that became so popular a weapon with the New Left, he tells of a "psychic therapy" session in which the participants sought release from their "childhood deprivation." He says, "I started shouting at my mother for the specific messages she gave me. 'Thanks, Mommy. You white-skinned no-good sexless asshole cap-toothed cancerous venom of a snake who destroyed me from birth...You taught me to hate myself, to feel guilty, to drive myself crazy,...to hate my body, to hate women...I have your self-righteous right-wrong should-should-not programming...with that stupid JUDGE inside me that I got from you. I don't see people as they are, but as they fit my standards, my self-righteous beliefs ...Oh, it is so liberating for me to tell the truth. MOMMY I AM GLAD THAT YOU DIED. IF YOU HAD NOT DIED OF CANCER, I WOULD HAVE HAD TO KILL YOU...You taught me to compete and compare, to fear and outdo. I became a ferocious achievement-oriented, compulsive, obsessive live-in-my-head asshole...Well fuck you, Mommy, fuck you in the ass with a red-hot poker." (Rubin's capitalization.) When we compare this passage with those I have quoted from Cohen and Bourne, we see that the conceptual content is the same. Rubin's, though, gives us insight into the nihilistic extreme to which those concepts – when articulated through the shock tactic of totally disregarding so-called "middle class" standards of expression – have been carried by the more militant members of the Left.[4]

2. The attack on the work ethic and on "middle class" moral constraints has gone hand-in-hand with objections to our culture's emphasis on material success.

John Dewey complained that "a regime of pecuniary profit and loss still commands our allegiance." He urged that "we question the worth of a dominantly money-civilization." John Dos Passos added that there was an "imperial American procession towards more money, more varnish, more ritz, that obsesses all our lives." During the late 1960's, Henry Fairlie compared the counterculture with his own youth, and wrote that "the young today, on the whole, despise business for the same reason that the young of my own day despised it: that it *seems* to be concerned only with making money by processes which *seem* to be intellectually and emotionally unsatisfying."⁵

3. A commercial, middle class society involves a peaceable day-to-day existence that has long struck many thinkers as intolerably mundane. Largely oblivious to the human drama that that life encompasses, these authors have felt a longing spiritually for "something bigger, more absorbing than individual lives."

Such a perspective was felt deeply by the adherents of the Romantic movement in the early nineteenth century. Thomas Carlyle yearned for "heroes" and considered the tradesman thoroughly mediocre. These attitudes reflected a resurgence of medieval and aristocratic values.

As secular religions, the totalitarian ideologies have yearned for a sense of transcendent destiny. In *Mein Kampf* Adolf Hitler angrily raised the rhetorical question of why he had been born in "an age of shopkeepers" rather than during the Wars of Liberation "when a man, even without a business, was worth something." In Communist writing, the "Bolshevik heroes" and the Stakhanovite heroes of self-sacrificing labor typify this commitment of the individual to the larger entity.

It is not surprising, then, that modern liberals have also reflected this yearning for a secular religion. Thus, Martha Higley wrote in *The New Republic* in 1931 that "the life of a large portion of the population is meaningless, because there is no centralizing force in their lives, no feeling that they are part of a social system greater than the individual unit." TRB complained in 1961 that "our culture has a genius for demeaning greatness."⁶

Although I believe that these complaints about the emptiness of bourgeois life miss a great deal of the meaning that is actually there, I have made the point that a free society *does* need, as much as any other, a transcendent sense of meaning. I agree with the other philosophies that a daily life based on small preoccupations is *not* enough in itself to satisfy humanity's basic psychic needs. The historic failure of bourgeois life in this dimension is a vitally important one. The blame for it, though, is only partly the bourgeoisie's. The social critics are blind to the fact that a significant cause of the failure is due precisely to the intellectual culture's own choices. That culture has for almost two centuries thrown itself into alienation when it could have served as a vitally important component of a liberal society (in the historic sense of "liberal") and have worked to provide such meaning.

4. An oft-repeated charge is that bourgeois society is "hypocritical." In his preface to *Civilization in the United States* in 1921, Harold Stearns said that one of the themes appearing in most of the book's thirty essays was "that in almost every branch of American life

there is a sharp dichotomy between preaching and practice." Anyone who lived through the New Left period of the late 1960's must certainly remember how often our society was charged with hypocrisy.[7]

It should be apparent, though, that hypocrisy, as a slippage between what is professed and what is actually done, is a universal human trait. It cannot be considered the exclusive possession of any particular culture. To stay on track, the discussion should debate the relative degree of hypocrisy.

I have not been able to find a detailed explanation of why modern liberalism feels that bourgeois society is more hypocritical than others. The absence of this explanation in the literature makes it a matter of conjecture.

My own analysis in the chapter on "Existential Problems in a Commercial Culture" in *Understanding the Modern Predicament* suggests that a special form of hypocrisy does exist within a commercial society. It arises out of the split that exists between the "extroverted outer flow" among people, which trivializes everything into what is pleasant, and the "radical solitude" of meaningful life to individuals. The very gregariousness that in so many ways makes our life pleasant also puts it under a veil of trivia. Real values are covered over and ignored. Anyone caring about those values will tend to think the resulting human relationships hypocritical.

The trivialization is a serious problem in the spiritual and intellectual life of our society. Whether, however, it creates a condition that justifies the contempt of intellectuals more than other cultures' hypocrisy does is another question.

5. The social criticism has created a caricature of middle class individuals that is closely associated with the complaints I have mentioned. It pictures the typical bourgeois as uninspired, insipid and preoccupied with money and social status.

The classic stereotype along these lines was drawn by Sinclair Lewis in his 1922 book *Babbitt*. Lewis' theme has been summarized by Henry May: "George F. Babbitt was a realtor in Zenith, Ohio...Essentially confused and timid, he joined in the town's scramble for social prestige, its false, gregarious jollity...." May says that "much the same picture of dulness and conformity was painted by other poets and novelists, by foreign lecturers like Andre Siegfried, and by sociologists like the authors of *Middletown*...."[8]

Because of the currency of this stereotype, it is no surprise that George Babbitt is virtually the same character as George Bernard Shaw's Mr. Burgess in *Candida*. According to Shaw's stage directions, Burgess is a man "made coarse and sordid by the compulsory selfishness of petty commerce...a vulgar ignorant guzzling man...."[9]

The stereotype appears again in Theodore Dreiser's *An American Tragedy* when Dreiser describes Roberta Alden's father and family: "Titus Alden was one of that vast company of individuals who are born, pass through and die out of the world without ever quite getting any one thing straight...A single, serious, intelligent or rightly informing book had never been read by any member of this family – not one. But they were nevertheless excellent, as conventions, morals and religions go – honest, upright, God-fearing and respectable."[10]

6. This caricature of the middle class has been accompanied by an equally slashing attack upon the rural American, who is often depicted as ignorant, provincial, vicious and narrowly limited by an anti-intellectual fundamentalist Christianity. H. L. Mencken wrote of "rustic ignoramuses" and said of William Jennings Bryan that he "seemed only a poor clod like those around him, deluded by a childish theology, full of an almost pathological hatred of all learning, all human dignity, all beauty, all fine and noble things. He was a peasant come home to the barnyard."[11]

This critique found its *cause celebre* in the Scopes trial in 1925 after John T. Scopes was charged with violating the Tennessee statute against the teaching of evolution. Clarence Darrow was the attorney for the defense, William Jennings Bryan for the prosecution. *The New Republic* editorialized that the statute had been "passed by the lunatic fringe – a broad one – in the Fundamentalist movement."[12]

It is worth noting that the critique has usually focused on the South, although it is actually broader than that would suggest. Tennessee Williams and Carson McCullers are authors whose works are central to the alienated portrayal of the South.

The intellectual culture's hostility toward what it considers a "hick" America is important if we are to understand the depth of the reservations that liberal intellectuals felt toward both Lyndon Baines Johnson and Jimmy Carter. Given the literary history of the twentieth century in the United States, Johnson and Carter were inevitably outsiders, no matter how liberal their programs and rhetoric. To the intellectual culture they were essentially "peasants come home to the barnyard."

7. Actually, of course, the alienation has been a general one, not limited to either the middle class or the rural American. It is a mistake to break it down too sharply into specifics. The larger alienation has been visible in countless ways, and I have discussed it extensively in my writing. I will illustrate it here by a relatively small example: the

inclination of liberal authors to blame the nation as a whole for the assassinations of John F. Kennedy and Robert Kennedy. In December 1963, right after the first assassination, TRB's alienation was apparent when he spoke of "this hapless situation, set off by a senseless horror in Dallas, where they breed such things. There is a crackpot hatred in America...." Then in June 1968, after the murder of Robert Kennedy by Sirhan Sirhan, a *New Republic* editorial said that the killing "tells us once more that we nurture in our society a disposition to violence." These are emotional outpourings expressed without regard to the specifics of the assassinations. They would hardly come from anyone who did not already feel deep alienation.[13]

8. Elitism will inevitably be an important characteristic of an intellectual culture that feels itself so superior to its milieu.

If this is surprising about American liberalism, it is only because liberals have so long been the ideological champions of democracy, material equality and compassion. These values have been dictated by the political, ideological imperatives of their alliance with the have-nots. At first, it seems incongruous that such a democratically oriented intellectual culture can also have been profoundly elitist. But anyone who thinks the various elements incompatible does not fully grasp the "layered" nature of liberalism.

"Majority rule" is supported whenever it is thought to lend itself to social legislation and to the forms of equality that liberalism pursues. Although liberalism sees itself as consistently democratic in the truest sense, majority rule, as such, will be subordinated to liberalism's other values if they conflict. One of the best examples is the Warren Court's striking down of Proposition 14, which was passed by an overwhelming majority in a referendum in California and that sought to repeal that state's open-housing law. Another is the Court's having invalidated various state referenda that sought to reinstate a geographical component in the make-up of state senates after the Court's reapportionment decisions. The fact that large majorities had voted a certain way was not seen to matter. Both "majority rule" and the doctrine so popular with liberals in the 1920's and '30's of "let the local majorities experiment" were subordinated by the liberal majority on the Court at that time. Although some justices continued to espouse the judicial restraint that they had preached while conservatives dominated the Court, the Warren Court's majority was given to judicial activism.

The alienation and elitism that I have illustrated in this chapter are also prepared to subordinate the values of democracy, equality and compassion to other values. There is no natural affinity of the intellectuals for the have-nots, whom they know to be even less given to intellectual values than the bourgeoisie. For a century and a half, the intellectuals and the have-nots have been ideological allies as the Left has sought coalitions against the predominant middle class culture. Because that is a long time so far as the perspective of any given person is concerned, the illusion is created that the connection is permanent. This illusion is the reason for the surprise and disillusionment that has followed in the wake of the actual behavior of Communist regimes, in which a brutal elitism soon becomes apparent. (Ironically, the elitism of the intellectuals is often replaced by that of a clique of political cronies, such as under Stalin. But if the analysis made by Konrad and Szelenyi is to be credited, there is later a tendency for an elite of at least technocratic intellectuals to assume power.)[14]

Modern liberalism and the Left's negative critique of the middle class is not primarily an opposition to the middle class's weaknesses and vices, but precisely to its strengths and virtues. True, it dislikes the intellectual, aesthetic mediocrity that arises out of the middle class's preoccupation with daily life and competitive success; but it also opposes the very value system of competition, of the work ethic, of family discipline. It sees no incongruity, given its willingness to mold itself to its tactical needs, in supporting and promoting (as our predominantly liberal media do) the hedonistic and vulgar sides of the middle class psyche. It is this combination of the intellectual culture with both black culture and middle class hedonism that has given rise to the predominant cultural tone in the United States in the twentieth century, especially since World War II.[15]

9. Throughout this discussion, I have referred to the "defiance of convention" which has often been one of the consequences of the assault upon middle class values. The passage by Jerry Rubin illustrated it starkly. Although liberalism itself is given to dissimulation to avoid confrontation, there is a direct connection between liberalism's critique of the society and these more extreme expressions of the critique.

In 1927, *The New Republic*, speaking of the American theater, said that "in its defiance of convention it has been expressing a widely prevalent revolt against the manners and values of previous generations." This revolt is intellectually, artistically related to the revolutionary theater of the New Left sixty years later.[16]

In 1932, Malcolm Cowley looked back to the time when Dos Passos was a student at Harvard immediately before World War I. It was the time of the "Harvard esthetes," who believed that "society is hostile, stupid and unmanageable; it is the world of the philistines...That the poet... should, in fact, deliberately make himself misunderstandable... That art...is the poet's revenge on society." Cowley spoke of the poet's flight into mysticism "by any means in his power – alcohol, drugs...." This was the same period that the Dadaist school in Europe was proclaiming art as a weapon against the bourgeoisie and against art itself.[17]

In *Exile's Return*, Malcolm Cowley explained that the Dadaist impulse had actually gotten started in Europe in the early nineteenth century. (It is no coincidence, of course, that that would correspond with the Romantic movement, with its deep revulsion against modernity and bourgeois culture.) In the same book, Edmund Wilson told how the nineteenth century author Flaubert "with several of his friends once visited a brothel in Rouen. On a bet, before them all, he made love to a prostitute without removing his hat or taking the cigar from his mouth. The gesture was something more than an ugly boast. It announced a furious contempt for everything held sacred by society."[18]

Years later, Eldridge Cleaver explained that this concept of "revenge upon the culture," applied in a racial context, lay behind why "I became a rapist." He said that "it seemed to me that the act of rape was an insurrectionary act. It delighted me that I was defying and trampling upon the white man's law, upon his system of values."[19]

10. A final point is important in its own right but is sufficiently different that it will also illustrate how far-reaching the implications of the rejection of American cultural values can be.

Liberal thought has often said that it wants to divorce "middle class" moral judgments from social policies directed toward the poor.

In part it has wanted to do so to "become more scientific." In Comte's three-part classification of historical stages, the scientific "positivist" phase would supplant the "metaphysical" phase that preceded it. Individual morality has been identified with the metaphysical phase (or with the theological phase, which was even earlier). An excellent example of the attempt to get away from so-called metaphysics and theology by applying a deterministic analysis to the exclusion of values is B. F. Skinner's *Beyond Freedom and Dignity*.

In addition to wanting to become clinically scientific, liberalism has had motives dictated by the tactical needs of its ideology in its quest for alliances with the poor. By negating "middle class" moral values, liberal ideology has accomplished two things: First, it has made it possible for itself to be easily empathetic toward the poor by rejecting the need to make adverse judgments. Then, in an associated step, it has made itself "the enemy of their enemies." It has been able to oppose those who *do* have adverse moral judgments to make. These two aspects affect a

*Liberalism in Contemporary America* 127

number of practical issues.

We have seen, for example, an editorial such as the one in *The New Republic* in 1968 in which the editors denounced specific policies that were based on moral evaluations. One was a Louisiana statute that made it a crime for someone to parent a second illegitimate child. Another was the rule which many states had adopted that provided that Aid to Families With Dependent Children would not be payable if there were an able-bodied man in the household. It is in the context of such issues that modern liberalism has established the web of "non-judgmental" programs that exist today. The result is that a humanitarian concern for the poor has been replaced by a paternalism that is extended as well to the irresponsible poor. For this and a number of other reasons, the problem of irresponsibility in its endless variety, of in-dwelling barbarism within civilization, is one of today's most intractable problems.

A lesser, but functionally very compelling, reason for the divorce from the so-called "middle class" principles of personal responsibility has been to make it possible for social workers and other professionals to establish a non-judgmental working relationship with the poor. If for no other reason than to encourage those who are irresponsible to seek counseling, and to continue with it once begun, a non-judgmental relationship is considered necessary between the counselor and the subject. This causes professionals in such fields constantly to seek ways to depersonalize (i.e., render deterministic) the explanation of the causes of the distressed condition of their subjects. (I recently attended a school meeting on the drug problem in which the audience was told over and over again that "neither the young person nor the parent is to blame" for the child's having become an addict. This was said in the abstract, as a general principle negating anyone's responsibility. The facts of any given case were abstracted away in favor of moral neutrality.)

Such a stance may or may not be conducive to effective counseling, but it clearly is predicated on the assumption that moral constraints, socially enforced, are no longer important to society. We can only hope that after a few years enough moral perspective will remain to allow our society to evaluate the effects of this assumption, and to adopt a different principle if it is found not to have worked.

## NOTES

[1] Henry David Thoreau, *Walden-Essay on Civil Disobedience* (New York: Airmont Publishing Company, Inc., 1965), p. 81.

[2] Morris Cohen is quoted in Henry May, *The Discontent of the Intellectuals:*

*A Problem of the Twenties* (Chicago: Rand McNally & Company, 1963), p. 23; New Republic, December 12, 1914, p. 21.

[3] New Republic, April 17, 1915, p. 7 of the Literary Supplement; New Republic, June 4, 1930, p. 68.

[4] Jerry Rubin, *Growing (Up) at 37* (New York: Warner Books, 1976), pp. 140-142.

[5] New Republic, April 24, 1929, p. 271; New Republic, April 16, 1930, p. 236; New Republic, April 8, 1967, p. 13.

[6] New Republic, June 24, 1931, p. 152; New Republic, January 23, 1961, p. 2.

[7] Harold E. Stearns (ed.), *Civilization in the United States* (New York: Harcourt, Brace and Company, 1922), p. vi.

[8] May, *Discontent of the Intellectuals*, pp. 30, 31.

[9] Another Babbitt-like characterization of American culture is summarized in the review of Sherwood Anderson's *Marching Man* in the September 29, 1917, issue of New Republic, p. 249.

[10] Theodore Dreiser, *An American Tragedy* (New York: The Heritage Press, 1962), p. 166.

[11] Mencken is quoted by May in *Discontent of the Intellectuals*, p. 27.

[12] New Republic, January 26, 1927, p. 260.

[13] New Republic, December 7, 1963, p. 30.

[14] George Konrad and Ivan Szelenyi, *The Intellectuals on the Road to Class Power* (New York: Harcourt, Brace, Jovanovich, Inc., 1979).

[15] Two qualifications should be made about what I have said in this paragraph: That my reference to black culture is by no means intended to be a universal condemnation of it; and that many dedicated members of the Left oppose the marriage with hedonism, wanting a purer method.

[16] New Republic, February 23, 1927, p. 6.

[17] New Republic, April 27, 1932, p. 303.

[18] Malcolm Cowley, *Exile's Return: A Narrative of Ideas* (New York: W. W. Norton & Company, Inc., 1934), pp. 148, 151.

[19] Ronald Berman, *America in the Sixties: An Intellectual History* (New York: The Free Press, 1968), p. 281.

# CHAPTER EIGHT
## Emphasis on Social Change

Modern liberalism has focused on the value of social change. To this end, it has stressed the impermanence of values and institutions. On issues of method, such as those involved in "civil liberties" and confrontational techniques, it has taken positions that facilitate change rather than impede it. It would not be off the mark to say that the emphasis on change has been as central to modern liberalism as the emphasis on stability has been to traditionalist conservatism.

The relationship of this focus to liberalism's tactical situation is apparent. Liberal thought has not relished the existing culture – has, in fact, been deeply alienated from it – and has been anxious to move to something else.

For most liberal thought, that "something else" has been, as we have seen, one form or another of socialism. Although this has not been nearly so true for the other components of the liberal coalition (such as the South, organized labor, the big city political machines, and the ethnic minorities) as it has for the intellectual culture, most of those other components have at least wanted an active program calling for social and legislative changes.

At the same time that liberalism has emphasized change, it has intuitively kept in mind its need for dissimulation. During most of modern liberalism's history, liberals have avoided directly advocating socialism. What has been needed, instead, has been a philosophical formulation that would focus on change *as a process* rather than as a conflict between well defined alternative systems. This explains why "pragmatism," American liberalism's most distinctive version of relativism, has been so popular within liberal thought. By denying theory and insisting that only the short-term and the concrete count, pragmatism has been consistent with the reluctance to reveal long-term aspirations.

This chapter's discussion of the liberal emphasis on change will examine four specific aspects of liberalism: the uses of pragmatism and of relativism; liberal educational theory; the role of "civil liberties"; and the liberal attitude toward confrontational techniques as catalysts of social change.

## Relativism and Pragmatism

In Chapter 10 of my book *Socialist Thought* I discussed the role that relativism has played in socialist thought. That chapter is important as background for our present discussion, since most of what I said there would apply equally well to an analysis of liberalism.

One of the points made there was that relativism arises in part out of the perspectives of science. Those who seek evidence and verification for their views are led to the "methodological individualism" of a Descartes and a Heisenberg. In addition, those who are primarily empirical come quickly to see that there is great variety within the world. Their studies constantly remind them that any particular set of values, institutions, laws or acculturations is simply one alternative among many.

This is illustrated by what John Chamberlain said about William Graham Sumner's sociological discussion in *Folkways*: "The one great idea that you take away from 'Folkways' is the idea of the relativity of cultures, the feeling that no custom or habit-pattern is right or wrong except in relation to a time and a place." Chamberlain's review was part of a *New Republic* series on the books that had most influenced liberal thought. Even though Sumner was a devout follower of Herbert Spencer's classical liberalism, his empirical relativism was congenial to liberal intellectuals, who have closely identified with the main trends of modern intellectuality.[1]

The rapid communication and travel that are available today constitute another major source of relativism. Local provincialisms become ever more difficult to sustain.

Because of these sources of relativism, it would be a mistake to attribute the modern relativistic philosophies exclusively to the tactical needs of the Left. Nevertheless, it would be an equally serious mistake to overlook the role played by the Left's needs, which have served as a third great source of relativism.

Eric Goldman was commendably candid in his book *Rendezvous With Destiny* about liberalism's tactical use of relativism as a "social acid." He said that liberals in the late nineteenth and early twentieth centuries found it necessary to attack the "steel chain of ideas" by which the American public was bound to classical liberalism. Goldman summarized this aspect of liberalism in the final sentence of his chapter called "Dissolving the Steel Chain of Ideas." He said that "between the depression of 1873 and the beginning of World War I, and especially during the early 1900's, these thinkers developed ideological acids capable of dissolving every link in conservatism's steel chain of ideas."[2]

Arthur Bestor discussed the same point in a *New Republic* article in

1955. He observed that "the alliance between pragmatism and liberalism was a fortuitous one, called forth by a particular historic situation...Pragmatism constituted, in essence, [a] sacred act *of intellectual spoliation.*" Speaking from a liberal perspective, he said that "it was *as a dissolvent* of untenable dogmas and misapplied certitudes that pragmatism served the liberal cause" (emphasis added). (It is worth noticing that he was not himself enthused about the relativism. He observed that pragmatism "revealed its fundamental inadequacy" in the late 1930's when it became necessary to articulate definite convictions to oppose the totalitarian systems. But we should notice, too, that there has been no repudiation of relativism by liberals in general. It has been used extensively in liberal ideology during the four decades since World War II.)[3]

We should not let it confuse us that Bestor's article uses the word "pragmatism" instead of "relativism." Pragmatism is nothing but the name given to the relativism that was put forward under that label by such thinkers as Charles Peirce, William James and John Dewey. Relativism without the label has continued to be used by liberalism as a "social acid" despite the reputed demise of pragmatism as such. When in the late 1960's we were told so often that "middle class values are just 'artificial structurings,'" we were being presented with a relativistic undercutting, even though nothing was said about pragmatism. In the 1970's we heard a similar argument, this time from feminists, that "the role assignments of 'masculinity' and 'femininity' are just artificial acculturations, with no inherent justification." Again, relativism was being used to dissolve people's attachment to existing norms. In both instances, it was quite successful. The relativistic undercutting has sufficient plausibility that most people, lacking a philosophical understanding of the values they hold, have no defense against it.

"Pragmatism," as such, is almost impossible to define, since, as F. C. S. Schiller said, there have been "as many pragmatisms as there were pragmatists." The entry by H. S. Thayer in *The Encyclopedia of Philosophy* traces the origin of pragmatism to the "Metaphysical Club" conducted at Cambridge in the 1870's by, among others, William James and Charles Peirce. Thayer says that James credited Peirce with having coined the name.

Readers who would like an introduction to the technical philosophical dimensions of pragmatism will do well to read Thayer's entry and the one preceding it by Gertrude Ezorsky on the "Pragmatic Theory of Truth." Dewey best expressed the technical aspects in his book *Logic: The Theory of Inquiry*.

Our concern here is with the application of pragmatism to social philosophy. This centers on John Dewey's version of pragmatism, since it was Dewey who used it to become perhaps the leading philosopher of liberalism. Peirce and James played no similar role.

As understood by liberal commentators, Dewey's pragmatism, which he preferred to call "instrumentalism," emphasized that knowledge is tentative and must come from an experimental attitude. Randolph Bourne praised Dewey for his "scientific method, with its hypothesis and bold experimentation." Morris Cohen thought its essence was that Dewey used ideas as "instrumental *for reforming the world*" (my emphasis). Dewey was consistent with this when he spoke of "a conviction that consequences in human welfare are a test of the worth of beliefs."[4]

This amounted to a value-laden flexibility, with an emphasis on the particular rather than the general. The values were those of liberalism. Dewey's pragmatism was a rationale for Fabian gradualism. We see these same ingredients in Charles Forcey's discussion of the views of Herbert Croly and Walter Weyl when he said that "pragmatism did not mean for [them]...mere expediency and drift...'The democracy, though compromising in action,' wrote Weyl, 'must be uncompromising in principle...and realized as opportunities permit.'" We should remember that Weyl considered himself a socialist; his reference to "democracy" was to the "industrial democracy" that was so popular at that time among British socialists and American liberals.[5]

It is no secret, of course, that John Dewey was also a socialist. The focus on experiment, on looking to social consequences, on judging ideas by their usefulness for social change, was ideal for an ideology that wanted to stress method, process and change while at the same time making its own criteria of social value the largely unarticulated measure for judging validity.

As a social philosophy, there was little that was new or profound about Dewey's pragmatism. His popularity as a social philosopher was due to his ideas' usefulness to liberalism. The same homage that was extended to Dewey as a philosopher was afforded to Oliver Wendell Holmes, Jr., for having applied relativism to law. Both men's positions must be understood in the context of liberalism's tactical needs at that time.

Even though "pragmatism" as a movement under that name may have died, references to the need to "be pragmatic" continued to be useful to liberalism after World War II. As we will see in the chapter on "the process of politicization," liberal thinking has seen virtually all human problems as appropriate subjects for governmental solution, preferably at the national level. The most direct way to address a problem was to establish an agency and to arm it with a few billion dollars. Whenever a conservative would object, he was implored to "forget that nonsense; be pragmatic." Direct action through government seemed much more immediate, "practical" and "compassionate" than to wait for people to work out their own problems or for the market to address them.

In this connection, it is worth noting that pragmatism is closely tied to at least three separate aspects of the modern mentality. It reflects the politicization that I have just mentioned. It relates, too, to the use of the state as a "direct action" tool, which is something that the Spanish philosopher Jose Ortega y Gasset considered in his book *The Revolt of the Masses* to be a major part of the primitive psychology of "the mass man." And it reflects the type of "rationalism" that has appealed to intellectuals of the Left, who have not thought in terms of simply using reason to create frameworks for otherwise unplanned human interaction.

A word of warning is in order, however. Many practical-minded people in American life have prided themselves on their "pragmatic" willingness to "solve problems." When a politician or a businessman calls himself "pragmatic," he usually means nothing more by it than that he is practical. He does not understand himself to be part of Dewey's movement, and he would certainly deny that he has any Fabian intentions. There is no particular ideological significance to the word "pragmatic" when it is used in that manner, other than that such a man's lack of general convictions will tend to make him a tool of whatever is fashionable during his lifetime (and in recent decades that has usually been "liberal").

Although what I have just said is true in its own way, I believe that this popular usage does have a dimension that is significant to our discussion of the ideologies. I made the point in my book about classical liberalism that individualistic liberalism was forced onto the defensive more than a century ago, and that that posture has kept it from being as reformist and as critical as it otherwise would have been. The theory of a free society in the classical liberal sense has accordingly not been developed in a fully adequate way. I am thinking especially of its failure to deal with the problems raised by market imperfections, although there are other issues that are equally affected.

If we understand this, it becomes evident that politicians and businessmen within our society have often felt a need not to adhere strictly to the too-narrow rationale that has been spelled out by free-market theorists. They have felt the insufficiency of that rationale.

Without an alternative theory of their own, they have justified their departure from the rationale by saying that they are "simply being pragmatic." It is likely that most such people have little, if any, socialist affinity; their common sense just tells them that they need to be free to act independently of a theory that most Americans have continued to embrace in general but have intuitively felt to be insufficient. Pragmatism's focus on the concrete allows a downplaying of theory. For liberals like Dewey, it has been a vehicle for bypassing conservative theory and for not having to articulate their own. For the average American, it has allowed a commonsense adaptation of inadequate theory to felt needs.

Another point about relativism that we should notice is that "true believers" within the American Left have often rejected relativism, just as they have rejected dissimulation. Such people have wanted to make a forthright statement of their values and social preferences. They have had a sense of the timidity and essential dishonesty of liberal dissimulation.

Thus it is that in 1932, during the period when liberal intellectuals were most moved to repudiate the dissimulation, Waldo Frank wrote with disgust about "that flabby relativism which goes by the name of liberalism in the West and which is so often nothing but a want of conviction...." Lewis Mumford, another who chafed in the same way, added in 1934 that the New Deal "is pragmatism in action: aimless experiment, sporadic patchwork, a total indifference to guiding principles or definitive goals." John Dewey, of course, would have denied that pragmatism as he favored it lacked goals, since he fully intended it to embody socialist values; but Mumford's statement illustrates the irritation that some felt.[6]

In the context of this debate, I should point out that it is entirely possible to be both a relativist and a devotee of theory, principles and long-term values – and to combine them without using relativism as a mask for unarticulated theories. I myself see real value in the methodological individualism of science and the cross-cultural awareness of empiricism. And yet I am attached to classical liberal values and to a modified form of classical liberal theory. My quarrel with relativism as it has been used by the Left in the past century is that it is intellectually insufficient when used as a debunking mechanism. This is because it is not enough to point out to somebody that "your values and institutions are just one cultural alternative among many" – and to let it go at that. It is incumbent upon a serious analysis to go further. It must examine the comparative utility of the various cultural alternatives for the service of a number of values that most human beings would agree are important to civilized life. Unless we are to assume that all alternatives are equally serviceable, this step is essential. But it is almost invariably omitted when relativism is used as a debunking tool.

A final point that I will mention has to do with the relativism that Eric Goldman refers to as "Reform Darwinism." He says that in the late nineteenth century liberalism countered the popularity of Herbert Spencer's individualistic "Social Darwinism" by advancing an opposing form of evolutionary theory. Spencer theorized in terms of the struggle of individuals, with the most fit surviving. Reform Darwinism spoke of the evolution of societies as a whole, moving from one phase to another.

It was the vogue at that time to express most things in an "evolutionary" context. What Reform Darwinism did was to restate the historicist thesis of the German Historical School in Darwinian terms. The content was the same. The German Historical School was arguing that cultures pass through phases, and that any given phase – such as the bourgeois period of the nineteenth century – had no rightful claim to permanence. Among other things, this provided the basis for an attack upon the claims of classical economics, which saw permanent validity in its descriptions of how a market economy works.

When John Dewey said that conservatism talked "as if the only individualism were the local episode of the last two centuries," he was simply repeating the critique made by the German Historical School. Lester Ward had made the same point in 1881 when he wrote that "all truth is relative. Doctrines that were true for one age cease to be true for a later one; principles which really worked the salvation of the last century cannot be utilized in the present one."[7]

Eric Goldman describes Reform Darwinism's emphasis upon the evolution *of institutions and cultures*: "Why not insist on thoroughgoing evolution and argue that contemporary institutions could and should change rapidly?...Why not, in short, work out a Reform Darwinism that would dissolve away conservatism's steel chain of ideas ...?" The result would be a philosophy that would "replace dreary inevitabilities with a philosophy of flux that justified experiment and change." From this, we can see that, despite the application of different labels over the past century in keeping with whatever was most in vogue, there is no significant difference between the German Historical School, Reform Darwinism, Dewey's Pragmatism, and the tactic of gradualism advocated by the British Fabian socialists.[8]

### John Dewey's educational theory

In addition to being a philosopher of pragmatism, John Dewey was the leading theorist for "progressive education." There is a great deal of similarity between the two. They are much the same thing, applied to different areas.

Just as with pragmatism, the emphasis within progressive education was upon flexibility, experiment, openness, a getting-away from the discipline and forms of the past. As with pragmatism, there was a socialist content, since the experimentation was not intended to be value-free. A third similarity was that the state would be a vehicle to accomplish these purposes; Dewey was quite clear about his willingness to use education for ideological indoctrination.

We see these elements in what Dewey himself had to say about the type of education he desired. That he wished to dissolve the connection between education and the existing social system appears from his comment in 1914 that "every ground of public policy protests against any use of the public school system which takes for granted the perpetuity of the existing industrial system...." That he wanted education to serve socialist values appears in statements such as the one in 1930 about the need to create "a new psychological and moral type." He desired "the creation of a type of individual whose pattern of thought and desire is enduringly marked by consensus with others, and in whom sociability is one with cooperation in all regular human associations." He called for "a new individuality...that is social."[9]

Morton White has described the thesis of Dewey's book *The School and Society* (1899), which White says was Dewey's "most widely read book and the earliest exposition of his theory of progressive education." White says that "Dewey's school was to be socially minded, imbued with the values of community life, rather than with the values of individual acquisitiveness." (We should notice that community values and "individual acquisitiveness" are seen as opposing values. Classical liberal individualism differs from socialist thought in considering them complementary. It thinks *both* important.)[10]

That Dewey was anxious to use education for ideological indoctrination is apparent from his statement that schooling should involve "indoctrination, or, if one prefer, teaching, with respect to preparation for a different social order."[11]

It was in 1928 that John Dewey wrote his series of six articles for *The New Republic* about Soviet education, reporting on his trip to Soviet Russia. A passage in his second article not only typifies the series in its mixture of caution and enthusiasm, but also shows how much he thought the Soviets were carrying out his educational goals: "In spite of secret police, inquisitions, arrests and deportations of Nepmen and Kulaks, exiling of party opponents,...life for the masses goes on with regularity, safety and decorum... *There is an enormous constructive effort taking place in the creation of a new collective mentality....*" (emphasis added) This is precisely the goal that he made central to progressive education.[12]

What are we to think of this? All cultures use their educational systems for the transmission of values. Children nowhere possess existential freedom. Although the New Left, reflecting anarchist thought, argued for such freedom, it is a "freedom" that would be inconsistent with maintaining an advanced civilization and even a free society. A middle class society rooted in classical liberal values uses family, church, school and other mechanisms to transmit its heritage. It does this every bit as much as Dewey or the Soviets would inculcate socialist norms. An objection to the indoctrination of children must be directed to the content of the indoctrination rather than to the fact that it occurs. But this does not mean that Dewey's proposed indoctrination should be accepted by us. It comes down to this: if we are socialists, we will welcome it; otherwise, we should very emphatically reject it.

Given a clear choice, most Americans would have rejected Dewey's educational theory, while the main intellectual culture would have embraced it. Consistently with liberal dissimulation in general, the socialist purpose was rarely revealed. Dissimulation has befogged liberal educational philosophy with the same ambiguity that has befuddled so many other issues. Nevertheless, despite the obfuscation and the pressures that the intellectual culture has been able to bring to bear upon people to accept liberal thinking under threat of otherwise not appearing sophisticated, a great many Americans *have* opposed progressive education.

A different set of issues is raised by the fact that liberalism has often sanctioned the use of the state and of the mass media for the ideological indoctrination of the *adult* public. At the height of the anti-Vietnam War movement, for example, the editors of *The New Republic* justified the politicization of the universities on the ground that, after all, "the times are abnormal." In 1977 the federal government sponsored a series of women's conferences leading to a large national conference. Gloria Steinem argued for the exclusion of conservative women: "The legal purpose of these conferences is to further the status of women and, therefore, there is no legal obligation to include representatives of groups who want to retard the status of women."[13]

Individual examples of this sort are insignificant, however, in comparison to the willingness of the intellectual culture to use television and film quite egregiously as propaganda vehicles for the Left. During my lifetime, the propagandistic content has been so blatant that I cannot help but feel that it demonstrates an almost complete lack of respect for the intelligence of the American public. This is an attitude that would be consistent with the cultural critique that liberalism makes and that I reviewed in the preceding chapter. Unfortunately, the critique seems in large measure an accurate one, since, despite the many conservative voices raised for many years against the propaganda, most people accept it without a second thought. (Those in the future who want to view examples of what I am talking about would do well to find an archive copy of the excellently made movie *Reds* – or, on a lower level, of the films *Poltergeist, Shampoo* or *Prophecy*.)

It would be utopian and perhaps not even sound to expect government as an institution (as distinct from the political leaders, who necessarily express views on controversial subjects) always to be strictly neutral with respect to the ideas that are currently under debate within a society, or to expect the intellectual culture wholly to eschew propaganda. Nevertheless, a free society should always to be concerned about the health of its processes of debate and discussion. There is basic inequity, as well as grave danger, in government's using tax money and its vast organizational strength to institutionalize a certain position that does not already enjoy a substantial consensus. And for the intellectual culture to approach the public forum with a partisanship that is so overwhelming that it colors and selectively censors all discussion, as the liberal media here during my lifetime, and especially during the 1960's and early '70's, is not consistent with a healthy marketplace of ideas.

It is appropriate to comment upon these aspects, despite (or even especially because of) liberalism's oft-repeated devotion to free speech. The actual performance of liberalism does not show its advocates to be more tolerant than are people who support most other points of view. It is worth remembering that there is a totalitarian Left which explicitly urges the repression of all non-socialist points of view. This was a position that was advocated prominently by the New Left philosopher Herbert Marcuse in his *Essay on Liberation*. It is the spirit reflected in the statement I just quoted from Gloria Steinem and in the 1990s' insistence on "political correctness" and "ethnic sensitivity."

### The role of "civil liberties"

American liberals have prided themselves on their support for "civil liberties." This is a term that they define differently than classical liberals define "liberty" in general. In common with democratic socialists, modern liberals intend the term to denote the freedoms associated with free speech and political participation as distinguished from property rights and freedom of contract. (The famous "Footnote 4" in Justice Stone's 1938 *Carolene Product* decision, which in effect laid down the rationale for liberal Constitutional doctrine during the decades after World War II, is a perfect example of this. It allows government free rein over property rights and market transactions, but offers a high degree of judicial protection to "insular minorities" and "the preferred freedoms" that make up the "processes of democracy.")

It is a serious mistake to believe that most of the proponents of an ideology are not sincerely committed to the values they espouse. This is certainly true with regard to modern liberalism's championing of civil liberties. Just the same, a complete understanding requires an awareness of additional aspects:

1. The liberties of speech and political participation are not simply values within a model of society that liberals favor; they also have an instrumental value. They are directly serviceable to the liberal desire for social change. Since they play a tactical role, it becomes important to examine the permanence of liberalism's attachment to them.

2. The enthusiasm that so many liberals felt toward the totalitarian Left during the 1930's, again during the late 1960's, and with the "political correctness" insistence of the early 1990's, suggests that, at least to a good many liberals, socialist values, when they appear within grasp, take priority over civil liberties and what have come to be called "human rights."

I recall an article by Joshua Kunitz in *The New Republic* in 1933 justifying the Soviet execution of six people for stealing and selling food. "That the decree is terribly drastic there can be little doubt. The Communists, however, believe it to be supremely just." Kunitz also justified a decree punishing "a single unexplained absence from work" by discharge, loss of living quarters and loss of ration card. "They had to be broken in, educated to a realization of their duties as Soviet citizens." In 1935, Anna Louise Strong, a frequent contributor to both of the main liberal journals, wrote about the Soviet concentration camps that "there are 'labor camps' in many parts of the country, as part of the Soviet method of reclaiming anti-social elements by useful, collective work."[14]

This gives us pause. Such passages directly contradict the liberal emphasis on civil and human rights. In my opinion, it would be a mistake to consider them aberrations. They are, instead, terribly meaningful glimpses into the hierarchy of values that exists within liberal ideology.

3. The tactical usefulness of these liberties almost certainly explains why liberals are willing to carry them beyond the limits that classical

liberals, who are also devotees of the same liberties, think desirable.

The Warren Court declared in the *Yates* decision that the abstract advocacy of revolution is protected by the principle of free speech. Only when this advocacy is followed with some form of action can it be considered illegal.

This is a principle that will appeal primarily to those who ignore important other values. It overlooks entirely the type of world in which this "abstract advocacy" may take place. The twentieth century world is one in which terrorist killings and kidnappings are rampant and in which totalitarian states with great military power have sought on ideological grounds to expand their power. Any group founded upon the "abstract advocacy" of violence stands as a ready reserve for terrorism and aggression. In case of war, it is an existing reservoir for espionage and sabotage. Under such circumstances, it is impossible to say that it does not at each moment constitute a "clear and present danger." (Sometimes I think that those who speak of "abstract advocacy" forget that it is assassination, mass carnage, destruction of property and the overthrow of free institutions that is being talked about. The word "abstract" seems to make it bloodless to them.)

In other connections, liberals have had little hesitation to affirm the need of a free society to protect itself. After Hitler gained power in Germany, a 1933 *New Republic* editorial asked appropriately: "Was not the ultra-liberal tolerance of this [Weimar] Republic largely to blame, which respected the right of association so scrupulously that it allowed the formation of party-armies?" A *New Republic* article by Stetson Kennedy in 1946 favored the mandatory registration of any group, such as the Ku Klux Klan, "having more than 20 members and requiring an oath as a condition of membership." Liberals acknowledge the right of a society, such as West Germany (and now in the unified Germany), to outlaw Nazi organizations. In stark contrast is Morris Ernst's 1949 argument that "I believe Communists have the right publicly to advocate the overthrow of the United States."[15]

## Attitudes toward confrontational techniques

Classical liberal theory has long seen coercion as the central problem among people. It seeks a society in which coercion is reduced as much as possible, with voluntary interactions accentuated. When a society actually exists that approximates these objectives, classical liberals identify with it, as distinguished from those who stand in an alienated relationship to it. They also think of its processes as sufficient to allow the expression of freedom.

Modern liberalism, on the other hand, has often endorsed methods of social change that are either coercive or confrontational. This posture is consistent with (a) their theoretical frame of reference, which does not see coercion as the central problem; (b) their alienation from the predominant society; (c) their impatience for more rapid social change than would come about without such techniques; and (d) their belief that there is a significant flaw in the communication that goes on in the absence of confrontation, since those wanting change do not otherwise seem to be able to "get the public's attention."

When I speak of coercive techniques, I do not mean that liberals have favored violence, at least directly. (My reason for qualifying the disclaimer will soon become apparent.) Coercion is a category that includes but is much larger than violence.

Labor conflict has been one of the areas in which this has been important. In the nineteenth century, classical liberals were favorable to "friendly societies," associations of workers who joined together for mutual support and improvement. They opposed, however, the "right to strike," since they saw a strike as coercive in the same way that a concerted boycott by suppliers is coercive. Modern liberalism, on the other hand, has been strongly influenced by the Left's perspective that workers are exploited by their employers, and has accordingly thought in terms of industrial conflict. It has sanctioned a number of coercive devices.

A passage from Herbert Croly's *Progressive Democracy* (1915), in which he described how workers could bring about a socialist "industrial democracy," illustrates this: "[Workers must engage in] warfare appropriate for the purpose. Their 'Constitution of Freedom' must be gradually extorted from their employers by a series of conflicts in which the ground is skillfully chosen and permanent defeat is never admitted. In that way only can the wage-earning class win effective power...Practically all of the wage-earners as a group should be unionized as the result of this warfare...."[16]

In 1936, the CIO's United Automobile Workers Union used the sit-down strike in the United States for the first time. Its members seized the General Motors plant in Flint, Michigan, for six weeks. Robert Morss Lovett justified this weapon in *The New Republic*: "...the sitdown strike [is] a weapon of industrial conflict. The right of non-working employees to occupy the plant...is one of the industrial liberties which are on the way to becoming legally recognized."[17]

The liberal call for class consciousness among workers and for coercive techniques failed to result in the great social divisions after World War II that it might have. This is due to the fact that instead of increasing in power, the union movement came to occupy a proportionally smaller place in American life. The intellectual culture began to view it with contempt precisely because it did not on the whole continue a militant posture expressing alienation and a desire for socialism. The liberal imagination was captured by such things as Cesar Chavez's angry "grape boycott," but this was on the periphery of the labor movement rather than central to it.

In the 1960's, the Civil Rights and anti-Vietnam War movements involved techniques of mass coercion and confrontation. Until they had escalated into the burning of cities and an underground terroristic movement of bombings and kidnappings, these techniques received widespread liberal support. As the methods became more extreme, much of the liberal sympathy withered away. But this withering took a long time in coming. It should not be forgotten how much the intellectual culture and the media supported the behavior of the "Yippies" in Chicago at the time of the Democratic convention in 1968. Not the revolutionary Left, but the Chicago authorities who responded to it, were the objects of the overwhelming opprobrium of the intellectual culture.

Probably the main residual of that period within liberal thought is the conviction that "non-violent direct action" is a legitimate means to provoke social change. This is inherent in the recent elevation of Martin Luther King, Jr., to the status of one of America's great heroes.

To place "non-violent direct action" in perspective, it will be well for us to recall the conservative viewpoint on Civil Rights: that, despite all imperfections, the main society was one that deserved fundamental support; that the condition of blacks had been improving dramatically, not worsening as the rhetoric of the Civil Rights movement had us believe; and that the most constructive and surest way for blacks to continue to progress was for them to continue on the road to self-development and to gain the respect of the white majority.

From that perspective, a great national agitation was precisely *not* the best way to seek change. Conservatives stood in horror at the violence that resulted from the frustrations and hatreds that the "non-violent" mass demonstrations occasioned. And conservatives thoroughly opposed the legislation that sought omnipresently to command non-discriminatory human relationships. Fortunately, the vast federal police power of surveillance and prosecution that this legislation implies has not, for the most part, been put to use. This is due, as I pointed out in Chapter 1, to our willingness to be hypocritical. The laws are on the books, but only partly enforced. This has made possible a *modus vivendi* that is tolerable precisely because of the hypocrisy's softening effect.

In contrast to the conservative perspective I have just described, modern liberalism welcomed both the legislation and a mass movement of confrontational "non-violent" demonstrations.

To assess the philosophy of "non-violence," we must realize that it goes in two directions at once. Its proponents genuinely desire, consistently with theories going back to Gandhi and Thoreau, to avoid committing any violence themselves. Their appeal is to moral strength through suffering. At the same time, they try in every possible way to build passions to a pitch at which violence by others is virtually inevitable. This violence is something they can hardly hope to control. The proponents of non-violence are quite aware that they are playing with fire. And although they fear the resulting violence, they often seek to use it to their advantage. Despite their protestations that they are divorced from it, their posture toward the violence is profoundly irresponsible.

All of these elements were apparent in Martin Luther King, Jr.'s, utterances. His genuine dislike for violence was evident when he said that "resistance and non-violence are not in themselves good. There is another element in our struggle that then makes [them] truly meaningful. That element is reconciliation."[18] At the very same time, though, his awareness of the violence that his methods could unleash was apparent when he added that "the tactics of non-violence without the spirit of non-violence may become a new kind of violence." He had to be fully conscious of the violence that agitation can produce, since he was still alive when one riot after another led to the burning of substantial parts of major American cities.[19]

King was often willing to use warnings of violence that might be committed by others as a weapon. Nat Hentoff wrote that King and others "warn of violence [that may be committed] if those victories are not large enough and do not come soon enough. The warning is partly in itself a tactic to frighten the white folks...." Such warnings should also be understood as essentially hypocritical. They were as much goads to and justifications for violence as they were genuine warnings. Edward Banfield pointed this out when he wrote that "one who said that if drastic measures were not taken to end injustice riots could be expected might be correct, but correct or not his words would help form an impression in the public mind that rioting is a natural and perhaps even laudable response to the continuance of an injustice."[20]

If the main culture were in fact despicable, as so much of the rhetoric of the 1960's described it as being; if blacks had not benefitted immeasurably from their presence in American society; and if their condition had not improved rapidly for several years prior to the stirring of the mass movement, the argument that a vast confrontational agitation was necessary would be considerably more compelling than it is. The support that modern liberalism gives to such methods is deeply at odds with classical liberalism. The difference is not a superficial one, but reflects their widely divergent worldviews.

Part of this divergence consists of the willingness by the Left, including modern liberalism, to drop the temporal context whenever it is expedient to do so. They then talk without reference to historical progression. Their historical relativity is abandoned in favor of utopian absolutes when that is useful in creating the critique that is so basic to the moral posture of one of the egalitarian movements. At such times, all perspective is lost, and no recognition is given to the fact that conditions for the particular group have actually been improving. The result is largely ideological fakery. It consists of a storm of cliches and emotions based on partial truths and on an intolerance toward any recognition of the unspoken truths. This process has, perhaps more than any other, given a neurotic, dreamlike quality to modern social philosophy and to the "pop liberalism" that episodically dominates our national mentality with one or another of its issues.

I should not close this discussion without observing that there has been dissent, some of it quite significant, within liberalism itself.

Supreme Court Justice Abe Fortas wrote a short book, for example, that sought to delineate strictly the appropriate bounds of civil disobedience. He argued that only the laws that are thought to be unjust should be disobeyed, and not others. He also believed that the activist must be willing to accept the penalties for violating the existing laws, however unjust.[21]

Much more significant dissent came from the "realism" injected, beginning in the mid-1960's, by those who eventually became known as "neo-conservatives." These thinkers refused to accept the illusions that had been built up as the ideological foundation for the civil rights movement. The main society, they saw, was not the entire cause of the plight of the Negro, but rather there was much that Negroes themselves could do to improve their own situation. Indeed, that situation would stay mired in difficulty until Negroes made that effort. This, of course, was a perspective that was totally at odds with the rationale for alienation and militancy. Instead, it called for constructive building.

# NOTES

[1] New Republic, May 31, 1939, p. 93.
[2] Eric F. Goldman, *Rendezvous With Destiny* (New York: Vintage Books, 1977), p. 81.
[3] New Republic, August 29, 1955, p. 18.
[4] New Republic, March 13, 1915, p. 155; New Republic, March 17, 1920, pp. 82-6.
[5] Charles Forcey, *The Crossroads of Liberalism* (New York: Oxford University Press, 1961), pp. 77, 78.
[6] New Republic, July 20, 1932, p. 256; New Republic, October 3, 1934, p. 223.
[7] New Republic, February 19, 1930, p. 14; Henry Steele Commager (ed.), *Lester Ward and the Welfare State* (Indianapolis: The Bobbs-Merrill Company, Inc., 1967), p. 23.
[8] Goldman, *Rendezvous With Destiny*, pp. 72-3.
[9] New Republic, December 19, 1914, p. 12; New Republic, February 19, 1930, pp. 14-15.
[10] Morton White, *Social Thought in America: The Revolt Against Formalism* (Boston: Beacon Press, 1957), p. 94.
[11] John Dewey, *Problems of Men* (New York: Philosophical Library, 1946), p. 50.
[12] New Republic, November 21, 1928, p. 12; the other articles appear in the issues of November 14, November 28, December 5, December 12, and December 19, 1928.
[13] New Republic, September 20, 1969, p. 12; Steinem was quoted in a Wichita Eagle-Beacon article in July 1977 about the Kansas Women's Weekend.
[14] New Republic, May 24, 1933, pp. 42-3; New Republic, August 3, 1935, p. 358.
[15] New Republic, May 31, 1933, p. 61; New Republic, July 1, 1946, p. 929; New Republic, January 31, 1949, p. 7.
[16] Herbert Croly, *Progressive Democracy* (New York: The Macmillan Company, 1915), pp. 390-1.
[17] Howard Zinn, *New Deal Thought* (Indianapolis: The Bobbs-Merrill Company, Inc., 1966), p. 215.
[18] New Republic, May 2, 1960, p. 16.
[19] New Republic, May 2, 1960, p. 16.
[20] Nat Hentoff, *The New Equality* (New York: Viking Press, 1964), p. 210; Edward C. Banfield, *The Unheavenly City, The Nature and Future of Our Urban Crisis* (Boston: Little, Brown and Company, 1970), p. 201.
[21] Abe Fortas, *Concerning Dissent and Civil Disobedience* (New York: Signet Books, 1968).

# CHAPTER NINE
## Legal Philosophy

The analysis that legal philosophers have made of the law over thousands of years has been formulated within a variety of cultural and ideological contexts. Jurisprudence accordingly includes much that can be considered apart from any particular ideology. Most jurisprudence is discussed as though it stands on its own, separate from time or place.

For many of the more important issues, however, this separateness amounts to a sterilization that is, in effect, a serious intellectual mistake. This is so because much of what is most meaningful about legal philosophy *does* relate intimately to the "ideologies," i.e., to the great systems of thought about politics and society. "Ideology," in a non-pejorative sense, plays a vitally important role. Each of the major worldviews necessarily has its own preferences about government and law. These preferences in part reflect the philosophy's vision of an ideal society and legal system. They incorporate the values, and the means to the attainment of those values, that the worldview considers desirable. In addition, they necessarily take tactical considerations into account, since each worldview exists within a certain time and place in competition with other forces and ideas.

The classical liberalism that formed the main American *ethos* during the nineteenth century had, as we will see, a distinct legal philosophy of its own. This was drawn from sources thousands of years old and was favored precisely because it would protect the system of limited government that classical liberalism favored. This legal philosophy was by no means a thing apart from classical liberalism's overall social philosophy. We will need in this chapter to gain an understanding of this "conservative" legal philosophy if we are fully to understand the attack that modern liberalism has made upon it.

The legal philosophy that modern liberalism has espoused has also been responsive to its larger philosophy's overall position and to certain tactical imperatives. This liberalism has needed an approach that would simultaneously (a) serve the active state that modern liberalism has favored, and (b) constitute an instrument for bringing about the Constitutional and legal changes that were necessary if the United States were to make the transition from limited government to an active state.

Not surprisingly, it has been relativism, applied to legal philosophy, that has served both of these needs. Relativism has accordingly been the main thrust of modern liberal legal thinking (although mixed from time to time with the particular absolutes to which liberals are wont to hold). This is why I have put this chapter immediately after my discussion of liberalism's use of relativism as a method of social change.

### The classical liberal Constitutional myth: a major barrier to modern liberalism

When I refer to the classical liberal Constitutional "myth," I am not using the word "myth" to undermine that position, but to point to the fact that classical liberalism invested the Constitution, and the American nation at large, with a system of values, meanings and ideals, all based upon classical liberalism's own worldview. Every philosophy seeks a similar investiture of meaning to events and institutions which, without such an imputation, would lack symbolic content. The struggle over legal philosophy between classical and modern liberalism has been a struggle between such systems. Modern liberalism has had its own myth to offer – its own perception of history, of what law ought to accomplish, of where it wants America to go. An interesting thing about such a struggle is that neither side is prepared to see that that is what the struggle is all about; each claims to have unmediated Truth on its side attesting to the self-evident validity of what it is asserting, and sees only the other as a product of human will.

When I say that classical liberalism clothed the Constitution with a certain meaning, I am referring to an extremely broad phenomenon rather than to the thinking of any particular group of men. What I have in mind is the "spirit of the age" of the late eighteenth and early nineteenth centuries, a time when the ideals of the Enlightenment burned brightest (although by the early nineteenth century they were coming under attack by the Romantic reaction in Europe). It will be impossible for anyone in the future to understand American history without appreciating the extent to which this spirit became immanent within the American people. As I have indicated before, this outlook and value system has continued as a major "underlay" throughout the twentieth century.

By no means was its acceptance unmixed or uncontested. The Burkeans are no doubt right when they point to a number of traditionalist values that have inhered in American life; the intellectual culture has stood outside for a century and a half thoroughly detesting the potency of classical liberal values; many issues have been argued out, and have been the subject of violent political controversy, without reference to larger principles; and hundreds of millions of people have gone about practical life without deep reflection concerning the milieu in which they have lived. Nevertheless, the liberal impulse, in the classical sense, has been a major part of American life. Modern liberals sensed this a century ago when they launched their attack upon the many links in what Eric Goldman has called "conservatism's steel chain of ideas."

The link that related to legal philosophy was especially important. Classical liberalism embraced the concept of the "Rule of Law" that went back as far as Pericles' "Funeral Oration" in Athens and that had received a powerful reiteration in the philosophy of John Locke. This was the conception of "law" as ideally meeting certain criteria: it would be a dependable framework of known rules, impartially administered and applying equally and more-or-less permanently as guideposts to action. These guideposts would bind both private citizens and the government, all of whom must "act within the law." Thus, the law would serve its normal functions of adjudicating disputes, militating against crime, providing principles of conduct, recognizing property and carving out a protected sphere for the individual. It would at the same time provide a major check against arbitrary action by government. The state, according to this ideal, would itself be subject to the established rules. And if it wished to change the rules, it could do so only by enacting rules that were declared in advance and that possessed the other characteristics required by the "Rule of Law."

Friedrich Hayek's book *The Constitution of Liberty* is an excellent discussion of the history of the Rule of Law ideal. For our purposes, we should note that he considered the distinctive American contribution to be the introduction of a written Constitution. When augmented by the doctrine of judicial review as proclaimed by Chief Justice John Marshall in *Marbury v. Madison*, the Constitution became far more than a mere grant of power to government; its contours channelized government, separated its functions, divided its powers, and limited it.

To the Jeffersonians in particular, the government that was created under the Constitution was limited to the "enumerated powers" (the functions spelled out by a list of specific responsibilities in Article I). There was also explicit recognition that individuals were to enjoy a general "liberty" that government could not validly abrogate. When in the ratifying conventions the objection was made that there was no "bill of rights," James Madison, whose name comes down to us as the "father of the Constitution," was reluctant to add one. He is said to have feared that the listing of certain rights would give rise to an inference that there were no others. (His concern was no doubt based on his awareness of the usual rule for interpreting documents, the legal doctrine of *ejusdem generis*, which says that general concepts are to be understood in light of any specifics that are mentioned.)

Accordingly, when eventually he undertook to draft the Bill of Rights as we know it today, Madison was careful to include the Ninth Amendment. From a classical liberal point of view, the concept expressed in the Ninth Amendment is fundamental to the American Constitutional scheme: it provides that "the enumeration in the Constitution of certain rights shall not be construed to deny or disparage others retained by the people." This expressly recognizes the existence of a reservoir of unspoken liberties. In turn, this raises the question of what content that reservoir is to have.

The Supreme Court began to address this question in the *Dred Scott* case in 1857. The facts of the case (relating to the return of a runaway slave) were such, of course, as to make it notorious as an affirmation of slavery and as a forerunner of the Civil War. But it had another side to it, one that is important to a free society in the classical liberal sense. Chief Justice Roger Brooke Taney, a leading figure in the Jacksonian party who had been appointed Chief Justice by Andrew Jackson in 1836, based the Court's opinion on the principle that the right to property is a part of the reservoir of protected liberties.

The Constitutional provision upon which Taney based this holding was the "due process clause" of the Fifth Amendment. Thereafter, the reservoir has been thought of as finding expression in that clause and in a similar one, applicable to the states, in the Fourteenth Amendment. Thousands of court decisions refer to the due process clauses and virtually none mention the Ninth Amendment. Although this seems odd, the reason for it is simple: that if a reservoir of liberties is taken to exist, as it must be in light of the Ninth Amendment, it is appropriate to consider it as within the purview of clauses that prohibit any deprivation of life, liberty or property without due process of law. The due process clauses are consistent with and presuppose the concept stated by the Ninth Amendment. After the Fourteenth Amendment was approved, there was an additional reason to use the due process clauses, since the two of them together apply to both the federal government and the states.

The articulation of classical liberal principles, at least by presidents, went into eclipse when the Civil War ended the ascendancy of the Jeffersonian-Jacksonian Democratic Party. Nevertheless, the legal profession and the Supreme Court continued to develop the Constitutional implications of classical liberalism. Christopher G. Tiedeman's book *Constitutional Limitations* (1886) is a excellent example. He saw law as, in effect, a science of liberty within a natural law context.

On the Supreme Court, there was, for a time, a struggle between Justice Samuel F. Miller, who wrote the decision in the *Slaughter House* cases and held to an expansive view of governmental power, and Justice Stephen J. Field, who wrote in dissent. Though Field was in the minority in those cases, his views soon became those of the majority, and the Supreme Court enunciated the principle of "freedom of contract" as a major economic liberty that was Constitutionally protected.

When the Court under Taney and Field gave Constitutional recognition to the rights of property and of freedom of contract, what it was doing was to include within the reservoir of unstated liberties the economic freedom that is so vital a part of classical liberalism. This could not have been surprising. Far from breathing "Herbert Spencer's *Social Statics*" into the Constitution in any narrow way, as Oliver Wendell Holmes, Jr., later charged, they informed it with the central core of liberalism in the classic sense. Freedom within a market has been as important to classical liberals as is freedom of speech or of religion. Indeed, the philosophy does not see freedom as a series of separate liberties, but rather as a unified system of personal freedom.

This libertarian construction of the Constitution similarly embraced the other concepts that have been central to the Rule of Law and to classical liberalism.

The presence of slavery and its aftermath in American history would seem to contradict the adherence to legal equality, but it is important to understand that these constituted an historically implanted exception that was in basic contradiction to the liberal principles that guided the society. Even though the United States had tremendous difficulty dealing with these problems, their presence does not render the liberal principles meaningless. Nor would it be correct to say that they were held to hypocritically. American law was quite consciously attached to the ideal of "equality under the law."

None of this is to say that American law in the nineteenth century formulated a perfect application of classical liberal principles. What I said earlier is pertinent here: that classical liberalism was itself insufficiently developed. It did not, and has not to this day, addressed all of the subtleties of social and economic questions. By the second half of the nineteenth century, classical liberalism had gone on the defensive and had lost its reformist edge. Its defensiveness caused it to give inadequate attention to the framework of law and institutions that is needed precisely as a part of a classically liberal society to facilitate the free interaction of individuals. A good deal of what free-market enthusiasts have considered "interventionism" has been at least in part a reaction to the absence of a thoroughly satisfactory framework. Certainly in the nineteenth century much work remained to be done.

In this section, I have described the nineteenth century classical liberal Constitutional position – one that I believe was very much in keeping with the principles of a free society. If, however, we wish not to lose sight of the mixed nature of the concrete realities of the late nineteenth century, we should notice that the classical liberal construction was not shared by all members of the Supreme Court. Looking back in 1940, Max Lerner considered Justice Miller very much a modern liberal hero for having opposed Justice Field's direction during the 1870's and 1880's. In 1915, *The New Republic* commented that the Court had been moving away from the classical liberal position, only to return to it with its decision in *Coppage v. Kansas*. Then in 1931, the editors commented again on how a "liberalization" had been underway but had stalled. John Marshall Harlan, who served from 1877 to 1911, and Oliver Wendell Holmes, Jr., on the Court from 1902 to 1932, were articulate opponents of the classical liberal interpretation. Because of this, it would not be correct to think that the entire Court moved from one ideology to another in 1937 when finally it began upholding the legislation of the New Deal. Modern liberalism had long been represented on the Court, and had had occasional majorities.[1]

**The legal, Constitutional needs of modern liberalism**
Since the rise of the Left in the early nineteenth century, there has always been significant support for a decentralized, non-statist socialism based upon cooperatives, communes, labor organizations, or the like. Modern liberalism showed an affinity for this type of socialism during its "industrial democracy" phase and during the years of the New Leftist counterculture. For the most part, however, modern liberalism has pursued a program of state intervention. It has seen the federal government as the principal instrument for social and economic progress.

Virtually all programs of state intervention in Europe and America during the nineteenth and twentieth centuries have embraced a legal philosophy that attacks the Rule of Law and argues for administrative and judicial flexibility. The opposition to preestablished rules to which government must itself conform has been the central characteristic of legal positivism, legal historicism, the free law school, and legal realism.

The Rule of Law criteria are exceedingly functional if the purposes are the classical liberal ones of establishing guideposts for individual conduct and of delimiting government. They are usually thought to get in the way if the desire is to vest free-wheeling power in government. (There is accordingly some irony in the piety with which modern liberals have pursued a "full enforcement of the law" in the Watergate and Iran-Contra cases. Their legalistic posture there has been at odds with the main thrust of their legal philosophy.)

In 1915 an article in *The New Republic* exulted that "this is fast becoming a government not of laws, but of men, perhaps really a government, after all, no longer a pious treasury of past generalizations." Rexford Tugwell argued for "a rule of men, not laws, if the right men are called to govern." Such statements as these involve a striking reversal of the classical liberal preference for "a Rule of Law, not of men." The body of American law is perceived as obstructive, and it is precisely the "rule of men" that is welcomed.[2]

Probably even more important than the need to free the state for flexible administration was modern liberalism's tactical need for a legal philosophy that would allow the existing body of law, and most especially of Constitutional law, to be circumvented without the need for formal amendment. Under the Constitution, the easiest way for an amendment to be adopted is for it to be proposed by a two-thirds vote of both houses of Congress and then approved by the legislatures of three-fourths of the states. Such a procedure is designed to require a substantial national consensus before an amendment can be enacted.

Since the Civil War, the amendment process has been successful primarily for the "democratizing" amendments. These have possessed a moral appeal that has enjoyed wide public support. They are the post-Civil War amendments dealing with slavery, the direct election of senators, the right of women to vote, the limitation of a president to two terms. The income tax amendment was passed, but without the public having any idea at the time that the tax would before long be raised to confiscatory levels. The Prohibition movement against alcohol, which was part of the Progressive thrust, was able to secure passage of the Nineteenth Amendment, but this was repealed within a few years.

For the most part, the revamping of American government from its classical liberal Constitutional base into a European-style social democratic state by Constitutional amendment has not been feasible for liberals, who have sensed the lack of a consensus sufficient to obtain passage of the necessary amendments. Even during the Great Depression in the 1930's, only passing attention was given to the possibility of validating New Deal-type legislation by Constitutional amendment. In 1915, *The New Republic* had recognized the difficulty when it called for making amendment easier. In 1918, Lewis Mayers wrote that "we encounter a constitutional obstacle, the extremely obstructive machinery of amendment." After World War II, TRB complained that "an honest rewriting of the Constitution is probably impossible."[3]

At the time he commented upon liberalism's inability to obtain amendments, TRB pointed openly to the implication for liberalism's tactical position. He said about the Constitution that "the sooner we circumvent it (i.e., 'stop standing on the letter') the better."

In so saying, TRB expressed the essence of modern liberal legal philosophy. The overriding tactical need has been to justify a loose construction. It has been to remove the Constitutional constraints upon governmental power without waiting for formal amendment.

The result has been a philosophy that (a) has raised flexibility and legal change to the highest value and (b) has simultaneously denied the validity of the classical liberal interpretation of the Constitution.

## The content of liberal legal philosophy

As I discuss the specific points made by liberal legal philosophy, I will quote extensively from what liberals themselves have said so that the texture of their point of view can be felt.

1. Before 1937, liberal justices used the concept of "judicial restraint" to implore conservative justices not to invalidate social legislation. Such a liberal justice as Felix Frankfurter became so imbued with the call for "judicial restraint" that he continued throughout his later years to believe that judicial restraint was the hallmark of liberal jurisprudence. It would seem, however, that Frankfurter's views reflected more an absorption of an erstwhile tactical position than an expression of the main liberal preference about the role of the Court. That preference has been for a political, activist Court. The "activist" majority on the Warren Court was what we might actually expect.

Liberal writing had long favored a politicized Court. In 1921, *The New Republic* said that "the radical view is that the Supreme Court is and ought to be a political body." It went on to say that this should involve "interpreting the Constitution and the law according to the spirit of the age, subject, of course, to certain elastic limits of legal plausibility." The next year, the editors wrote that law should be considered "an instrument of progressive social engineering." In 1930, they argued that "the truth is that the Supreme Court is a supreme policy-making body."[4]

This was consistent with Jerome Frank's later praise of the thesis expressed by Charles Curtis in *Lions Under the Throne*. Here is what Frank had to say about Curtis' position: "With respect to constitutional questions, the Supreme Court, he says, is not a court. Its power to nullify legislation compels it, he asserts, to be primarily a peculiar kind of political agency, although legal tradition requires it to talk as if it were a judicial tribunal. Thanks to Mr. Justice Holmes, this approach to constitutional decisions is now openly accepted by the Supreme Court justices...."[5]

As with other aspects of liberalism, the open radicalism of the 1930's offers a window into the ultimate preference. A *New Republic* editorial in 1935 called for replacing the Supreme Court with a "Supreme Planning Council." "This policy-making body...must differ from the Supreme Court in essential respects. It should act before the event, not after...It should consist, not of precedent-minded logicians, but of experts in social and economic management...In other words, instead of a Supreme Court we ought to have a Supreme Planning Council." The reason, they said, is that "there is no hope of gradual evolution towards an effective socialism within the existing framework of the United States...To have a socialist society we must have a new Constitution."[6]

The preference expressed in 1935 is the same as the one voiced by William Beaney and Alpheus Mason, two writers prominent on behalf of liberal legal philosophy, in their 1968 book *The Supreme Court in a Free Society*. They said that by the early 1940's, under a liberal majority, "the Court had apparently accepted the collectivist theory of government. Social democracy could be achieved...."[7]

2. Modern liberals have constantly stressed the mutability of law and the power of judges to disregard precedents.

In *The New Republic* in 1918, Lewis Mayers spoke of "the time-honored method of gradually wearing down constitutional restrictions – the President and Congress taking the initiative with unconstitutional legislation and the Supreme Court reluctantly 'distinguishing' out of existence the constitutional obstacle." This is the spirit in which liberal writing has so often quoted Chief Justice Charles Evans Hughes' dictum that "the Constitution is what the judges say it is." In *Equal Justice Under Law*, published under the auspices of the Foundation of the Federal Bar Association, the authors quoted Holmes to the effect that the "Constitution is an experiment" and praised him as having "inspired generations of lawyers to shun classic attitudes of jurisprudence and recognize that law changes with society's needs."[8]

The stress on change and arbitrary judicial power is what makes Oliver Wendell Holmes, Jr.'s, definition of law so popular in liberal legal writing. He said that "the prophecies of what the courts will do in fact, and nothing more pretentious, are what I mean by law." We can imagine that future legal thinkers will find this definition deliberately reductionist. It is utterly banal in its over-simplification of the legal process. But its serviceability to liberal ideology is that by centering upon the empirical question of "what judges do in fact," it treats as irrelevant the Rule of Law definition of law. This is that law is the body of statute and precedent – i.e., the rules that have been set down in advance--to which lawyers and judges recur when they ask each other "what does the law say?" with regard to a point at issue.[9]

3. I mentioned earlier that an important element of liberal thinking has been the denial of the validity of the classical liberal construction of the Constitution. As with so many of these points, Justice Holmes made the leading statement. Holmes denied the core of classical liberal doctrine – that economic freedom is an essential part of Madison's reservoir of liberties – when he wrote that "a constitution is not intended to embody a particular economic theory" and that the Constitution "is made for people of fundamentally differing views." He said essentially the same thing, although more cleverly and with greater sophistry, in his famous statement that "the Fourteenth Amendment does not enact Mr. Herbert Spencer's *Social Statics*." Chief Justice Harlan Fiske Stone made a similar argument when he wrote that "the Fourteenth Amendment has no more embodied in the Constitution our preference for some particular set of economic beliefs than it has adopted, in the name of liberty, the system of theology which we may happen to approve." (The analogy to religion is plausible only superficially. A classical liberal would agree that the Constitution does not dictate a specific economy; but he would say that it dictates a system of economic *freedom*, just as it commands a system of religious freedom.)[10]

4. A corollary has been the charge that classical liberal jurists were "activists" when they construed the Constitution as they did.

Thus, Mason and Beaney charge that these judges made themselves "virtually a superlegislature." Justice Holmes wrote that "the dogma, Liberty of Contract,...is merely an example of doing what you want to do, embodied in the word liberty." Justice Frankfurter said that "between the presidencies of Grant and the first Roosevelt, *laissez faire* ... was imported into the Constitution." And, speaking of the judges who in the 1930's considered much of the New Deal's legislation unconstitutional, Arthur Schlesinger, Jr., commented that "far from being engaged, as they supposed, in a process of immaculate interpretation, the conservative four, like the liberal three, were reading their own notions of social wisdom into a designedly ambiguous charter of government."[11]

5. In the passage I have just quoted from Schlesinger, he acknowledges that the liberal judges were "activists." It is curious that the literature damns conservatives for what it considers their activism, while praising modern liberal judges for theirs. A double standard is applied about the validity of activism, even assuming the correctness of the liberal charge that a classical liberal construction of the Constitution amounts to judicial activism. The double standard is accounted for by the fact that modern liberals *like* the purposes for which the liberal justices have been activists, while they dislike those of the conservatives.

Such a double standard reflects the common human tendency to employ whatever arguments are handy, regardless of consistency. Mason and Beaney have offered the only attempt I have seen to rationalize it: "The thought of the so-called [liberal] activists...seems to be that though the Constitution does not embody, as Holmes said, any particular *economic* philosophy, it does incorporate a particular political theory... Judicial self-restraint does not mean that the Court is paralyzed. 'It simply conserves its strength,' as Attorney-General Jackson put it, 'to strike more telling blows in the cause of a working democracy.'...The 'self-restraint' banner raised in 1937 has not blinded Chief Justice Warren's Court to certain positive responsibilities." The upshot is that these justices think the Constitution *does* embody some theory – but just not the central principles of classical liberalism.[12]

6. An important part of the attack upon the classical liberal interpretation of the Constitution was the economic determinist argument that the Founding Fathers were motivated not by a sincere idealism, but by their own economic self-interest.

J. Allen Smith launched the attack in 1907 with his book *The Spirit of American Government*. Eric Goldman writes that Smith "brought down upon the Framers...the onus of greed." Smith's thesis, he says, was that "the Framers were profit-minded and little else." Arthur A. Ekirch, Jr., says that Smith's book "influenced among other progressives both Theodore Roosevelt and Robert M. LaFollette." He observes that "the book...weakened the case for conservatives' devotion to the sanctity of the Constitution."[13]

The person most famous for this debunking is Charles Beard, whose *An Economic Interpretation of the Constitution* was published in 1913. Beard argued that "the members of the Philadelphia Convention ... were, with a few exceptions, immediately, directly, and personally interested in, and desired economic advantages from, the establishment of the new system. The Constitution was essentially an economic document...A large propertyless mass was, under the prevailing suffrage qualifications, excluded at the outset from participation...."Writing in *The New Republic* in 1944, Goldman said that "it reduced the abstractions of conservatism to the special pleading of a special economic group. Little wonder that the Beardian economic interpretation became the bulldozer of liberalism...."[14]

It is no accident that the books by Smith and Beard appeared around the time of the Muckraker era. After World War I, liberal thought began to reflect some awareness of the over-simplification inherent in such debunking. In 1922, Zechariah Chafee penned an intelligent piece for *The New Republic* critical of the reductionism inherent in applying a purely economic determinism to judges' decisions (which was the specific issue his article addressed).[15]

7. Unfortunately, it is rare for the advocates of any one philosophy really to understand another philosophy's point of view. In general, modern liberal thinkers have had no empathetic understanding of why American conservatives have held the beliefs and values they have, any more than conservatives have put themselves into liberals' thinking.

Modern liberal legal commentators have shown almost no awareness of the idealism that supports the Rule of Law and its embodiment in the written Constitution. Such an awareness has not been evident in any of the passages I have quoted in this chapter so far.

Probably the most egregious example of imputing every motive to an opposing philosophy except a sincere adherence to a set of perceptions and values is Jerome Frank's book *Law and the Modern Mind*. Frank excoriated the Rule of Law criteria as "mechanical jurisprudence." Although not a psychiatrist, he reflected upon every conceivable psychoanalytical explanation for why lawyers, judges and the public value certainty in the law. People, he said among other things, apparently want the law to serve as a "father figure." Through it all, Frank showed a resplendent shallowness – a partisanship unleavened by any apparent awareness of the history of the Rule of Law going back to the Greeks or of the reasons that those who wish to limit the state through law have given for their views.

Of course, this is what Smith and Beard were doing, too, with their economic determinism, albeit without the elaborate trappings of pseudo-psychoanalysis. None of them ever considered classical liberal legal philosophy *on its merits*. They contented themselves with considering only straw men or reductionistically understood motives.

This is revealed in the caricatures that liberal writing has painted of conservative views and personalities. Arthur Schlesinger, Jr., wrote, for example, that conservatives saw judges as "the infallible expositors of an unchanging document." This transforms the classical liberal preference for adherence to a body of precedent in Constitutional law into a parody of the Catholic doctrine of papal infallibility. It is hard to imagine that any serious conservative thinker has ever claimed infallibility for judges.

The combination of partisanship and limited understanding has resulted in virtually all conservative judges being belittled in liberal literature as dull and intransigent, while liberal judges have been praised as brilliant and courageous. For example, Oliver Wendell Holmes, Jr., has come down to us as "the Great Dissenter." The description given of him in the Foundation of the Federal Bar Association's book is "philosophic dissenter." Notice how that same book characterizes the four conservative justices' dissent from the rulings that began to uphold New Deal legislation in 1937: "*Stubbornly* the 'four horsemen' dissented."[16]

The same book speaks of Justice John Marshall Harlan's writing "a fighting dissent." He "won fame as a defender of democracy" and fought "an ardent battle for civil rights." Along with Holmes, he is said to have been "one of the great dissenters." Other liberal justices are praised along the same lines: Chief Justice Warren was a "champion of civil liberties" and Justice Abe Fortas a "champion of individual liberties." Schlesinger describes Justice Harlan Fiske Stone as "tough, articulate [and] passionate."[17]

Here, in contrast, is Schlesinger's description of the four conservative justices in the 1930's: Justice Willis Van Devanter was lucid and knowledgeable in person-to-person dealings, but was struck by "an awful paralysis" so far as writing opinions was concerned. Justice James C. McReynolds was a surly anti-semite who used an undistinguished "scissors and paste" technique in writing opinions. Justice George Sutherland was the most able, but "evidently nothing happened after the eighteen eighties to cause him to doubt" the writings of Thomas Cooley and Herbert Spencer. Justice Pierce Butler was bellicose, "a bruiser, burly and contentious, untiring at his desk, bullying in conference, vigorous and dogmatic in his opinions." In all, compared to a sparkling set of liberal justices, they were either intellectually mediocre or personally undesirable, or both.[18]

There would be little reason to note this partisanship if it did not have a broader significance. It is important for anyone reading liberal legal philosophy to realize that the authors are creating their own myth, which is populated by its own heroes and villains. An objective scholar will need to understand that the liberal analysis is far from dispassionate. And someone wanting to decide which of the competing legal philosophies deserves support will essentially have to decide which overall philosophy he favors, since the legal philosophies are merely applications of the larger philosophies. Having made this decision, he will see that the myth that has been formulated by that philosophy is serviceable to the perceptions and values it supports, and will probably find reason enough to favor that myth.

### From judicial restraint to judicial activism

Until the New Deal, most social legislation came from the states rather than from the federal government. Accordingly, the tactical need for liberals was for the Supreme Court to take a "hands off" attitude toward state legislation. This gave rise to what J. Joseph Huthmacher has called "the Brandeisian idea that the states should be afforded the utmost freedom to 'experiment.'" The theme of "let the local majorities experiment" was then picked up by Franklin Delano Roosevelt. Eleanor Roosevelt wrote that "it is quite probable that Franklin derived his concept of the forty-eight states as experimental laboratories from his study of Justice Brandeis' writings and opinions."[19]

During the 1930's, once Roosevelt was in the presidency, the focal point for activity became the federal government. Until 1937, modern liberals remained basically in the minority on the Supreme Court. In that context, liberalism's most pressing tactical need was to call for "judicial restraint." This position was calculated to take the Court, dominated by conservatives, out of the equation. The situation changed radically after 1937. The conservative justices left the Court. It wasn't long before all of the justices were liberals in the pre-1937 sense.

What tactical need was there then for "judicial restraint"? None at all. Liberals had the power to be activists if they wanted to be. What occurred is an oddity that speaks well for the integrity of such a justice as Frankfurter, who continued to preach the doctrine of judicial restraint even after the tactical need for it had vanished. A split developed among the liberal justices. They slowly formed into blocs based, respectively, upon judicial activism and judicial restraint.

The years of the Warren Court, starting in 1953, represented the predominance of the activist bloc. The majority's judicial philosophy during those years was radical: precedent and 160 years of history were not to stand in the way of what was, strangely enough, an elitist imposition of the dogmas of a "popular democracy." The decision in *Reynolds v. Sims* about the reapportionment of state senates illustrates this radicalism. Throughout American history, the states (except Nebraska with its one-house legislature) had patterned their senates after the United States Senate in the sense that geographical units, not simply population, were given representation. The United States Senate was the product of the "Connecticut Compromise" between the large and the small states in the Philadelphia convention. When in the 1960's the Warren Court held that state senates had to be based upon a "one man, one vote" system of equal representation, there could be no pretense of basing the decision on anything in American history. In addition, the Court had to overrule a century-and-a-quarter old doctrine called the "political question doctrine," which held that any issue about whether a state government was meeting the requirement of having a "republican form of government" was up to Congress, not the Court. Since there was neither history nor precedent to support the Court's decision in *Reynolds v. Sims*, it is clear that the Court had come quite openly to the philosophy that "the Constitution is what the judges say it is."[20]

And yet, the Warren Court, radical in method, did not go to the outer limits of Constitutional change. Its innovations largely had to do with issues that were essentially peripheral. It would have been easy, for example, to move major functions that had traditionally been governed by the states to the federal government by handing down a series of decisions saying that each area needed a "uniform national rule." (The "concurrent powers doctrine," enunciated by Chief Justice Taney before the Civil War, says that the states can continue to act in an area that is within the purview of the federal government if Congress has not pre-empted the field and if the Court has not held that a uniform national rule is needed. Since virtually all state jurisdiction exists only by virtue of the concurrent powers doctrine now that the post-1937 Court has held that the federal government has ubiquitous jurisdiction, the survival of the traditional functions of the states depends upon the willingness of Congress and the Court to allow them to continue.)

I do not mean to say that the Warren Court was all sound and no fury, but only to indicate that in content its record was not as radical as its reputation. As the cutting edge of liberal activism during that period, however, the Warren Court must nevertheless be considered, for good or for bad, to have been a major agent in causing the social turmoil that rocked the country during that period. In turn, the Burger Court, which followed the Warren years, was a factor in settling the country down.

When Richard Nixon became president, he announced that he would appoint justices who were committed to "judicial restraint." This was not in itself necessarily an effort to reinstate the pre-1937 classical liberal construction of the Constitution. Rather, it could very well mean no more than a reversion to the philosophy that the liberals themselves had espoused prior to 1937, which was the philosophy of judicial restraint that Justice Frankfurter had continued to support. Some of President Nixon's appointments were of that nature; some, especially of Justice Rehnquist, were more ideologically conservative (although his conservatism, and nominee Robert Bork's later, was hardly what we might expect: both have adamantly opposed embracing the pre-1937 classical liberal construction). Because of the appointments made recently by conservative presidents, it will take several years for a majority of liberal activists to dominate the Court again.

## America's Third Constitution:
## "Footnote Four" in the Carolene Products Case

As the years have gone by and the original Constitutional scheme has become more and more distorted as a result of the Court's special solicitude toward "minorities," it has become apparent that the rationale laid down by Justice Stone in his famous "Footnote Four" in *United States v. Carolene Products Co.*, 304 U.S. 144 (1938) has, in effect, constituted a "third Constitution" for the United States.

The original Constitution, of course, was the one that emerged from the Constitutional Convention in 1787, as amended by the Bill of Rights. It's plausible to argue that a "second Constitution" came into being as a result of the Thirteenth, Fourteenth and Fifteenth Amendments following the Civil War, since they were so far-reaching. And in 1938 the Court, in the opinion written by Justice Stone, laid down a revolutionary paradigm that has now governed us for more than half a century.

What Footnote Four said, in so many words, was that governments could do virtually anything they wanted with regard to economic relationships (the vast area encompassing private property and contractual freedom), because legislation in that area would henceforth be subject only to a "rational basis" test. Since a "rational basis" can be discovered for almost any measure, a court thereafter would almost never overturn such legislation. This gave governments – state and federal – a free hand, contrary to the earlier classical liberal limitation upon them. Three other areas of governmental activity, however, would be subject to meaningful court scrutiny, with the effect that the Court would serve as a substantial protector against majorities as to them: where a specifically enumerated right is involved, where something relates to democratic process, and where the rights of "discrete and insular minorities" are concerned.

This has given rise to our "double track" system of Constitutional rights, as distinct from a unified system. The mainstream society has virtually no judicial protection from governmental power; at the same time, certain specific liberties are given exaggerated emphasis (as where the First Amendment is said to bar a libel suit against a cartoon depicting Rev. Jerry Falwell having intercourse with his mother), and minorities have stringent protection that others don't receive. In keeping with the spirit of Justice Stone's rationale, legislation has followed (such as that in most states that is held to prohibit men's service clubs) that has amplified the dual system.

This, in large measure, is what the conservative majority will have to grapple with in the 1990's and the years beyond.[21]

# NOTES

[1] New Republic, October 14, 1940, p. 531; New Republic, January 30, 1915, p. 4; New Republic, June 3, 1931, p. 56.

[2] New Republic, January 9, 1915, p. 8; Rexford G. Tugwell, *The Battle for Democracy* (New York: Columbia University Press, 1935), p. 94.

[3] In 1936, Lloyd Garrison proposed a Constitutional amendment to give the federal government general power to promote the economic welfare; New Republic, January 29, 1936, p. 329. New Republic, January 23, 1915, p. 3; New Republic, August 17, 1918, p. 74; New Republic, February 28, 1949, p. 3.

[4] New Republic, July 13, 1921, p. 177; New Republic, February 22, 1922, p. 353; New Republic, February 26, 1930, p. 30.

[5] Jerome Frank, *Courts on Trial* (New York: Atheneum, 1967), p. 311.

[6] New Republic, June 12, 1935, p. 117.

[7] William M. Beaney and Alpheus Thomas Mason, *The Supreme Court in a Free Society* (New York: W. W. Norton & Company, Inc., 1968), pp. 232, 310.

[8] New Republic, August 17, 1918, p. 73; The Foundation of the Federal Bar Association, *Equal Justice Under Law* (Washington: National Geographic Society, 1965), pp. 67, 72.

[9] Quoted in Jerome Frank, *Law and the Modern Mind* (Garden City: Anchor Books, 1963), p. 134.

[10] Quoted in Foundation of the Federal Bar Association, *Equal Justice Under Law*, p. 72.

[11] Beaney, Mason, *The Supreme Court*, p. 231; Felix Frankfurter, *Mr. Justice Holmes and the Supreme Court* (Cambridge: Harvard University Press, 1961), pp. 63, 62; Arthur M. Schlesinger, Jr., *The Politics of Upheaval* (Boston: Houghton Mifflin Company, 1960), p. 459.

[12] Beaney, Mason, *The Supreme Court*, p. 312.

[13] Eric F. Goldman, *Rendezvous With Destiny* (New York: Vintage Books, 1977), p. 113; Arthur A. Ekirch, Jr., *The Decline of American Liberalism* (New York: Longmans, Green and Company, 1955), p. 184.

[14] Charles Beard's conclusions are quoted in Goldman, *Rendezvous With Destiny*, p. 117; New Republic, November 27, 1944, p. 696.

[15] New Republic, June 7, 1922, p. 36.
[16] Foundation of the Federal Bar Association, *Equal Justice Under Law*, pp. 68, 83.
[17] Foundation of the Federal Bar Association, *Equal Justice Under Law*, pp. 59, 68, 126, 129; Schlesinger, *Politics of Upheaval*, p. 464.
[18] Schlesinger, *Politics of Upheaval*, pp. 455-457.
[19] J. Joseph Huthmacher, *Senator Robert F. Wagner and the Rise of Urban Liberalism* (New York: Atheneum, 1968), p. 185; Foundation of the Federal Bar Association, *Equal Justice Under Law*, p. 53.
[20] Reynolds v. Sims, 377 U.S. 533.
[21] My discussion in this chapter is similar to that contained in my article "Myths and American Constitutional History: Some Liberal Truisms Revisited" in the Fall 1978 issue of *The Intercollegiate Review*, pp. 13-23. My views about what would be best for the future conservative direction of the Court were stated in broad outline in the paper I delivered to the annual meeting of the Philadelphia Society in April 1981. That paper is currently unpublished.

## CHAPTER TEN
## Liberalism and the Modern Corporation

The corporation has been the dominant form of business entity within modern capitalism. That, of course, would be reason enough for it to have received considerable attention from the social philosophies. But there has been an additional reason: the attention has been heightened by the fact that there have been major schools within both socialist and modern liberal thought that have looked upon the large corporation as a stepping-stone to a collectivist economic system.

Because each of the philosophies has been vitally interested in the role of corporations and other economic aggregates, the subject has come up in my books discussing the other ideologies. Those discussions are an important backdrop for this chapter. They should be consulted if a reader wants a more complete understanding of the issues raised by the other philosophies.[1]

Earlier in the present book I discussed the competing liberal attitudes toward corporations when I reviewed the Progressive period and the New Deal. The present chapter, of course, deals with the issue for its own sake in light of its importance within liberal philosophy. In this discussion, I will try to avoid repeating the earlier material beyond what is necessary to allow the issue to be understood as a whole.[2]

As part of reviewing the New Nationalist school, we will examine what I call "the Berle-and-Means thesis," which alleges a crisis of legitimacy within the modern corporation. We will see, too, how the New Left, reflecting the attitudes of nineteenth century decentralist socialism, levelled a powerful attack upon what it called "corporate liberalism" or the "military-industrial-political complex."

### The New Nationalist perspective

To understand one of the main liberal schools of thought regarding the modern corporation, it is important to know something about the history of socialist thought. In *Das Kapital*, Karl Marx wrote about how capitalism reaches a transitional phase to socialism through the corporate form. As a large number of investors place their capital in a corporation that is managed by others, thereby making a passive investment, the capital, Marx said, becomes "directly endowed with the form of social capital as distinct from private capital, and its undertakings assume the form of social undertakings as distinct from private undertakings." He referred to this as "a necessary transitional phase" that points toward worker control when finally the corporation is converted "into the property of associated producers, as outright social property."[3]

Although Edward Bellamy's theoretical system was somewhat different from Marx's, this point about the corporation was the keystone of Bellamy's expectation that corporate capitalism would evolve into socialism. In *Looking Backward* (1888), Bellamy projected a future in which business would become so consolidated that it would be run as "one great business corporation." Then the state would become "the one capitalist in the place of all other capitalists, the sole employer, the final monopoly in which all previous and lesser monopolies were swallowed up...The epoch of trusts had ended in The Great Trust." The reader will recall that his book, which is among the more influential in the intellectual history of the United States, was a futuristic description of how a socialist society would come about and could be expected to function.[4]

Bellamy became the leader of a movement known as "Nationalism." In his introduction to the 1960 republication of Bellamy's book, Erich Fromm explained what Bellamy meant by this label. Fromm wrote that Bellamy "called this movement 'nationalist,' referring by this word both to the nationalization of all means of production and to the fact that only this form of society could bring about the rich flowering of a nation's life."[5]

We have seen how during the Progressive period a movement called "the New Nationalism" arose out of the interplay between Herbert Croly and Theodore Roosevelt. The principal expression of this position was in Croly's book *The Promise of American Life* (1909). It was a natural heir to Bellamy's perspective. It too looked forward expectantly to the continuing consolidation of corporate capitalism; it saw that consolidation as the main chance for government to absorb the corporate system into a comprehensive scheme of national policy; and it too held to an ultimate socialist aspiration.

The difference between Bellamy and Croly was the difference between those who were openly socialist and those who, by adopting dissimulation and a generally unacknowledged Fabianism, fashioned that unique ideological animal known as the American liberal. There is no question but that Croly yearned for socialism. His book *Progressive Democracy* (1915) embraced, as we have seen, the Guild Socialist enthusiasm for worker-control. But Croly was the master dissimulator – a subject about which I have already cited ample detail.

Again it is important to recognize that not all who have followed the New Nationalist tradition within modern liberalism have been socialists. In my discussion of the New Deal, we saw that there were several sources for the call for consolidated business. These even included important business elements. Such elements have differed from those who are socialists over an essential point: the business sources have generally wanted the consolidation to serve the purposes of business; those who have been socialists have wanted the consolidation to be the vehicle for central state planning and for worker control.

Examples of the attitudes of those members of the liberal intellectual culture who have embraced the New Nationalist perspective are easy to find. An unsigned article in *The New Republic* in 1925 illustrates the preference for the large corporation over small-unit capitalism: "Can we force a return to the dominance of the small independent baker, grocer, druggist? Would the public benefit if we could?...A splitting up of the large company would destroy the economies. To get anywhere we must turn away from the old trust-busting tradition towards profits taxation, or price regulation, or public ownership, or consumer ownership." (The reader will notice the reference to "consumer ownership," which within socialist thought has been an alternative to worker ownership.) This article is consistent with Croly's view in *The Promise of American Life* that "the process of industrial organization should be allowed to work itself out. Whenever the smaller competitor of the large corporation is unable to keep his head above water with his own exertions, he should be allowed to drown."[6]

In this context, the stockholder's role would be minimal, becoming that simply of a bondholder receiving interest on the money advanced. (Even this was a concession to the American political realities. In England, the socialist R. H. Tawney called for the expropriation without compensation of the stockholder. Tawney was, by the way, a frequent contributor to *The New Republic*. In keeping with the dissimulation, he held such views in check in his articles for American publication. Liberal intellectuals were, of course, fully aware of what he was saying in his books.) A 1931 *New Republic* article called for "public control in the public interest" and went on to say that "in determining 'public interest,' first consideration [should] be given to the workers in the industry, second to the consuming public, and third to the active management. The interest of the investors [should] be recognized only to the extent of a reasonable rate of interest on the actual investment in the enterprise."[7]

Liberals have for the most part been discrete in their statements about how much the giant corporations are then to be socialized. (As with the dissimulation in general, though, they have let down their guard on a number of occasions, especially although not exclusively during the more radical periods.) A statement by T. K. Quinn in *The New Republic* in 1961 has been typical: "Powerful, giant, private corporations cannot safely continue to be treated as wholly private institutions...In addition to the establishment of a Price and Wage Board, we should now reconsider such proposals as public representation on the boards of directors of the biggest corporations." TRB chimed in in his weekly column a week later: "Corporations...are becoming so big and powerful as to warrant a quasi-governmental status with the kind of supervision applied to other federal agencies." In his book *The New Industrial State* in 1978, John Kenneth Galbraith wrote: "If the mature corporation is recognized to be part of the penumbra of the state, it will be pressed more strongly to the service of social goals."[8]

We know from our earlier review of post-World War II liberalism that the more-or-less futile search for identity by liberals during the 1970's and 1980's has entailed renewed interest in the entire range of options that were considered by liberals during the 'Teens and 1920's. There has been considerable ferment for worker control, with the Japanese system of participatory management and life-time worker security serving as at least one of the models in light of Japan's success. The literature has repeatedly brought up the idea of government or consumer or worker representatives on corporate boards of directors, and has often referred to the European principle of "co-determination." This reference is a favorable one, since it evokes the example of the European social democracies. We know, of course, that the idea has also been popular within the main totalitarian movements of the twentieth century.[9]

A substantial literature has grown up during the past several years about "corporate social responsibility." This literature presupposes a liberal point of view; it calls upon corporations to serve voluntarily as major social service agencies, and to perform a great many functions that do not relate, except indirectly through the goodwill that may be generated, to the task of creating a return on their stockholders' investments. An academic discipline has sprung up within the schools of business in our universities, and classes in social responsibility have been made a required part of business curricula. Within schools of accountancy, a subdiscipline of "social accounting" has developed, and seeks ways to measure just how "socially responsible" each corporation is. Efforts are made to plug this accountability into government, so that the federal government can monitor and regulate the social-service activities of business.

To the extent such an *ethos* can be created and the government gotten involved in requiring and monitoring it, the "social responsibility" approach is another of the efforts to absorb corporations into the state. As such, it is fully in line with the New Nationalist tradition.

To the extent, however, that it constitutes an effort to prevail upon business voluntarily, and without oversight, to perform the functions that liberals have wanted the welfare state to perform, it is something that would have been viewed with contempt by most pre-World War II liberals. T. K. Quinn was speaking very much within this tradition when he wrote in 1961 that "America cannot depend upon any fictitious Corporation Conscience or permit the domination of any private power." He called upon the federal government itself to exercise the functions that he considered primarily governmental. It is worth remembering that after the Progressive movement had ended liberals came to excoriate the idea of "moral do-goodism." Consistently with socialist theory and the deterministic perspective of so much social science, they wanted a system of entitlements. These would replace charity and "unplanned, unpredictable" voluntary programs.[10]

Another concept that originates in the New Nationalist position is the idea of "yardstick" firms. Melville J. Ulmer has said that the idea originated with Walter Durand in *The New Republic* on May 26, 1926. In recent years, John Kenneth Galbraith has been a strong supporter of the concept. (It seems ludricuous, now that Communism has collapsed in Eastern Europe and the Soviet Union, that anyone would suggest looking at a state-operated enterprise as a measure of how well a private enterprise is doing. But that is what the "yardstick" idea proposed.)[11]

### The Berle-and-Means thesis

There is a part of the New Nationalist tradition that should be discussed separately because it occupies a distinct place in the literature. This is the analysis that is attributed to A. A. Berle, Jr., and Gardiner C. Means, and which they stated in their famous book *The Modern Corporation and Private Property* in 1932.

It has been commonplace in liberal writing since 1932 to refer back to the Berle-Means book as though the analysis originated with them. No doubt a great many of the writers who make these references are not aware that the analysis that Berle and Means made was already quite old by the time they elaborated it. But even if this is true, the focus on Berle and Means is one of the best examples of liberal dissimulation; it puts a twentieth century American liberal source in the place of the various nineteenth century socialist authors who advanced the same ideas well ahead of Berle and Means. Since many American liberals, especially in the 1930's, were intimately conversant with socialist writing, including Marx's *Das Kapital*, the conclusion is inescapable that this substitution was essentially dishonest, arising from a desire to be less than candid about the socialist origins of a major liberal analysis. A good portion of this obfuscation can be attributed to Berle and Means themselves. It was hardly an accident that Berle and Means did not footnote to Marx, G. D. H. Cole, Thomas Kirkup and others.

The Berle and Means thesis, as I summarized it in my book *Socialist Thought*, is that in large business corporations the control is no longer in the hands of the owners, the stockholders. "Control," the thesis says, "may be held by the directors or titular managers who can employ the proxy machinery to become a self-perpetuating body, even though as a group they own but a small fraction of the stock outstanding." This means that the managers are "irresponsible," since they are not effectively accountable to the stockholders. In turn, this is said to falsify one of the basic assumptions upon which a system of private property is based – the assumption of owner control. Berle and Means suggested that this makes the corporation more "quasi-public" than private.[12]

As a solution for this alleged irresponsibility, Berle and Means, in common with New Nationalists in general, called for marrying the modern corporation to the state, making the corporation an instrument of social policy. "Neither the claims of ownership nor those of control can stand against the paramount interests of the community...(T)he 'control' of the great corporations should develop into a purely neutral technocracy, balancing a variety of claims by various groups in the community and assigning to each a portion of the income stream on the basis of public policy." Other than perhaps the statement I have just quoted, there was no clarion call for government ownership; Berle and Means were committed to a dissimulative style and were willing to go only as far as Croly had gone in *The Promise of American Life*, with broad suggestions in favor of governmental absorption. But the direction in which they pointed was unmistakably socialist.[13]

At the beginning of this chapter's section on New Nationalism, I quoted a passage from Marx's *Das Kapital* that contains all of the same ideas (but without the dissimulation). It is worth noting that the British socialist G. D. H. Cole had stated the thesis in his book *Labour in the Commonwealth* – and had even considered it a "commonplace." He said that "it is, of course, commonplace that the development of capitalism and the growth of joint-stock enterprise have more and more divorced the ultimate ownership from the actual control and management of industry." In addition to seeing the thesis in the writings of Marx and Cole, I have noticed it in Thomas Kirkup's *History of Socialism* – published *in 1909*.[14]

The thesis was also common currency in American liberal writing long before Berle and Means. In an 1895 article, Lester Ward quoted statements by J. R. Commons, made of course at an even earlier time, expressing the analysis. Jerome Frank, ignoring Marx and the other openly socialist authors, traced the thesis back to Thorstein Veblen. Writing in 1938, Frank said that "Veblen was the pioneer thinker. Repeatedly he pointed out the rise of 'absentee ownership' as an inherent and significant aspect of the growth of the giant corporations...Two of his disciples, Berle and Means, recently gave us striking statistical evidence of Veblen's thesis."[15]

The thesis had in fact received considerable attention in *The New Republic* during the 'Teens and 1920's. The first article I have noted was in an issue just three months after the journal began. John Maynard Keynes authored one of the many articles when in 1926 he wrote of "the tendency of big enterprise to socialize itself." He said that "a point arrives in the growth of a big institution...at which the owners of the capital...are almost entirely dissociated from the management." Berle himself was actively promoting the analysis in an article as early as 1921.[16]

When we evaluate the merits of the analysis, we see immediately that the thesis offers one of the better examples of how an idea can gain almost universal acceptance by containing just enough of the truth to enjoy a superficial plausibility. The thesis is repeated uncritically by a great many authors. This includes the literature that is read in the colleges of business (which, as to their faculties, are not necessarily hothouses of conservatism).

It is foolish, however, for anyone to accept the Berle-and-Means thesis who is otherwise committed to a market economy. The analysis is only partly an observation of fact and is primarily a rationale for the state's absorption of large corporations.

The thesis' plausibility comes from its latching onto the fact that, in the absence of unusual circumstances, a widely diffuse body of stockholders, most of whom do not own enough stock to have a substantial interest in company affairs, cannot do otherwise than rubber-stamp the actions of the existing management. Unless there is a major stockholder revolt, the existing management is easily able to gain reelection and the ratification of its policies.

It does not follow, though, that the managements of large corporations are for that reason "loose cannons" – "unaccountable" and "irresponsible." Nor does it follow that one of the basic premises of the theory of private property is falsified by the fact that there is a separation between ownership and control.

The justification, so far as the theory of property is concerned, is in the freely arrived at contractual relationships through which the stockholders have come to vest control in the management. Classical liberalism, the philosophy most devoted to private property and the market economy, recognizes "freedom of contract" as a central principle. It has no bias against "a separation of ownership and control" – such as occurs in any bailment, lease or (from the settlor's point of view) trust – so long as the relationship is the product of voluntary contract.

It is, instead, socialist thought that has always had the bias against "absentee ownership." It is a misstatement to say that the modern corporation's separation of ownership and control violates classical liberal suppositions; it would, however, be accurate to say that it violates those of socialism. (I am aware that John Locke, the major classical liberal thinker of the seventeenth century, justified private property in a way that left unresolved the question of absentee ownership, since his analysis was rudimentary within the context of his discussion of rights arising out of "a state of nature." What he would have said about more extended forms of property if he had addressed them is, of course, a matter of conjecture. The classical liberal position is the product of a great deal of thinking that goes well beyond Locke on this point.)

So far as the accountability of corporate management is concerned, it comes in the marketplace, not primarily at stockholders' meetings. Business firms rise and fall according to the flow of equity and debt capital. Most certainly there is a "survival of the fittest" among firms – and consequently among the managements that head them. The argument that managers are insulated from this is an argument that in the short term a management team can bleed a company, oblivious to the fact that the firm is losing its place. But managers who take that attitude are making themselves vulnerable to a hostile take-over: outside financiers see that a firm is performing less well than its prospects would seem to justify, and are accordingly willing to acquire the firm for its profit-potential; and the stockholders, if they are dissatisfied with the existing management, are anxious to sell.

It is also true that the courts provide some remedy for minority stockholders in cases where the management has been given more to spoliation than to promoting the business's interests. I don't emphasize this, since it never seems to me that litigation is more than a pale substitute for a satisfactory reality. But there is no reason to think that the reality is not essentially satisfactory. The issue of management spoliation hardly receives any attention in public discussion – including among investors of all types –, and this leads me to infer that it cannot be a genuine problem. Our media have by no means lost their interest in good "muckraking" where it is available, which it would be if that sort of abuse were common.

At any time that such a problem does actually come to exist, those who favor the market system will be well advised to reexamine the institutional-legal framework for corporations to be sure that existing management is still subject to market forces. The defenses against hostile take-overs should never be allowed to become so effective that they insulate bad management from challenges. Adjustments in corporation law to assure this should not be interpreted as attacks upon the corporate system, but as ways to assure its viability.

If corporate managers were mainly looters, such a situation would indicate a major deviation from a classical liberal atmosphere. Individualistic liberalism presupposes a high ethical level. Ethics are to be socially inculcated and enforced through family, school, church and peer group. There has been a significant undermining of this ethical context due to a number of factors: the relativism of modern liberalism; the "do your own thing" libertarianism of the New Left and even of a good many superficial thinkers on the right; and the hedonism that arises out of the mixture of our intellectual shallowness and our affluence. If "corporate looting" ever becomes a significant problem, much of the cause will be attributable to these factors, not to an inherent flaw in the structure of corporate capitalism.

Before we leave the Berle-and-Means thesis, it is worth noting that there have been important variations of it. Probably the most significant of these are the "New Class" analyses, which assert that in modern life both the state and the large corporation are effectively in the hands of a uniform culture of technical, bureaucraticized intellectuals. This was the theme of John Kenneth Galbraith's *The New Industrial State* (1978). "The decisive power in modern industrial society is exercised not by capital but by organization, not by the capitalist but by the industrial bureaucrat ... There is no name for all who participate in group decision-making or the organization which they form. I propose to call this organization the Technostructure." Needless to say, Galbraith, a leading "liberal" at the same time that he is a self-proclaimed socialist, sees no "function" served by stockholders in such a setting.[17]

### Overt calls for nationalization

While the New Nationalist school has used dissimulation to place at least a thin veil over the socialist content of its proposals, it is significant that liberal writing has on many occasions called for the outright nationalization of major industries in the United States. As early as 1883, Lester Ward looked forward to government operation of "all private enterprises which concern the general public," although he said that first "there must be a gradual maturing of the conditions."[18]

During its first month of publication in November 1914, *The New Republic* called for the eventual government ownership of the railroads, with control in the workers. "The nationalizing of the railroads has a chance of converting them into genuine agencies of the national economic interest." The journal repeated the call in 1923 and 1931. In the 1920's, liberals were enthusiastic about the Plumb Plan "for national ownership of the railroads and operation by a 'tripartite' board representing management, labor and the public."[19]

There has been a long-term campaign for the public ownership of utilities and of hostility toward private utility companies. After the election in 1948, TRB praised President Truman by saying that "now we have in the White House a man with the most radical platform in presidential history...Truman advocates government ownership and operation of transmission lines from government dams right up to the consumers' electric stoves." We recall, of course, the many proposals for "valley authorities," with their vast implications for regionally implemented socialism.[20] Also included in the call for nationalization have been the telephone and telegraph systems. In 1918, *The New Republic* said that "for a generation the sentiment for government telegraphs has been growing."[21]

Government ownership has been urged for mines and natural resources. In 1923, *The New Republic* reported the results of a poll showing that "the sentiment of liberals continues overwhelmingly in favor of public ownership of mines...." For many years, the United Mine Workers called for the nationalization of the mines. Robert Marshall advocated government ownership of forests in a 1934 article. In 1946, the editors favored the continued federal ownership "of the rich submerged oil lands off the coasts."[22]

In 1924, *The New Republic* came out in favor of governmental construction of homes, arguing that private enterprise builds homes only for the wealthy. In 1948, Henry Wallace argued that private home-construction had "failed miserably," and wanted a government program, in cooperation with business, to build 4 1/2 million homes.[23]

In 1928, Paul Blanshard called for municipal ownership of funeral businesses. We recall how the original thinking for the T.V.A. included government ownership of a variety of small businesses.[24]

Banking is among the more significant areas for which nationalization has been urged. In 1933, *The New Republic* editorialized that "the most desirable form of banking would obviously be a single, nationwide, government-owned and operated enterprise." A year later, the editors said that "*The New Republic* [has] long [been] an advocate of complete socialization of banking...."[25]

Soon after World War II, however, a distinct change in feeling toward nationalization occurred among European socialists and consequently among American liberals. The Socialist International downplayed it at the time of the International's rebirth in 1951. In 1959, the German Social Democrats abandoned nationalization, except with regard to energy. The experience in England when the Atlee government tried nationalization after World War II was almost immediately seen as unfavorable. In addition, the resurgence of nineteenth century-style decentralist socialist thinking within the Left after the events of 1956 caused a movement away from "state socialism," with which nationalization is necessarily identified.[26]

### The New Freedom's perspective

The "New Freedom," a name associated with Louis Brandeis and Woodrow Wilson, denotes a school of thought that contrasts with New Nationalism in its views about big business. This school has not favored the existence of immense corporations. It has not seen big business as a stepping-stone to socialism, and has not generally seen significant economies of scale in large enterprises. What the New Freedom has favored has been a "regulated competition," through which government plays an active role in assuring the existence of truly competitive markets. It has favored the nationalization of an industry where such competition cannot be maintained, and it has called upon the state to perform the many functions of the welfare state.

The combination of these ingredients was present, as an example, in a book by Paul Douglas, later a United States Senator, in 1935. Broadus Mitchell's review said that Douglas "urges breaking up as many monopolies as possible ... Where this policy fails ... ownership will have to be socialized."[27]

Woodrow Wilson is, along with Brandeis, considered the original champion of the position, but a reading of his 1912 campaign speeches shows him to have been given to platitudes that were far from clear in content. His performance as president was quite mixed on this issue.

We have seen how Franklin Delano Roosevelt began strongly in favor of the New Nationalism, and then, although perhaps remaining a New Nationalist at heart, switched to a not-very-resolute New Freedomite position in what is called the "Second New Deal."

There has been considerable activity in favor of New Freedom-style measures since World War II, probably reflecting a natural liberal preference for limiting the role of big business if it does not appear feasible at a given time to place large corporations under the wing of government. In 1945, Alvin Hansen proposed changing the patent law to make "available all inventions and new processes to any user upon payment of a reasonable royalty." In 1946, Senator James Murray of Montana proposed a plan in Congress for stronger anti-trust enforcement – with the alternative being public control. In the late 1940's and early 1950's, Senator Estes Kefauver headed a committee in the Senate that called for stricter anti-merger rules. Kefauver, too, called for the licensing of patents. In 1950, *The New Republic* advocated the regulation of prices and wages where a large corporation's dissolution is not technically feasible.[28]

In 1960, Paul H. Douglas and Howard Shuman asked rhetorically: "Why...should not the giant industries be split up into almost as many companies as there are production units?" In 1972, Peter Barnes reported that Senator Harris had introduced legislation to break up corporations in concentrated industries. During the presidential campaign that year, Senator McGovern came out for a war against mergers. John M. Blair's book *Economic Concentration* (1972) advocated "breaking up GM, GE and the others into their constituent parts," according to Bernard D. Nossiter.[29]

A *New Republic* article in 1974 reported that "Senator Philip Hart (D. Mich.), chairman of the antitrust subcommittee, is pushing for legislation that, for the first time, would make market dominance a basis for breaking up large firms in such oligopolistic industries as autos, steel, aluminum, chemicals, drugs, electrical machinery, computers, communications equipment and energy."[30]

In 1978, Morton Kondracke told his readers that "[Senator] Edward Kennedy favors...a break-up of the big oil companies," along with "deregulation and increased competition." The following year, Lester Thurow reported that Kennedy offered a bill to bar conglomerate mergers where the companies had assets or annual sales exceeding two billion dollars.[31]

In 1982, Mark Green, in his book *Winning Back America*, called for statutorily established criteria about size: "Whenever a firm, or up to four firms, controls 50 percent of a market, it would have to be decentralized into smaller units unless they could argue by a preponderance of the evidence that economies of scale required their size." Green also called for progressively higher income tax rates for corporations, depending upon their size and market share.[32]

It is worth pointing out that conservative thought includes its own division between supporters and opponents of vast corporate size. Many classical liberals argue that growth to any size is a matter of right, and that in any case the problem of bigness has been exaggerated. They argue that market processes, in the absence of governmental favoritism for some economic groups over others, will produce a healthy situation.

Other classical liberals, however, believe that the health of the market and of a free society is best served by size limitations, and argue that the legal framework of a free society can rightfully state such limits. I count myself among the latter group, since I believe that a market system, to function at its best, requires more of a "framework" of laws and institutions than many market enthusiasts are willing to admit. I would point to the fact that corporate size has given the Left some of its best ammunition against the market, and for many has provided a potential vehicle for collectivization.

# NOTES

[1] See Dwight D. Murphey, *Burkean Conservatism and Classical Liberalism* (Washington: University Press of America, 1982), pp. 426-428; Dwight D. Murphey, *Socialist Thought* (Washington: University Press of America, 1983), pp. 279-281.

[2] The earlier discussions in the present book are at pages 40-45 and 53-55.

[3] Karl Marx, *Das Kapital*, Vol. 3, Chap. 27; the passage is quoted in Maurice Cornforth, *The Open Philosophy and the Open Society* (New York: International Publishers, 1968), p. 191.

[4] Edward Bellamy, *Looking Backward* (New York: Signet Classic, 1960), pp. 53, 54.

[5] Bellamy, *Looking Backward*, p. xvi.

[6] New Republic, October 21, 1925, p. 214; Herbert Croly, *The Promise of American Life* (New York: The Macmillan Company, 1914), p. 358.

[7] New Republic, March 25, 1931, p. 144.

[8] New Republic, April 3, 1961, p. 10; New Republic, April 10, 1961, p. 2; John Kenneth Galbraith, *The New Industrial State* (Boston: Houghton Mifflin Company, 3rd ed., 1978), p. 408.

[9] As to worker control, see Mark Green, *Winning Back America* (Toronto:

Bantam Books, 1982), pp. 42, 43, 52, and New Republic, November 25, 1981, p. 29. As to co-determination, see New Republic, November 24, 1973, p. 17, and Green, *Winning Back America*, pp. 44-45.

[10] New Republic, June 5, 1961, p. 12.

[11] New Republic, January 5, 1974, p. 14; New Republic, September 8, 1973, p. 29.

[12] A. A. Berle, Jr., and Gardiner C. Means, *The Modern Corporation and Private Property* (New York: The Macmillan Company, 1956), p. 5.

[13] Berle and Means, *Modern Corporation*, p. 356.

[14] G. D. H. Cole, *Labour in the Commonwealth* (London: Headley Bros. Publishers, Ltd., no date given), p. 107; Thomas Kirkup, *History of Socialism* (New York: The Macmillan Company, 1909), p. 356.

[15] Lester Ward, *Lester Ward and the Welfare State*, Henry Steele Commager, editor (Indianapolis: The Bobbs-Merrill Company, Inc., 1967), p. 186; Jerome Frank, *Save America First* (New York: Harper & Brothers Publishers, 3rd ed., 1938), p. 282.

[16] New Republic, January 30, 1915, p. 8; New Republic, February 6, 1915, p. 7; New Republic, July 14, 1920, p. 198; New Republic, August 4, 1920, p. 280; New Republic, September 29, 1920, p. 112; New Republic, Sept. 7, 1921, p. 37.

[17] Galbraith, *New Industrial State*, pp. xv, 74, 409.

[18] Ward, *Lester Ward*, p. 55.

[19] New Republic, November 21, 1914, p. 12; New Republic, February 7, 1923, p. 266; New Republic, July 25, 1923, p. 238; New Republic, June 10, 1931, p. 85.

[20] New Republic, Nov. 28, 1914, p. 29; New Republic, Nov. 15, 1948, p. 3.

[21] New Republic, July 6, 1918, p. 275.

[22] New Republic, July 11, 1923, p. 164; New Republic, February 6, 1924, p. 268; New Republic, June 27, 1934, p. 176; New Republic, Sept. 23, 1946, p. 374.

[23] New Republic, March 5, 1924, p. 41; New Republic, March 1, 1948, p. 10.

[24] New Republic, August 22, 1928, p. 17.

[25] New Republic, March 15, 1933, p. 118; New Republic, Sept. 5, 1934, p. 89.

[26] New Republic, August 6, 1951, p. 10; New Republic, Nov. 30, 1959, p. 8.

[27] New Republic, August 28, 1935, p. 81.

[28] New Republic, January 1, 1945, p. 11; New Republic, January 21, 1946, p. 75; New Republic, January 13, 1947, p. 30; Estes Kefauver, *In a Few Hands: Monopoly Power in America* (New York: Pantheon Books, 1965); New Republic, January 16, 1950, p. 9.

[29] New Republic, September 26, 1960, p. 18; New Republic, January 22, 1972, p. 19; New Republic, June 24, 1972, p. 23; New Republic, December 9, 1972, p. 26.

[30] New Republic, July 6, 1974, p. 17.

[31] New Republic, Sept. 23, 1978, p. 12; New Republic, April 28, 1979, p. 10.

[32] Green, *Winning Back America*, pp. 47, 49.

## CHAPTER ELEVEN
## The Process of Politicization

After all that we have seen about modern liberalism's relationship to socialist aspirations, it would hardly seem necessary to include a chapter on "the process of politicization." A discussion of "politicization" will have the advantage, however, of talking about liberalism in the form in which it has been most directly perceived by the American public. Since dissimulation has obscured liberalism's socialist core, the public has seen liberalism primarily as a movement that has pressed insistently for what we might call the "de-privatization" of most human problems. A great many aspects of the human condition – problems that in the past and within the perspective of classical liberalism have been seen as private, to be solved or suffered by the individuals themselves – have been redefined as public in nature, to be addressed by a combination of social science and the state. In this light, liberalism has constituted an on-going process of absorption of the private into the public.

Such a process relates directly to liberalism's underlying socialist premises and to the gradualistic Fabian method. We will not fully understand it, though, if that is all we notice about it. We must appreciate the dimension that brings together social science, the state, and the rationalism of intellectuals who wish to impose order on the subjects they study. *The New Republic* was seeing liberalism in this light when in 1920 it spoke of "liberalism [as] the offspring of the coalition between science and humanism." When this mixture is combined with a willingness to use the state as something of a "social church," the result is what Hubert Humphrey referred to as "the humanitarian state."[1]

Through most of the twentieth century this process has produced some major secular trends in the political sphere: the size and power of the state have increased enormously; this power has become centralized as liberalism has sought to focus it in the national government; and much of the newly-found power has come to reside in the hands of the "expert" in the many independent agencies and the bureaucracy.

There are two points that should be mentioned before we begin our discussion of this process. The ideology of the Left calls into being an alliance of the intellectuals with the "have nots," and invokes the power of the state, of a movement, or of a collective of one sort or another on behalf of this alliance. This in itself accounts for much of what I have just described. And yet there is more. Reformers such as Dorothea Lynde Dix campaigned for state-supported asylums for the insane before the Civil War. Could this be attributed to "an alliance with the have-nots"? Maybe very indirectly, as an offshoot of the mental set that resulted from the alliance that was in fact coming into existence; but certainly there was no evident political or power-enhancing value to the intellectual from an alliance with the insane. Such a movement points to the other factors that this chapter will explore.

The second point is that both the Left and modern liberalism have had an anti-statist dimension. This is a dimension that has certainly not predominated; but it is one that should be kept in mind if we are not to oversimplify. Much nineteenth century socialist thought talked in terms of decentralized collectivism: communes, mutual associations, cooperatives, and the like. We have seen that this was important to the Guild Socialist movement in England and to the "industrial democracy" vogue within American liberalism around the time of World War I. Another major source was the anti-modern, anti-scientific, anti-rational Romantic movement that was so powerful in Europe after the disillusionment with the French Revolution. This was to become a central inspiration to the New Left, a diverse phenomenon which included significant elements repudiating both rationality and the "rational state" that springs out of the desire to "rationalize society."

### The intellectual, social mindscape
### that underlies the absorption

There is a passage in Lester Ward's *Applied Sociology* (1906) that is one of the best examples I have seen of the mentality that has mixed science, a planning-type rationalism, and the state in a process that absorbs all of life into it. Ward wrote that "legislation will consist in a series of exhaustive experiments on the part of true scientific sociologists and sociological inventors working on the problems of social physics from the practical point of view. It will undertake to solve not only questions of general interest to the state,...but questions of social improvement, the amelioration of the condition of all the people, the removal of whatever privations may still remain, and the adoption of means to the positive increase of the social welfare, *in short the organization of human happiness*...." (Emphasis added)[2]

This is precisely what Ivan R. Dee had in mind in 1973 when he wrote that "politically such men as Chase, Soule, Alfred Bingham and Adolf Berle longed for a coherent social order, a rational community that would be 'liberal in strategy, socialist in ultimate aims.'" Dee added that "this is why the seeming confusion of the [Franklin] Roosevelt administration bothered many intellectuals."[3] It is also what Kimball Young had in mind when he described John Dewey's main thesis: "when we learn to observe, correlate and deduce laws of social phenomena, we shall be able to construct a consciously controlled society."[4]

One nuance of all this was that the image of a thoroughly planned society led the intellectual culture to its embrace with the Soviet Union. For many, the infatuation persisted for as long as thirty years. In 1957, Gus Tyler wrote that "for many years – almost up to the present – it was widely believed that, whatever the faults of the Soviet Union, it was dedicated to true internationalism, national autonomy and cultural equality...Then too there is the captivating illusion popular for a time among Western progressives that intelligence and human engineering had come into their own with the Five Year Plan."[5]

This infatuation was shattered eventually by a number of events, but the one that most shocked the scientific-rationalist mentality that I am now discussing was the Lysenko affair. In 1949, Julian Huxley wrote in *The New Republic* that "the U.S.S.R. has officially rejected some of the essentials of scientific method itself." The Soviets, holding to a view that science reflects "the class struggle" and that there are such things as "bourgeois science" and "proletarian science," suppressed Mendelian genetic theory for several years after World War II. The theory formulated by Trofim D. Lysenko that an organism passes environmentally-acquired properties on to the next generation was given official Soviet sanction. To scientists around the world, this seemed an unpardonable injection of dogmatic ideology into science, comparable to some of the worst actions of the medieval Church.[6]

Another nuance is that the mentality makes certain assumptions about human nature. These are assumptions that are not universally accepted. We see the contrast if we compare the views of, say, Ralph Waldo Emerson and Bruce Bliven. In early 1915, Percy H. Boynton wrote in *The New Republic* that Emerson had held back from the pre-Civil War reform movements because he felt "that in considering man as a plastic thing they were all in error." Bliven, on the other hand, wrote in 1931 that "If anyone observes that 'you can't change human nature,' the only intelligent answer is...'Yes, you can so.' Human nature is one of the most malleable things in the world." The Bliven viewpoint is consistent with Ward's and Dewey's, as well as with that of such a thinker as B. F. Skinner, who in *Beyond Freedom and Dignity* postulates a system in which human beings are the subjects of deterministic manipulation.⁷

### Identification of private conditions as scientific, political problems

The essence of what I have called "the de-privatization" was expressed by C. Wright Mills when he wrote that "it is the political task of the social scientist – as of any liberal educator – continually to translate personal troubles into public issues." This is a process that has been at the heart of American liberalism. We recall how Senator Edward Kennedy once made a trip to Alaska and in effect discovered the plight of the Eskimos, for the solution of which he then urged a federal program. He was actively engaged in "translating personal troubles into public issues." To a classical liberal, the "plight" of the Eskimos would seem to follow from their choosing to live within the Arctic Circle; he would see it as an unenviable condition – but not as a subject for political solution.⁸

Examples can be cited endlessly, since the Ward, Dewey, Mills rationale envisions the broadest possible embrace of the human condition. Walter Mondale (U.S. Senator and 1984 Democratic presidential nominee) commented, say, on the plight of rural migrants: "They move all over. They belong nowhere. They don't vote. Often their children don't even go to a school. It's a disgrace...These people just go on being exploited." I would direct the reader's attention to the last point, the reference to "exploitation." The idea that millions of people are trapped and exploited, and that the state serves a liberating function as the vehicle for overcoming the exploitation, is one of the key concepts in the ideology of left-wing socialism, such as we see it, say, in the writings of Ferdinand Lassalle. (I say "left-wing" socialism because rightist forms of socialism tend to seek collectivism on other premises, such as a tribalistic appeal to a nation or a race rather than to the "have-nots" as such.) Since much of what we are discussing is a seamless web, the interconnection between exploitation theory and the process of politicization cannot be surprising. In the 1990's, the general public has shown an awareness of this century-and-three-quarters-old theme when popular writing speaks of liberalism's current "victimology," which seeks to interpret many people's situation as that of "victims."⁹

The discovery of "problems" often reflects a utopian mentality that drops the historical context. The process is then oblivious to the fact that instead of becoming worse, the particular condition has often been improving. Action is called for to solve "problems" that have been fading out rather than increasing. Probably the most important example of this has to do with the condition of blacks immediately before the Civil

Rights movement began. Anyone listening to the rhetoric of the movement would not have known that there had been a substantial improvement in that condition. Another example was the legal prohibition of child labor. Such a prohibition only became thinkable, and politically possible, when affluence had risen to a level at which families could afford not to have their children work. The whole movement to abolish child labor was necessarily a "tag-end" movement, coming as the "problem" was already disappearing. Along the same lines, the "Occupational Safety and Health Act" (OSHA), establishing a structure for minute safety standards in places of employment, was passed after industrial accidents had been *on the decline* for several years.

Edward C. Banfield has cited the "school dropout problem" as an example. "At the turn of the century," he says, "when almost everyone was a 'dropout,' the term and the 'problem' did not exist. It was not until the 1960's, when for the first time a majority of boys and girls were graduating from high school and practically all had at least some high school training, that the 'dropout problem' became acute."[10]

Modern social science has fashioned various intellectual tools to serve the combined needs of rationalistic empiricism and politicization. It is not coincidental that statistics developed as a discipline in response to the planning requirements of the German state during the Cameralist period. L. L. Bernard and Jessie Bernard inform us in their *Origins of American Sociology* that "statistical work was early developed in Europe, and especially in Germany in the seventeenth and eighteenth centuries, due to their strong emphasis upon state administration. The Cameralists found quantitative measurement and recording indispensable to efficient administration...."[11]

Daniel Patrick Moynihan has written about the United States that "the national government began compiling economic statistics that were to make economic planning feasible years before such planning became politically acceptable." He goes on to say that "the truth of John Kenneth Galbraith's observation remains: statisticians are key actors in the process of social change...." Galbraith, he says, attributed this to the fact that "it is often only when it becomes possible to measure a problem that it also becomes possible to arouse any political interest in solving it." I would add that the process is more subtle than this last comment suggests: before there is even a perceived need to "arouse the public," a human condition must come to be seen as a collective "problem." Statistics, bringing together many otherwise isolated cases into a perceivable aggregate, are at the heart of that transmutation.[12]

Other techniques that have been developed both as modes of

analysis and as planning tools have been input-output analysis and its descendant, linear programming. Jacob Oser tells us that "input-output analysis would have been irrelevant in the days of atomistic competition and laissez faire." He cites its uses in a modern corporate setting, but adds that it "is probably more useful in a socialist economy than in one based primarily on private enterprise." We are told by Heinz Kohler that linear programming "is a lineal descendant of input-output analysis" and "was developed in 1939 by Kantorovich in the USSR."[13]

### The split within the intellectual culture over social science

Much of American social science has possessed a distinctly liberal content, both because of the worldview its practitioners have held and because of the process I have just described. This is true generally despite the fact that many social scientists have taken seriously the teachings of Max Weber to the effect that sociology should be value-neutral. Philip M. Hauser has made a telling point in this regard. He says that "my training in sociology at the University of Chicago during the late twenties and early thirties led me to accept the Weberian model of sociology. That sociology was a science, not a vehicle for social action, was a tenet of faith on the part of the faculty...." He adds, however: "Yet, ...it was clear that many members of the faculty...were making major contributions to action programs...I reconciled the apparent contradictions...by accepting the proposition that the sociologist could play multiple roles...." I do not mean to overlook the fact that a number of social scientists have been one form or another of conservative. These would not wish to be included within my general description. But they will almost certainly agree with the description I am giving of the impact of social science in general.[14]

Even though most American social science has been related to liberalism and to the de-privatization, there has been a wide difference in the way members of the Left have perceived it. This is a difference that almost certainly tells us more about those making the critique than it does about social science itself. Those who have been well attuned to the Fabian process and have been willing to bear with the reverses that liberalism has suffered will have had no difficulty seeing the main bulk of social science as an ally. Those, on the other hand, who have been more impatient, as the more overtly alienated and socialist have been wont to be, will have found the "scientific neutrality" and gradual politicization almost intolerably slow. One would expect them to denounce American social science as having been insufficiently socialist.

Many modern liberals have praised social science's contribution to liberalism. Herbert Croly wrote of "the idea of a social science which would be useful in supplying a technique of social progress." In 1926, *The New Republic* was effusive about the development of social work as a profession: "The forward rank of social workers is creating a new technique, a new philosophy, and a new spirit which, if it succeeds in winning the day, will transform old-style philanthropy into a genuine social therapeutics." I recall how George Soule made himself one of the main protagonists for "national planning," to which "professionally qualified experts...putting together the statistics" were essential.[15]

There has been a steady drumbeat of criticism, however, by those who have wanted an overt expression of "values," heavily socialist in orientation, rather than a "scientifically neutral" approach. We are mistaken if we think that such criticism arose mainly during the years of the New Left. It has been in evidence for many years; the New Left merely continued an existing critique.

In 1931, Benjamin Ginsburg had this to say in a review in *The New Republic* of a book about social science: "One begins to wonder whether there is not also present a motive of social conservatism, a motive which uses social science as a sort of Penelope's web to put off the demands of the suitors for social reform." He criticized a "policy of providing millions for research and not one cent for philosophy."[16]

It is interesting that, from a conservative point of view, I have made the same criticism of the positivist fashion that is insisted upon in high school debate competition. The national debate topic has almost invariably centered on one socialistic proposal or another. Students tell me that they are discouraged from arguing on the basis of social and political values, and that they must confine their arguments to matters of cost, administrative feasibility, and the like. In that context, the positivism is a way of "doing without *conservative* values." It may seem strange that leftist critics would complain of a lack of socialist values in the broader realm of social science. To understand it, we need to remember their impatience with dissimulation and gradualism. It is a matter of the perspective that the observer brings to the critique.

John Dewey himself was dissatisfied with the non-socialist preoccupations that he saw in the social science of his day. In 1931, he wrote bitingly about "the present zeal for 'fact finding.'...For the most part, the data...are not social facts at all. For their connection with any system of human purposes and consequences, their bearing as means and as results upon human action, are left out of the picture." He wanted social science to be much more consciously geared toward "social planning and control."[17]

In a *New Republic* article in 1933, George E. Novack applied a Marxist perspective to severely criticize the mathematical economics of Walras, Jevons, Marshall and Clark. He said that this economic theory was too abstract, having "only the remotest connection with the real capitalist world of class societies and imperialist states, overproduction and recurrent crises...." The "unacknowledged premise," he said, is "that there was nothing fundamentally wrong or unjust about the operation of the price system...." In 1938, Max Lerner authored a review of a book by Robert S. Lynd about the social sciences. Lerner complained about "American social scientists keeping their placid tenor amid disaster," and spoke of "the fairly patent fact that the 'detachment' and 'objectivity' that they have exacted of themselves have been excuses for keeping quiet... devices for saving their skins."[18]

In 1957, Merle King posed the question "What of social scientists?" He said that, "confusing form for content, they assume that resort to the forms of the calculating machine, the questionnaire, the interview, and the quantified formula indeed will enable them to travel toward the future with the natural scientists and engineers." To King, their "visions [were] blocked by a massive wall of technology, science, mathematics and expertness." He wanted more "vision," less technique.[19]

The New Left, which had begun germinating by that time, continued this theme. Years later, Morris Dickstein said "I can remember the impact that C. Wright Mills' work had on us as undergraduates in the late '50's. He seemed like the one bold spirit in the gray, gray crew of American social science." Mills' position was summarized by Staughton Lynd in 1962: "C. Wright Mills has called modern American social science 'an elaborate method of insuring that no one learns too much about man and society.' Mills argues that the great tradition of George, Bellamy and Veblen has disgraced itself by turgid definition-splitting on the one hand, and the statistical exegesis of trivia on the other."[20]

Edward Chase joined in the criticism in 1968 when he wrote about "academic economists who insulate themselves from troublesome doubts about fundamentals by their absorption in econometrics and data manipulation." In 1975, Martin Duberman referred to "the sharp challenge of recent years to the claims of 'value-free,' 'objective' social science."[21]

A substantial part of the New Left's criticism took on a different tone from that which we have just traced back to the 1930's. The "counter-cultural" side of the New Left was not mainly criticizing the lack of an effectively socialist social science; instead, drawing deeply from sources in the early nineteenth century's Romantic revolt against modernity and the Enlightenment, it was in profound opposition to the very existence of science, technology and rationalism. In 1968, Martin Duberman said of "today's student radicals" that "their disgust with traditional procedures is grounded in a growing distrust of rationality itself." Duberman looked on this favorably, saying that it meant that the activists wanted men "to become something more than minds."[22]

New Left activist Jerry Rubin said it most graphically: "Abstract thinking is the way professors avoid facing their own social impotence. Our generation is in rebellion against abstract intellectualism and critical thinking. We admire the Viet Kong guerrilla, the Black Panther, the stoned hippie, not the abstract intellectual vegetable."[23]

A more thoughtful, literary expression of the same perspective came from Theodore Roszak in *Where the Wasteland Ends*. Roszak said that from "the Romantic movement...we inherit a stubborn counter cultural resistance to the pre-eminence of science." He argued for a return to a magical, mystical way of seeing the world, and said that "it is the culture of science from which we must liberate ourselves." He spoke of "urban-industrial society [as] having hopelessly lost touch with life lived on a simpler, more 'primitive' level, and [as being] convinced beyond question of the omnipotence of technical intelligence." Roszak concluded that "we should undertake to repeal urban-industrialism as the world's dominant style of life" and substitute an "anarchist brotherhood and sisterhood" that would be "shot through with mystical sensibility."[24]

During the radical resurgence of the 1960's, the proponents of "behavioral science" were spurred to a point at which they were bidding to become the *avant garde* of academic radicalism. This was especially in evidence in the mid-western College of Business in which I was teaching. The movement was reflected in Reed Whitemore's observation in late 1969 that "social and behavioral scientists are ambitious and expansionist. They see their revolution coming."[25]

As the New Left faded rapidly after the tumultuous events of the spring of 1970, American radicalism retreated into various forms. One of the more important of these was the rise of academic Marxism, which prefers to call itself "radicalism". As early as April 1969, Martin Duberman was able to speak of "a new generation of radical academics." An organization called U.R.P.E. (for "the Union of Radical Political Economy") has published a prolific literature.[26]

Before I leave this subject, I should interject that some of the criticism of social science has been of a sort that would have been present even in the absence of ideological motivations. Various commentators within liberalism have been fully aware of the pseudo-scientific quality of much of the work that is done, and of the stifling neo-Scholasticism and credentialism that is imposed. Thus, Benjamin Stolberg wrote in 1922 that "the truth is that to compare actual to social science,...without an acute sense of poetic license is to commit one of the gravest of fallacies." Under the unfortunately partisan-sounding title *Social Sciences as Sorcery*, Stanislav Andreski has written an elaborate and thoughtful dissection of the trivia that so commonly clogs the social sciences as we came to know them during the middle half of the twentieth century. Here is a representative statement from his critique: "What is particularly dismaying is that not only does the flood of publications reveal an abundance of pompous bluff and a paucity of new ideas, but even the old and valuable insights which we have inherited from our illustrious ancestors are being drowned in a torrent of meaningless verbiage and useless technicalities."[27] Irving Kristol has told how the statistical method has been abused and has become a vehicle for ideology rather than of science: "That the concept of poverty should be continually and vigilantly redefined so that 20 percent of the population is always 'poor' is a function of ideology, not sociology." He points out that this reflects the attitudes of people who are "considerably more interested in the perpetuation of a critical attitude toward liberal-capitalist society than in any particular set of objective accomplishments."[28]

### The rise of the social-scientific professional

What I have described has become an institutionalized part of American society. Beginning with the formation of the distinct branches of social science in the late nineteenth century, every part of social science and of social work has become the domain of its own profession and bureaucracy. Referring to "the young economists who in 1885 founded" the American Economics Association, *The New Republic* in 1915 commented that "it is to these innovators...that we owe the fact that today the specialized economist...is at work for the state, the industrial corporation and the trade union." The journal saw clearly the implications for liberalism: "Social work will be a vocational school where the community learns constructive collectivism."[29]

No doubt this institutionalization can be seen as "in aid of democracy." That it can also become an elitist threat to it became apparent quite early. In 1915, a *New Republic* article called for teachers to share power over the schools with the elected Boards of Education. It is an easy matter to see the professional as more qualified than outsiders representing an amorphous and "not specially qualified" public. In the United

States, we have insisted that military professionals remain subordinate to civilian authority; a similar subordination of domestic "experts" to elected representatives is not so easy to recognize as a democratic imperative, or to delineate once it has been recognized.[30]

Despite the institutionalization, which suggests that the processes of "social therapeutics" have become regularized, the divisions within the American Left and within the groups that have constituted its alliance have been such that the road has not been one of smooth acceptance. The radical Left has upon occasion attacked social workers as representatives of the bourgeois establishment. As early as 1917, for example, Rebecca West complained that in England "the welfare worker is a failure...The welfare workers are drawn almost as exclusively as the philanthropic workers from the middle classes. Labor regards this with a resentment that is entirely reasonable."[31]

Even those who have been the subjects of social work, as so many blacks have, have been bitter critics. Reporting on the Watts ghetto shortly after its 1965 riot, Lewis Yablonsky wrote that "there was a uniform attitude that people trying to do social work in the neighborhood who lived outside were 'fools,' to be exploited as much as possible." In his "autobiography," Malcolm X said that "if ever a state social agency destroyed a family, it destroyed ours...They had looked at us as numbers and as a case in their book, not as human beings." There is, of course, a lesson in this: harmony does not inevitably exist between a professionalized Welfare State and its beneficiaries.[32]

### The effects of the de-privatization on American political life

It is in its political effects that the process I have described has been most obvious to the American people. The ideology that has sought the centralization of functions in the national government has had a distinct aversion to local or private or market solutions to the problems it has perceived. In this, it has differed sharply from classical liberalism, which sought solutions precisely in those areas.

If a classical liberal, for example, were to look at the history of labor-management relations and were to hope for the improvement of the condition of labor as it existed in the nineteenth century, he would welcome the development of job-related amenities by private employers. In contrast, here is the reaction that *The New Republic* expressed in 1915 to any improvement that came from a private employer: "The despot becomes benevolent. Hospitals, swimming pools, Y.M.C.A.'s, 'profit sharing,' are bestowed, evidently in complete oblivion of the fact that there would be little manhood in men who accepted these benefits at the price of submission."³³

A classical liberal approves of private education as an expression of freedom and as a decentralization of power over the public's thinking. Here, though, is what another 1915 editorial said in *The New Republic*: "Universities, whether supported by the state or privately, are becoming too vitally institutions for public service to be much longer directed on the plan of a private corporation...Irresponsible control by a board of amateur notables is no longer adequate for the effective scientific and sociological laboratories for the community that universities are becoming."³⁴

Before Medicare was established, conservatives preferred the Kerr-Mills Act of 1960, under which the federal government would subsidize a state-initiated insurance plan, operated through a private insurance company, for elderly persons in medical need. Eric Goldman tells us that "proponents of Medicare responded in unveiled disgust." They preferred a program that was both compulsory and federal.³⁵

During most of the twentieth century, this preference has caused liberals to take a dim view of state and local government. The exceptions have come during the periods, such as the 1920's, in which liberal action has been blocked at the federal level. The more usual view was stated by William Orton when he wrote that "mobilization [for social purposes] is frustrated by the existence of forty-eight separate political and legal jurisdictions...American liberalism...must undoubtedly look increasingly toward the federal power, the only power that is adequate to the largest problems." With this as the premise, it is no wonder that in 1935 *The New Republic* was able to call for "a new form of government that will...abolish the present states..., substituting flexible regional divisions." This was consistent with Herbert Croly's views years earlier. Charles Forcey has summarized those views: "Since the states were largely artificial political units with no real relation to industry, Croly suggested that they be deprived of virtually all control over economic matters. To the towns and the cities would be given the control or ownership of local utilities, while the rest of the economy would be regulated by a much strengthened government in Washington." In *Progressive Democracy*, Croly had written that "the state governments will be needed and valued, not as independent and coordinate centres of authority, but as parts of an essentially national system."³⁶

Nor were these views held only by liberals in Croly's generation. In 1966, Walter Heller described the "federalism" he favored: "States and localities...will continue to be the service centers through which important national purposes are achieved." This subordination of the states to federal policy has become quite pronounced – and continued even under the Reagan and Bush administrations. (We recall, for example, how the Reagan administration used strings attached to federal spending as a way to force the states to change their laws about the age at which young people were allowed to drink beer).[37]

Why has modern liberalism favored centralization? For a combination of reasons. First, the influence of the intellectual culture can most effectively be brought to bear at the national level. Second, as some of the commentators themselves have stated, the type of planning liberalism has wanted does not lend itself to geographical limitations coinciding with state boundaries. Third, the statistical aggregation of erstwhile individual problems into collective problems provides no rationale for decentralized solutions. Fourth, there has over a long period of time been a progressive weakening of local loyalties, and of the romance of providing local political leadership, due to such objective factors as increased mobility, broadened communication, and the like. And fifth, the quality of local and state leadership has for over a century been notoriously low, a fact that reflects perhaps more than anything else the unwillingness of most people even in a democracy, absorbed they are by their daily lives, to devote any time (or contribute any money) to politics.

In addition to liberalism's movement away from the local and state units of government, liberal thought has had as one of its premises the assumption that little or nothing will get done without "planning." Senator Hubert Humphrey was thus able to look out upon the world, armed with statistics about current numbers of graduates, and say that "the cold fact is that the number of engineering graduates is declining--as are Ph.D.'s in education and government. We cannot permit this to continue." To Humphrey, there was no "invisible hand" that leads to the automatic flow of resources in response to the free choices made by many individuals. This is one of the profound differences between Humphrey's brand of liberalism and that of the classical liberals, such as Adam Smith and David Ricardo. Those who see chaos in the marketplace of free choices are bound to seek order in other ways.[38]

Another example can be seen in the statement Senator Edward Kennedy made on June 17, 1971. "Between now and the year 2000," he said, "the population of America will increase by nearly 100 million people...The increased population is the equivalent of building 200 new cities with populations of 500,000 or 100 new cities with populations of 1 million. In fact, the development of such new cities, using advanced new technologies and systems analysis, may be the most important

## Liberalism in Contemporary America

challenge we face...." This passage illustrates not only the absence of a "vitalist perspective" (which looks to the on-going vitality of private processes) within modern liberalism, but also the mentality of planning and of a collectivistically applied social science.[39]

The result of all this has been that modern liberalism has, at least until its post-New Left disillusionment, called for an ever-expanding role for government. I compare this to "blowing air into the balloon." Many of the specific programs have been of a "foot-in-the-door" nature, carrying an intent that they be expanded once they are started. In 1964, TRB spoke of "the steady expansion of government," and said that "there is no doubt in my own mind that this expansion ought to go on, and will go on." A description of the specific programs could fill several volumes.[40]

Before the collapse of liberal morale in the 1970's and '80's, there was an assumption of irreversibility – that a governmental function, once embraced, would not, indeed could not, be abandoned. Henry Fairlie could say in 1966 that "departments like Health, Education and Welfare are developing a character which will survive changes in the political climate." He described at least one of the factors that would press for permanence and growth when he said that "the lever of federal funds, once it is given to a bureaucracy, is unlikely to be left unused for very long." Another factor of perhaps equal importance has been that each program has developed its own constituency – and voting bloc. This has placed a premium on political opportunism and has made political competition increasingly difficult (or well-nigh impossible) for those not given to the opportunism of a "spend and elect" politics.[41]

It is a mistake to think that federal power has been manifested even primarily through direct legislation. Ubiquitous webs of influence and control have come into being.

There has been a universe, so to speak, of regulation coming out of the massive independent agencies, to which vast realms of power have been delegated. In 1915 *The New Republic* exulted about the Federal Trade Commission Act that "a Democratic Congress has actually delegated the broadest kind of personal discretion to a commission of 'experts'" and that "the Act achieves a very happy but a most amazing delegation of legislative function."[42]

In addition, intricate control has been exercised through strings attached to spending. "Affirmative action" programs have been probably the foremost example of this. Every firm that has had government contracts of a certain size has had to have an "affirmative action plan" for the recruitment of minority employees. It has been required that part of the firm's plan be that the businesses with which the firm deals must also have a plan. The principal lever for the enforcement of all of this has been the threat of cutting off government funds and contracts.

Another avenue has been through abjuring all pretense of neutrality in taxation. The tax system has existed only partly to raise the hundreds of billions of dollars that have been needed to fund governmental programs; it has equally been adapted to "social intervention," by which countless activities are encouraged and many others discouraged.

The Jacksonians before the Civil War argued strenuously against the use of the tariff for other than the raising of revenue, and feared the "consolidation" that would result from unrestrained federal spending. But the high-tariff parties during American history always favored the use of taxation for interventionist, not simply revenue-raising, purposes. This was one of the leading issues throughout the nineteenth century.

Then, relating to a more modern context, we were told by Felix Frankfurter that "Theodore Roosevelt was the first President avowedly to use the taxing power as a direct agency of social policy." Robert LaFollette, another of the major figures of the Progressive era, said in his *Autobiography* that "I argued openly that the Constitution authorized the federal government to use the taxing power, that there was no limit to that power for police purposes...." In 1935 *The New Republic* advocated an interventionist system of taxation when it called for "a thoroughgoing program of social reform through taxation."[43]

## The loss of confidence; the
## critical reevaluation after 1965

As a result of the divisions within the American Left during the 1960's, a fact of considerable significance was reported by James MacGregor Burns in March 1968: "For the first time in decades the power of the Presidency is undergoing critical reevaluation by American liberals...Liberal political scientists are reconsidering the need for institutional checks and balances against the man in the White House."[44]

The old magic was gone. Implicit faith was no longer reposed in the presidency, as Burns' statement shows – or in any of the rest of the massive federal enterprise. Many of the factions on the Left began seeing the gigantic apparatus as evil or incompetent or both. There was a turn inward, as during the 1920's, and toward proposals for decentralized collectivism, such as worker control.

Lee Benson voiced a common New Left theme when he wrote that "1968 showed that the fatal weakness of modern bureaucracies is precisely their inability to satisfy humanist needs." A *New Republic* editorial in 1970 reported that "black America's confidence in the national government has rapidly, dangerously diminished." In 1972, TRB told his readers that "there is an undercurrent of disassociation, a feeling almost of despair that it really won't matter much. This lack of confidence in the capacity of government to solve problems is rather terrifying." *The New Republic*'s editors in 1974 stated the problem this way: "[The] national Democratic party has a tradition of benevolent big government. But how sure can our 1976 candidate be that an extension of the New Deal, the New Frontier, the Great Society, will produce more well-being for more people or a federal bureaucracy that's more responsive and benevolent?"[45]

In May 1980, attempting to explain why Senator Edward Kennedy "is simply out of his time," Henry Fairlie said that "there seems at last to be an end to the belief in the ability of quick if not deep or penetrating minds – seducible or purchasable or both – to identify real problems and their possible political resolution." Then in December 1984, following Senator Walter Mondale's defeat by President Reagan the month before, a *New Republic* editorial declared that "the old liberal confidences...now lie shattered...We will have to admit [that] there may be some problems that can't be solved, even with...a hefty bit of cash." "American liberalism," the editors said, "is in crisis."[46]

# NOTES

[1] New Republic, June 30, 1920, p. 139; Hubert H. Humphrey, *The Cause is Mankind* (New York: MacFadden Books, 1965), p. 21.

[2] Lester Ward, *Lester Ward and the Welfare State*, Henry Steele Commager, ed. (Indianapolis: The Bobbs-Merrill Company, Inc., 1967), p. 368.

[3] New Republic, July 28, 1973, p. 32.

[4] Harry Elmer Barnes, ed., *The History and Prospects of the Social Sciences* (New York: Alfred A. Knopf, 1925), p. 185.

[5] New Republic, November 4, 1957, pp. 12, 14.

[6] New Republic, December 5, 1949, p. 11.

[7] New Republic, January 30, 1915, pp. 16-18; New Republic, December 23, 1931, p. 151.

[8] Louis A. Zurcher, Jr., and Charles M. Bonjean, ed.s, *Planned Social Intervention* (London: Chandler Publishing Company, 1970), p. 14.

[9] New Republic, December 25, 1971, p. 22 (Senator Mondale is quoted by Robert Coles).

[10] Edward C. Banfield, *The Unheavenly City* (Boston: Little, Brown and Company, 1970), p. 20.

[11] L. L. Bernard and Jessie Bernard, *Origins of American Sociology* (New

York: Thomas Y. Crowell, 1943), p. 807.

[12] Zurcher and Bonjean, *Planned Social Intervention*, p. 43.

[13] Jacob Oser, *The Evolution of Economic Thought* (New York: Harcourt, Brace & World, Inc., 2nd ed., 1970), pp. 298, 299; Heinz Kohler, *Welfare and Planning: An Analysis of Capitalism Versus Socialism* (New York: John Wiley & Sons, Inc., 1966), p. 106.

[14] Zurcher and Bonjean, *Planned Social Intervention*, p. 27.

[15] New Republic, June 18, 1918, p. 168; New Republic, June 2, 1926, p. 48; New Republic, March 4, 1931, p. 62.

[16] New Republic, March 11, 1931, p. 104.

[17] New Republic, July 29, 1931, p. 276.

[18] New Republic, July 19, 1933, p. 258; New Republic, July 5, 1939, p. 257.

[19] New Republic, April 8, 1957, p. 15.

[20] New Republic, January 29, 1977, p. 36; New Republic, March 12, 1962, p. 30.

[21] New Republic, February 24, 1968, p. 37; New Republic, March 8, 1975, p. 23.

[22] New Republic, June 2, 1968, p. 27.

[23] Jerry Rubin, *Do It!* (New York: Simon and Schuster, 1970), p. 213.

[24] Theodore Roszak, *Where the Wasteland Ends* (Garden City: Doubleday & Company, Inc., 1972), pp. xxv, 37, 73, 414, 425, 428.

[25] New Republic, December 20, 1969, p. 21.

[26] New Republic, April 19, 1969, p. 30.

[27] New Republic, December 13, 1922, p. 75; Stanislav Andreski, *Social Sciences as Sorcery* (London: Andre Deutsch Limited, 1972), p. 11.

[28] Irving Kristol, *Two Cheers for Capitalism* (New York: Mentor Book, 1978), p. 202.

[29] New Republic, January 2, 1915, p. 9; New Republic, August 28, 1915, p. 108.

[30] New Republic, April 3, 1915, p. 229.

[31] New Republic, October 13, 1917, pp. 298-300.

[32] New Republic, January 1, 1966, p. 10; Alex Haley and Malcolm X, *The Autobiography of Malcolm X* (New York: Grove Press, 1965), pp. 21, 22.

[33] New Republic, January 30, 1915, p. 6.

[34] New Republic, July 17, 1915, pp. 269, 270.

[35] Eric F. Goldman, *The Tragedy of Lyndon Johnson* (New York: Dell Publishing Co., Inc., 1969), p. 341.

[36] New Republic, January 29, 1930, p. 267; New Republic, June 12, 1935, p. 117; Charles Forcey, *The Crossroads of Liberalism* (New York: Oxford University Press, 1961), p. 33; Oser, *Evolution of Economic Thought*, p. 37.

[37] Walter W. Heller, *New Dimensions of Political Economy* (New York: W. W. Norton & Company, Inc., 1967), p. 123.

[38] Humphrey, *The Cause is Mankind*, p. 40.

[39] Thomas P. Collins and Louis M. Savary, ed.s, *A People of Compassion: The Concerns of Edward Kennedy* (New York: The Regina Press, 1972), p. 82.

[40] New Republic, October 31, 1964, p. 12.
[41] New Republic, January 1, 1966, p. 19.
[42] New Republic, January 9, 1915, p. 8.
[43] Howard Zinn, *New Deal Thought* (Indianapolis: The Bobbs-Merrill Company, Inc., 1966), p. 359; Robert M. LaFollette, *LaFollette's Autobiography* (Madison: The University of Wisconsin Press, 1968), p. 53; New Republic, January 30, 1935, p. 319.
[44] New Republic, March 16, 1968, p. 25.
[45] New Republic, January 18, 1969, p. 20; New Republic, July 18, 1970, p. 8; New Republic, January 1, 1972, p. 6; New Republic, June 29, 1974, p. 6.
[46] New Republic, May 31, 1980, pp. 18, 19; New Republic, December 10, 1984, p. 12; New Republic, December 10, 1984, p. 9.

## CHAPTER TWELVE
## The New Left I

A violent storm swept over American life in the second half of the 1960's and the first years of the '70's. For those within the alienated Left, it was a thrillingly exhilarating time of uninhibited militancy and mass support that for most ended in fragmentation, exhaustion and despair. For many liberals, less militant, it began hopefully as the expression of several good causes, but became a time of soul searching and anguish that left most of the old certainties profoundly shaken.

For Americans of conservative values, it was a frightening time during which a chasm opened up to reveal all of the barbarism that lurks so close to the surface even in advanced civilization. It was a time of the unthinkable, and of general complicity in the unthinkable. They came to see how tenuous was the hold that the American people of the mid-twentieth century, shallowly rooted and lacking in an intellectual culture appropriate to a free society, had upon fundamental values. The threat to those values no longer came as much from the ever-expanding power of government as from cultural solvents that dissolved the bonds of loyalty and trust that hold a free society together. To such Americans, it was a scarring time left nothing ever again quite as it was before.

This was a decade during which paradoxically, in a high tide of moral catharsis, millions joined hands communally to damn everyone else and the society as a whole. The movie "Network" told it all: millions throwing open their windows and shouting, in unison with all the others, "I'm madder than hell and won't take it any more."

Three different but intertwined revolutions raged at once: what we might for convenience call the Red, the Black and the Green. A resurgent radicalism from the far Left made up the Red; the splintering factions of the Civil Rights movement made up the Black; and the Green was formed of the startling mixture of moralism, ascetic renunciation, hedonism and anarcho-communism that made up the "counter-culture."

From the description I have given, it might seem that this great spasm was an entirely American phenomenon. To think so would be a serious mistake. The Red and the Green revolutions can hardly be understood without an appreciation of their continuity with forces that had long been at work within the world Left and of the corresponding movements that were occurring contemporaneously in Western Europe and the Third World. The term "New Left" is sometimes used to refer only to what I am calling the "Red" revolution, but it and the counter-culture of the Green revolution constituted together a major resurgence of alienation from the far Left as it existed in the years immediately following the death and disgrace of Stalin.

We can fit the pieces together from the elements that have already been relevant to our discussion of American liberalism. The revolutionary ferment during these years was not something *sui generis*. It was one of the manifestations of the complex mixture that we must fathom if we are to understand the modern predicament.

We have seen how for a century and a half the world intellectual culture had stood outside the predominant commercial, bourgeois civilization. Intellectuals who supported the *ancien regime* formulated an elaborate philosophical defense of medieval values and set them off against the "Philistine" civilization that had supplanted the old order. Other intellectuals used the same revulsion to create the world Left. As an alienated sub-culture, the intelligentsia then sought allies among all disaffected or unassimilated groups. Socialist projects of many kinds, fragmented but united in their hatred of "bourgeois" civilization, came into being. The Romantic movement gave rise to an atavistic renunciation of Reason and of modernity, and contributed immensely to the illiberal clamor that Julien Benda described in his *Les Trahison des les Clercs*. These were the forces that pulsed out of Europe, half-overwhelming the classical liberal vision that had itself led, and continued to offer, a revolution in favor of democracy and individual freedom.

These gigantic forces provide the backdrop for what I call the "inherent presence" of both the radical Left and the counter-culture (itself a part of the radical Left) within all advanced Western societies during the nineteenth and twentieth centuries. If ever it has seemed that they have been absent, the absence has been an illusion, a failure to see what at times is a quiescent core of alienation, militancy and withdrawal. That core will remain present until the alienation of intellectuals withers and ceases to be a major fact in our culture – an event so momentous that we will rightly be able to say that we will have passed into a new period of history.

An appropriate but inherently unfavorable analogy comes to mind. Those who favor the Left don't like it; others find it graphically descriptive. It has to do with the similarity between this "inherent presence" of radical militancy and of the counter-culture to the herpes virus. The virus never leaves the host individual, but lives unnoticed at the juncture of a nerve and the spinal cord until, under the right circumstances created by weakened body resistance or some other catalyst, the virus moves down the nerve to erupt violently at the surface of the skin. During periods when the sores are not in evidence, it is a mistake to think the virus is gone. It has simply retreated up the nerve to the spinal cord.

This movement of attack and withdrawal is analogous to a phenomenon that I have referred to as part of the psychology of the American Left, including modern liberalism. There is an alternation that consists of a period of yearning-for-activity, followed by one of intense movement and agitation, which in turn gives way to a time of disillusionment, fatigue and withdrawal. We have seen how this cycle has repeated itself through a century and a half of American alienation, reflecting the psychology of the intellectual. If we treat the yearning as the beginning of a cycle, we can say that the American Left ran through an entire cycle between the years 1956 and 1975.

There is perhaps no better example of the yearning with which it began than the passages that Arthur Schlesinger, Jr., wrote in *The New Republic* in June and July 1956. In June, he said that "I feel that an injection of anarcho-syndicalist revolt – dissent for dissent's sake – would...be enormously helpful in our increasingly homogenized culture. The attack against the Establishment has been going on for some time in Britain. We have our own Establishment, and it needs to be attacked too." Then in July he added that "of the varieties of intellectuals, the sort America most needs at this moment is precisely the opposite of *Time*'s Man of Affirmation...One begins to feel that in the cloying atmosphere of 1956 any assertion of individuality, no matter how crude or vulgar, tends to be liberating...We need more people who don't give a damn and can awaken responses in us."[1]

It is improbable that Schlesinger could even remotely foretell how "crude and vulgar" the militancy of the 1960's would become, but we can see in his statements – in 1956! – the deep psychological impulse that moved the Left toward its great spasm of activity, both in the form of a renewal of a radical critique and of the counter-culture. It is especially significant that this yearning-for-activity was voiced by a leading liberal, not just someone who had long been a part of the far Left.

We can draw still another important fact from Schlesinger's 1956 statements. It is that the spasm was not a product of the "catalysts" – the confrontations of the Civil Rights movement, the movement against the Vietnam War, the concern over the "environment" – to which it is so often ascribed. From Schlesinger's comments and other evidence that we will review, we will see that the movement was well under way within the world Left, and in the United States, before those catalysts came on the scene. What the catalysts *did do* was to provide vehicles for mass support. They lent "warm bodies" to a force that found its core in the alternating cycle through which the alienated intellectual culture passes.

### "Inherent presence": the radical Left

One of the oddest statements I have seen by a serious thinker is Michael Harrington's observation in 1969 that "this radical generation is virgin-born and has no ideological parents." Although it is true that many of the militants of the New Left were not well read, in countless ways they were the inheritors of the preceding century-and-a-half's legacy of alienation and socialism.[2]

According to Malcolm Cowley in 1977, "several leaders of campus rebellions were the sons or daughters of old-time radicals." Irving Howe informs us that during the 1950's "those who left the [Communist] party or its supporting organizations because they feared government attack were often people who kept, semi-privately, their earlier convictions." He tells how the catalysts called them back to activity: "As soon as some ferment began in the civil rights movement and the peace groups, these people were present, ready and eager."[3]

It is no coincidence that the rhetoric of the Henry Wallace third-party presidential campaign in 1948 had the same tone and content that the New Left's rhetoric had a decade later. We recall how deep the generalized distrust was that the New Left created toward American institutions. Here is what Vincent Sheean reported in November 1948: "It is in the radical tradition...to charge venality...But the Wallace campaign has generalized the technique into a wholesale insemination of distrust which...would make our processes of government invariably suspect to a considerable minority of our young people." It is a fair inference that this "considerable minority" played no small role in the New Left, which, after all, began to emerge within less than a decade after the Wallace campaign. One such person was Staughton Lynd, who according to Jack Newfield went from being "a national youth leader in the Henry Wallace campaign of 1948" to someone "whom *The New York Times Magazine* correctly termed 'elder statesman and doyen theoretician of the new Left.'"[4]

The core of radical thinkers who in the late 1950's germinated the American New Left were, in fact, already active together in the mid-1940's. Dwight MacDonald, who was still around to sign a 1930's-style Manifesto supporting the "Chicago Eight" after the violent confrontation between the Yippies and the Chicago police at the time of the 1968 Democratic convention, started the radical journal *Politics* in 1944. C. Wright Mills and Paul Goodman, the two who were most prominent in creating the American New Left in the second half of the '50's, were among the first to contribute articles to MacDonald's journal.[5]

One of the leading hotspots of New Left activity in the 1960's was at the University of California at Berkeley. For most Americans, those events erupted, as it were, from a vacuum. But here is what Andrew Kopkind told the readers of *The New Republic* in 1966: "For ten years a loose community of radicals has been growing in the San Francisco Bay area...Starting with the remnants of the old base carved out by Jack London, then by Harry Bridges and the Longshoreman's Union, the newer radicals began their careers demonstrating against the Un-American Activities Committee, then the Caryl Chessman protest and the formation of a student political organization called SLATE at Berkeley in 1957; the civil rights sit-ins in San Francisco followed, then the Free Speech Movement, and the VDC" (the Vietnam Day Committee).[6]

The anti-Vietnam War movement during the 1960's had important antecedents in the radical "peace movement" of the 1930's and 1940's. One part of the "peace movement" had long been from the radical Left; another part had consisted of the various "peace churches" (which, even though they should be carefully distinguished from the Left as such, have often reacted to the Cold War environment since World War II by identifying closely with the radical Left in its defense of revolutionary movements in such places as El Salvador and Nicaragua).

Before World War I, European and American socialists had made "peace" a major part of their program, based on their Marxist supposition that the proletariat's interests were international and that proletarians would have no reason to fight on anyone's side in what would necessarily be a struggle among governments representing the bourgeoisie.

During the interregnum between the world wars, leftist thought was heavily "neutralist." It remained so until events in the second half of the 1930's dragged most leftists into the conflict with Hitler. In his book *Rebels Against War: The American Peace Movement, 1941-1960*, Lawrence S. Wittner says that in 1935 60,000 college students took part "in a 'strike' against war." Many of them took the "Oxford oath," which swore an "absolute refusal to serve in the armed forces." (The taking of this oath reminds us that there was a comparable radical peace movement in England, showing the international flavor of these movements.)[7]

Some of those who were most closely identified with the "peace movement" never did support the war against Hitler. David Dellinger, later a leading activist within the New Left and one of the Chicago Eight defendants in 1968, remained a committed pacifist even during World War II. Wittner says that in 1943 "in the Newark slums an ex-divinity student and Socialist, Dave Dellinger, and a handful of other revolutionary pacifists organized the People's Peace Now Committee to press for an immediate end to the war."[8]

Thousands of "Conscientious Objectors" were incarcerated in camps and prisons during World War II. According to Wittner, "prison life provided a vital fund of experience that pacifists drew upon in postwar struggles," especially in developing "non-violent methods of protest." Wittner says "the steam went out of radical pacifism" between 1948 and 1956, but that "a small band of isolated pacifists" spent those years formulating theory: they "subjected America's role in the international power struggle to a critical reexamination."[9]

Then in 1956 the journal *Liberation* was founded "by a small group of radical pacifists." It expressed several themes that were to become important to the New Left: "utopianism, anarchism, non-violent revolution, civil rights, the Third Camp, and...peace." Wittner says that "beginning in 1957 the American peace movement underwent a revival." In 1963, an advertisement for *Liberation* claimed that the journal had been "the most referred to spokesman for the nonviolent movement in all its aspects – in civil rights, in the peace movement, in labor."[10]

All of this fed into the anti-Vietnam War movement in the mid-1960's. So that we appreciate the continuity, we should notice that in 1963, which was before America's involvement in the Vietnam War had heated up, an advertisement in *The New Republic* for the War Resisters League included the circular "peace symbol" that became so well known to Americans later in the decade. Another *New Republic* advertisement, this time for S.D.S. (Students for a Democratic Society), which was arguably the central New Left organization, said in 1965 that the S.D.S. was working to "create an independent, radical peace movement."[11]

Thusfar, I have told enough to suggest the continuity that existed between American radicalism in the 1930's and 1940's and the later beginnings of the New Left. Considerably more detail could be given, but my purpose is to explain the continuity of the ideas rather than to seek an encyclopedic discussion of the people and events.

Another dimension providing continuity with the world Left was the international one. Some of the important aspects of this dimension will become apparent when in the next section we review the "inherent presence" of a counter-culture within Western radicalism.

Other vitally important international links stemmed from the trends that emerged within the Left after World War II. In 1956, Nikita Krushchev denounced Stalin in his famous "secret address" to the 20th Soviet Party Congress. This was combined with the repression of the "Polish October" in 1956 and with the crushing of the Hungarian Revolution by Soviet tanks in late 1956. For many, these events sealed the long decline of Soviet influence within the world intellectual movement. As we have seen, there had been many earlier shocks: the purge trials; the persecution and murder of Trotsky; the Hitler-Stalin Pact; the Soviet aggressions against Poland, Finland, Latvia, Estonia and Lithuania; the Lysenko affair; and the development under Tito of a form of Communism that was not totally dominated by the Soviet Union. The split between the U.S.S.R. and Communist China was to provide another.

Although the U.S.S.R. remained a continuing source of orthodox Marxism-Leninism (except perhaps in the eyes of the Chinese), these events splintered Marxist thinking in the West. One of the important consequences was the rise of what has become known as "humanistic Marxism." Signs of it began in the late 1930's. It stresses Marx's early writings and focuses on such concepts as "reification" and the "alienation of the worker from his work." This brand of Marxism was given a boost by Erich Fromm when in 1961 he republished Marx's early essays. It has been a significant part of Western Marxist thought ever since.

More important to the New Left, however, was the rise of charismatic, Romantic revolutionaries in the Third World. Although these figures – such as Fidel, Che, Mao and Ho – were mostly tied to the Soviet Union, they appeared energetic, untainted and fresh. It was from their inspiration that, as Mark Rudd wrote in 1969, "we learned...the great truth stated by Chairman Mao Tse-Tung, 'Dare to struggle, dare to win.'" Irving Howe has concluded that "most of the 'new leftists' have identified...with the harder, more violent, more dictatorial segments of the Communist world."[12]

When the split occurred between Communist China and the Soviet Union, many revolutionaries in the Third World became associated with the Chinese, while others retained their tie with the Soviet Union. This became one of the sources of ideological fragmentation that contributed to the eventual collapse of the New Left.

C. Wright Mills was one of those who felt a strong affinity for the Soviet bloc. Irving Howe says that Mills travelled to Europe in 1957 and came back "impressed by the industrial achievements of the communist nations." Mills "wanted to see a new alignment of 'the left,' sort of an informal Popular Front that would include intellectuals who were to one or another extent sympathetic to the Communist bloc."[13]

The international origins of the New Left thus reflected the continued vitality of the world Left after the Second World War despite all of the "shocks" that had rocked the earlier faith in the Soviet experiment. Even though the democratic socialist movements in Europe moved away from Marxism, the shift did not imply an evaporation of the radical Left.

### "Inherent presence": Antecedents of the "counter-culture"

The "counter-culture" has been another side of the Left. By treating it separately, I do not mean to suggest that it has been something distinct from the Left. The pre-World War I crowd in Greenwich Village, for example, was intensely committed to radical theory and action at the same time that it was wrapped up in a "culture of radicalism" that involved a lifestyle that was distinctly counter to "bourgeois" values.

Even though the committed theorist-activist and the denizens of the counter-culture have both been parts of the Left, and have sometimes even been the same people, there has been a long-standing tension between these two styles. The disciplined leftist often scorns what he sees as the dissipation of the energies of those who express their alienation by "opting out." If he is a Marxist, as virtually all are, he has a theory of revolutionary development that tells him what forces will be most conducive to success. This usually assigns no place to the mere bohemian.

Throughout history, there have been sub-cultures of withdrawal. As conditions worsened with the impending collapse of the Roman Empire, most ancient philosophies preached withdrawal as the way to escape. The asceticism of the early Christians provides many examples of individuals who renounced not only the existing civilization, but worldly life itself. The doctrines of Augustine, which remained most influential within Christianity for eight centuries, preached withdrawal. Monastic life was a prominent part of the Middle Ages.

The stage was set for a similar pattern in the early nineteenth century when European thought moved sharply into a renunciation of modernity and of the existing culture. Theodore Roszak's New Leftist *Where the Wasteland Ends* is a foolish but literate explanation of the tie between this "revolt against Reason" and the counter-culture of the 1960's.

Not only did Romanticism give rise to an impulse toward withdrawal (which we will see had been manifested in the German Youth Movement when we discuss it next), it provided much of the intellectual rationale that was continued by the American counter-culture of the 1960's. An example is evident in what Leo Stein said about John Ruskin in 1919 on the 100th anniversary of Ruskin's birth. "He soon came to see," Stein said, "that the bitterest enemy to beauty in life was the factory system and the modern industrial organization." As Roszak said, "Romanticism is...a critical counterpoint to the imperial advance of science." He spoke of "their challenge to science and industrialism" and "their loathing for system, abstraction, routine, in their passion for free self-fulfillment." The sophisticated denunciations of modern life that came so freely to the lips of those within the "hippie culture" of the '60's were not formulated out of thin air by nineteen and twenty year olds; they were ideas that had been articulated in a vast literature a century before.[14]

Some of the earliest manifestations of a counter-culture were the various "utopian communities" of the nineteenth century. But perhaps the first open counter-culture as we think of it was in Greenwich Village prior to World War I. Lewis Coser tells us that "young men and women...began flocking to Greenwich Village about 1910" with an "implied commitment to a lifestyle." "Bohemia," Coser says, "attempts to create countersymbols and a special and distinct culture of rebellion. The Village provided a refuge from middle class philistinism and permitted the widest experimentation in dress, sexual mores, and life styles generally...For a few years the Village embodied the full flowering of an intellectual, artistic, political, and emotional counterculture that gave sustenance and support to the assault against the dominant values of nineteenth-century America."[15]

This continued during the years of disillusionment after World War I. William Harlan Hale told the readers of *The New Republic* in 1931 that "carried on the wave of post-war revolt in thought and morals, the students of the early twenties were the last word in radicalism...Everyone remembers...the baggy trousers, the collegiate semi-bohemianism." In 1923, H. M. Kallen had told of "rebellious youth," of which he said that it "has no alternative ideal to present. Its spirit is discontent; its cry: There is no good in the institutions of modern life."[16]

In *Exile's Return*, Malcolm Cowley summarized the ideas that moved the counter-culture of the early 1920's. The similarity to the ideologically anarchic, hedonistic "flower children" of the 1960's is apparent: "...the system of ideas...could roughly be summarized as follows: 1. If...children are encouraged to...blossom freely like flowers, then the world will be saved by this new, free generation. 2. The idea of self-expression...3. The idea of paganism. – The body is a temple...to be adorned for the ritual of love....5. The idea of liberty. – Every law, convention or rule of art that prevents self-expression or the full enjoyment of the moment should be shattered and abolished...6. The idea of female equality."[17]

This was the time of the "Lost Generation" and of the flight to

Europe. The spirit of that time continued, for some, into the 1930's. A product that later became important as a source of the New Left was Henry Miller's *The Tropic of Cancer*, published in 1934. Edmund Wilson said that this book was ignored by the activist radicals of the 1930's as representing "the decadent expatriate culture."[18]

In the late 1930's as catastrophe after catastrophe shook the Left, Malcolm Cowley wrote that "I notice that many writers are drawing back – either into ultra-radical idleness or else into an assortment of mysticisms, cynicisms and revolutions of the pure word." George Soule reported a similar phenomenon in 1946.[19]

Thus we see that my phrase "inherent presence" is aptly applied to the counter-culture. At varying levels, anti-bourgeois withdrawal has been a permanent part of the Left in the twentieth century. Later when I describe the Beatniks of the 1950's and the Hippies of the 1960's, the description will not be of something startlingly new, but of an "ultra-radical idleness," to use Cowley's expression, that has been one of the principal styles of alienation.

### An ominous forerunner: The German Youth Movement before and after World War I

I remember what an electric effect it had upon the national meeting of the Philadelphia Society in 1968 when a speaker read the following passage from Ludwig von Mises' *Bureaucracy* – which had been published in 1944! It was as though Mises had been describing the youth culture of the New Left. Mises' language makes his own revulsion clear, an attitude shared by the conservatives who heard the passage:

> In the decade preceding the First World War Germany...witnessed the appearance of a phenomenon hitherto unheard of: the youth movement ... In bombastic words they announced the gospel of a golden age. All preceding generations, they emphasized, were simply idiotic; their incapacity has converted the earth into a hell...Henceforth the brilliant youths will rule. They will destroy everything that is old and useless,...they will substitute new real and substantial values and ideologies for the antiquated and false ones of capitalist and bourgeois civilization...We are the deadly foes of the rotten bourgeois and Philistines....
>
> The chiefs of the youth movement were mentally unbalanced neurotics. Many of them were affected by a morbid sexuality, they were either profligate or homosexual...The only trace they left were some books and poems preaching sexual perversity.[20]

I have described the German Youth Movement in *Understanding the Modern Predicament*, and will repeat enough here only to lay the foundation for a comparison with the New Left. There are excellent books by Howard Becker and Walter Laqueur describing the Youth Movement in detail.

Here is some of the discussion from my earlier book: "The Movement's first phase was that of the *Wandervogel* between 1896 and 1919. The second was the Bund...which continued from 1919 until the Movement was absorbed into the Hitler Youth in 1933...Alienation from the bourgeoisie was the consistent thread. Laqueur says that 'the *Wandervogel* chose the other form of protest against society – romanticism. Their return to nature was romantic, as were their attempts to get away from a materialistic civilization, their stress on the simple life, their rediscovery of old folk songs'...Becker says...that 'German youth of Karl Fischer's day loathed and hated the world of their elders.' (I would necessarily have us ask how it happened that so many young people were suddenly independent philosophers having so great a sensibility to higher and finer values. Instead of reaching this subtle and extensive analysis themselves, they no doubt picked up the entire body of values and social critique from the alienated intellectual generation that preceded them....)"[21]

A difference between all of this and the later New Left was that the totalitarian ideologies that the Youth Movement's members proclaimed were drawn from a wide variety of left-and right-wing socialisms, whereas the New Left drew exclusively from the many factions of the far Left. We recall that in Germany after Hegel movements of Leftwing Hegelians championed ideas of class struggle and that movements of Rightwing Hegelians championed ideas of racial struggle. Both were equally antithetical to the bourgeoisie and to liberalism in the classical sense. Both were in evidence in the German Youth Movement.

In 1969, Michael Miles reported in *The New Republic* that "cultural historians have compared it [the New Left] to the Russian nihilists; social historians compare it to the Nazi paramilitary organizations of the 1920s. 'There is, they say, the same obsession with direct action, the myth of violence, the revolutionary claims without substance.'" (It is relevant that both Hitler and Mussolini's movements were initially youth movements, and shared the characteristics I have described.)[22]

## NOTES

[1] New Republic, June 4, 1956, p. 20; New Republic, July 16, 1956, p. 17.
[2] New Republic, February 8, 1969, p. 30.

[3] New Republic, August 20, 1977, p. 37; Irving Howe, *Steady Work: Essays in the Politics of Democratic Radicalism, 1953-1966* (New York: Harcourt, Brace & World, Inc., 1966), p. 48.

[4] New Republic, November 1, 1948, p. 19; Jack Newfield, *A Prophetic Minority* (New York: The New American Library, Inc., 1966), pp. 194, 195.

[5] New Republic, August 9, 1969, p. 5; Lawrence S. Wittner, *Rebels Against War: The American Peace Movement, 1941-1960* (New York: Columbia University Press, 1969), p. 94.

[6] New Republic, June 4, 1966, p. 17.

[7] Wittner, *Rebels Against War*, p. 7.

[8] Wittner, *Rebels Against War*, p. 56.

[9] Wittner, *Rebels Against War*, pp. 92, 228.

[10] Wittner, *Rebels Against War*, pp. 237, 240; New Republic, August 31, 1963, p. 36.

[11] New Republic, September 28, 1963, p. 22; New Republic, October 30, 1965, p. 2.

[12] Carl Oglesby, ed., *The New Left Reader* (New York: Grove Press, Inc., 1969), p. 312; Irving Howe, *Steady Work*, p. 73.

[13] Irving Howe, *Steady Work*, p. 247.

[14] New Republic, February 8, 1919, p. 52; Theodore Roszak, *Where the Wasteland Ends* (Garden City: Doubleday & Company, Inc., 1972), pp. 278-9.

[15] Lewis A. Coser, *Men of Ideas: A Sociologist's View* (New York: The Free Press, 1965), pp. 111, 113.

[16] New Republic, May 13, 1951, p. 348; New Republic, January 10, 1923, p. 168.

[17] Malcolm Cowley, *Exile's Return* (New York: W. W. Norton & Company, Inc., 1934), pp. 69-70.

[18] New Republic, March 9, 1938, p. 140.

[19] New Republic, November 9, 1938, p. 23; New Republic, August 5, 1946, p. 146.

[20] Ludwig von Mises, *Bureaucracy* (New Haven: Yale University Press, 1946), pp. 94-5.

[21] Howard Becker, *German Youth: Bond or Free* (New York: Oxford University Press, 1946); Walter Z. Laqueur, *Young Germany* (New York: Basic Books Publishing Co., Inc., 1962); for my quotations from my earlier discussion, see Dwight D. Murphey, *Understanding the Modern Predicament* (Washington: University Press of America, 1982), Chapter 16.

[22] New Republic, April 12, 1969, p. 17.

# CHAPTER THIRTEEN
# The New Left II

### The Green revolution: the counter-culture

On November 16, 1952, *Time* magazine carried an article "This is the Beat Generation," describing the forerunners of what became known as the Beats or Beatniks. Jack Newfield later told of "an underground subsociety that developed about 1953, was mythicized by the Beat novelists and poets, and quickly spawned colonies."[1]

It has been said that the "Beats" did not assume a distinct identity until after the appearance of Jack Kerouac's novel *On the Road*, which is referred to as "the Bible of the Beat Generation." This book's influence should not be taken as a sign of any particular merit; to someone outside its *ethos* it is a rather undistinguished telling of the story of a drifter; but the extent of its influence does point to the receptivity in the 1950's of a certain type of literary individual who was ready, as so many had been in the past, to respond to a message of withdrawal.[2]

Despite the importance that is assigned to Kerouac, we should augment this with an awareness that the movement was international in scope and reflected the contributions of several authors and influences. In what follows, we will simultaneously discuss Beat culture and these sources.

In his *The Beat Generation*, Bruce Cook has described contributions by William Carlos Williams, Gary Snyder, Allen Ginsberg, John Clellon Holmes, Kenneth Rexroth, Diane diPrima (who he says wrote a "scandalous, semipornographic little book, *Memoirs of a Beatnik*), Gregory Corso, and William S. Burroughs. Jack Newfield has said that "the Beat Generation was partly a small literary faction...Kerouac, who according to critic Seymour Krim 'single-handedly created the Beat Generation,' was the leader. The more gifted followers included Allen Ginsberg, the Jewish-radical-mystical- homosexual from Paterson, New Jersey." Newfield describes "the Beats' mysticism, anarchy, anti-intellectualism, sexual and drug experimentation, hostility to middle-class values, and idealization of the Negro and of voluntary poverty."[3]

One of the more famous works within the movement was Ginsberg's poem *Howl*. Bruce Cook informs us that it was "written during a long weekend spent in his room under the influence of various drugs – peyote for visions, amphetamine to speed up, and dexedrine to keep going." He tells us that Ginsberg's mother had emigrated from Russia and "became involved in radical politics and eventually a member of the Communist party." Cook calls Ginsberg "the Beat Generation's Walt Whitman."[4]

The reference to Ginsberg's mother simply reenforces our awareness of the tie that all of this had to earlier radicalism. Cook interviewed Gary Snyder and quoted him as saying: "Formative influences?...well, that's kind of funny. I guess my grandfather, the one up in Washington, was pretty important. He was a Wobbly, dues-paying member of the Industrial Workers of the World ...The old I.W.W. mythology became very important to me as I grew up in the Northwest."[5]

When he interviewed Kenneth Rexroth, Cook "asked if he felt the western radical tradition was important to the development of the Beat thing...'Oh, sure. No doubt about it. It goes back to Jack London and the I.W.W....there was a lot of native radical feeling out here...good old-fashioned anarchist-pacifist...There were a lot of things happening back then...for instance, all the Conscientious Objectors...San Francisco was within hitchhiking distance of half the C.O. camps in America."[6]

Cook considers it "an accident of time" that a movement similar to the Beats was occurring in England, which he describes as "a group of young English writers – which their press had dubbed the Angry Young Men." He sees no real relation between these and the Beats. He also gives short shrift to the fact that, as he says, "there were Dutch Beats, Turkish Beats, French Beats, and German Beats." But I consider Cook's conclusion a serious mistake; these phenomena were by no means disassociated, especially if we see them as part of a common heritage of anti-bourgeois alienation. Referring in 1959 to "today's 'lost generation' in England," Edmund Wilson was right, it seems to me, when he said that "our 'beat' generation here more or less corresponds to them. These anti-social writers are typical of the world in its present state."[7]

We see the ideological similarity from Wilson's comment that "the appearance of this phrase 'the Establishment' in England is very significant." Oddly, he added that "I don't think that in this country we could talk about anything equivalent." It wasn't long before reference to "the Establishment" was a standard part of the New Left's rhetoric in the United States. Wilson then spoke of "Jean Genet, the French writer, who carries the anti-social attitude farther than any of the rest." It would be a mistake to overlook the contribution of alienated French authors, especially Genet and Camus.[8]

The French philosopher Jean Paul Sartre believed Genet's "masterpiece" to be "Our Lady of the Flowers." Stanley Kauffmann would later look back and call Genet "a genius of homosexuality, who has also been a prostitute and a professional criminal (ten convictions for theft)." Robert Brustein said of Genet that his "most important ideological influence, aside from de Sade, is the tradition of French pornography." "For Genet...all functions are the manufacture of fakery and sham, and the artifice of the brothel is identical with the make-believe of the world. If the whorehouse is a mirror of society, society, in turn, reflects the whorehouse." To this, Victor Lange has added that Sartre valued Genet's work because "he regards his notorious life of crime and homosexuality as a significant and entirely legitimate form of anti-bourgeois action."[9]

As the counter-culture continued to develop in this country, Paul Goodman was another leading influence. (I will mention C. Wright Mills in another connection.) His works included *Growing Up Absurd*, consisting of articles authored between 1956 and 1960, and his later *Utopian Essays* and *Seeds of Liberation*. In *Growing Up Absurd*, Goodman wrote that "the Beat Generation has contrived a pattern of culture that [turns] against the standard culture." He said that "characteristics of the present-day poor are essential in Beat culture. As, contrariwise, are the organizational characteristics of being hip and convinced that society is a Rat Race. But finally, there are essential traits...[that comprise] the essential morality...One striking trait is nonconformism and tolerance in sexual and racial questions and behavior." Speaking of the Beats' language, he said that "the paucity of its vocabulary and syntax is for the Beats essentially expressive of withdrawal from the standard civilization and its learning." He went on to say that "they have the theory that to be affectless, not to care, is the ultimate rebellion."[10]

As we proceed into the 1960's, there was so much writing of this sort that it becomes arbitrary to pick just a few selections for comment. I will nevertheless point to Joseph Heller's *Catch 22*, about which Robert Brustein wrote in 1961 that "through the agency of grotesque comedy, Heller has found a way to confront the humbug, hypocrisy, cruelty, and sheer stupidity of mass society." Brustein said the book "is one of those sublime expressions of anarchic individualism...Heller has come upon a new morality based on an old ideal, the morality of refusal."[11]

A vast literature developed over the ensuing fifteen years. The literature that was primarily oriented toward the counter-culture came to include such works as Theodore Roszak's *The Making of the Counter-culture* and *Where the Wasteland Ends*; Ken Kesey's *Sometimes a Great Notion*; Charles Reich's *The Greening of America*; Norman Mailer's *The White Negro*; Abbie Hoffman's *Revolution for the Hell of It*; Norman O. Brown's *Life Against Death* and *Love's Body*; Anthony Burgess' *A*

*Clockwork Orange*; and Timothy Leary's *High Priest* and *The Politics of Ecstasy*. Among the journals, *The Realist* is generally considered to have been the most representative counter-cultural vehicle. There were hundreds, if not thousands, of "underground" newspapers and journals.

### The ideology of the Red revolution

Leftists take seriously the differences that for a century and a half have raged within the Left over such matters as method, ultimate social model, historical rationale, and which coalitions to form. To those involved in the New Left, the distinction between what can be described as the "soft" or "Green" Left of the counter-culture and the "hard" or "Red" Left of those who preferred greater discipline and organization seemed very real. Anyone who is not "of the Left," however, will be justified in seeing these as intramural disputes among people whose ideas and emotions were in most respects similar. Even though I am separating "the ideology of the Red revolution" into a different section from the counter-culture, the reader should not conclude that the two were sharply different in their thinking.[12]

Although I would have us keep in mind the common ground that existed between these factions, a student of the subject needs to know that there were a number of specific viewpoints. There was no universally recognized version of "New Left" thought. I will not attempt a review of the versions put forward by the many factions, since the fine details of the doctrinal disputes on the Left are not important to the analysis I am making. A good reference for such a review is Kenneth and Patricia Dolbeare's *American Ideologies*.

Newfield says that in the late 1950's "a New Left began slowly to take root, nourished by the pacifist and socialist British New Left of the Aldermaston marches and the *New Left Review*; by the Beasts' private disaffection from and rage at the Rat Race; by the Cuban revolution; and by the writings of such men as C. Wright Mills, Albert Camus, and Paul Goodman." Peter Clecak, in his *Radical Paradoxes: Dilemmas of the American Left, 1945-1970*, attributed the New Left's thinking to four "plain Marxists" – C. Wright Mills, Paul Baran, Paul Sweezy and Herbert Marcuse.[13]

In early 1958, Frederick L. Schuman reported in *The New Republic* that "C. Wright Mills sees the U.S. and the U.S.S.R. as both 'overdeveloped' and 'superior' nations dedicated to 'technological prowess' and the blind worship of 'the science Machine'." This was one of the first references to Mills in that journal. Mills' famous "Letter to the New Left" appeared in England's *New Left Review* (which had begun publication in

January 1960) in the fall of 1960. The importance of Mills to the New Left was underscored by Ronald Berman in 1968 when he wrote that "Mills' 'On the New Left,'...on the subject of ideology at least, has become the *Das Kapital* of the present radicalism." Mills was the sociologist who gave form to the New Left's attack on the Establishment as involving a "military-industrial-(and political)" triad.[14]

Phillip Abbott Luce, who was one of the leaders of the Chinese-oriented Progressive Labor faction of the New Left until his break from it in February 1965, wrote that "by the fall of 1958...most of the young radicals that I knew were searching for a program of initiating a New Left in America." He pointed to the beginning of the Marxist journal *Studies on the Left* in 1959 as having "expressed the views of the emerging New Left." He has added that C. Wright Mills was "one of the first American political mentors of the new era."[15]

Earlier I quoted Arthur Schlesinger, Jr.'s, statements – penned in 1956! – expressing his yearning for a new radical movement. In my reading of *The New Republic*, I found that the first statement of a comprehensive New Left position in that journal appeared in the issue of October 20, 1958. Philip Green showed the new passion there when he spoke of the "stirrings of critical thought" about "the ugly botch we call our 'way of life.'" He denounced "the damned Organization...the system," and said that "our society...is materialistic, technology-worshipping...Our vaunted stability is composed partly of war preparedness, and partly of anti-social waste...[The] citizenry is becoming progressively unenlightened, an object of cynical manipulation...."[16]

It is important to focus on these early statements because they show that the alienation and ideology of the New Left came into existence well before America's involvement in the Vietnam War and even before the radicalization that occurred through the confrontations of the Civil Rights movement. Only the mass support was added later.

These developments are consistent with the opinion expressed by Irving Howe that it was not the new "humanistic Marxism" – which was burgeoning in eastern Europe and among some intellectuals in the West – that mainly influenced the New Left's Red revolution. I earlier quoted Howe's comment that "most of the 'new leftists' have identified...with the harder, more violent, more dictatorial segments of the Communist world." Thus, in 1966 Christopher Lasch could say that "the New Left in general more and more identifies itself with Castro, Guevara, Regis Debray, and Ho Chi Minh." And he pointed out that the "black power" ideology, which spearheaded the more militant part of the Black revolution, had come to represent more than just "a revival of Afro-American nationalism," transcending issues based solely on race to become a part of the "romantic anarchism" of the New Left.[17]

This is reflected in *The New Left Reader*, which was published by the Grove Press in 1969 and consisted of articles going back to 1958. Included were pieces by C. Wright Mills, Herbert Marcuse, Frantz Fanon, Fidel Castro, Malcolm X, Huey Newton, Rudi Dutschke, Daniel and Gabriel Cohn-Bendit, and Mark Rudd. Such a compilation shows not only the "hard" nature of the leftism involved; it also shows the global nature of the "Red" side of the New Left. This corresponds to the international dimensions of the counter-culture, which I discussed earlier. Dutschke was a leader of the German New Left; the Cohn-Bendits, one of whom was "Danny the Red," were part of the French; and Frantz Fanon focused on the example of the Algerian revolution.

Herbert Marcuse was a professor of philosophy at the University of California in San Diego. His thinking was heavily steeped in Marxism, although there was also a substantial admixture of Bakunin, Rousseau and Fourier. Orthodox Communists denounced him as "petit-bourgeois" and considered him a "revisionist." Marcuse has been referred to as the intellectual mentor of Angela Davis.[18]

The thesis of Marcuse's book *One Dimensional Man* is that modern industrial, capitalist civilization is suffocating the human potential by obliterating values that are not part of its system. In *An Essay on Liberation*, Marcuse argued that modern society has lost touch with the original, socialist nature of man. (Here we see Rousseau's very considerable shadow.) He argued that the workers within capitalism, who traditionally have been the principal revolutionary hope for orthodox Marxists, have been lulled to sleep by a manipulative affluence. "The masses themselves are forces of conservatism and stabilization." Since they would no longer be the source of an anti-capitalist revolution, he looked hopefully to "the young middle-class intelligentsia" and to "the ghetto populations" as catalysts for revolution among a newly sensitized majority. "The political consciousness exists among the nonconformist young intelligentsia; and the vital need for change is the very life of the ghetto population." He saw that "at present in the United States, the black population appears as the 'most natural' force of rebellion." "The Cuban revolution and the Viet Cong have demonstrated: it can be done; there is a morality, a humanity, a will, and a faith which can resist...capitalist expansion."[19]

Although Marcuse saw great value in the counter-culture's reorientation of consciousness, he was no friend to "the wild ones and the noncommitted, the escapists...."This is why I am discussing him as on the

Red, not the Green, side of the New Left.[20]

The revolutionary nature of his message is clear from what I just quoted. His totalitarian nature was especially evident in his essay "Repressive Tolerance." He argued that the very "tolerance" that democratic society encourages has been one of the manipulative factors that have lulled the masses to sleep. He called for a "liberating tolerance" that would encourage all views from the Left and suppress all conservative views. "Liberating tolerance would mean intolerance against movements from the Right, and toleration of movements from the Left."[21]

Despite Marcuse's affinity for the Fidel Castro's and Ho Chi Minh's of the Soviet bloc, there were certain elements in his thinking that justified placing him within a "new" Left. He could speak in post-Stalinist terms of "the repressive Stalinist development of socialism"; and he could say that "the new radicalism militates against the centralized bureaucratic communist as well as against the semi-democratic liberal organization. There is a strong element of spontaneity, even anarchism, in this rebellion...Therefore the aversion against preestablished Leaders, apparatchiks of all sorts, politicians no matter how leftist."[22]

Nevertheless, the word "new" was appropriate only to those whose memories were short. The revival of "romantic anarchism" was in most ways a harking back to the wilder varieties of nineteenth century socialist thought. When at last the Soviet Union had lost its role as the focus for emulation, Bakunin and Fourier stood ready to fill the void.

### A time of intense activity

I will not attempt an exhaustive review of the events of the 1960's, but will give only enough of the detail, drawn primarily from my notes from *The New Republic*, to paint a picture of those tumultuous years and to highlight any important observations about the content:

• In August 1960, an article by David Evanier spoke of "the sit-ins of the Negro students in the South, followed by the heroic demonstrations against the Un-American Activities Committee in San Francisco."[23]

• Advertisements appeared in *The New Republic* in November 1960 for the S.D.S. journal *Venture*; in April 1962 for the "radical journal" *Studies on the Left*; in September 1963 for *Liberation*; in January 1964 for the counter-cultural journal *The Realist*; and in July 1964 for *The Psychedelic Review*.

• Andrew Kopkind reported that the League for Industrial Democracy was sponsoring the Students for a Democratic Society. "In the summer of 1962, the new SDS students met near Port Huron, Michigan, and approved a statement of ideas and principles. The 'Port Huron Statement' is the seminal document of the new left – or 'the movement.'" He told of the rapid spread of S.D.S. chapters and the beginning, in early 1964, of "SDS projects in a number of Northern cities" to organize among poor whites. Tom Hayden had drafted the Port Huron Statement, and then became an organizer in Newark. In April 1965, the S.D.S. sponsored the "March on Washington to End the War in Vietnam."[24]

• In July 1963, Reese Cleghorn wrote that "today the banner taken to jail [by participants in the Civil Rights movement] is usually that of the Student Non-Violent Coordinating Committee [SNCC]... born of the 1960 college student sit-ins, cut free by its young leaders' decision not to accept direction from older organizations or Dr. King...." Two years later, Andrew Kopkind described SNCC as "the most radical civil rights group...It is anarchic rather than monolithic." He reported that SNCC had no desire to work within the Democratic party, wishing rather "to demolish it."[25]

• At the Democratic National Convention in August 1964 the Mississippi Freedom Democrats demanded to be seated in place of the regular-party delegation, and then, in the words of Andrew Kopkind, "rejected a compromise that would have given them 'tokenism.'" Despite the Johnson administration's success in securing the enactment of civil rights legislation, the conflict at the 1964 convention was looked back upon later by black militants as having indicated their inability to trust, and to work with, "white liberals."[26]

• In early 1965, an editorial told of the Berkeley sit-in in December 1964 at which 800 students were arrested after occupying the campus' administration building. In an article, Robert Brustein said that "these two revolutions – the Negro and Sexual (or Homosexual) – are currently supplying the major dialogues of our time." [It is a sign of the enormous variety within this radical resurgence that I have not previously found occasion to emphasize the "homosexual revolution," as such.][27]

• An editorial in April 1965 reported that "among styles of protest [the teach-in against the war in Vietnam] is all the rage this month" on the campuses at Michigan, Berkeley, and the like.[28]

• An advertisement in June 1965 told about Saul Alinsky's efforts to build "FIGHT, a militant Negro organization," in Rochester. Alinsky was the author of the 1946 book *Reveille for Radicals*, which advocated organizing "conflict groups." "A war," he had said, "is not an intellectual debate, and in the war against social evils there are no rules of fair play." James Ridgeway wrote in 1965 that "Alinsky would not be in Rochester were it not for the Council of Churches...various denominations had put

up the first part of a total of $100,000...."[29]
- In December 1965 Kopkind described the November "March on Washington" by 30,000 anti-war activists. "The weekend was an informal first Party Congress of the 'New Left.'" Instead of reporting strength, however, he told of fragmentation and lack of purpose. "There was a mood of uncommon pessimism...The students find they have no workable program for effecting the changes ...The frustration is particularly apparent in the tension between the radicals and the liberals." Speaking of the march's National Coordinating Committee, he said that it was a "recreation of the sectarianism of the left of the 'thirties...There were the Trotskyists – all 28 flavors...the Stalinists...the Maoists...the Russian revisionists...the Castroites....Many had allegiance to Students for a Democratic Society."[30]
- *The New Republic*'s first alienated "ecology" editorial (although it did not use the term, which had not yet caught on) appeared on June 25, 1966. By the end of the decade, and especially during the winter of 1969-1970, "the environment" became the focus for an hysterical attack on American life. The *Environmental Handbook*, rushed to print in time for the massive "Earth Day" protests that took place on April 22, 1970, spoke in tones of doom, saying "time is running out." In the Foreword, Garrett De Bell italicized his warning that "a year is about one-fifth of the time we have left if we are going to preserve any kind of quality in our world." Don Marquis said "america [sic.]...is dying because of the greed and money lust of a thousand little kings who slashed the timber all to hell and would not be controlled." Another author spoke of "smashing the worms of capitalism and totalitarianism." In *The New Republic*, Wayne Davis rung his hands "...as the curtain gets ready to fall on man's civilization." It was too late to save ourselves, he argued, unless we give up capitalism. "Let no one make the mistake of thinking we can save ourselves by 'cleaning up the environment.'" Only governmental ownership of land and resources offered any hope.[31]

It is worth observing that to the true devotees of the Red revolution the ecology craze seemed a harmful digression. Instead of indicating strength, it was a harbinger of loss of purpose and of fragmentation.
- In July 1966, an editorial commented that "in the space of three years, ghetto riots have become part of America's summer scene." The Watts conflagration was in 1965. In 1966, there were "riots" (if mass burning is truly rioting) in Chicago, Cicero and Harlem. In 1967: Newark, Detroit, Minneapolis, Plainfield (New Jersey), Hartford, Kansas City (Missouri), Waterloo, and Cambridge (Maryland). And these are just the riots that *preceded* the assassination of Martin Luther King, Jr.,

in April 1968.³²
- Phillip Abbott Luce had been among the many "radical youth" who had gone to Cuba for inspiration after Castro's victory there. He called Cuba "the Mecca of the early New Left." Even though the emphasis later shifted to the Vietnamese and Chinese Communists, it is worth noticing that, according to an unnamed reviewer in *The New Republic*, "in late November of 1969 216 young Americans, black and brown and white, left for Cuba by way of Mexico; and in February of 1970 687 more left – followed later that year by another group of 409."³³
- The project called "Vietnam Summer," with a peace group hiring 2,000 full-time field workers, took place at Cambridge in the summer of 1967. It was patterned after the 1964 "Freedom Summer." There had been a flow of activity from the militant Civil Rights movement to the anti-Vietnam War movement.³⁴
- One of the wilder spectacles occurred in 1967 with "the New Politics Convention." In a report to *The New Republic*, James Ridgeway told how the convention was attended by black nationalists, members of the W.E.B. DuBois Clubs (the Communist youth organization), the Communist Party, peace activists, "people from SDS, various community workers, southern student organizers, and a large contingent who had come from the Vietnam Summer project." Ridgeway observed that "the Communists...were out in the open for the first time in years," but added that "they were the most conservative element present."³⁵

Just how the convention managed to be held is a question, judging from Ridgeway's report. The black militants, he says, tried to get the blacks to leave; others formed a "white radical caucus, split off from the blacks; and "some jews [who] had financially supported the convention...walked out." It is interesting that Martin Luther King, Jr., the so-called apostle of "non-violence," gave the keynote address. Ridgeway mitigates this, so far as King is concerned, by pointing out that the speech was "such a bore to the delegates," but another report says the delegates responded enthusiastically.³⁶

Ridgeway viewed the convention with despair. "For some of us who have held out hope for the future of the radical reconstruction of America, our despair was...in quite suddenly realizing that neither the new nor the old left takes America seriously...It is indeed the worst of times, and the National Conference of New Politics destroyed what was left of our hope and we are alone." One can understand his despair, since the convention was one of the most bizarre gatherings ever held.³⁷

- In early 1968, Michael Miles reported that the S.D.S. had adopted Marxism, together with a non-exclusionary policy toward the Communists. Thus the New Left reversed the position taken by American liberals through the Americans for Democratic Action in 1947 and 1948. The A.D.A. had stood for the refusal of liberals to "cooperate with" Communists. In my chapter on "Liberalism and a World in Revolution," we will see how important that issue has been throughout the world.[38]

• In April 1968, Daniel Zolo reported that "a violent students' revolt began about seven months ago in all major Italian universities," based on "non-orthodox Marxists" who looked to Che Guevara. Then in June of the same year, Robert Greenstein told of the student revolt in West Germany, led by Rudy Dutschke and based on the doctrines of Marcuse, Mao, Ho Chi Minh, Che Guevara and Rosa Luxembourg. An article by Peter Brooks in July 1968 told of the May revolt by French students, which expressed "the tradition of 'creative anarchy,'"[39]

• In May 1968, Dotson Rader and Craig Anderson gave an account of the rebellion at Columbia University. They said that a "small group of students, led by Tom Hayden,...had stormed Math Hall on Thursday night and secured it for the liberation." The "students" remained in the hall, "building barricades, pulling up the tiles...." On Tuesday, April 23, "approximately a hundred radical students, lead by Mark Rudd, chairman of SDS, had marched on Morningside Park." Eventually, "plainclothes police forcibly entered Low Library, using their night sticks to break through the crowd of professors who had blockaded the entrance...SDS had won a clubbed and outraged faculty to its side."[40]

The Columbia revolt is analytically significant for at least six reasons. First, it shows that the militant "student" activity was neither spontaneous nor a response to police provocation. Rader and Anderson reported that "months before, at an SDS conference in Maryland, the decision had been reached to take physical control of a major American university this spring." Second, it shows that the "issues" that were taken so seriously by the media and by academia were mere sham: "The ... issues were pretexts. The point of the game was power. In the broadest sense, to the most radical members of the SDS Steering Committee, Columbia itself was not the issue."

Third, the fact that professors blockaded the building demonstrates the role of militant leftist faculty during those years. Fourth, in the comment about SDS's having "won an outraged faculty to its side" (necessarily those who were not already militant, such as the ones doing the blockading), we see the process of "radicalization" which was deliberately created by the confrontation and which no doubt served as one of its main purposes.

This relates, fifth, to a structural fact about modern society that is important in understanding the 1960's: that the intelligentsia, being attached to the Left, was prepared to articulate a high moralistic defense of the militants and an equally moralistic attack upon the police, the national guard, or any other representatives of the established order. Thus, despite everything they have told us, Rader and Anderson were able, incredibly, to reach the conclusion that "*police* violence was *unprovoked* and unlimited" (emphasis added). At the same time, the predominant society, having very little by way of an intellectual culture to speak for it, could rally no moral defense of itself and no articulation of a rationale on its own behalf. This led, in large measure, to the majority society's paralysis and moral equivocation.

My sixth point relates to this. It is that the processes of orderly society were bared as being more tenuous than we are accustomed to imagine. The social cements are not to be taken for granted; they can readily disappear. To those who value a free society, this is perhaps the most frightening single fact demonstrated by the New Left.

• Similar episodes, with similar responses, occurred at many other places, including Harvard in early 1969. After black militants took guns into Willard Straight Hall at Cornell, the editors of *The New Republic* made the typical moral inversion: "The black students at Cornell, or at least some of them, had their reasons for thinking they might need to defend themselves against violent attack."[41]

This voices a perspective that has been inherent in the Left's view of the world for more than a century: The masses, exploited, are no more than exercising their dignity as human beings by rising up; it is the bourgeoisie, in putting down the revolution, that commits the violence.

• The Columbia, Harvard and Cornell episodes served as a paradigm for the confrontation between the militants and the police in Chicago at the time of the 1968 Democratic National Convention. Except for a few admissions here and there, the intellectual culture has insisted to the American people that "Chicago" represented the beating of "kids" by the "brutal Chicago police." Several prominent "liberals" – including Michael Harrington, Jules Feiffer, Nat Hentoff, Christopher Jencks and Norman Mailer – signed a 1930's-type manifesto that appeared as an advertisement in *The New Republic* on August 9, 1969. It defended the "Chicago Eight" defendants and said that "both the mass media and the government's own Walker Report made it clear that the principal responsibility for acts of violence that occurred in Chicago last August lay with the Chicago authorities."[42]

Here, though, is how James Ridgeway, *The New Republic*'s correspondent, described the events in Chicago right after they occurred: "The strategy was to confront the Chicago police, and thereby demonstrate that America was a police state...The radicals talked enthusiastically about little acts of violence...to provoke the police and manipulate the liberal McCarthy youth into their ranks. In effect, the idea was to simulate a little guerrilla war...Chicago smelled of revolution." This was consistent with Jerry Rubin's boasts in *Do It*!: "Sunday night a police car drove through Lincoln Park. From every direction the yippie's own brand of rock music started: the rhythm of rocks rending cop-car metal and shattering windshields. The Battle of Czechago was on."[43]

• During the second half of the 1960's, the various revolutions going on simultaneously under the New Left banner were torn by fragmentation and eventually by disillusionment and fatigue. During the summer of 1970 following the incident at Kent State in May 1970, various fragments of the Red revolution went underground and formed the basis for the bombings and kidnappings of the 1970's. A great many of the militants, and especially those involved in the counter-culture, withdrew into mystic fads and cults. Others "went straight," and this included, with some, going into electoral politics.

• There were also during the second half of the 1960's some major developments within the Black revolution. The goal of "integration," which had received the imprimatur of the United States Supreme Court in *Brown v. Board of Education* in 1954, came under attack from the more militant blacks. An article in *The New Republic* in late 1966 spoke of "the myth that integrationist measures are bringing better housing to the Negro poor." In January 1967, Kopkind reported Stokely Carmichael's views about the Great Society's "War on Poverty": "The war on poverty may give some black people some of the things they need, but to Carmichael it keeps them under white manipulation...What galls SNCC people most is the way white radicals seem to have treated SNCC as a kind of psycho-therapy, as a way to work out problems of alienation and boredom." This points to a double split that was occurring: between integrationist blacks and separatist blacks; and between whites and blacks within the Civil Rights movement. "What is happening now," Kopkind said, "is that many of those whites feel hopelessly rejected by their Negro friends." Simon Lazarus would later speak of "the sharp turn toward separatism and violence taken by SNCC in 1967." He mentioned "SNCC's scorn for moderates like Martin Luther King – on the ground that the latter direct their appeals to whites rather than blacks."[44]

• A final development is that there had been a flow of energy from the early Civil Rights movement to the anti-Vietnam War movement. Kopkind told in 1965 how many of those who had participated in the anti-war March on Washington that year had earlier taken part in the 1963 civil rights March on Washington and had been at Selma. This is consistent with Barry Kalb's observation in 1969 about one of the women in S.D.S.: she was "a veteran of the Southern Christian Leadership Conference, SNCC, the Mississippi Freedom Democratic Party, the National Mobilization Committee to End the War in Vietnam, and SDS." Ronald Berman quoted Mario Savio as having said that "last summer I went to Mississippi to join the struggle there for civil rights. This fall I am engaged in another phase of the same struggle, this time in Berkeley."[45]

## The collapse of the New Left

To an outsider the New Left appeared to collapse suddenly and dramatically between the end of the academic year in May 1970 and the beginning of the fall semester. Great spasms of activity had accompanied the events of the spring, which had included the observance of Earth Day on April 22, the demonstrations that followed the United States armed forces' invasion of the North Vietnamese sanctuaries in Cambodia, and the outcry that followed the National Guardmen's opening fire at Kent State University. Radicals urged renewed vigor in the fall, including a shutting down of all universities; but the movement, strangely enough, lost all its impetus. The masses were gone. Slowly the realization dawned that a major change had occurred. What remained were the bombings and kidnappings by those who "went underground," the flight of many thousands into mysticism and the occult, the turning of others to electoral politics, and the rise of "women's liberation" as the principal issue on the Left during the 1970's.[46]

The suddenness of this collapse was something of an illusion. The New Left had been dissolving internally for as long as five years, although it would be arbitrary to assign a beginning date. As we review the causes of the collapse, we will see that many of them had been underway since the mid-1960's. The New Left was, in the Marxist phrase, collapsing "from its own contradictions." (It would be a mistake, of course, to assume that the New Left fully "had its act together" at any one time and then began to collapse from there. Because of this, there is some artificiality in thinking in terms of a collapse. We do, however, seek to understand the New Left's downward, rather than upward, trajectory, and its eventual demise.)

There were at least nine causes, and almost certainly more, that contributed to the eventual evaporation of the New Left. Needless to say, several are related.

1. *The militants' fatigue.* Michael Unseem conducted interviews among the militants and found that by early 1969 one-fourth had dropped out. Some, he said, told him that they were "suffering from general exhaustion."[47]

The phenomenon of "tired radicals" corresponds to a like phenomenon during the 1920's, after the intensity of the Progressive years. After recounting the effort of those years, George Soule said in 1931 that "the effect of all this upon us differed according to the individual. Some became 'tired radicals' and surrendered by going out for conventional success." According to L. Otis Graham, Jr., a symposium in 1926 on "Where are the Pre-War Radicals?" cited "the high personal cost..., costs both financial and professional" as a cause of their disappearance.[48]

2. *The intellectuals' cycle: a time for withdrawal.* I discussed this theme earlier, tracing it back as far as Emerson's generation. We see the withdrawal part of the cycle taking effect in Charles Kerr's April 1970 statement that "Robert Brustein would have young radicals lower their voices and settle down to a 'revolution of the spirit.'" In so urging, Brustein was following in the footsteps of Herbert Croly in the 1920's.[49]

3. *The public's fatigue.* In its very first editorial in its opening issue in November 1914, *The New Republic* attributed the loss by Progressive candidates in the 1914 elections to the fatigue the public felt toward political agitation. Can we doubt that the public who laughed at the antics of a Bruce and a Rubin in the 1960's would come to feel a similar fatigue after several years of New Left agitation? The human factors stay much the same from one episode to another.[50]

4. *The displacement of moderates.* Like slapstick as a form of entertainment, in which the old devices after a while stop startling, the New Left had to keep increasing its militance and its shock techniques to hold the attention of its audience (especially since the young in an age of television had become accustomed to rapidly changing images). And, too, those who were caught up in it were propelled to more and more extreme conduct. Jerry Rubin says that "By 1970 there was tremendous pressure on all activists to translate their radical talk into action – shoot a gun or plant a bomb." The "going underground" with terroristic activity by the end of the 1960's was a predictable product of these forces.[51]

The effect, however, was slowly to lose the support of the "moderates" and those who shrunk from violence. Rubin writes that "most of us were not ready for an armed confrontation with the state. I felt that I was being set up for martyrdom by death or jail." In addition to militants like Rubin, there were the people who had "supported the goals of the New Left" while only mildly "faulting the means." Some were moderates out of wisdom, some out of the timorousness that had so long set American liberals apart from the remainder of the Left.[52]

Thus Robert Greenstein reported in June 1968 that the German movement under Rudi Dutschke was incurring "the alienation of liberals... who dislike the authoritarian style." Recalling a scene reminiscent of the Nazis, Greenstein said "the end of the Vietnam Congress...is a case in point...SNCC representative Dale Smith jumped on a table and raised a clenched right hand. Virtually every one of the 3,000 German students rose from his seat. Three thousand right fists shot up and down together, as students chanted in unison with Smith, 'Burn, baby, burn.'"[53]

5. *Sectarianism; sterile factional in-fighting*. The Left's fragmentation has been a source of great weakness for over a century. Although for a while it added to the range of New Left expression, it was a major factor in the eventual collapse.

In 1965, Andrew Kopkind told about the debate over "how far radicals can go in accepting liberal forms of action," thus revealing a split between the moderates and the revolutionaries. In 1969, it was reported that many within the New Left sympathized "with the Arabs as part of the romanticized third world," and a year later Reed Whittemore commented that "the Middle East struggle...is dividing the left ideologically." When we realize how much of the traditional Left has been Jewish, we know how significant a division this represented. The foreseeable split between the disciplined Left and the undisciplined romantic anarchist also developed. Michael Miles wrote in early 1969 that "at Berkeley...there is an open split between radicalism with a rational analysis and program and 'militancy' empty of political content." Other disputes simply reflected old sectarian differences: Barry Kalb reported in July 1969 that "The National Office group of the SDS last week informed the [Peking-oriented] Progressive laborites that they were no longer members of the family. Each party thereupon elected a slate of officers; each called itself 'the real SDS'." Several years later *The New Republic* looked back and added an additional split to the list: "Black leadership in this country has been splintered and quiescent since the assassination of Martin Luther King, Jr."[54]

6. *Lack of revolutionary commitment on the part of the rank-and-file*. We see the seeds of a major problem for the New Left in the comment by the editors of *The New Republic* in 1967 that "the overwhelming majority of the 150,000 Americans who took part in antiwar demonstrations in New York and San Francisco on April 15 almost certainly knew nothing, and probably care less, about what went on behind the organizational scenes." The New Left was, for a time, able to draw large

crowds, but these did not consist of committed cadre. They could be, and were, there one day – and not the next.[55]

The same point was made in *The Nation* about the black side of the New Left. In a 1972 article entitled "Where Did Their Revolution Go?," the author wrote that "the explanation would be that there simply never was a 'black revolution.' There was militancy...but never much of a genuine revolutionary conviction on the part of most black students."[56]

This lack of commitment could be due to a number of causes, but we might conjecture that perhaps Sombart's "schoals of apple pie and ice cream" were coming back to haunt the New Left.

7. *The annual loss of continuity among college students*. The New Left of the second half of the 1960's was largely centered in the universities. The annual graduation of approximately one-fourth of the students, including always those who were older, makes continuity difficult. This should not obscure the fact, of course, that the New Left did have an inner core of full-time militants, such as the ubiquitous Tom Hayden.

I have seen no study concerning it, but I have wondered whether the younger brothers and sisters of the students of the late 1960's perhaps reacted negatively to the antics of their older syblings, so that when they arrived at college they were not so inclined to continue the agitation. This would be an interesting area for empirical study.

8. *Removal of the catalysts*. The alienated core of the Left gains wide public support when it exploits issues that can bring in others who deeply feel their own interests at stake. Both the "black" and the "red" revolutions involved "catalysts" of this sort. In each case, the catalyst gradually disappeared. Despite the calls by black militants for more, the civil rights legislation enacted under the Johnson administration, including especially the Voting Rights Act of 1965, went far toward satisfying the needs that moderate blacks had perceived.

The mass movement faded, too, as the Vietnam War ceased being an issue. As early as June 1968, Richard Anthony and Phil Semas told *The New Republic*'s readers that "SDS support... [has been] drifting away in response to the McCarthy candidacy and the Paris peace talks."[57]

9. *A rallying of the forces loyal to the existing society*. Eventually signs began to develop of an articulated defense of American society. After Kent State, Andrew Greeley wrote that "it doesn't take those patriotic parades of 'hard hats' to demonstrate that there is immense dissatisfaction in the country with 'radical protest'" Then Greeley noted something that to him seemed quite incredible: "The outrage in academia notwithstanding, it appears that more than half of the American people blame the Kent State killings on the students themselves!"[58]

# NOTES

[1] Jack Newfield, *A Prophetic Minority* (NY: New Amer. Lib., 1966), p. 45.
[2] New Republic, November 8, 1980, p. 24.
[3] Newfield, *Prophetic Minority*, pp. 44, 45, 47.
[4] Bruce Cook, *The Beat Generation* (New York: Charles Scribner's Sons, 1971), pp. 64, 113, 28.
[5] Cook, *The Beat Generation*, p. 32.
[6] Cook, *The Beat Generation*, pp. 32, 59-60.
[7] Cook, *The Beat Generation*, pp. 21, 155; New Republic, March 30, 1959, p. 14.
[8] New Republic, March 30, 1959, p. 14.
[9] New Republic, November 23, 1963, p. 23; New Republic, May 3, 1975; New Republic, March 28, 1960, p. 21.
[10] Paul Goodman, *Growing Up Absurd* (New York: Random House, 1956), pp. 64, 65, 175, 281.
[11] New Republic, November 13, 1961, p. 12.
[12] In my discussion here, I am using the word "Green" in the sense Charles Reich used it in *The Greening of America* to denote the counter-culture, and not directly in the sense that the term was used by the "Green" faction (an anti-nuclear movement) in Europe in the 1980's. It is perhaps unnecessary to explain that the word "Red" as I am using it in these chapters on the New Left is intended more broadly than just to denote the Communist Party or even pro-Soviet groups.
[13] Newfield, *Prophetic Minority*, p. 21; for a review of Clecak's book, see New Republic, January 5, 1974, p. 29.
[14] New Republic, February 3, 1958, p. 15.
[15] Phillip Abbott Luce, *The New Left* (New York: David McKay Company, Inc., 1966), pp. 51, 47, 54.
[16] New Republic, October 20, 1958, pp. 19, 20.
[17] Irving Howe, *Steady Work: Essays in the Politics of Democratic Radicalism, 1953-1966* (New York: Harcourt, Brace & World, Inc., 1966), p. 73; Christopher Lasch, *The Agony of the American Left* (NY: Vintage Books, 1969), pp. 130, 131.
[18] New Republic, December 24, 1977, p. 36.
[19] Herbert Marcuse, *An Essay on Liberation* (Boston: Beacon Press, 1969), p. 80, 51, 58, 81.
[20] Marcuse, *Essay on Liberation*, p. 60.
[21] Herbert Marcuse, essay entitled "Repressive Tolerance" in *A Critique of Pure Tolerance* (Boston: Beacon Press), pp. 90, 109.
[22] Marcuse, *Essay on Liberation*, pp. 85, 89.
[23] New Republic, August 8, 1960, p. 13.
[24] New Republic, June 19, 1965, pp. 15-19.
[25] New Republic, July 20, 1963, p. 15; New Republic, April 10, 1965, pp. 13, 14.
[26] New Republic, December 11, 1965, p. 17.
[27] New Republic, March 27, 1965, pp. 6, 26.
[28] New Republic, April 17, 1965, p. 9.
[29] Saul D. Alinsky, *Reveille for Radicals* (Chicago: University of Chicago Press, 1946), pp. 153, 154; New Republic, June 26, 1965, p. 16.

[30] New Republic, December 11, 1965, p. 15.

[31] Garrett De Bell, ed., *The Environmental Handbook* (New York: Ballantine Books, 1970), pp. xiv, vii, 2; New Republic, January 10, 1970, p. 15.

[32] New Republic, July 30, 1966, p. 5.

[33] See *Venceremos Brigade: Young Americans Sharing the Life and Work of Revolutionary Cuba*, no individual author given; Luce, *The New Left*, p. 60; New Republic, July 10, 1971, p. 28.

[34] New Republic, May 27, 1967, p. 5.

[35] New Republic, September 16, 1967, pp. 9-11.

[36] New Republic, September 16, 1967, pp. 9-11.

[37] New Republic, September 16, 1967, p. 12.

[38] New Republic, February 3, 1968, pp. 25, 22.

[39] New Republic, April 27, 1968, pp. 16, 17; New Republic, June 8, 1968, pp. 18-20; New Republic, July 6, 1968, p. 25.

[40] New Republic, May 11, 1968, pp. 9-11.

[41] New Republic, May 3, 1969, p. 5.

[42] New Republic, August 9, 1969, p. 5.

[43] New Republic, September 7, 1968, p. 11; Jerry Rubin, *Do It!* (New York: Simon and Schuster, 1970), p. 170.

[44] New Republic, December 17, 1966, p. 20; New Republic, January 7, 1967, p. 18; New Republic, January 13, 1968, pp. 28, 32.

[45] New Republic, December 11, 1965, p. 18; New Republic, July 5, 1969, p. 12; Ronald Berman, *America in the Sixties: An Intellectual History* (New York: The Free Press, 1968), p. 161.

[46] Regarding the desire to shut down all universities, see New Republic, September 12, 1970, p. 19.

[47] Michael Unseem, *Conscription, Protest, and Social Conflict* (New York: John Wiley & Sons, 1973), pp. 276-277.

[48] New Republic, January 21, 1931; L. Otis Graham, Jr., *An Encore for Reform: The Old Progressives and the New Deal* (New York: Oxford University Press, 1967), pp. 162-163.

[49] New Republic, April 25, 1970, p. 29.

[50] New Republic, November 7, 1914, p. 4.

[51] Jerry Rubin, *Growing (Up) at 37* (New York: Warner Books, 1976), p. 93.

[52] Rubin, *Growing (Up) at 37*, p. 93.

[53] New Republic, June 8, 1968, p. 20.

[54] New Republic, December 11, 1965, p. 17; New Republic, February 15, 1969, p. 9; New Republic, March 21, 1970, p. 32; New Republic, April 12, 1969, p. 18; New Republic, July 5, 1969, p. 11; New Republic, Sept. 17, 1977, p. 6.

[55] New Republic, April 29, 1967, p. 3.

[56] The Nation, Vol. 215, p. 272.

[57] New Republic, June 29, 1968, p. 13.

[58] New Republic, June 27, 1970, p. 14.

# CHAPTER FOURTEEN
## The New Left III

### The New Left's methods

One of the issues that have fragmented the Left for a century and a half has related to which methods are both justifiable and effective in bringing about social change. It is not surprising that a variety of methods were used by the different factions of the New Left. We will discuss the Dadaist method; the "non-violent" method that was derived from Thoreau and Gandhi; and violence. We have already seen a fourth method: protest by withdrawal.

1. Most Americans are not aware that the "comical" method that was used so effectively, especially among the young, by many New Left militants has had a long history within the Left. I will refer to it as "the Dadaist method."

Before I trace its origins, we should first see how it was used by the New Left. The following examples, even though they will only cite specific instances, represent an extensively used style. They should be sufficient to illustrate both the method and the intentions behind it:

• A *New Republic* article in 1964 reported that Lenny Bruce "turned up in court looking like a bearded rabbi in the garb of the concentration camp."[1]

• The Free Speech Movement at Berkeley asserted a right to use obscene language, which in turn became useful for its shock value and its symbolic shattering of what the Left likes to call "bourgeois" norms. Stanley Kauffmann reported in 1968 that the Canadian Broadcasting Corporation refused to carry an item "because it contains – often – the words 'fuck' and 'bullshit.'" [It is relevant to my later discussion of the complicity of liberalism with the New Left that Kauffmann went on to say – in *The New Republic* – that "I hope that at least some members of the CBC felt that this decision was a fucking disgrace."][2]

• In early November 1970, David Sanford reported from Kent State University that "last Saturday the Yippies staged a carnival on the famous Kent commons to raise bail money. They sold commie pinko bubblegum for a penny, fished for fake dope, threw painted rocks at paper pigs, and built a 10-foot penis out of papier-mache."[3]

• The entire "movement" was seen as part of an on-going "happening" of "guerrilla theater." It consisted not only of startling behavior, but of a complete cultural identification. The outspoken Jerry Rubin stated the rationale: "We were a religion, a family, a culture, with our own music, our own dress, our own human relationships, our own stimulants, our own media...Long hair is communication...We longhairs recognize each other as brothers in the street...Man was born to let his hair grow long and to smell like a man...We even smell our armpits once in a while." He showed how much of this was acting for effect when he said that "an event happens when it goes on TV and becomes myth...The presence of a camera transforms a demonstration."[4]

In his 1934 book *Exile's Return*, Malcolm Cowley traced the development of the Dadaist technique. "Tristan Tzara says that Dada was born in 1916...He wrote the *Dada Manifesto* in March, 1918...All over Europe Dadaist groups had sprung into being, and everywhere they spread the same pattern of childishness and audacity...But the history of Dada was in reality much longer. Its existence was rendered possible by a succession of literary schools beginning before the middle of the nineteenth century." It was then that Cowley quoted Edmund Wilson about the episode in which the French writer Flaubert had made love to a prostitute in front of his friends "without removing his hat or taking the cigar from his mouth." Flaubert's purpose, Wilson had said, was to "announce a furious contempt for everything held sacred by society."[5]

Kenneth Coutts-Smith's book *Dada* gives the history of the post-World War I Dadaist movement. "The most obvious aspect of Dada...was a savage anarchism, a deliberate programme designed to undermine the moral and social assumptions of existing middle class society." Among many examples, he cited a 1920 art exhibit in which patrons entered through a public lavatory and were then confronted "by a young girl dressed as for her first communion who suddenly began to recite obscene verses."[6]

Oddly enough, American precedents include Huey Long. A 1935 *New Republic* editorial commenting on Long's assassination said that he "used the manners of a clown to achieve his ends...He concealed his furious energies and hatreds beneath...an act of deliberate buffoonery." We have already seen the influence that the I.W.W. (Wobblies) had as a source of the New Left. It is pertinent that in 1948 in *The New Republic* Wallace Stegner described Joe Hill, a "folk hero" of the Wobblies, as having had "the poet's knack of self-dramatization. His whole conduct during his trial was dramatic...." In my discussion of the origins of the counter-culture, we saw the importance of Jean Genet's influence. Those of us who recall the tumultuous "revolutionary theater" of the 1960's will know what

Robert Brustein had in mind when he spoke of "the boiling 'total theater' of Artaud."[7]

All of this lent itself to an ideological characteristic of the New Left about which I have not yet commented. I have in mind the role that exaggeration played in the ideology – a super-inflation of every American defect.

Marcuse, for example, was capable of describing American society as one "which compels the vast majority of the population to 'earn' their living in stupid, inhuman, and unnecessary jobs; ...which is infested with violence and repression while demanding obedience and compliance from the victims of violence and repression...." Robert Theobald said in 1968 that "we have something like six to nine months to make visible the beginning of a change...If trends continue to develop as they are presently developing, we will move into a fascist police state in this country." Also in 1968, William Barrow reported in *The New Republic* that "the so-called 'militants' long ago gave up expecting anything other than efforts at genocide from the white majority." And the journal's own Robert Brustein, in 1964 before he eventually turned against the more extreme elements of the New Left, had described the United States this way: "What has been the most characteristic pattern of American history? The commission of some crime, paid for with a hundred years of remorse."[8]

As a result of its method, alienation and ideology, the New Left, with a great deal of liberal complicity, built a fantasy-world which it then projected onto American society. The amazing thing is that it was all granted a *prima facie* plausibility at the time by the media, academia and public acquiescence. Those who opposed it had few avenues of expression.

2. The Civil Rights movement made extensive use of the technique of "non-violent protest." The same method was later used in the anti-Vietnam War movement in the sit-ins and lie-ins.

There is obviously a broad continuum of possible activity within what might be called non-violent protest. It can range from the normal processes of speaking-up in a free society to the mass seizure of public and private property. When it is carried to the extent of mass action that involves the seizure of property and the building of intense emotions within large numbers of people, it is properly considered a revolutionary technique. This is, in fact, precisely what David Dellinger considered it, as we see from the title of his book *Revolutionary Nonviolence.*

This militant, revolutionary form of non-violence has a long history. It is usually attributed to Gandhi, although Gandhi is said to have drawn inspiration from the United States' own Henry David Thoreau, who wrote his "Essay on Civil Disobedience." Sorel's "General Strike," in which all of a country's workers would go on strike simultaneously, was certainly in the tradition. The United Auto Workers' sit-down seizure of the General Motors plant in Flint, Michigan, in 1936 is another example.

I have already discussed "non-violence" in detail in my chapter on liberalism's attitudes toward methods of social change. (See Chapter 8.) I made the point there that the advocates of non-violence are often willing to create the setting in which violence is bound to occur. In the context of the New Left, we can see that the seizure of university administration buildings, sometimes by people with weapons, is "non-violent" only if we are willing to accept the sophistry, which we heard voiced in connection with the Columbia seizure, that it is *the police* who, by responding on behalf of the larger society, commit the violence.

The hypocrisy of so much of the "non-violent" movement is seen when we consider, too, that Dellinger's book *Revolutionary Nonviolence* was published *in 1970* – after the bombings had started and after a large number of American cities had undergone riots and mass burning. To extend one of Oliver Wendell Holmes, Jr.'s, analogies, this is like continuing to shout "Fire!" even *after* the crowd has started to stampede in a theater. Thus Tom Hayden told how activists planned a "demonstration" the *day after* the Newark riot.[9]

"Non-violence" is widely misunderstood by many who praise it as a method. The term suggests that the method is a mild one consistent with the framework of a free and orderly society. When "non-violence" is used on behalf of revolution against a free (albeit imperfect) society, however, and involves substantial coercion, violation of law, denial of public and private property rights, and a building of mass emotions to a pitch at which it is foreseeable that violence will result, it should be seen in a very different light. It then bears the same relationship to violence that gross negligence (defined in law as "doing something highly dangerous without caring") bears to intentional harm.

3. On March 28, 1970, *The New Republic* reported six bombings, of which three "were unmistakably revolutionary." A month later, Robert Brustein told how "recently, three young people blew themselves up on W. 11th St. with bombs, said to be intended for Columbia University." Brustein, who by that time had become an opponent of the extremists, spoke of "the atrocities being prepared by Americans in the name of 'revolutionary idealism'" [although, to show that he wasn't letting such thoughts go too far, he was careful to point out that the atrocities were no more than on a par with "atrocities" Americans were committing in

Vietnam].[10]

In September 1970, Stephen Solomon reported an "18-month wave of fire-bombings" at the University of Wisconsin. This had culminated in the now-infamous terrorist attack in which "an explosives-laden truck destroyed [a] building, [and] killed a young physics scholar." In the same issue, Albert A. Eisele wrote from Minnesota that there was "a deep insecurity and even fear about violence." "This was sickeningly brought home when dynamite bombs smashed the federal office building...and a downtown department store." Significantly, he pointed out that Senator Hubert Humphrey called on "true liberals" to "condemn criminality."[11]

Fortunately for Americans, the violence ebbed away during the 1970's instead of building. Terrorism, including truck-bombings, became common in Europe and the middle-East during the 1980's, largely from the same types of leftist guerrilla organizations – such as the Red Brigades in Italy – that were beginning to form in the United States. A significant portion of this terrorism came from Soviet client-states such as Syria and Lybia. This informs us that it is a technique that is not unique to the Bakuninist-style Left but is also one of the weapons in the arsenal of the Soviet bloc. Although terrorism is used by individuals and groups outside the Left, and is thus a commentary on the general level of civilization in the way that Jose Ortega y Gasset considered so important, it is a mistake to think that much of it is not related to alienation and Leftist ideology. We saw this in 1970 when Eldridge Cleaver, in a book published by McGraw-Hill, declared that "we have to fight a revolutionary struggle for the violent overthrow of the United States government and the total destruction of the racist, capitalist...power structure."[12]

### Liberalism's relationship to the New Left

One of the factors that muted the New Left was that eventually even a good many American liberal intellectuals turned against it. Certain individuals and parts of the "liberal coalition" had been against it all along. And yet, one of the more important facts to note in an analysis of the New Left, especially in a book about liberal thought, is the liberal intellectual culture's complicity with it. (The word "complicity" is not value-free and is not intended to be.)

The New Left received vitally important institutional support from liberal sources. It is likely that without this support the movement would have been severely limited.

We have seen how the Council of Churches put up $100,000 in Rochester to support Saul Alinsky's activities. Jerry Rubin boasted about how much financial support he was receiving: "After some of my speeches on campus, the students would close down the school with a strike, or blow up the ROTC building, or riot. Meanwhile, I was being paid $500 to $1,000 from the official student organization for giving the speech." I myself resigned from the Wichita State University Forum Board Committee in protest over its funding of an on-campus showing of revolutionary films featuring Angela Davis. In July 1968, Paul Marx told the readers of *The New Republic* that many of the "community action organizations" established by the Johnson administration as part of its War on Poverty "have on their payrolls radicals who advocate tearing down the whole society."[13]

But even more important was the moral support given by the liberal intellectual culture. This is readily seen in *The New Republic*. Following the seizure of the chief administration building on the Berkeley campus in December 1964, a *New Republic* editorial applauded the students. In July 1965, D. W. Brogam reported in a review of Michael Harrington's *The Accidental Century* that "Mr. Harrington is afraid not that we will be faced with a revolutionary situation, but that we won't, that the unemployed...will be...docile." After *The New Republic* ran a series of "personal statements" by "young radicals" in late 1965, Harrington commented that "whatever their shortcomings, the New Leftists hold out the hope for a renewal of American social criticism and action." In January 1967, Stanley Kauffmann wrote that "a good deal of the Young Generation's behavior is admirable and promising, much of it is at least comprehensible, and most of it is preferable to the torpor that prevailed in the Eisenhower years."[14]

The first strong denunciation in *The New Republic* appeared in an editorial on August 5, 1967, which said that "'Burn this town down' is the shout of the angry, exalted young Brown Shirt ...it leads to madness." Thereafter, we might expect to have seen a consistent opposition by the editors to at least the more extreme part of the New Left. This is especially so since the editors clearly perceived the danger; in July 1968, they said that "as in the pre-Civil War period, the American political system may not be able to withstand the strains put upon it. One can foresee the possibility that our major parties may again be incapable of containing violent pressures from below, that the government elected in November may be impotent and our internal conflicts irreconcilable."[15]

Despite this awareness, it was just two months later, in September 1968, that Kauffmann made his statement about a decision by the Canadian Broadcasting System being a "fucking disgrace," language that must certainly have been intended to show his and *The New Republic*'s "solidarity" with the very movement the editors saw threatening civil war. In the following issue, an article by Marcus Raskin bitterly denounced Democratic liberalism as having "transformed the society into an authoritarian one which stood on the legs of the labor bosses, the large corporations, the military and the city bosses."[16]

In April 1969, an editorial described the seizure of University Hall at Harvard. It followed the usual line of blaming the police for the ensuing violence, saying they "went beserk." A few pages later, an author wrote that "even when they strike out in apparently un-American directions – tribal living and doped mysticism ... – they do so in the pioneer spirit of discovery." Then a couple of weeks later the editors supplied their apologia for "the decision of black militants at Cornell to bring guns into Willard Straight Hall," saying, as we saw earlier, that they "had their reasons for thinking they might need to defend themselves...."[17]

Even after the editors began to denounce the revolutionary movement with somewhat more genuine feeling, as they finally did in November 1969, and they said that "those who preach or practice violence in this country are nihilists and fools," they were willing to run an advertisement for *Ramparts* in April 1970 that said that "the students at Santa Barbara who burned down the Bank of America probably did more to save the environment than all of the Teach-Ins and Survival Fairs put together." And in 1972 the editors were appalled that "there is persuasive evidence that the FBI undertook a massive surveillance program to keep tabs on most of the dissident political groups...." They thought it reprehensible that the main society should protect itself, even by surveillance, against what they themselves had thought was an impending civil war.[18]

### The host culture

We cannot fully understand the New Left, however, unless we fathom the weakness of the main culture. The series of books of which this is the final volume has largely been an effort to explain that weakness. I have elaborated upon both the peculiar nature of modern intellectual culture and upon the essential "infancy" and "immaturity" of humanity even during the modern age. As I grow older, I see nothing to contradict the analysis I made of that immaturity in *Understanding the Modern Predicament*. (I would remind the reader, of course, that I hold to a mixed, rather than to an Augustinian or Hobbesian negative, view of human nature.)

One of the more important weaknesses of American society during the period was, of course, the continuing failure of a "bourgeois" culture to generate a sufficient intellectual culture to (a) give its fundamental values a voice and (b) provide it with the constructive criticism that it will always need. It is this void that created the "silent majority." Tens of millions of people had no bent toward, nor means of, articulating ideas in support of American society during the years of the onslaught.

This gave rise, in turn, to several additional phenomena: One was that, hearing only the exaggerated drumbeat of the Left, a great many average Americans, including especially the young, grew spongy in their commitment to values that have been of the utmost importance to the classical liberal underlay that has sustained American freedom. Another was the mechanism I have already mentioned: that the New Left could count on an articulated moralistic response from the media and academia even for the worst outrages, while the representatives of the main society were subject to derision.

A third effect was the impact on American foreign policy and the conduct of the war in Vietnam. Fifty-five thousand young Americans died in a war for which the true purpose, which was anti-Communist, was not articulated even by American presidents until it was almost over. It was the division internally within the United States, and not the prowess of the North Vietnamese on the battlefield, that caused the United States to lose the war. (I say "lose the war" advisedly. The delay from 1945 to 1975 that the French and American resistance caused in Communist expansion almost certainly prevented a victory by Communism throughout Southeast Asia. It was during that period that the Indonesians overthrew a Communist-dominated regime, and the delay gave Thailand and India many valuable years of respite. Unfortunately, the "dominoes" did fall in Laos and Cambodia, leading to a holocaust which in terms of percentage of the population outdid the enormities of Hitler, Stalin and Mao. When liberals even today point out how "the dominoes didn't fall" after the collapse of South Vietnam, seeking thereby to prove how right they were in their condemnation of the war as an unnecessary intervention by the United States, they are guilty of the most unspeakable moral obtuseness, since they are wilfully ignoring this holocaust.)

The counter-culture in particular drew upon the hedonism, the moral shallowness and the lack of roots in twentieth century America. It was a strange mixture, this combination of drugs and sex, overweening moral sensibility and outrage, and pretentious mouthing of Leftist cliches and slogans. These were people to whom it meant nothing that the raised clenched fist had been a Communist symbol in countless parts of the world for half a century or that the slogan "All power to the people" was a direct pick-up of the Leninist slogan "All power to the soviets." It turned out that shallow hedonists make bad revolutionaries. What is very little acknowledged is that they also make bad citizens of a free society.

This is the mentality that has lent itself to the many fads of ideology. Nothing has been able to stand in their way, thus verifying Alexis de Tocqueville's observation a century and a half ago that there is nothing quite so omnipresent and suffocating as majority opinion in a democracy. The fads have been both large and small, and have usually been formed of a mixture of fatuous ideology and hedonistic self-interest. While a fad is "in" there is no truth that can be put up against it; everything outside it is written off as outmoded and, worse, as a sign of bigotry. (It is now considered "sexist" – a new slogan – to use the pronoun "he" to designate a person of unspecified sex.) It is no wonder that Ben Wattenberg could exclaim in 1970: "Crisis. Crisis. Crisis. That so very much of this is preposterous...should come as no real surprise to those who follow the fads of crisis in America."[19]

The spring of 1970, when Wattenberg made his remark, was no doubt among the worst periods for it. But in general we can say that we breathe a neurotic atmosphere. Public discourse is reduced to what will fit the fixation of the moment, and the media so penetrate our lives with all of this that the content of private existence is profoundly discolored. What is worse, the great positive values of high civilization are all but forgotten in the ubiquitous wash of mediocre music, mediocre theater, mediocre television, mediocre writing, incomprehensible art. Technique is everywhere valued, but without aesthetic judgment. The intellectual culture's anti-bourgeois values come together with the public's disregard for taste to produce, what? – the zoot-suiter of the 1940's, the beads and bell-bottoms of the 1960's, the shaved temples of the punk-rockers of the 1980's, and a public that smiles indulgently upon it all.

Our affluence makes possible an ever-increasing quantity of everything, and productions of all kinds are done on a scale that would have dazzled earlier generations. Fortunately, a lot of good work, and even some great and memorable work, is done as part of the sheer volume. It would be an amazing fact that would itself require explanation if so many millions of people, trained so highly in technique, were not to allow some real sensibility to shine through a certain fraction of the time. And, too, there are individuals who separate themselves from the flood. It is not, however, the good or the great work that sets the tone of contemporary culture.

This vacuity translates, too, into a willingness of Americans to allow themselves to be "used" by movements that they do not bother to understand. Irving Howe spoke of "a kind of complicity [that is] set up between the outraged and/or amused urban middle class and the rebels of sensation." This lays the foundation for political and social instability such as we saw during the 1960's and could see again.[20]

## The continuing residuals and effects of the New Left

Virtually all the factors I have discussed are present, some of them at a muted level, today. The great question is what is happening within the intellectual culture. The alienation still burns within a good many, especially among the academic Marxists, but in the 1980's the overall tone was quieter, more accepting, than it was at any time in my lifetime. (It is a mistake to think the intellectual culture was quiescent in the 1950's; it wasn't. It burned with alienation while I was on the Colorado University campus between 1951 and 1954.)

The New Left's slashing attacks on the "Establishment" and on "interest-group liberalism," together with the "do your own thing" combination of hedonism and anarchist ideology, set the stage, paradoxically enough, for liberalism's loss of faith in itself, for the questioning of the assumption that a government program is the solution to all problems, and for the success of conservatism in the 1980's (a success that was probably delayed by Watergate). What no amount of conservative warning and exhortation could accomplish, the New Left brought about in a flood. It would be too much to say that the Reagan and Bush administrations were "residuals" of the New Left, but they are certainly among the "effects."

The main "residuals" we see today are cultural. There has been an evangelical Christian movement against pornography, say, but it has barely been able to dent the public's apparent desire to acquiesce in, and even to encourage, the cultural slide. Dress and entertainment continue to show the influences of the 1960's.

There are conservative authors who purport to see a great conservative intellectual resurgence. If there is one, I (writing first in 1986 and then in 1991) do not see it, other than marginally. And the failure of conservatism, most particularly in the form of a renewed classical liberalism, to light a fire in the minds especially of the young means that the problematic nature of "bourgeois civilization" remains uncorrected. Without intellectual ferment on behalf of the values of the main society, the Reagan presidency is almost certainly bound to have been an interregnum based upon circumstance and a remarkable personality. Where we are going is an open question formed out of the weakness of both the Left and the Right and the indifference of a practical, life-absorbed people, a people that is rapidly changing in its composition. This is a theme upon which I have touched before, but which deserves reiteration.

During the years since the first edition of this book appeared, liberalism's multiculturalist attack on mainstream society has grown in force. It is especially dangerous since long-term demographic trends offer to strengthen it during the years ahead. The alienation may yet win by swamping out the culture it hates so much.

## NOTES

[1] New Republic, September 12, 1964, p. 13.
[2] New Republic, September 21, 1968, p. 42.
[3] New Republic, November 7, 1970, p. 17.
[4] Jerry Rubin, *Do It!* (NY: Simon and Schuster, 1970), pp. 55, 93, 97, 107.
[5] Malcolm Cowley, *Exile's Return: a Narrative of Ideas* (New York: W. W. Norton & Company, Inc., 1934), pp. 148, 151.
[6] Kenneth Coutts-Smith, *Dada* (New York: E. P. Dutton and Co., Inc., 1970), pp. 22, 116-117.
[7] New Republic, September 18, 1935, p. 146; New Republic, January 5, 1948, p. 24; New Republic, January 22, 1966, p. 24.
[8] Herbert Marcuse, *An Essay on Liberation* (Boston: Beacon Press, 1969), p. 62; Robert Theobald, *An Alternative Future for America* (Chicago: Swallow Press, 1968), pp. 47, 48; New Republic, April 20, 1968, p. 13; New Republic, October 31, 1964, p. 85.
[9] Tom Hayden, *Rebellion in Newark* (NY: Random House, 1967), pp. 24-25.
[10] New Republic, March 28, 1970, p. 5; New Republic, April 25, 1970, p. 30.
[11] New Republic, September 19, 1970, pp. 12, 19.
[12] Lee Lockwood, *Conversation with Eldridge Cleaver/Algiers* (New York: Delta Books, 1970), p. 54.
[13] Jerry Rubin, *Growing (Up) at 37* (New York: Warner Books, 1976), p. 90; New Republic, July 6, 1968, p. 31.
[14] New Republic, March 27, 1965, p. 6; New Republic, July 24, 1965, p. 26; New Republic, February 19, 1966, p. 20; New Republic, January 28, 1967, p. 26.
[15] New Republic, August 5, 1967, p. 6; New Republic, July 27, 1968.
[16] New Republic, Sept. 21, 1968, p. 42; New Republic, Sept. 28, 1968, p. 17.
[17] New Republic, April 26, 1969, pp. 6, 21; New Republic, May 3, 1969, p. 5.
[18] New Republic, November 15, 1969, p. 9; New Republic, April 18, 1970, p. 5; New Republic, January 29, 1972, p. 11.
[19] New Republic, April 4, 1970, p. 18.
[20] Irving Howe, *Steady Work: Essays in the Politics of Democratic Radicalism, 1953-1966* (New York: Harcourt, Brace & World, Inc., 1966), p. 59.

## CHAPTER FIFTEEN
## Liberalism and International Affairs

In this discussion of liberalism's thinking about international affairs, we will again need to differentiate between the thinking of the liberal intellectual culture and the positions taken by liberal presidents. Here, as elsewhere, liberal politicians have stayed much closer to majority opinion. Liberal thought, as such, has been much further to the left.

So far as the intellectual culture is concerned, it would be surprising if its outlook on world affairs had not been formed from the same elements as its ideology in general. The liberal intellectual culture has been as far to the left in its attitudes toward foreign policy as it has toward other things.

True, there has been an anti-Communist wing within liberalism. In the July 1947 issue of *Foreign Affairs* George F. Kennan enunciated the containment doctrine, which was behind the policy of most liberal presidents and politicians during the Cold War. American organized labor, one of the elements in the liberal coalition, has for the most part been adamantly anti-Communist. Senator Henry Jackson, who had strong ties to organized labor, is often cited as one of a number of liberal leaders who have been strongly anti-Communist. It is especially worth noting that the Americans for Democratic Action (ADA) was established right after World War II precisely as a vehicle for liberals who did not want to collaborate with Communists.

The main thrust of the liberal intellectual culture, however, has been much further to the left. The extreme leftward orientation of liberal thought on international affairs has a chilling effect on dispassionate discussion. A direct statement, all in one place, of the liberal intellectual culture's positions will almost certainly shock most Americans. It will even shock liberals themselves; consistently with the dissimulation that is so basic to their posture, liberals instinctively prefer (and have come to expect) that such views will be expressed so transparently only in liberalism's "in-house" literature. To defer to that preference, however, would keep us from completing our study of liberal thought.

Because the formative influences of domestic and world attitudes have been the same, we can expect the main contours to be:
- That liberal thought has held to a fundamentally Left-oriented point

of view toward the world at large, but without continuing after World War II to see the Soviet Union as a champion. This included an ever-recurring tolerance toward Communist regimes (including even the Soviet Union). Exceptions occurred if in a given case a regime did something quite recent to outrage liberals or to make that tolerance more than ordinarily impolitic.
• That the outlook has reflected the divisions that have plagued the Left. In foreign affairs this has appeared mainly in the tension between the traditions of pacifism-neutrality and of Progressive-style, idealistic internationalism.
• That liberal thought has been ready, so far as Europe and the Third World are concerned, to see value in democratic socialism, in "non-alignment" and "neutralism," and even in Communist regimes when they fit into the pattern of "pluralistic Communism." (The latter refers to the pattern that emerged with Tito in Yugoslavia and with the Chinese after their split with Moscow.)
• That the thinking has included a variety of alienations: against the residuals of Western influence as they have appeared in the form of the last vestiges of nineteenth century colonialism; against non-Communist and non-socialist regimes whenever they have seemed especially vulnerable to criticism; and, perhaps most important of all, against American policy whenever that policy reflected, as it so often did, an anti-Communist purpose.

## Several conceptual elements

1. Probably the most important conceptual element in the main line of liberal thought about international affairs after World War II was its conviction that for one reason or another Communism was not a significant problem. Although "Russian nationalism," seen as acting under the rubric of Communism, was seen as something that should be countered, Communism as an expansionist totalitarian ideology was considered more of a phantom of conservatives' imaginations.

This premise lay behind many of the statements about Vietnam. In 1971, Senator Frank Church said that "the threat of Communism in the third world is exaggerated...for many countries radical revolution is the only real hope...." Two years earlier, *The New Republic* had quoted Walter Lippmann as saying that a Communist South Vietnam "won't make very much of a difference." In 1972, the editors wrote that "no considerations of national interest or moral imperative required the United States to designate the Vietcong and Hanoi as an enemy and to move militarily against them." A short time before the collapse of South

Vietnam in 1975, TRB was able to write that "if Congress cuts off aid hostilities probably will stop. Communists will win. How bad is that?"[1]

We know, of course, the overwhelmingly favorable liberal perception of the Soviet Union during the three decades after the Bolshevik Revolution. This perception suffered some very real shocks in the late 1930's, but it was substantially rehabilitated during World War II. The Cold War that followed put a damper on that enthusiasm, and an anti-Communist side to liberal thought was manifested in the Americans for Democratic Action. But the enthusiasm continued, for those further left, under Henry Wallace's leadership. In December 1946 – at the highest point of Stalin's Gulags – the extent of Wallace's self-deception was revealed by his statement that "today democracy is a universal ambition. The Soviet government no longer prides itself on the Dictatorship of the Proletariat."[2]

The persistence of this illusion among a great many liberals is shown by Louis J. Halle's observation in 1960 that "the simple geographic image of the expanding Communist 'empire'...is too simple. (Is it one 'empire'? Does it include Yugoslavia?...China?)." In 1973, Stanley Karnow said about the 1950's and early 1960's that "Eisenhower and Kennedy were battling against monolithic communism long after the Sino-Soviet dispute proved that *the international Red menace was a myth*" (emphasis added). In May 1977, President Jimmy Carter declared that "we are now free of that *inordinate fear of Communism* which once led us to embrace any dictator" (emphasis added).[3]

2. One consequence has been the double standard that has existed in liberal attitudes toward Nazism and fascism, which were correctly perceived as despicable and expansionist, and Communism.

To refresh ourselves about the early background, we should compare the attitudes toward the two systems in such a year as 1933. This was the year in which in Soviet Russia variously estimated millions of peasants were deliberately starved to death to overcome the opposition to the collectivization of agriculture. *The New Republic* ignored the slaughter. Within a few months after that dreadful winter of 1932-33, however, it was moved to condemn "Hitler's anti-Jewish campaign, which is on the whole the most uncivilized episode in modern history." The condemnation of Hitler was, of course, justified even though Hitler's anti-Jewish efforts were just in their beginning phase; but the selective perception, which has shielded Communism from being similarly condemned, must be understood as a central fact about the liberal intellectual culture's view of the world. (Photographs of the starving peasants would no doubt have created just as stark as image as the later photographs showing emaciated inmates at Auschwitz.)⁴

I have commented previously that the 1930's "provides a 'window' into liberal thinking." A candid explanation of the double standard, which will be helpful in understanding attitudes expressed throughout the fifty years that followed, was provided in a *New Republic* editorial in 1935. The editors said that "those who are more tolerant of the Soviet Union than of Nazi Germany or Fascist Italy are so because they sympathize with the main objectives and the chief policies of the workers' republic...To attempt to establish a classless society...is quite a different thing from enforcing industrial autocracy based on private ownership of the means of production." This explanation was given in response to a letter from William Henry Chamberlin in which he had demanded to know: "What is the background for the double standard of morals that not a few American and British radicals have consciously or unconsciously set up, one for Russia, one for the rest of the world?"⁵

The editors had more to say about this in late 1936: "Those individuals go seriously astray who announce that they are opposed to the dictatorships both of fascism and communism. The fascist dictatorship is an end in itself; the dictatorship of the proletariat is a means to a very different end." They spoke of Communism's being only in its "transition stage." A year later, Matthew Josephson added that "to liken the labor dictatorship of Stalin to the more opportunistic dictatorships of Mussolini or Hitler reveals a crudeness of judgment...."⁶

In 1943, a *New Republic* editorial praised the editors of *Time* magazine for an article about the Soviet Union. "The editors do not let what happened to the kulaks [peasants] overbalance the fact that Russia solved one of her gravest problems by collectivizing agriculture." Again we see the counterpoise of an extreme insensitivity toward Stalin's crimes and condemnation of Hitler's; a few months later, an editorial said that "the greatest tragedy of modern times is the murder of Jews and other victims by Hitler."⁷ In 1946, as we emerged into the postwar era, Joseph and Stewart Alsop wrote that "only a fool could fail to recognize the difference between the fascist system and the Soviet system, which though brutal in method, is entirely civilized in its basic concepts."⁸

In 1949, E. H. Carr wrote in *The New Republic* that Stalin's "own contribution to collectivization was the courage, determination and ruthlessness with which the policy was carried out and without which it could not have succeeded." It is hard to imagine similar virtues – about policies that killed millions of people – being attributed to Adolf Hitler.⁹

In 1956, Eric Bentley wrote that "Bertolt Brecht...was a Communist, and I am anti-Communist...yet I had the experience of being his political enemy and his personal friend...." We should ask ourselves whether a similar relationship would have been tolerable for Bentley if Brecht had been a Nazi. Again, it reflects the double standard.[10]

In 1961, after Patrice Lumumba's assassination, a *New Republic* editorial said that "Lumumba...was a very human African national whose association with the Soviet Union was pragmatic rather than ideological." We can recall no similar rationalization justifying Vidkun Quisling's collaboration with Nazism in Norway.[11]

In 1963, Graham Greene reported that "the huge crowd that gathered before the monument to Marti to hear Castro's three-hour speech on July 26 was not the regimented or hypnotized crowd that used to greet Hitler."[12]

This attitude certainly lay behind *The New Republic*'s 1967 editorial that argued that "fortunately, Mr. [Lyndon] Johnson is willing not to let his Vietnam obsession get in the way of better relations and increased trade with Russia, even though Russia is helping arm people we're fighting."[13]

3. The result of this abstracting-away of the problem of Communism was that liberal thought *tended to interpret the world in pre-World War I terms*. Instead of a world beset by an expansionist totalitarian ideology, the world was seen as one of contending nation-states, of national suspicions and jealousies, of arms races arising out of nothing more substantial than provincialism and jingoistic posturing. The solutions that seemed applicable to such a world were obvious: more cultural exchanges, more mechanisms for "improving understanding," the expectation that an international organization such as the United Nations should have been able to serve as a truly meaningful instrument for peace, the pursuit of arms limitation treaties, and the like.

These would have made real sense if the pre-World War I syndrome had indeed been the central problem. If, however, expansionist totalitarianism was the overriding source of difficulty, creating a "protracted conflict" that was fought, in effect, on a worldwide scale at a number of different levels, these things trivialized and misdirected the response to it. Constantly to urge "detente" and "improved understanding" with regard to a system that all the while was subverting every vulnerable society that was not already within the circle of its totalitarian ideology was to act on illusion, not reality.

4. As we saw in our discussion of the origins of the New Left, a radical peace movement has long been in existence, fed partly by the Left and partly by the "peace churches." This has stressed pacifism and neutrality. It is worth noting that this peace movement is at its core

something very different from the messianic "Progressive-style" liberalism that favors foreign intervention if it approves the particular cause. For most purposes, these positions overlapped during the Cold War, since neither wanted America to be the leader of an adamant anti-Communism.

The distinction between the two lines of thinking was tellingly apparent, however, with regard to the response to the Nazi threat in the late 1930's. This has been the subject of James J. Martin's two-volume *American Liberalism and World Politics, 1931-1941*. I will illustrate it simply by taking the example of *The New Republic*'s stance toward Brazil in 1938 and 1939 when Brazil was threatened with a Nazi take-over. American policymakers were considering an intervention to prevent that from happening.

The Left was acutely aware of the despicable nature of Nazism and of its dangers to other peoples. It harbored no illusion about it comparable to that which it has held about Communism. If we were to go on the hypothesis that illusion has been the main obstacle to a willingness to support anti-totalitarian action, we might expect that the liberal intellectual culture would have supported an anti-Nazi intervention in Brazil. An intervention would have been consistent with the views of non-pacifist liberals, as we see from the fact that in 1915, before it became pacifist, *The New Republic* called for American intervention in Mexico because of internal conditions there.[14]

By 1938, however, *The New Republic* had for several years adhered to a pacifist-neutralist position. The point worth noting here is that *The New Republic* remained consistent with that stance even in the face of Nazi expansion. The editors opposed an anti-Nazi intervention in Brazil.[15]

We know from this episode and from substantial other evidence that the pacifist-neutralist tradition has been powerful within liberal thought. It would accordingly be a mistake to think that the illusion about Communism has been the only source of liberal thought's apparent weakness in the face of Communism.

5. This mix of ingredients has led liberal thought to welcome the prospect of a world in which most of the nations would be either democratic socialist (and neutral toward what liberal thinkers see as primarily a struggle between two contending superpowers) or "independently Communist." What to conservatives is unthinkable was to liberal thought a fully acceptable solution to the world's post-World War II plight.

It became clear quite early that liberal thought would welcome the spread of democratic socialism. In September 1945, a *New Republic* editorial said that "the scene is being set for a great experiment in democratic socialism, perhaps covering all of Europe, alongside the differently oriented Soviet experiment." In 1947, Michael Straight wrote that "a great democratic, socialist force in the world today could isolate Soviet nationalism and American reaction. It could expand into a world society, bringing peace." In 1957, an editorial criticized the anti-socialist policy that underlay American aid to India. In 1961, TRB wrote that "we bow down to the sacredness of private property and yet almost certainly an adequate revolution in Latin America must stand private property on its head."[16]

At the same time, liberal thought saw great value in the "pluralization" of Communism through movements and regimes that were not strictly subject to Moscow's direction. It was even argued that the creation of a Communist regime, such as in Angola, could be a good thing, provided it was "independent." In January 1950, the editors of *The New Republic* urged the American people to "distinguish between Communist-type revolutions and Kremlin-directed revolutions."[17]

In 1968, TRB wrote that "the theory was that there was a global communist conspiracy – but this evaporated when Moscow and Peking split." In 1977, Hans J. Morgenthau referred to "the polycentric character of Communism" and said that "the real issue...is not whether a certain government professes and practices Communism, but to what extent a government's foreign policy supports the foreign policies of the Soviet Union or of other governments hostile to the United States."[18]

This thinking was pursued by Zbigniew Brzezinski, the principal architect of President Jimmy Carter's foreign policy. In 1962, Brzezinski argued that containment and liberation "have ceased to be relevant. Both were based on the premise that there is a united Soviet bloc." He called for a policy of "differentiated amity and hostility [to] consolidate differences within the Communist world." During the Carter presidency, Stanley Hoffmann wrote that "Brzezinski saw the world as far too diverse and complex to be managed by a Kissingerian balance-of-power system." This worldview explains Andrew Young's actions as ambassador to the United Nations during the Carter administration.[19]

The third aspect was liberalism's readiness to see vast portions of the globe declare their "neutrality." So much of the world was included in this that, if the liberal intellectual culture's wishes had been fulfilled, the United States would have come to stand alone, stripped of allies.

In 1950, Michael Straight argued that "if Nehru could help to bring China out of the Soviet orbit and into an Asiatic bloc, the neutrality of Asia might not be too high a price to pay...." In 1957, the editors wrote that "what is needed, basically, is...a new Asian policy, one that does not assume that 'neutralism' helps Communism." In 1958, they said that "the main reason for our loss of influence in the Middle East and Asia was the attempt to extend the alliance system to areas whose peoples did not feel threatened by Russia – the Baghdad pact and SEATO, followed by an interpretation of the Eisenhower Doctrine as something on which the Middle Eastern states had to declare 'for' or 'against.'"[20]

In 1958, George F. Kennan's "disengagement" proposal was discussed. It involved having the Soviet Union withdraw from Eastern Europe and the United States from Western Europe. *The New Republic* supported the proposal, calling for a Europe that would be both neutral and free of nuclear arms. Consistently with its serving as an intellectual clearing house for liberalism, which means that some articles were at odds with the journal's editorial positions, *The New Republic* included an article by Eugene V. Rostov in March 1959 that pointed out that "such a policy would shift the balance of power against us appallingly."[21]

In his book on Walter Lippmann, Hari N. Dam says that "in June 1960, Lippmann wrote an article urging a reappraisal of the policy of containment initiated under the Truman Doctrine... In view of the nuclear parity between the two [super]powers, the most prudent policy would be to promote neutrality among the peripheral states."[22]

Shortly after John F. Kennedy's inauguration, a 1961 editorial said that "Mr. Kennedy is espousing a new U.S. doctrine around which a new non-Communist coalition can be formed – the integrity of neutralism." Later that year, Denis Warner wrote that "there is nothing wrong with neutrality; it is no longer considered 'immoral.'"[23]

Meanwhile, the Soviet Union had sought to advance the movement toward "non-alignment." In 1967, Ernst Halperin wrote that "in 1956 Khrushchev sought to legitimize his new policy of encouraging 'non-alignment.'" He even went so far as to say that Khrushchev had considered Castro's victory in Cuba a "bitter setback" to Khrushchev's larger strategy of seeking the neutralization of all of South America.[24]

In 1962, *The New Republic* called for settling the Vietnam War by neutralizing South Vietnam. This took the form in September 1963 of a call for "uniting the country" *under Ho Chi Minh's rule*, at which time "he could become another Tito" [i.e., independent Communist].[25]

They advocated all of this despite the fact that "non-alignment" soon came to bear the same relationship to Soviet Communism as "fellow-travelling" did during the 1930's. In 1961, Walter Z. Laqueur and Alfred Sherman described a meeting of the "non-aligned" countries held in the (Communist) city of Belgrade: "For many American well-wishers of the newly independent countries of Africa and Asia, the meeting of the 'non-aligned' in Belgrade came as a shock...Tito's stand at the conference, which was the most obdurately anti-Western on all questions, should serve as a reminder that Yugoslavia is a Communist state...The Cuban performance lent further weight to the belief that for all practical purposes the country's leaders at present are wholly identified with the Communist bloc and that their adherence to the flexible principle of non-alignment is a matter of temporary expedience."[26]

A 1958 *New Republic* editorial described Nasser's ostensible "neutrality" in Egypt: "We are neutralist but we fervently hope that the Soviet bloc will defeat the imperialist West...We are not Communists; we only want to establish a popular democratic society on the pattern of Mao's China." Another editorial, in 1971, described the scene as "cheers and dancing in the aisles of the General Assembly" when finally Communist China was given a seat and the Republic of China was ousted.[27]

All the while, Moscow and Peking were each taking advantage of this moral and intellectual weakness by treating Asia, Africa and Latin America as a "soft underbelly" for Communist subversion. Moscow worked to build up its traditional bases for revolution among the workers, seeking to tie its worldwide network to Soviet foreign policy; Peking nurtured those who sought "revolution now." In 1962, the *New Republic* reported that "in the last few years the Chinese have trained thousands of Spanish and Portuguese agents who have traveled all over Latin America." In 1967, Bjorn Kumm spoke of "North Vietnam, where the hard core Bolivian guerrillas were sent for training...." Kumm said that "it is known that [Che] Guevara appeared at a secret meeting in Prague in early May 1965...[with] a group of Bolivians who were later to become the nucleus of the guerrilla force." We know, of course, that Guevara was later killed fighting as a guerrilla leader in Bolivia.[28]

6. An important part of all this received growing attention in conservative circles starting in the mid-1980's. It is that one of the premises of the worldview has been that there was a moral equivalency between the Soviet Union and the United States.

In light of all that I have covered, it should probably be considered an improvement, from the United States' point of view, even to be considered morally equivalent to the Soviet Union. There were many years during which the world intellectual culture gave the Soviet Union far the better of it.

Nevertheless, the fact that "moral equivalency" could be entertained as a notion after the world had seen the depths of the Soviet dream demonstrates how skewed such a perception is. That after the purges, the Gulags, the crushing of Hungary and Czechoslovakia and Afghanistan, it was still possible for the Soviet Union to have any moral stature at all is perhaps the best example I know of of what Ayn Rand called "moral counterfeiting." It is another manifestation of the attitudes I have been tracing. At the same time, to place the United States on a moral par with the Soviet Union, even at what is for the Soviet Union an inflated level, is a function of the abiding hatred that lies at the heart of the world Left.

The concept of "moral equivalency" was used to disarm any anti-Communist action or attitude. In 1960, TRB wrote that "we can't abide the thought of Cuba going Communist; doesn't that help give us an idea of the way Red China feels about Capitalist Quemoy and Matsu and Formosa?" Then in 1961 TRB wrote that "the U.S. has been complaining of the Soviets' recent airlift into Laos, a country into which we ourselves dumped a third of a million dollars, nearly all military." The editors added to the theme a couple of months later: "The President is correct when he says that the Communists 'send arms...to every troubled area.' But it is only part of the truth. For this is what the United States has been doing since the start of the Cold War...." In 1970, the editors argued that "as long as this country keeps 400,000 or even 200,000 troops in South Vietnam...it cannot convincingly claim that the Russians have no right to put 8,000 or even 12,000 troops in Egypt."[29]

7. These attitudes led to bitter criticism of all anti-Communist efforts. It is a mistake to think that the criticism arose mainly out of the circumstances of a given case. Jeane Kirkpatrick was electrifying with her speech to the 1984 Republican National Convention in which she denounced those "who always blame America first." She put her finger on one of the many aspects of the ideological syndrome I am describing.

8. An extremely important part of all this was the way liberal thought reacted to revolutionary situations throughout the world. Because of its importance, this will be the subject of the next chapter.

9. There are a number of corollary issues, each significant in itself. One of these had to do with the often-mentioned "principle of non-intervention." Another had to do with what the American attitude should be toward non-Communist governments that were for one reason or another undesirable. (The questions of democracy and of "respect for 'human rights'" were rarely raised about Communist governments, so it has been non-Communist governments that, interestingly enough, have constituted the "universe of discourse" here.) A third pertains to what is derisively called "the domino theory."

Most liberal thought gravitated in the late 1930's to a position favoring the Allies' eventual war against Hitler; and we have seen that *The New Republic* favored intervention in other countries on moral or humanitarian grounds prior to 1920. But, with these as the main exceptions, the overwhelming refrain within liberal thought has been that there is no right to intervene in another country for any reason internal to that country. The international nature of the Communist problem has not been thought to make an overwise "internal" issue an "external" one.

A few examples of how the "principle of non-intervention" was applied will suffice: A *New Republic* editorial in 1927 criticized American domination of Nicaragua and the Phillipines, speaking of "American imperialism." In 1929, the editors were displeased that "the Monroe Doctrine has come to mean the 'right' of the United States to police the western hemisphere." Many years later, in 1961, TRB wrote that "the State Department ejaculated – 'Communism in this hemisphere is not negotiable.' What virtue! What stupidity! It means that we deny the sovereignty of Latin nations to choose their government." In 1965, the editors argued that "sending 25,000 American servicemen to the Dominican Republic violated the O.A.S. charter." In 1978, TRB called the DeConcini reservation to the Panama Canal treaty "arrogant" for "asserting the U.S. right to intervene after the year 2,000 to keep the canal open." In 1980, an editorial said that Americans should apologize to the Iranians for having interfered in Iran's affairs "to shore up a despotic regime." Liberals have roundly condemned the involvement of the Central Intelligence Agency in the overthrow of Salvador Allende in Chile to prevent the Communization that he was openly carrying out. The Reagan administration's invasion of Grenada after the Communist take-over there has been condemned.[30]

It would be misleading, though, to conclude that this represents a genuinely held principle of "non-intervention," except for liberals who are actually a part of the pacifist-neutralist tradition. We have already seen how in 1915 *The New Republic* criticized Woodrow Wilson's "hands-off" policy toward Mexico's turbulent internal situation. The editors argued that "an unalterable rule of non-intervention ignores the truth...that no country can in the long run be allowed to behave as it pleases without regard to the interests and standards of other nations." Later that same year, in connection with the Turks' massacre of the Armenians, they held that "the dogma that all governments are sovereign and that intervention is never justified...is of course an impossible doctrine...."[31]

It has mainly been hypocrisy, rather than a well-reasoned return to the principles that *The New Republic* stated in what I have just quoted, that has underlain liberalism's long-standing attack upon Apartheid in

South Africa and the attack by the Carter Administration on "human rights abuses" by non-Communist governments in several countries. Unless racial discrimination can be considered "external" in a way that Communism cannot, there is no basis, consistently with the pure principle of non-intervention that the liberal intellectual culture has espoused for so long, for the article by Ian Robertson and Phillip Whitten in an April 1968 issue of *The New Republic* entitled "The Olympics: Keep South Africa Out!" In 1980, Bernard-Henri Levy wrote passionately that "the time has come to reestablish in the world, in its most desolate corner, the principles of an entirely different internationalism: the internationalism of human rights and of help for the tortured." At least so far as non-Communist governments were concerned, but only as to them, the principle of non-intervention had been repudiated.[32]

Except with a few purists, principles such as "non-intervention" have been instruments of ideological convenience. I would be the last to suggest that hypocrisy is embraced exclusively by American liberalism; but we are foolish if we do not take into account the extent to which liberal thought has applied double standards.

"Non-intervention" is closely related to the second of the three areas that I am now discussing. This is the question of how the United States and the world community should react to "undesirable" regimes. We will see that here too there has been enormous inconsistency.

Immediately after Mao completed his conquest of the Chinese mainland in late 1949, *The New Republic* called for the United States to win back the "friendship of the Chinese people" by extending diplomatic recognition to the newly-created People's Republic of China and by engaging in trade. Again in 1958, and at various other times as well, the editors called for recognition of Red China and its admission to the United Nations. Obviously these attitudes were calculated not to take into account the holocaust that occurred under Mao (in which, according to *Time* magazine's report after Mao's death, a variously estimated 10 to 60 million Chinese were put to death following the Communist takeover) or the lack of democracy under his regime. The principle that called for ignoring such matters had been enunciated years before when *The New Republic* wrote that "we have opposed this policy of making diplomatic recognition the equivalent of moral approval...."[33]

This should be compared with Harold L. Ickes' position in 1949 that "Franco's Spain should not be admitted to the United Nations or the North Atlantic Pact unless it genuinely adheres to democratic principles." Over the years, liberal thought has applied a similar moral sensibility to Nationalist China, Rhodesia, South Africa, the Shah of Iran, the regime of the Greek colonels, the Pinochet government in post-Allende Chile, the Marcos regime in the Phillipines, and several others. It has amounted, of course, to a selective morality; but our purpose right now is to see how it raises havoc with the principle, often asserted, that moral considerations should not affect America's willingness to recognize, to trade with, and otherwise to share a world with a given regime.[34]

A thread of consistency did appear back in 1933 when *The New Republic* argued for the recognition of Hitler's regime, at which time it pointed out that the journal had always held that moral considerations should not stand in the way of recognizing Soviet Russia. We have already noted how *The New Republic* did hold consistently to a pacifist-neutralist position in 1938 about taking action against Nazis in Brazil, so we know that consistency is possible. But whether the position taken about recognition of Hitler in 1933 represented a true consistency, or merely a tactical one in light of the journal's passionate affinity for Soviet Russia at that time and desire for American recognition of its government, is a matter of conjecture. It would have been too directly self-contradictory to have argued opposing rationales in so brief a period.

The third point among those I am now discussing relates to the shifting positions on what liberals have called "the domino theory."

Liberal rhetoric often spoke of "the domino theory" in its criticisms of the Vietnam War, both during the war and since, and also in connection with the threats posed by Communism in South and Central America. The concern that a Communist victory in one place would threaten adjacent areas was made to sound far-fetched, a remote conjecture. This was accomplished by demoting the concern to the status of a "theory." An example occurred in 1970 when Salvador Allende took office in Chile with an openly announced program for Communizing the country. A *New Republic* editorial said that "the White House...put forward a new Latin-style domino theory, according to which Peru, Bolivia and Argentina... might be the next three countries to fall."[35]

Oddly, this rhetoric was accepted at face value in much public discussion, despite the fact that the concern that the "domino theory" reflected was a valid one. In several connections where there was no ideological reason to denigrate the concern, liberal thought has itself used the point – and has taken its validity for granted as a mere fact of common sense. In 1937, a *New Republic* editorial about Spain observed that "if Franco wins, the war-willing powers will be immensely encouraged for their next aggression." In 1967, the editors asked the readers to "imagine the world as it would have been had Israel lost on the battlefield or remained passive...The Middle East would have become an exclusive Soviet preserve." In 1980, an editorial said about the Soviet invasion of Afghanistan that it was not "by itself, that important. The danger is that for destabilizing – or actually attacking – neighboring areas that are important, specifically Pakistan and Iran." (Interestingly, the so-called "domino theory" was applied in these last two instances even to Communist expansion. I have never seen an explanation within liberal writing of why the "theory" is thought to make perfectly good sense in certain circumstances, but in others, such as in Southeast Asia and Central or South America, to be obviously stupid.)[36]

### Consequences of the worldview

The next chapter deals with "Liberalism and a World in Revolution." I will then discuss the consequences of the liberal worldview as they have been felt in a number of different countries. In the present chapter, I will mention only certain consequences that will not fit into that discussion. Needless to say, a brief space won't allow an attempt to be exhaustive.

A major result of the self-deception can be seen in America's failure to have fought World War II with political objectives in mind. We "won the war" but "lost the peace" in a way that was a disaster for hundreds of millions of people and the free world. Garet Garrett pointed to a startling fact: "When the Yalta Agreement was signed [in February 1945] the number of people in the Communist world was hardly more than 200 million. Five years later it was 800 million...."[37]

Our leftist-spawned illusions about Stalin's dictatorship were such that we forcibly returned a reported two million Russians to the Soviet Union at the end of the war. A review in *The New Republic* in 1978 said that "Nikolai Tolstoy's *The Secret Betrayal* may well be the most authoritative accounting of the monstrous repatriation to the Soviet Union of more than two million Russians living (mostly imprisoned) in the countries liberated by the western allies at the end of World War II."[38]

In Volume I of *The Gulag Archipelago*, Aleksandr Solzhenitsyn, who spent years in Stalin's labor camps, commented about this and other associated events: "In their own countries Roosevelt and Churchill are honored as embodiments of statesmanlike wisdom. To us, in our Russian prison conversations, their consistent shortsightedness and stupidity stood out as astonishingly obvious. How could they, in their decline from 1941 to 1945, fail to secure any guarantees whatever of the independence of Eastern Europe? How could they give away broad regions of Saxony and Thuringia in exchange for the preposterous toy of a four-zone Berlin, their own future Achilles' heel? And what was the military or political sense in their surrendering to destruction at Stalin's hands hundreds of thousands of armed Soviet citizens determined not to surrender? They say it was the price they paid for Stalin's agreeing to enter the war against Japan. With the atom bomb already in their hands, they paid Stalin for not refusing to occupy Manchuria, for strengthening Mao Tse-tung in China, and for giving Kim Il Sung control of half Korea!"[39]

Solzhenitsyn tells how the entire army of Russian soldiers under General Vlasov who had defected and had been fighting against the Red Army were tricked into thinking they were surrendering to the English when in fact they were being turned over to the Red Army.[40]

During World War II, Heinz H. F. Eulau wrote prolifically for *The New Republic* favoring a postwar domination of Eastern Europe by the Soviet Union. In April 1944, he wrote that "Soviet influence in future Balkan politics is natural...Those who raise the cry of 'Soviet imperialism' fail to understand that the overwhelming majority of the common people in the Balkans do not fear Soviet influence." In August 1944, he wrote that "Poland will be in close alliance with the USSR and form an integral part of the security system which the Soviet Union is building up in Eastern Europe under her hegemony." A month later, Jerome Davis told the journal's readers that "the Soviet Union wants to work with the rest of the world. In the postwar world she doesn't want to foist communism off on other nations...." In April 1945, a contributor with the initials E. L. P. spoke of "the Anglo-American Russia-haters [who] bewail the allegedly undemocratic lot of the Eastern European countries under the Soviet heel...." In July of the same year, the *New Republic*'s editors said that "the Russia-hating American press has long argued that once anybody got into the clutches of Soviet Russia, he was never again permitted to escape. For the record, let it be noted that this seems to be false so far as it concerns the Poles."[41]

The lack of geopolitical strategy within the Roosevelt administration reflected this outlook. A *New Republic* editorial in June 1945 told the story: "While Roosevelt was alive he acted as mediator between two stubborn men, Churchill and Stalin...who clashed...notably as to whether the Anglo-American invasion of Europe should be in the Balkans, as Churchill wished, through territory which the Russians regard as their sphere of influence, or through France." It was Stalin, not Churchill, who, with Roosevelt's decisive vote, won this argument. The decision in favor of Operation Overlord, the invasion of Normandy, consigned Eastern Europe to Soviet domination, since it was the occupation by the Red Army, even more than any decision made at Yalta, that determined the fate of those countries.[42]

In a 1957 book, Rexford Tugwell discussed the decision to invade Normandy rather than to attack through Eastern Europe: "The Americans were still wary of Churchill,... being fearful that he would soon begin, as usual, to find reasons for postponement...He did now suggest that going north to meet the Russian...drive somewhere in the Balkans would be a way of preventing future trouble in Europe." Tugwell said that "Marshall and Hopkins were his [Churchill's] active counters. Their acceptance of Russia as an ally was much more sincere than that of the British...."[43]

W. W. Rostow told about yet another facet of this strategic struggle in a book in 1960. He said that "the United States did not support Churchill's efforts in 1945 to seek Anglo-American victory in the race for Berlin and Prague or encourage his notion that Western troops withdraw to the occupation areas in Germany only when the Yalta provisions concerning the method of forming the Eastern European governments were actually carried out."[44] Senator Robert A. Taft observed that "our troops could have reached Berlin before the Russians if they had not been called back. We withdrew from Dresden and Leipsig, which we had already occupied. General Patton would have been in Prague the next day, but he was called back so that Czechoslovakia could surrender to Russian generals, and his own book shows that he was not pleased with the recall."[45]

After Eastern Europe fell into Stalin's grasp, *The New Republic* began the process (which in the next chapter we will see became part of an often-repeated cycle) of regretting it. In November 1945, the editors reported that "the Soviet government has exercised terrific pressure on the countries liberated by the Red Army – Rumania, Bulgaria, Yugoslavia, Hungary, Czechoslovakia, Poland and Austria –...It has used techniques of political control which are objectionable to democratic nations." But the editors asked, "Can it be blamed?...If we would share the [atomic] bomb with them..., our opposition to Russian-controlled governments in Eastern Europe might carry real weight." Even in late 1947, the best face was being put on things. *The New Republic* ran an article by Owen Lattimore, later of China fame, that said that "it may be that the Czechoslovakian Communists, heartily backed by the Soviet Communists, are giving a thorough trial run to a policy of suggesting, to the nation's neighbors, that socialism and eventual communism can be reached by an easy transition, with prosperity all along the way and without massacre or coercion."[46]

# NOTES

[1] New Republic, November 13, 1971, p. 13; New Republic, September 27, 1969, p. 8; New Republic, May 13, 1972, p. 8; New Republic, February 1, 1975, p. 2.

[2] New Republic, December 16, 1946, p. 789; New Republic, March 24, 1947, p. 12.

[3] New Republic, February 29, 1960, p. 14; New Republic, September 8, 1973, p. 18; New Republic, June 4, 1977, p. 8.

[4] New Republic, June 7, 1933, p. 84.

[5] New Republic, February 27, 1935, pp. 61, 77.

[6] New Republic, December 9, 1936, p. 160; New Republic, December 1, 1937, p. 107.

[7] New Republic, April 5, 1943, p. 428; New Republic, February 7, 1944, p. 164.

[8] New Republic, September 16, 1946, p. 322.

[9] New Republic, November 28, 1949, p. 21.

[10] New Republic, August 27, 1956, p. 19.

[11] New Republic, February 20, 1961, p. 6.

[12] New Republic, November 2, 1963, p. 17.

[13] New Republic, April 22, 1967, p. 4.

[14] New Republic, January 23, 1915, p. 7; see also New Republic, October 9, 1915, p. 245, regarding the massacre of the Armenians by the Turks.

[15] New Republic, February 9, 1938, p. 4; New Republic, December 7, 1938, p. 127; New Republic, November 22, 1939, p. 137.

[16] New Republic, September 3, 1945, p. 272; New Republic, December 29, 1947, p. 9; New Republic, September 23, 1957, p. 4; New Republic, May 8, 1961, p. 2.

[17] New Republic, January 23, 1950, p. 6.

[18] New Republic, January 20, 1968, p. 6; New Republic, January 22, 1977, p. 54.

[19] New Republic, March 26, 1962, pp. 13, 14; New Republic, July 29, 1978, p. 20.

[20] New Republic, November 20, 1950, p. 14; New Republic, June 24, 1957, p. 8; New Republic, June 2, 1958, p. 4.

[21] New Republic, January 6, 1958, p. 3; New Republic, March 2, 1959, p. 23.

[22] Hari N. Dam, *The Intellectual Odyssey of Walter Lippmann* (New York: Gordon Press, 1973), pp. 152-153.

[23] New Republic, April 3, 1961, p. 3; New Republic, September 25, 1961, p. 13.

[24] New Republic, November 27, 1961, p. 11.

[25] New Republic, March 12, 1962, p. 4; New Republic, December 15, 1962, p. 5; New Republic, September 14, 1963, p. 5.

[26] New Republic, September 25, 1961, p. 9.

[27] New Republic, March 10, 1958, p. 4; New Republic, November 6, 1971, p. 9.

[28] New Republic, January 29, 1962, p. 6; New Republic, Nov. 11, 1967, p. 15.

[29] New Republic, August 29, 1960, p. 2; New Republic, April 3, 1961, p. 2; New Republic, June 5, 1961, p. 4; New Republic, August 1, 1970, p. 5.

[30] New Republic, January 12, 1927, p. 203; New Republic, January 30, 1929, p. 286; New Republic, May 8, 1961, p. 2; New Republic, May 15, 1965, p. 1; New Republic, April 22, 1978, p. 2; New Republic, March 8, 1980, p. 6.

[31] New Republic, January 23, 1915, p. 7; New Republic, October 9, 1915, p. 245.

[32] New Republic, April 13, 1968, p. 12.

[33] New Republic, September 26, 1949, p. 6; New Republic, June 16, 1958, p. 4; New Republic, June 21, 1933, p. 138.

[34] New Republic, May 30, 1949, p. 15.

[35] New Republic, November 7, 1970, p. 9.

[36] New Republic, January 13, 1937, p. 315; New Republic, June 17, 1967, p. 1; New Republic, January 26, 1980, p. 8.

[37] Garet Garrett, *The American Story* (Chicago: Henry Regnery Company, 1955), p. 349.

[38] New Republic, December 1, 1978, p. 51.

[39] Aleksandr I. Solzhenitsyn, *The Gulag Archipelago* (New York: Harper & Row, 1974), Thomas P. Whitney, trans., Vol. I, pp. 259-260.

[40] Solzhenitsyn, *Gulag*, Vol. I, p. 259.

[41] New Republic, April 3, 1944, p. 462; New Republic, August 7, 1944, p. 157; New Republic, September 4, 1944, p. 277; New Republic, April 25, 1945, p. 555; New Republic, July 16, 1945, p. 59.

[42] New Republic, June 4, 1945, p. 771.

[43] Rexford G. Tugwell, *The Democratic Roosevelt* (Garden City: Doubleday & Company, Inc., 1957), pp. 621-622.

[44] W. W. Rostow, *The United States in the World Arena* (New York: Harper & Brothers, 1960), p. 184.

[45] Senator Robert A. Taft, *A Foreign Policy for Americans* (Garden City: Doubleday & Company, Inc., 1951), p. 54.

[46] New Republic, Nov. 5, 1945, p. 589; New Republic, Sept. 22, 1947, p. 7.

# CHAPTER SIXTEEN
## Liberalism and a World in Revolution

Enormous tragedy came to the world after 1917 from the fact that liberal thought, with regard to one country after another that came under attack from Communist revolution, followed a discernible pattern starting with illusion and ending with an admission of horror. The cycle was repeated many times. The ultimate recognition of the horror did not prevent the illusion that begins the cycle from being present again and again with regard to later Communist revolutions in other countries.

This chapter will review the positions of the liberal intellectual culture before, during and after the revolutionary challenges to Russia, Spain, Western Europe, Greece, China, Taiwan, Korea, Guatemala, Cuba, Guinea, the Dominican Republic, Vietnam, Chile, Rhodesia, Nicaragua, El Salvador, South Africa and Grenada. In several cases we will be able to see the playing out of the entire cycle. In others, such as where the revolution did not succeed or is still in progress, the situation will have lent itself to only part of the cycle.

By limiting my discussion to the countries and areas named, I do not mean to suggest that there have not been others. My primary concern, as it has been throughout this book, is to analyze and illustrate the ideological elements rather than to write an exhaustive history.

### Stages in the cycle of liberal response

Without caring to reach a round number for its own sake, I have identified ten related but separate components of the liberal intellectual culture's response to leftist revolutions as they have occurred throughout the world:

1. Most especially since World War II, the world Left, including the American liberal intellectual culture, has held many non-Communist countries in what we might call "simmering contempt." Accordingly, it would not be accurate to say that liberal thought has ever fully accepted the *status quo* within them. But it is significant that with others, at least until a revolution has gotten underway, the existing society and its government have been accepted, despite their imperfections, as normal parts of the world community.

Chiang Kai-shek and his government in China offer a good example.

In August 1943, a *New Republic* editorial praised Chiang as both a man of action and a thinker. "The meliorism of Thorstein Veblen and J. A. Hobson he finds in harmony," the editorial said, "with the best present tendencies in Chinese thought."[1]

2. After the revolutionary attack on a country has begun, the liberal attitude toward the country has changed to a dramatic condemnation. The existing regime has then been painted in the darkest colors. Those identified with the government and opposed to the revolution have been pictured as corrupt oligarchs whose repressions and violations of human rights have made them examples of unmitigated evil.

If we pursue the Chinese example a step further, we see that in May 1944, just a few months after the praise I have just quoted, *The New Republic*'s TRB began to talk about "the anti-democratic movement in China...the heavy censorship...the disregard of the tragedy of the poor" and another article spoke of "the autocratic, one-party rule of [Chiang's] Kuomintang." We know with hindsight that these were the opening volleys in what became a decades-long campaign of vilification that painted Chiang and the Kuomintang as reactionary and that continued long after Chiang and his army had retreated to Taiwan.[2]

3. In casting the existing government in this light, liberal thought has abandoned the cultural relativity that it has used in so many other connections. The regime has been judged not in the context of its own society, with its unique history and conditions, but by an ideal standard.

Even more importantly, the regime has been judged without regard to the fact that it has by that time become embroiled in combatting riots, anarchy and organized revolution under what have inevitably been conditions of internal war. Again with regard to China, the effects of many years of war and inflation upon the Chiang Kai-shek government were ignored. In a perceptive comment, Freda Utley observed that "to ascribe the defeat of the Chinese National Government to its 'corrupt and reactionary' character is to beg the question. What is required is an examination of the causes which led to the frustration of the great national renaissance led by the Kuomintang in the 1920's and 1930's...It was useless to expect that an economically backward country, exhausted from an eight-year war with Japan and currently involved in an undercover war with Russia, could, almost overnight, set up a 'democratic' government. Add to these drawbacks the fact that China had no past experience of representative government."[3]

South Vietnam provides another example. The distortions imposed upon the society by the systematic assassination of thousands of village chiefs and other leaders were never considered. In June 1961, President

Kennedy spoke of 4,000 civilian officials having been assassinated in the preceding twelve months – a horrendous fact, if we think about it. The statistics about the dead might briefly be recited, but then the successors of the dead leaders were themselves condemned as venal and unrepresentative. In the same month that Kennedy told of the assassinations, an article in *The New Republic* accused the South Vietnamese government of "lies and fakery," of being "undemocratic" and of using "connivance and force to prolong its life." The unspoken assumption was that such a bleeding was of no consequence and that the government should be judged just as though it had never happened.[4]

In each case, the existing governments have been judged by criteria that Americans would apply to, say, an American presidential administration. This has subsumed, as well, a country not torn by internecine hatreds. No doubt such a standard has been used with considerable cynicism by the intellectual culture, which is hardly so naive in other connections. Such a standard has been a natural one in the twentieth century American context. It has been able to play upon the simple-mindedness and provincialism of millions of Americans. There have been many, some of them on the edge of the intellectual culture and others simply members of the public at large, who have prided themselves upon keeping their minds fully attuned (without so much as a moment's genuine thought) to the twists and turns of fashionable opinion. In countless ways, people of this sort have made themselves the instruments of propaganda and ideological bias.

4. At the same time as a country's existing regime has been condemned, the leftist revolutionaries have been lavishly praised. The Communist and totalitarian nature of the revolution has almost invariably been denied. The "national liberation front" has been pictured as democratic, led by men who have represented a people in revolt against intolerable conditions. By this process Mao became an "agrarian reformer" and Fidel a romantic swashbuckler. While the revolution is seen as an explosion resulting from the indignation of exploited masses, the central role of the intelligentsia and of trained Marxist-Leninist cadre within it is given scant attention.

5. A point that should be considered separately, for emphasis if for no other reason, is that in most cases the precise nature of the revolutionary movement has been obscured by the fact that the "social democratic" Left throughout the world has been willing (beginning with Russia in 1917) to join in a United Front with the Communist Left. This coalition of the various segments of the Left is what has made it possible to say that "only a part of the revolution consists of Communists" and to

treat as mere speculation the concerns of anti-Communists about whether the Communists will control the revolution after it succeeds.

The ambiguity created by this collaboration was one of the more important facts about the world after World War II. It meant that in one revolutionary situation after another public opinion within the free world was unable clearly to identify its enemy. The effect has been devastating. The support of the social democratic Left not only helped the revolutionary movements materially and politically; it contributed immensely to a semi-paralysis on the part of the non-Communist world.

• The collaboration was the factor that more than any other laid the foundation for the moral and intellectual uncertainty that the free world, and especially the American public and the Congress of the United States, experienced about resisting Communist expansion. This resulted in serious internal division, such as existed in the mid-1980's about American policy toward the Sandinista regime in Nicaragua. (The Boland Amendment prohibiting assistance to the Contras, who were fighting the Sandinistas, set the stage for the Iran-Contra Affair, with the prosecutions of administration leaders that has continued into the '90's.)

• The result was the lack of an articulated anti-Communist rationale for American policy in such a place as Vietnam. In March 1967, TRB wrote that "we are not there to prevent South Vietnam going Communist. ('We do not seek to impose our political beliefs upon South Vietnam,' says the President [Lyndon Johnson] categorically.) ... What are we there for, then? Mr. Johnson tells us. It is terribly simple. It is to give 'a concrete demonstration that aggression across international frontiers is no longer an acceptable means of political change." President Johnson was choosing to rationalize the war in terms of a post-World War I "Kellogg-Briand" type of thinking, in which the problem was seen as one of aggressive nation-states attacking one another. Johnson was playing to the Left and to the ambiguity within American public opinion, deliberately avoiding an anti-Communist rationale.[5]

• These factors in turn led to an irresolute response to Communist revolutionary attacks upon the free world.

• Although Americans found it most comfortable to pull back mentally into the comfortable routine of their own lives, the fact remained that since 1939 hundreds of millions of people had been lost to Communist domination. One country after another had succumbed to one-party Marxist-Leninist dictatorship. Our mental defenses are such that it seems almost ungracious to recall their names: Estonia, Latvia, Lithuania, Poland, Hungary, Czechoslovakia, Yugoslavia, Rumania, Albania, China, North Korea, North Vietnam, South Vietnam, Laos, Cambodia, Angola,

Mozambique, Ethiopia, Rhodesia, Cuba, Nicaragua, Afghanistan....and others. But of course these are not just names; they are whole peoples who came to live under a totalitarian system.
• There was an increasing isolation of the United States within a world that, to the extent it was not Communist, had become ever more hostile and "neutral." The French refusal to allow American warplanes to fly over its territory to make the retaliatory raid on Libya in 1986 was symptomatic of this shift. The change reflected more than just the decisions of politicians. It manifested their awareness of opinion within their respective countries. (This is an isolation that fortunately has been ameliorated by the dramatic collapse of Communism.)

Because of what I have just mentioned, we should recall the division that occurred within American liberalism at the end of World War II. At that time, the Americans for Democratic Action (ADA) was formed primarily to represent liberals who opposed "working together" in the same organizations with Communists. The Progressive Citizens of America (PCA), which provided the vehicle for Henry Wallace's presidential candidacy in 1948, represented those further to the Left. Its supporters included Communists and those who were willing to continue the old United Front coalition that had been so important in the 1930's.

This seems simply a footnote in American history, but the principle should long have been considered, for the reasons I have just mentioned, one of the most crucial issues in the world after World War II. Unfortunately, most (although not all) of the world's "social democratic" Left took the position of the PCA. Even more fatefully, the American liberal intellectual culture encouraged it in this. The principle of non-collaboration was largely lost sight of after the debate over it in the late 1940's. As we saw in our discussion of the New Left, the principle was abandoned in the 1960's. Further, we saw in our discussion of liberal attitudes toward world affairs that liberal thought encouraged the collaborationist posture of the so-called "non-aligned" factions throughout the world. The failure to insist upon a moral imperative of non-collaboration marked the intellectual bankruptcy of American liberalism and of the social democratic Left in the world arena.

6. The sixth component in the cycle was an active opposition to any support for the existing government in its struggle against the revolution.

This opposition was rationalized in a number of ways: the denial of the "domino theory" allowed liberals to argue that the loss of the particular country would have no further ramifications, so that any intervention by the United States was not really justified by our national interest. The concept that the revolutions were "just civil wars between the existing government and factions that are actually nationalist, and to whom Marxism-Leninism is simply a facade" had the same effect. And the perception of the unworthiness and corruption of the existing government meant that support, if given, could be made to seem both wasted and morally reprehensible.

We saw this opposition to support wherever the existing regime sought American backing. Countries to which this applied included Russia (with regard to Western assistance to anti-Communist forces in the post-1917 civil war in which Lenin succeeded in consolidating his power), Greece, China, Korea (before the North Korean invasion), Taiwan, Quemoy and Matsu, Vietnam, Guatemala, the Dominican Republic, and El Salvador. In addition, the liberal intellectual culture opposed any effort to overthrow a Communist regime once it was in place. We recall the condemnation of such efforts in Cuba, where they did not succeed, and in Chile and Grenada, where they did.

7. Once the Communist revolution had taken the particular country, liberal thought urged a friendly posture toward the revolutionary regime. The hope was expressed that the revolution would either (a) prove itself not truly to have been Communist, or (b) be tamed by the conciliatory gestures and thereby become one of the "independent Communist" regimes within a pluralistic rather than a monolithic Communist system.

8. Closely related to this seventh point was the consequent blaming of the United States for the hostility that followed between it and the Communist regime. The hostility, the argument ran, was the product of the American government's not having been conciliatory enough.

We recall how the United States was blamed for not having cultivated Ho Chi Minh as a Vietnamese "nationalist" after World War II. According to this argument, the American government was responsible for the Communist nature of Ho's regime. (The fact that Ho was a Moscow- trained revolutionary and that Walter Briggs pointed out in a 1948 issue of *The New Republic* that he was "fanatically loyal to Moscow" was considered irrelevant to this line of reasoning, which was not based on evidence but upon ideologically induced sophistry.)[6]

Along the same lines, Samuel Shapiro wrote in *The New Republic* after Fidel Castro's victory in Cuba that it was Eisenhower's hostile policy that had driven Castro "into the arms of Nikita Krushchev." We heard a similar argument about the Sandinistas in Nicaragua, despite the Carter administration's extensive efforts to cultivate a friendly relationship both before and after they took power. Such a conciliatory policy was followed until the Reagan administration decided to stop most American aid because of the Sandinista government's supplying of arms to the leftist guerrillas in El Salvador.[7]

9. Finally, at the end of the cycle, there has been a belated recognition that in fact the Communists have used the revolution to impose a dictatorship and oppressive conditions.

It took many years for this realization to sink in with regard to the Soviet Union, which is where the cycle probably played itself out over the longest time. Usually it was much quicker. A year and a half after the victory by Mao in China in late 1949 a *New Republic* editorial told for the first time about "the Chinese Communist terror campaign," and finally in 1955 Robert C. North told the readers that "from the day of its establishment the Chinese Communist government has functioned as a police state patterned after the Soviet model."[8]

Not long after Castro's victory in Cuba, George Sherman wrote that "I came away from Cuba profoundly disturbed...by the growth of totalitarian organization." And after the Sandinista takeover in Nicaragua, we eventually saw the *New Republic* article in October 1983 entitled: "Darkening Nicaragua: Still not Totalitarian, but the Drift is Disturbing."[9]

10. A tenth point about the cycle is one that I mentioned at the very beginning of this chapter: that the ultimate realization of the Communist nature of the revolution and of the totalitarianism that it imposed did not prevent the cycle from being replayed, with the beginning illusion fully intact, when the next country came under attack. It was as though the illusion was so strong that it could not be dispelled by experience. Only the horror itself dispelled it – and then only for the particular case. The Chinese experience, for example, was no help to liberals in understanding the assault upon Cuba or Vietnam. And neither of these was any help in understanding Chile or Nicaragua.

After a country was lost to Communist brutality, there was no introspection within liberal literature, no self-examination in which an admission of error was made.

For several years, fashionable opinion throughout the world has been clamoring to pull down the South African government. No responsibility whatsoever is being shown about what will take its place. The fact that one bloody dictatorship after another, Marxist or simply personal, has come into being throughout Africa out of the ruins of a departed Western influence counts for nothing. The system of Apartheid is seen simply as an unmitigated evil. American celebrities and young people, without having taken the least effort to study the history of South Africa and to understand the extreme difficulty of its multiracial situation, have demonstrated outside the South African embassy in Washington, worn white armbands at college graduation ceremonies, and congratulated themselves on the humanity of their position. If history teaches any lessons at all, it is that these same people will in a few years, without any introspection into the role they themselves played, throw themselves into a generous effort for humanitarian aid to alleviate "starvation in South Africa," just as they did not long ago for Ethiopia. (It is significant that during all of the clamor for aid to the millions starving in Ethiopia, almost no attention was given to the fact that there was a Communist government there. Even in that instance, the ideological insistence upon not learning from experience was apparent.)

### Several revolutions: examples of the liberal cycle

The elements of the cycle appeared in connection with a series of countries:

*Russia.* In 1918, after Lenin overthrew the democratic socialist Kerensky regime that supplanted the Czarist government, H. N. Brailsford urged the West to desist from attacking the Bolsheviks. His rationale was that if the Bolsheviks were assured of the safety of socialism within Russia, they would not need to become aggressive. The *New Republic*'s editorials opposed the Western nations' "indefensible and mischievous policy of military intervention" against Lenin's regime.[10]

A 1939 article by John Chamberlain put part of the blame on Western nations for Stalin's collectivization of agriculture, which included the liquidation of the kulaks. "In 1927," he said, "just before embarking on the first Five Year Plan, the Bolsheviks hoped to get capital from the Western nations. But the capital was not forthcoming...The gosplanners were forced to divert most of the available Russian manpower, [with] nothing much to pass on to the farmer for his grain." This, he said, led to events that culminated in the decision to collectivize. Such an argument corresponds to the phase in the cycle in which the abuses of the Communist regime are said to be due to the non-Communist world's not having been sufficiently supportive.[11]

We know, of course, that the world intellectual community's perception of the Soviet Union eventually soured, which corresponds with the end of the cycle. Representative of this was the reference in *The New Republic* in July 1948 to "the vast forced labor system" within the U.S.S.R.

*Spain.* In March 1936, a *New Republic* editorial reported that a United Front coalition was in power in Spain, consisting of "Left Republicans, Socialists, Communists and Anarcho-Syndicalists." Throughout the

Spanish Civil War, the journal supported the Left without objecting to the collaboration of the democratic socialist factions with the Communists and the anarcho-syndicalists.[12]

While opprobrium was heaped upon Franco's side, the Left was praised. The *New Republic*'s statement that "if Franco wins, the war-willing powers will be immensely encouraged for their next aggression" saw fascist expansion as a bad thing, for example. But the editors treated Communist expansion as a different matter. The editors chose to overlook the implications of Leon Trotsky's prediction, which had been reported in *The New Republic* itself in 1931, "that Spain would be 'next'" for the Communists.

*Western Europe; France.* In a discussion of the "underground resistance [against the Nazis] in Europe," a *New Republic* article in 1942 praised the Communists active in the resistance. In keeping with the phase in the cycle in which liberal thought obscured the nature of the revolutionaries, he denied the seriousness of their Communist faith: "The Soviet Union and the Communist Parties in Europe are not preaching Communism or social revolution. But they are advocating anti-fascist revolution and the restoration of democratic government and human rights and liberties...." In February 1944, a *New Republic* editorial reported a rumor that the State Department opposed arming the French underground "because some of its members are Communists." "If this charge is true," the editors said, "it represents a genuine low mark in stupidity."[13]

To appreciate the importance of this tolerance toward Western European Communists and of the willingness to see them armed, we need only note the *New Republic*'s own observation, made in 1950, that "the loss of Western Europe [would be] irreparable for the Free World." The comment was made while rationalizing the acceptability of losing Asia, but we can draw from it the awareness, however belated, of how crucial it was that Western Europe not be seized by the Communists at the end of World War II. This recognition can be assigned to the "realization" phase.[14]

*Greece.* In *The New Republic* in March 1947, Henry Wallace set forth an argument based on the same phase that we just saw with regard to Western European Communists, of again obscuring the nature of the threat posed by the revolutionaries. He argued that the Greek Communists "are largely Communists because of their extreme misery and have little ideological knowledge of what communism is."

An editorial incorporated two aspects of the cycle. It opposed the

Truman Doctrine's assistance to Greece in its fight against the Communist insurgency, and damned the non-Communist regime as composed of "the survivors of an old and wretched order – the royalist officeholders pledged to King George II of Greece." Freda Kirchwey in *The Nation* added her own contribution to the phase that condemns the non-Communist government. She argued in 1948 that the Truman Doctrine had been a "failure" because it had kept in power "a cruel, corrupt oligarchy that survives on terror."[15]

By 1952 *The New Republic* entered upon the "realization" phase (although it was helped in this by its break with Henry Wallace). An article by Thomas R. Phillips pointed out that "control of Greece would have extended Soviet influence into the Eastern Mediterranean and would have isolated Turkey, the Middle East and the Suez Canal."[16]

*China.* In 1931, Malcolm Cowley reported about the Chinese Communists that "Communism has captured a generation of Chinese intellectuals." The same year, William Prohme told readers of *The New Republic* that "several thousand villages are under this Soviet rule," which he said was a good thing because "non-resident landlords no longer exploit the endless labors of the farmers." In 1936, an editorial argued that the Chinese Communists were free of Russian control, citing a report by Edgar Snow that "he found no Russian Communists whatever with the army."[17]

The campaign to blacken the name of Chiang Kai-shek began near the end of World War II. *The New Republic* made Richard Watts, Jr., its leading author on China, and in numerous articles he condemned the Chinese Nationalists and praised the Communists. In May 1945, he reported something "upon which all the American visitors to Yenan [the Communist headquarters] during the summer and fall of 1944 seemed to agree...that these so-called Communists were concerned, not with collectivizing China, but with building a progressive, democratic, non-feudal, unified nation." He argued that "their current aims and tendencies are in the direction of agrarian democracy rather than collectivization." Such passages illustrate again, of course, the early phase during which the Communist nature of the revolution is denied or sugared over. At the same time, those opposing the Communists were dripping with evil; in the article immediately following the one by Watts that I have just quoted, Agnes Smedley told the readers of *The New Republic* about "Kuomintang concentration camps" and speculated: "How many men and women have been done to death in these camps or in the dark cells of Kuomintang prisons, mankind will never know."[18]

The next phase – or rather one that ran along concomitantly – was to oppose American support for the anti-Communist side. A *New Republic* editorial in August 1945 said that "it is to be hoped that American policy...will not uphold Chungking against the Communists as another 'bulwark against Communism.'" In a long series of convoluted developments, this was accepted by the Truman administration as its policy, as we see from the fact that in July 1947 an editorial reported that "about a year ago, the State Department, bolstered by [General George] Marshall's concurrent opinion, decided that Chiang's government was hopeless as an instrument for counteracting Communism in Asia. It decided to fulfill the promises made after V-J Day, but to make no new commitments of aid."[19]

Immediately after Mao's victory, an exultant headline for a book review by Edgar Snow declared that "In China the People Decided." But as we have seen from Robert C. North's 1955 comment about "a police state patterned after the Soviet model," the "realization" phase eventually set in. This awareness did not lead to introspection about liberalism's role, however, or to an admission of error. Thus, a *New Republic* editorial in 1975 was able to say that "the U.S. made a mistake in Vietnam that it had averted in China. Thanks to the wisdom of Gen. George Marshall...the U.S. turned away from the Chinese civil war and left Chiang to his fate."[20]

*Formosa/Taiwan*. After Mao's 1949 victory on the mainland of China, a *New Republic* editorial predicted "that Formosa will fall to the Communists by a combination of popular revolt and transfer of allegiance by its naval and air-force commanders." In August 1950, the journal criticized General Douglas MacArthur for establishing a liaison with Chiang on Formosa and voiced its opposition to American involvement in the defense of the island. TRB at the same time called it "the ultimate cost of McCarthyism" that "Truman paid the GOP price for Congressional unity [by having] included Formosa in our defense program." But then, after the "realization phase" set in with regard to Communist China, an article by Clarence Decker said that Formosa was "a beacon of hope to the Communist-oppressed Chinese on the continent."[21]

*South Korea*. At the time of the fall of the Chinese mainland to Mao, a *New Republic* editorial remarked passingly that "Korea...soon will pass under Communist control." In *The China Story*, Freda Utley told how "Syngman Rhee's [non-Communist] government, like Chiang Kai-shek's, was called reactionary, tyrannical, corrupt and undemocratic...In Korea, as in China, willingness to collaborate with Communists was regarded as the hallmark of a democrat...The 1949 United Nations commission on Korea regretfully reported that the South Korean government had been 'uncooperative.' The evidence...was its refusal to 'participate in official discussions with the [Communist] North looking to unification." She related how in the July 17, 1949, issue of the *New York Compass* Owen Lattimore wrote that "the thing to do is to let South Korea fall, but not to let it look as though we pushed it. Hence the recommendation of a parting gift of 150 million dollars."[22]

In the meantime, the ideologically induced illusions of the Truman administration set the stage for the North Korean invasion of the south on June 25, 1950. In 1947, General Albert C. Wedemeyer's report had sought to dispel any illusion. He told of the Soviet Union's building up of North Korean forces. Wedemeyer wrote that "the Soviet-equipped and trained North Korean Peoples' army of 125,000 is vastly superior to the United States organized constabulary of 16,000 Koreans, equipped with Japanese small arms. The North Korean Peoples' army constitutes a potential military threat to South Korea, since there is a strong probability that the Soviets will withdraw their occupation forces and thus induce our own withdrawal."[23]

It is one of the great tragedies of the period that Wedemeyer's warning went unheeded. Chesly Manly has written that "as predicted by General Wedemeyer, the Soviet government, on September 18, 1948, informed the United States that the withdrawal of its occupation forces from North Korea would be completed by the end of December, 1948. In the General Assembly, the Russians were demanding withdrawal of the American forces from South Korea. The United States soon complied. On June 29, 1949, the U.N. commission reported that it had verified the withdrawal of American occupation forces."[24]

This withdrawal in the face of Communist military superiority was coupled with still another failure. Freda Utley wrote that "not only was the American Army withdrawn from Korea in the summer of 1949, the military aid voted for Korea by Congress in 1949 was not delivered."[25]

The next step was that Secretary of State Dean Acheson declared in January 1950 that our defense perimeter included Japan, Okinawa and the Phillipines. "We thus made it clear," Senator Robert A. Taft wrote later, "that we would not defend South Korea if attacked." But of course Acheson's statement was merely an important capstone to a policy that in substance had already been carried out.[26]

Senator Taft understood the link between liberal illusion and American policy. He said that "the Korean war and the problems which arise from it are the final result of the continuous sympathy toward communism which inspired American policy."[27]

*Guatemala.* The Eisenhower administration intervened to prevent a Communist victory in Guatemala. The critique in *The New Republic* was voiced by David L. Graham when he wrote that "to a man, Guatemalans and Latin Americans remember the Liberation as a violent, American-engineered overthrow of a legal government."[28]

*Cuba.* In Cuba, as in China, the entire cycle ran its course. In February 1958, before Fidel Castro's victory, Daniel N. Friedenberg attacked the non-Communist president, Fulgencio Batista, in *The New Republic* as "a thug called an anti-Communist." An editorial in the same journal in January 1959 repeated the common theme: "Batista's regular army was not only venal, but incompetent and cowardly."[29]

American policy responded to such liberal criticisms in the usual way. A *New Republic* editorial in April 1958 reported that "two weeks ago the [State] Department imposed an embargo on further shipment of arms to Batista (as well as on arms to the rebels)." The editors added that "it might soon be incumbent upon us to put pressure on Batista to give way and get out...." David Morris looked back in 1968 and said that "it took an arms embargo and a complete break between the United States and Batista to give Castro sufficient momentum to overcome the established regime...The United States in 1958 was ambivalent toward Castro, and large segments of the liberal policymaking establishment (e.g., CIA) supported him."[30]

The concomitant sugar-coating of the Communist revolutionary movement is nowhere better evidenced than the same editorial in April 1958. It said that "to hint that Castro is a 'revolutionary' in any Marxist sense, or is the enemy of the United States and a friend of the Russians is silly." In January 1959, the editors spoke of "the absence of any evidence of significant Communist penetration of the Castro movement." Even though they were speaking in terms of an "absence of evidence," they explained away some that was quite material: they argued that "neither Castro's brother Raoul nor his Argentine adventurer-lieutenant Che Guevara – often described as pro-Soviet – are powerful enough (or pro-Communist enough) for alarm."[31]

Herbert Matthews of *The New York Times* was central to this sugar-coating. William L. O'Neill writes that "when...Matthews met Castro in the Sierra Maestra on February 17, 1957, he described Fidel as nationalistic, socialistic, anti-American, and noncommunist." O'Neill adds about Castro that "in 1959 he repeatedly denied being a communist, in 1960 he no longer bothered. Later he announced that not only was he now a communist but always had been."[32]

After Castro's victory, there was the usual period of rosy expectation, followed by the slow acknowledgment that his regime was indeed Communist. We recall that Castro soon executed a large number of opponents. Robert Taber came to his defense in *The Nation* in early 1960: "The question remains whether it would have been possible to implement the program which has given the Cuban masses their first glimpse of hope...by less arbitrary, more conventional methods. One concludes, however reluctantly, no." But *The New Republic*'s editors showed the beginning tremors: "Cuba's leaders have unquestionably given grounds for uneasiness...." Nevertheless, they were still able to say that "Castro's is a nationalist revolution...." By October 1960, Daniel Friedenberg was telling the readers that "I am not saying that Fidel Castro is a Communist, but that in every way he supports Soviet imperialism." Finally, a month later, *The New Republic*'s Gerald W. Johnson was at last ready to declare that "Communism has crossed the Atlantic and now squats 90 miles off-shore."[33]

Next, the argument was made by Samuel Shapiro in *The New Republic* that it was Eisenhower's unfriendly disposition that had forced Castro into the Soviet orbit. The solution, Shapiro argued, was to be conciliatory, not anti-Communist: "The only sensible course open to us is one of patience [and] forebearance...." It was predictable that *The New Republic* would be bitterly critical of the Bay of Pigs invasion's attempted overthrow of the Castro government. Indeed, it was the ambivalence of the Kennedy administration, manifested by the last-minute withdrawal of American air support, that assured the failure of that invasion.[34]

*Guinea.* In June 1960, Robert C. Good provided an interesting specimen of the liberal illusion in a *New Republic* article entitled "Is Guinea Communist?" After reciting: • that "virtually every ministry [of the government] has some Czech advisers;" • that the Soviet Union had made the government a $35 million loan; • that "Communist China will soon start a large demonstration scheme in rice culture;" • that "more than fifty percent of Guinea's trade is now committed to the East;" • that "Guinea increasingly is sending its students to the East to pick up generous scholarships offered by Communist governments;" • that "Guinea's leaders have been schooled in left-wing labor groups. They are Marxian socialists;" and • that "Guinea seeks a centralized society, a monolithic party, a state-directed economy;" Good said that "despite all this, my conclusion is that Guinea has not 'gone Communist.'"[35]

*Dominican Republic.* In May 1965, a *New Republic* editorial spoke skeptically of "its [the Johnson administration's] claim that Communists had 'infiltrated' the Dominican revolt and were rapidly rising to the top." The editors concluded that "sending 25,000 American servicemen to the Dominican Republic violated the OAS charter."[36]

*Vietnam.* As is to be expected, the cycle went full circle as to Vietnam.

The initial acceptance of the existing regime appeared somewhat obliquely in a comment by Joseph Buttinger in *The New Republic* in 1955 that "the French have tried to get rid of Premier Ngo Dinh Diem because they cannot use him for their policy of appeasement."[37]

From at least 1957 on, however, *The New Republic* followed the pattern of painting the blackest possible picture of the successive non-Communist governments. The journal rampaged against Diem, even calling for and then justifying his assassination; but neither did it see any good in the later governments. This was compounded by the usual failure to feel any empathy toward a society bled and forced into counter-measures by terrorism and guerrilla attack.

An article by David Hotham in 1957 criticized the widespread arrests "and imprisonment without evidence and without trial of persons suspected of being Communists or 'enemies of the State.'" In January 1961, Denis Warner wrote that under Diem "democratic institutions, such as free elections, have been turned into a farce. Imprisonment is the punishment for criticism." In June 1961 TRB told of President Kennedy's report of the 4,000 assassinations of South Vietnamese leaders within the preceding twelve months; and in the same month Adrian Jaffe and Milton C. Taylor complained of the lack of democracy and the use of the secret police by the South Vietnamese government. In December 1961, Frank C. Child wrote that "South Vietnam is a police state with...secret police harrassment, arbitrary arrest and police brutality...."[Child did not reflect upon what *any* society, including our own, would resort to to protect itself if there had been the killing, even within the one-year period cited, of 4,000 of, say, its cities' mayors and aldermen.][38]

In August 1963, a *New Republic* article by Erich Wulff implored that "Vietnam will fall into chaos if Diem does not resign, and soon." Then in October, Ho Thong Minh wrote that "the current situation renders imperative the overthrow of the Diem regime; for this the Vietnamese Army will be the ineluctable instrument." This was followed in short order, of course, by Diem's actual assassination; and on November 16, 1963, a *New Republic* editorial praised the assassination, saying that "the coup...obliges us to admit that there are two kinds of military putsches: 'bad' ones which have not received Presidential encouragement; 'good' ones which enjoy such sanction. The effect of that on would-be military dictators from Togo to Honduras will bear watching." Ironically, John F. Kennedy's own assassination occurred six days later.[39]

Without looking back at the journal's own role, a *New Republic* editorial in September 1966 said that "ever since the Kennedy administration permitted Diem to be assassinated in 1963, successive governments in Saigon have been too weak to dare to contemplate negotiations." Then the condemnations of the new government began. In September 1967, an editorial referred to the Thieu-Ky regime as a "puppet military government." In 1970, the editors spoke of "the fiction that the Thieu regime is the only one which could and should represent the people of the South, and that its survival is a sacred trust."[40]

Meanwhile, the revolutionary movement was given the usual sugar-coating. Since Ho was clearly a Communist, other pretexts than a full denial were used. In the early 1950's, *The New Republic* said that "Ho has become a hard-core Communist." But in 1965, the editors were calling the war a mere "civil war." In 1969, Walter Lippmann made his statement that if the Communists won "it will be...more or less like Yugoslavia is Communist, relatively speaking, and it won't make very much of a difference." Senator Fulbright argued that the war was "a civil conflict in which Communism is and always has been secondary to the drive for national independence."[41]

As in other countries, this perspective led many liberals to oppose American aid to the non-Communist side. In 1950, even at the time when *The New Republic* was acknowledging the hard-core Communism of Ho Chi Minh, the editors argued that aid to Ho's opponent, Bao Dai, would be "going back to a policy that has been a disastrous failure before." Later in 1950 the editors were saying that "further losses in Asia...will be costly but not irreparable. Only the loss of Western Europe is irreparable for the Free World." In 1957, David Hotham opposed all military aid and made an argument that would seem especially strained to today's public opinion, that the West's nuclear umbrella was the primary factor with which to restrain North Vietnamese aggression.[42]

It is little known in the United States that a major turning-point of the Vietnam War was brought about through very much the same mechanism that led to the North Korean attack upon South Korea. President Lyndon Johnson, reflecting liberal attitudes and playing presidential-election politics, announced during the 1964 campaign that the United States would stand back. Acting upon this premise, Ho Chi Minh changed the nature of the Vietnam War by sending his own regular army troops into the South. The war on that side had until then been fought by the Viet Cong, the Communist guerrilla force in the South. Here is Dave Richard Palmer's analysis from his *Summons of the Trumpet: A History of the Vietnam War from a Military Man's Viewpoint*: "That very August [of 1964],...President Johnson had announced publicly that he would not consider bombing North Vietnam or 'committing American boys to fighting a war that I think ought to be fought by the boys of Asia to help protect their own land.' Just as the North Koreans...had become convinced that the United States would not make a stand for Korea, so was North Vietnam convinced fourteen years later that America would not fight for Vietnam." Palmer says that "by committing its regular forces...Hanoi dramatically altered the entire thrust and scope of the conflict. It was a key command decision. Indeed, it may well have been *the* key command decision of the war."[43]

The tragedy reached its culmination in 1974 and early 1975. In November 1974, Fred Branfman reported that "Congress cut military aid to Vietnam from $1.6 billion requested to $700 million appropriated, economic aid from $750 million to under $450 million...." In February 1975, TRB exulted that "if Congress cuts off aid hostilities probably will stop, Communists will win. How bad is that?" Gareth Porter told how Theiu was complaining that the Paris Accords, which left regular North Vietnamese forces in the South, threatened the existence of the South Vietnamese government. We know the rest of the story: the South, together with Laos and Cambodia, fell to the Communists in the spring of 1975. North Vietnamese tanks entered Saigon as helicopters evacuated the last Americans from the embassy rooftop.[44]

During the years since that terrible spring, frequent reference has been made to "the lessons of Vietnam." As we will see from liberal attitudes toward leftist revolutionary challenges arising to such countries as Nicaragua and El Salvador, the lessons, as understood by most liberals, have not called for introspection. Instead, liberals have understood the lessons to confirm how right they were in holding the views that made up the cycle.

*Chile*: The first reference I noticed about Salvador Allende in *The New Republic* was in an editorial in 1964. It expressed the characteristic view that blames the supposed intransigence of the United States for any leftist's becoming a revolutionary. "Will Dr. Allende, if he wins," the editorial asked, "be turned into another Castro by U.S. stiffness?"[45]

In 1967, Joseph A. Page referred to Allende and spoke of "an exaggerated spectre of Communism." He told of "...FRAP, the name given to a coalition of the Socialist and Communist Parties." His words show not only the typical sugar-coating, but also the role that a United Front of socialists and Communists played in creating an arguable ambiguity.[46]

In August 1970, Georgie Anne Geyer told *The New Republic*'s readers that "when asked whether he [Allende] would create a 'popular democracy' and *a one-party socialist state*, he said that the election is 'not an electoral fight but the definitive battle,' that there would be a 'change of regime and of system'" (emphasis added). An editorial in November said that "an unabashed Marxist is inaugurated this week as President of Chile." Despite this awareness and what Allende himself had said about creating a one-party state, the editorial put things in the best possible light: "Allende is too aware of the limits of the possible in Chile to attempt imposing a rigid totalitarian structure on pluralistic Chile." William R. Long added that "only the most excitable anti-Marxists believe that Allende wants to establish a dictatorship of the proletariat, at least in the first years of his term."[47]

Allende himself continued to make his intentions clear. In May 1971, he praised Castro and told how he looked forward to revolution throughout Latin America: "The Cuban revolution is a national revolution, but it is also a revolution of the whole of Latin America. It has shown the way for the liberation of all our peoples." Nevertheless, *The New Republic* never acknowledged the danger. In September 1973, after Allende was killed in the coup that toppled his regime, an editorial commiserated that "the fact that Allende was toppled by a military junta is a tragedy for Chile..." He wasn't really for Communism, just socialism: "Allende's program was to put Chile on the road to socialism." (Perhaps for sake of analysis we should for a moment assume the correctness of this view that "only" socialism was involved. It has been hard to imagine *The New Republic* declaring it a tragedy for any regime that is not on the Left to be overthrown, in Chile or anywhere else, that declared itself intent upon creating a "one-party state.")[48]

After 1973, it was commonplace within liberal writing to declare Allende's anti-Communist successors "repressive and incompetent" and to blame the United States for assisting in Allende's overthrow. His failure to complete his consolidation of power meant that the usual realization that comes from hard reality never had a chance to command an acknowledgment from them.[49]

*Rhodesia*: The cases of Rhodesia and South Africa are somewhat different from the others. The white-minority rule over blacks has made it even more plausible to condemn the existing regimes. Assisted by this, the same cycle of illusion and irresponsibility has been present. The very real question, raised by the experience of several other African nations, of whether a black government, even though it would represent a majority, would be able to maintain adequate standards of civilization – for blacks as well as for whites – has not seemed relevant when condemning the "white minority." The main object has been the destruction of the white regime without regard to whether chaos or dictatorship might rise from the ashes.

Worldwide pressure was for several years brought to bear on Ian Smith to turn power over to a black majority. Milton Viorst told in 1975 how "it's been almost a decade since Rhodesia...declared its independence of Great Britain...Since then, it has lived in diplomatic isolation, and under the shadow of the United Nations economic embargo." A *New Republic* editorial used language in 1978 of a severity that it has rarely, if ever, applied to the world's worst butchers: "There is probably no way to exaggerate the malignancy of Smith's 13-year rule of Rhodesia. His regime was created in the name of white supremacy."[50]

The pressure eventually brought a new constitution under which the erstwhile Marxist guerrilla leader Robert Mugabe became the prime minister. An Associated Press dispatch on July 7, 1985, reported that "Prime Minister Robert Mugabe, more powerful than ever after a landslide election victory, vowed Saturday *to create a one-party state* in the next five years" (emphasis added). It went on to say that the country was "dividing...on clearly tribal lines."

*Nicaragua*: For several years, following the usual pattern, liberal writers attacked the anti-Communist Somozan government. "The United States," *The New Republic* said in 1978, tracing this country's support of non-Communist regimes over several decades, "is deeply implicated in the suppression of the Nicaraguan people."[51]

The same editorial sugar-coated the Sandinista revolutionary challenge, citing, as has so often been the case, the ambiguity of the revolutionary situation: "Certainly there are hardened Communists among the leaders of the Sandinista guerrillas, but it is not a foregone conclusion that they would rule Nicaragua if Somoza decided to leave the country."[52] The usual result followed from this illusion. "The Carter administration," the editorial said, "has stopped military aid to Somoza and in July the Senate wisely ended U.S. training of the Somoza National Guard. Economic aid continues...."[53]

After the Sandinistas won, the Carter administration tried the expedient that liberal thought favored: to secure the independence, if not the good will, of the revolutionary regime by showing every possible sign of friendship. Shirley Christian reported in 1981 that "the United States is trying to balance the Cuban influence and the less obvious Soviet presence with a large aid program." It didn't work. She went on to say that "a substantial portion of it [the aid program] was suspended recently by the Reagan administration...over the issue of arms supplies to Salvadoran guerrillas." In 1983, Robert W. Tucker told how "the Carter Administration went to some lengths to show its goodwill and desire for normal relationships. The government of Managua responded in a manner that was bound to put it on a collision course with Washington, and did so well before the present [Reagan] administration came to office."[54]

We saw earlier how the eventual "realization" set in. In October 1983, *The New Republic* published Ronald Radosh's article entitled "Darkening Nicaragua: Still not Totalitarian, but the Drift is Disturbing."[55]

But there was nevertheless the usual opposition to efforts to displace the Communist regime. In April 1983, Morton Kondracke wrote in *The New Republic* that "the United States is risking disaster – another Bay of Pigs and possibly worse – by giving aid to rightist guerrillas bent on overthrowing the government of Nicaragua." The Boland Amendment was passed by Congress prohibiting aid to the anti-Sandinista forces. When Oliver North and others sought a way around this, they were prosecuted. All charges were dropped against North in September 1991 after years of what can only be called political persecution.[56]

*El Salvador*: Contrary to the pattern, *The New Republic* hasn't sugar-coated the guerrillas in El Salvador, although at the height of revolutionary activity it painted a black picture of the non-Communist alternative. In November 1982, the editors conjectured that "the people of El Salvador may be caught between a Fascist rock and a Communist hard place."[57]

The liberal pattern of denial was present, however, as we see from Robert W. Tucker's reference in late 1983 to "a growing number of administration critics" whose "common point of departure is that we have no valid and certainly no vital interest in opposing the emergence of radical governments in Central America." Tucker himself suggested a sharing of power with the guerrillas. After the election of Napoleon Duarte as a centrist and moderately leftist president, the liberal media were largely silent about El Salvador. The Reagan administration continued, however, to feel the pressure of divided American opinion.[58]

*South Africa*: The system of racial separation in South Africa called

Apartheid came to be well-nigh universally condemned during the 1970's and 1980's. This condemnation has been driven to the point at which, whether the purpose is admitted or not, the prospects for South Africans of all races are bleak: either a "voluntary" destruction of the advanced industrial civilization to accommodate black majority rule, or a revolution encouraged and supported by much of the world.

The condemnation marks the acceptance of a principle that has certainly not been universally agreed to until recently and which is of dubious merit. It is one that is almost certainly embraced hypocritically by many who proclaim it. What I am referring to, of course, is the principle that there can be no racial separation within a society without that being *per se* unjust. (I am aware that criticism is made of the particular incidents of the racial separation in South Africa, such as the proportion of the land set aside for blacks. But I feel certain that those who are pressing the condemnation would agree that they mean to condemn the principle of Apartheid, not simply the form it has taken.)

It was not all that many years ago – in 1961 – that Harry Oppenheimer was able to write in *The New Republic* that "it would be quite wrong to think of their apartheid philosophy, in theory anyhow, as either willfully stupid or immoral." He pointed out that "partition has, after all, been applied as a last resort in quite a few parts of the world." The difficulties he saw in South African Apartheid were not moral, but practical. For Oppenheimer to express such views today would brand him a moral leper.[59]

The position expressed by Oppenheimer was also stated by Leonard Fein in *The New Republic* in 1977, not in connection with South Africa but in relation to Jewish opposition to racial and sexual "affirmative action" in the United States. "Jews know that there is such a thing as group culture," he said, "and that the culture of the group – for better, for worse – makes the goal of integration as it is sometimes understood a totalitarian goal." And yet, an editorial a month later was able to say that "South Africa is in danger of placing itself outside as an entire society, by defining the human race in terms that everyone else now rejects."[60]

The moral clamor that has been raised against South Africa seems to me to include substantial ingredients from the cycle of illusion that we have examined in this chapter. It is a matter of alienation and ideology rather than of reliance upon a sound and long-established moral principle. This is not to say that I consider the Afrikaners blameless. Their mistake, it seems to me, was to think that they could "have their cake and eat it, too." They have welcomed the presence internally of an ever-growing black population for the labor that it could provide, while they have also hoped to maintain a white society based upon a European model. In the long run, these are incompatible. An analogy would be the mistake European countries made in thinking that they could establish colonies, as the English did in America, and keep them wedded to the mother country after they had grown and matured. There are realities that, once they have developed, have ineluctable consequences.

It is worthwhile to be aware that "mistakes" about such things usually never come to a head for decision at any one time so that responsibility for them can be assigned to specific leaders. They creep up as part of an historical development. I do not know enough about South African conditions in 1948 to have an opinion about whether that year could have been an effective "hour of decision." The Afrikaners, descended from the Dutch, were assuming power and were then instituting the Apartheid system. Whether it would have been a viable option to have worked to limit the black population over the long run is not altogether clear. Culturally, the Afrikaners have long considered physical labor beneath them. It is possible that there would have been no constituency politically for limiting the growth of the black population. And if that path was not open, history and their own characteristics had locked them into the problem they now face.

The questions that constructive people should be asking about South Africa today are: Will even the blacks be better off, in terms of freedom or material well-being, if the Republic of South Africa is destroyed either by negotiation or revolution? and, if the answer to that question is negative, What evolutionary changes should be encouraged within South Africa to create an accommodation that will be acceptable to all of the diverse racial groups? It is relatively certain, however, that anyone pursuing this moderate course, which is essentially what the Reagan administration wanted to follow, would be excoriated by those who have been chanting, in effect, for the destruction of South Africa.

*Grenada*: In 1983, during the Reagan administration, the United States invaded the Caribbean island of Grenada after one Marxist government had been supplanted in a coup by another, more militant, Marxist faction. American medical students on the island were rescued, preventing a possible situation comparable to the hostage-taking in Iran during the Carter administration. After an interregnum of a few months, the island was made an elective democracy.

In keeping with the accommodation that American politicians have insensibly made to the liberal illusions, even the Reagan administration did not think it possible, at least initially, to justify the invasion in anti-Communist terms. Instead, it based its rationale on the danger to the American students. This reason was by no means far-fetched, but it was almost certainly not the principal motive.

Typically, the liberal intellectual culture took the dimmest view of the American intervention, although the success and popularity of the invasion within the country at large put a damper upon the condemnations (just as later the success of Desert Storm took the impact out of the movement against the war with Iraq). The tone of *The New Republic*'s reaction is indicated by the following passage from an editorial: "The United States invaded Grenada to rescue Americans...It is a mere excuse. There is no evidence that American nationals, many of them medical students in St. George's, were in any peril." We are interested in the tone, but we should recall that we have seen the claim of "no evidence" before, such as with regard to Cuba about whether Castro was a Communist. The editorial was correct in saying that the rescue of the students was not the main motive; but that there was "no evidence" that the students were in danger makes little sense. The American people had vivid memories of the Iranian hostage episode.[61]

### Conclusion

My analysis of the liberal cycle relating to Communist revolutionary attacks upon non-Communist nations is not meant to suggest that there would have been simple solutions in those countries if only the liberal illusions had not been so pervasive. Even the greatest clarity would not have done away with the Communist thrust. Nor would it have cured the weakness of what has come to be known as the Third World.

Nonetheless, a great many of those peoples would almost certainly have avoided subjugation to Communism. It is worth asking how much the weaknesses within pre-Communist Vietnam would have contributed to Communist victory if China, the colossus to the north, had not already fallen to the Communists. How great would the threat to El Salvador have been if Cuba and then Nicaragua had not succumbed? Each successive revolution did not occur in a vacuum, but with the support of a then-expanding Communist world.

## NOTES

[1] New Republic, August 30, 1943, p. 269.
[2] New Republic, May 8, 1944, p. 628; New Republic, May 29, 1944, p. 729.
[3] Freda Utley, *The China Story* (Chicago: Henry Regnery Company, 1951),

pp. 55, 58.

[4] New Republic, June 5, 1961, p. 2; New Republic, June 19, 1961, pp. 17, 20.

[5] New Republic, March 25, 1967, p. 4.

[6] New Republic, December 13, 1948, p. 16.

[7] New Republic, February 6, 1961, p. 16; New Republic, October 24, 1983, p. 26; New Republic, July 18, 1981, p. 19.

[8] New Republic, May 21, 1951, p. 7; New Republic, July 4, 1955, p. 20.

[9] New Republic, October 24, 1960, p. 15; New Republic, Oct. 24, 1983, p. 7.

[10] New Republic, March 9, 1918, pp. 167-170; New Republic, April 6, 1918, p. 280; New Republic, February 8, 1919, p. 38.

[11] New Republic, September 6, 1939, p. 123.

[12] New Republic, March 25, 1936, p. 182.

[13] New Republic, Sept. 14, 1942, p. 311; New Republic, Feb. 7, 1944, p. 163.

[14] New Republic, December 18, 1950, p. 7.

[15] New Republic, March 17, 1947, p. 12; New Republic, March 24, 1947, p. 6; The Nation, Vol. 166, p. 341.

[16] New Republic, January 21, 1952, p. 15.

[17] New Republic, July 8, 1931, p. 205; New Republic, August 12, 1931, p. 334; New Republic, December 30, 1936, p. 256.

[18] New Republic, May 28, 1945, pp. 735, 747.

[19] New Republic, August 27, 1945, p. 236; New Republic, July 21, 1947, p. 14.

[20] New Republic, Nov. 7, 1949, p. 18; New Republic, April 19, 1975, p. 7.

[21] New Republic, December 12, 1949, p. 6; New Republic, August 21, 1950, p. 5; New Republic, August 14, 1950, p. 3; New Republic, Jan. 12, 1953, p. 14.

[22] New Republic, October 31, 1949, p. 6; Utley, *The China Story*, pp. 87-90.

[23] Chesly Manly, *The Twenty-Year Revolution from Roosevelt to Eisenhower* (Chicago: Henry Regnery, 1954), pp. 174, 175.

[24] Manly, *Twenty-Year Revolution*, p. 176.

[25] Utley, *The China Story*, pp. 89, 90.

[26] Senator Robert A. Taft, *A Foreign Policy for Americans* (Garden City: Doubleday & Company, Inc., 1951), p. 59.

[27] Taft, *A Foreign Policy*, p. 60.

[28] New Republic, September 16, 1957, p. 9.

[29] New Republic, January 26, 1959, p. 5.

[30] New Republic, February 17, 1958, p. 14; New Republic, April 14, 1958, p. 4; New Republic, November 16, 1968, p. 28.

[31] New Republic, April 14, 1958, p. 4.

[32] William L. O'Neill, *Coming Apart: An Informal History of America in the 1960's* (Chicago: Quadrangle Books, 1971), pp. 36, 38.

[33] The Nation, Vol. 190, p. 63; New Republic, May 30, 1960, p. 8; New Republic, October 10, 1960, p. 11; New Republic, November 21, 1960, p. 10.

[34] New Republic, February 6, 1961, p. 16; New Republic, April 17, 1961, p. 3.

[35] New Republic, June 13, 1960, p. 11.
[36] New Republic, May 15, 1961, pp. 1, 6.
[37] New Republic, February 28, 1955, p. 9.
[38] New Republic, November 25, 1957, p. 14; New Republic, January 30, 1961, p. 8; New Republic, June 5, 1961, p. 2; New Republic, June 19, 1961, p. 17; New Republic, December 4, 1961, p. 14.
[39] New Republic, August 31, 1963, p. 14; New Republic, October 12, 1963, p. 19; New Republic, November 16, 1963, p. 3.
[40] New Republic, September 17, 1966, p. 5; New Republic, September 2, 1967, p. 7; New Republic, May 2, 1970, p. 7.
[41] New Republic, April 24, 1950, p. 6; New Republic, December 18, 1965, p. 6; New Republic, September 27, 1969, p. 8; New Republic, Dec. 20, 1969, p. 6.
[42] New Republic, February 13, 1950, p. 9; New Republic, December 18, 1950, p. 7; New Republic, November 25, 1957, p. 14.
[43] Dave Richard Palmer, *Summons of the Trumpet: A History of the Vietnam War from a Military Man's Viewpoint* (NY: Ballantine Books, 1978), pp. 90, 80.
[44] New Republic, November 23, 1974, p. 11; New Republic, February 1, 1975, p. 2; New Republic, February 8, 1975, p. 19.
[45] New Republic, April 11, 1964, p. 6.
[46] New Republic, December 23, 1967, p. 30.
[47] New Republic, August 29, 1970, p. 10; New Republic, November 7, 1970, p. 9; New Republic, November 28, 1970, p. 8.
[48] New Republic, May 22, 1971, p. 30; New Republic, Sept. 22, 1973, p. 7.
[49] New Republic, January 17, 1976, p. 20.
[50] New Republic, March 29, 1975, p. 10; New Republic, Oct. 28, 1978, p. 6.
[51] New Republic, September 16, 1978, p. 5.
[52] New Republic, September 16, 1978, p. 5.
[53] New Republic, September 16, 1978, p. 5.
[54] New Republic, July 18, 1981, p. 19; New Republic, October 24, 1983, p. 26.
[55] New Republic, October 24, 1983, p. 7.
[56] New Republic, April 25, 1983, p. 8.
[57] New Republic, November 22, 1982, p. 9.
[58] New Republic, October 24, 1983, pp. 24, 31.
[59] New Republic, February 20, 1961, p. 17.
[60] New Republic, Oct. 15, 1977, p. 17; New Republic, Nov. 12, 1977, p. 6.
[61] New Republic, November 21, 1983, p. 8.

## CHAPTER SEVENTEEN
## Liberalism and Anti-Communism

During the twentieth century, civilization has been threatened by two totalitarian ideologies. One was defeated rather quickly in a World War and is remembered with universal loathing. The other, despite suffering a great many "shocks," mostly self-inflicted, continued for many years before starting to crumble. For seventy years it expanded *vis a vis* the non-Communist world. As this is written in 1991, it is still not possible to speak of Communism as having fully collapsed, since Communism oppresses over a billion people in China and elsewhere. Whatever becomes of it, its expansion was a major fact of the twentieth century. The relationship of modern American liberalism to that expansion is important in any review of liberal intellectual history.

In face of this expansion, it might have been expected that all of the non-Communist world would have come together in a common cause against the common enemy. Nothing would have been more natural or justifiable. According to this expectation, the non-Communist governments and peoples, despite the diversity that otherwise separated them, will have had one thing at least in common: their mutual antagonism to Communism as a totalitarian ideology.

It is essential for our analysis to recognize the validity and importance of anti-Communism. A study of the relationship of modern liberalism to anti-Communism is significant only to the extent that anti-Communism was important. And to anyone who equally opposed brutal totalitarian systems of all types, an antagonism to Communism was every bit as important and valid as opposing Nazism in the 1930's and 1940's. It was both a civilizational necessity and a moral imperative.

From our review of the history of liberal thought, we would have to say that between 1917, the year of the Bolshevik Revolution, and approximately 1947, a period of thirty years, the main thrust of modern liberal thought, certainly as evidenced in *The New Republic* and *The Nation*, was not anti-Communist at all. Nor was it tolerant toward those who were. The liberal intellectual culture during those years overwhelmingly attacked any sort of anti-Communist as a "Red baiter."

There were inevitably individual exceptions, although during those years they did not substantially influence the tone and content of liberal discourse. We know, too, that in the late 1930's and early 1940's the Soviet purges, the persecution of Trotsky, the Hitler-Stalin Pact, the joint Nazi-Soviet attack on Poland, and the Soviet invasions of Finland and of Estonia, Latvia and Lithuania sent many former Communists and fellow-travelers reeling. Some then became strongly and permanently anti-Communist. Although shaken, the main liberal intellectual culture found it possible, however, to renew its emotional bond with the Soviet Union when World War II rehabilitated the Soviet image.

It is one thing, of course, to speak of the liberal intellectual culture; it is another to refer to the many other elements within the "Democratic" or "liberal" coalitions, which were themselves identified with liberalism as a political movement. My subject in this book is liberal thought, and so my focus is upon the intellectual culture, not upon all aspects of the broad political movement. The generalization I have made about the intellectual culture does not describe, for example, the great majority of Democrats. No one, for example, took more abuse for precisely their anti-Communism than the successive Democratic Congressmen, including such a man as Martin Dies of Texas, who for several years headed the House Committee on Un-American Activities.

After World War II, the picture with regard to the intellectual culture was considerably more complex. There were a great many more liberal thinkers who felt themselves distinctly separated from Communism. I have in mind such a figure as Sidney Hook, who though a declared socialist was also an articulate enemy of Communism. The Americans for Democratic Action was founded immediately following the war for the express purpose of opposing any further United Front with Communists. (We have seen that this principle was abandoned, though, during the period of the New Left in the 1960's. And we have also seen that non-Communist leftists in several of the revolutions around the world have received liberal sympathy despite their failure to maintain a distinct separation from Communists.)

What I seek, however, is a generalization about the intellectual culture's main thrust during the forty years after World War II. During those years, liberal thought argued for what it called a "more intelligent" form of anti-Communism. As we've seen, it argued that Communism could be tamed and preempted only by a world composed mainly of neutralist and of either democratic-socialist or independently Communist states. This worldview put the liberal intellectual culture into a sympathetic relationship with all parts of the world Left except a narrowly defined Soviet bloc. Since much of the world socialist movement was willing to collaborate with Communists and the true "independence" of any given Communist regime was necessarily questionable, the "anti-Communism" of the liberal intellectual culture after World War II was obscured by the ambiguity within the world Left itself.

At the same time, the liberal intellectual culture considered any form of anti-Communism that did not embrace the world Left misguided and even vicious. Liberals argued that any "reactionary" form of anti-Communism would be counter-productive, in that it would only alienate the Fidel Castros and Indira Gandhis of the world – i.e., the "independent Communists" and "neutralists." Moreover, it felt that such an anti-Communism would be worse than Communism itself. We have already examined the attitudes that downplayed the problem of Communism and treated it as virtually non-existent. To anyone holding such a perspective, the real problems in the world came from the many non-Communist regimes that are "venal, corrupt and repressive," or that were at the very least "unjust." The result was that the emotions of the liberal intellectual culture became most heated not toward Communism, but toward anti-Communists and a good many non-Communist governments.

If, then, we compare the period of 1917-1947 with the four decades that followed, we find: that both periods shared a consistent anti-anti-Communism; and that so far as its own position *vis a vis* Communism was concerned, the liberal intellectual culture during the later period moved only incrementally to the right. It remained on the far Left, disassociating itself only from what had become most disreputable.

The intellectual culture's attitudes impacted profoundly on the other elements of the liberal coalition. Most liberal political leaders, such as Adlai Stevenson, Hubert Humphrey and Henry Jackson, shared the country's general anti-Communism. And yet this should not obscure the effect that the ambivalence that was interjected by the intellectual culture had upon American politicians in general, and especially upon liberal politicians. Even though the United States occupied an historic role as the principal defender of the free world against Communism, the "anti-Communism" that was manifested by its government and by liberalism as a political and popular movement was during most of the post-World War II period apologetic and half-hearted.

### Specific aspects of the relation to anti-Communism

1. *The downplaying of Communism, while virtually all anti-Communists were subjected to unmitigated attack.*

An attitude that ran through the literature for many years was that Communism was not a significant problem, but was an exaggerated "Red bogey" conjured up by those who were hysterical and over-reactive. This downplaying of Communism was accompanied by an attack against almost all anti-Communism.

That this attack was so continuing and widespread tells us something important: that it had very little to do with the alleged clumsiness or insensitivity of any particular anti-Communist. This is true even though in each instance the attack took the form of a criticism of the specific type of anti-Communism. It is a mistake to think that the liberal intellectual culture objected only to sorts of anti-Communism that were "unfair" or "unfounded" or "abusive." The attack was so general that every form of anti-Communism was subjected to it. I can't hope to cite the instances exhaustively, but will give enough examples to illustrate the long-term, impersonal nature of the liberal intellectual culture's anti-anti-Communist position. The examples will also show that the attack on anti-Communists was equally violent both before and after World War II – with the exception that there were fewer such attacks after the mid-1950's precisely anti-Communism itself had largely been silenced.

- *The New Republic* carried an article in 1928 that denounced "professional patriots," who were said to have had "anti-Russian prejudices." In 1929, an editorial chided school authorities for opposing the formation of a Young Pioneer [Communist] group in a high school.[1]
- In May 1930, an editorial spoke of "the good old Red bogey" and called anti-Communism "witch-hunting." Later that year, an article by Conrad Seiler entitled "The Redmongers Go West" attacked the committee headed by Congressman Hamilton Fish that was investigating Communist activities in Los Angeles.[2]
- In early 1933, at the very time when thousands of Communist Party members poured into Ukrainian villages to enforce Stalin's decision to starve several million peasants to death, an unsigned review in *The New Republic* attacked a book by Dr. William I. Robinson for its "truculent" criticisms of the U.S.S.R.[3]
- In 1935, a *New Republic* editorial attacked the trial of eighteen radicals in Sacramento under a criminal syndicalism statute. "The real crime of these eighteen defendants is not being Communists – which they are – but fighting for decent wages and working conditions." An article by Ethel Thornbury in June of that year called the members of a Wisconsin state senate committee "witch hunters" for investigating Communism at the University of Wisconsin. Then in August, the editors wrote about "Red baiting in the A.F. of L.," arguing that Communists should not be excluded from unions.[4]

- In 1937, an editorial spoke of "a Red-baiting session of Fordham University alumni." In 1938, the editors wrote that "witch-hunting has no place in the progressive labor movement."⁵
- In 1939, the editors urged readers to send money to *The New Masses*. They said that "a real fight for the freedom of the press is going on down at the offices of *The New Masses*, the only national Communist weekly...Well-to-do America is letting *The New Masses* starve, by not advertising in it, not buying it and not mentioning it."⁶
- Also in 1939, an editorial charged that "the Dies Committee has been trying to smear the American Youth Congress as a Communist group." [Notwithstanding their charge of "smear," an editorial in July 1940 reported that "the convention of the Youth Congress was dominated by Communists as previous ones have been."]⁷
- In 1941, Bruce Bliven reviewed Eugene Lyons' *The Red Decade*, attacking Lyons for his "heavy-handed ruthlessness...His fanaticism like theirs, only turned inside out."⁸
- In 1942, the editors wrote of "the irresponsibility of the Dies Committee" and said "Go away, Mr. Dies; go away."⁹
- In 1943, they complained that "Robert Morss Lovett has at last resigned his post in the Virgin Islands," saying that "Dr. Lovett has been hounded from office by a small group of witch-hunters in Congress... They falsely charge him with being a Communist." Significantly, they added: "Even if the charge were true...."¹⁰
- In 1944, an editorial said that Congressman "Dies has never understood the principles of fair play...We hope...that Congress will put his committee [in]...the ash can."¹¹
- In 1945, a *New Republic* review attacked a book by William Henry Chamberlin, which said "largely devotes itself to belaboring Soviet Russia." Another review said that Alexander Barmine "claims a special competence for his hatchet-job on the Soviet Union by virtue of his career as Red Army officer, industrial leader and diplomat."¹²
- In 1946, F. L. Schuman wrote this about Victor Kravchenko's *I Chose Freedom*: "Take one Soviet renegade. Mix with several professional Russophobes. Stir well...The latest spicy dish from the Red-baiters' kitchen purports to be an autobiography of Victor Kravchenko, industrial engineer and Red Army captain, who fled...on April 4, 1944."¹³
- In 1947, an editorial called it "anti-Red hysteria" when Secretary of State George Marshall fired ten State Department employees. That same year, Bruce Bliven wrote of "many liberals and progressives everywhere terrorized into silence, with witch hunts...." Henry Wallace wrote that "the American imperialists who masquerade as defenders of American

democracy against the Red menace...are interested in extending... the area of human exploitation."[14]
• After Congressman Martin Dies retired, Henry Wallace attacked his successors in 1947, speaking of "the intimidating tactics of Thomas, Rankin and the House Un-American Activities Committee."[15]
• In 1948, Daniel S. Gillmor said that 125 government employees were fired between 1942 and 1947 for disloyalty. This, he argued, was a case of "guilt by association." A week later, an editorial charged the Truman administration with "guilt by association" when Attorney General Tom Clark listed thirty-two organizations as subversive. Also in 1948, a *New Republic* editorial charged the New York City Board of Education with "bigotry and hysteria" for "attempting to bar from the teaching profession in New York known Communists or suspected Communists."[16]

## 2. *The crushing of Senator Joseph McCarthy.*

It should be noted that everything that I have just cited occurred *before* Senator Joseph McCarthy began his crusade against Communists in government in February 1950. Everything that was eventually said about Senator McCarthy had already been charged against countless other anti-Communists.

This record places Senator McCarthy's career and character in a different light than his current infamy dictates. The record I have just traced shows that Senator McCarthy would be painted in the blackest terms regardless of the merits of his case or the validity of his methods. In 1938, J. B. Matthews published *Odyssey of a Fellow Traveler* where he told of his own movement to anti-Communism after several years as a leading figure in Communist "front" organizations. What he said *in 1938* fits Senator McCarthy's case twelve years later: "Any critic of Communism who hopes to escape the charge of red-baiting by holding his criticisms rigidly within the bounds of fact and good temper is simply deluding himself...Any criticism of communists is, *per se*, red-baiting."

This caution is important for any scholar now or in the future who wants to make an objective evaluation of Senator McCarthy's anti-Communist crusade. Such an historian will have to set aside all preconceptions based on the Senator's present reputation. From my own study, I believe that four main conclusions follow from an objective analysis:
• First, that, contrary to accepted opinion today, Senator McCarthy's "methods" were, with only minor exceptions, legitimate, and were the same as those that liberals themselves had long favored in the investigation of other subjects.
• Second, that his personal style had both good and bad aspects. He

was an articulate, militant slugger, consistently with having been a Marine and prize fighter. His appearance and demeanor were gruff (which was played upon unmercifully by the cartoonist Herblock, who always pictured him with a heavy five-o'clock shadow). These things were objectionable to people who especially valued (or claimed to value) gentility – which is, after all, properly to be valued. On the other hand, he needed every bit of his prize-fighter temperament if he were to champion the anti-Communist cause. Such an effort would have to challenge the Left's illusions about Communism – a superhuman task. And it would need to articulate anti-Communism *as a moral issue*, so that Communism would come to be seen in the same light as Nazism. In doing these things, McCarthy was going against an enormous force. It meant facing all the abuse that the liberal intellectual culture would inevitably muster. The abuse eventually dispirited and killed him. But until it did, he fought a harder fight than anyone had before or has since.

• Third, that the cause he championed was of the utmost validity and importance. When Senator McCarthy raised the issue of Communism as a moral imperative and insisted that it was not to be evaded through illusion or a desire to enjoy the comfort of a false moderation born out of blindness and insensitivity, he spoke for hundreds of millions who no longer had a voice to speak for themselves. His enemies, on the other hand, arose from two main sources. The first consisted of those who clung to or wished not to acknowledge the illusions of the Left. The second were a breed that was all-too-common in twentieth century America: the millions who congratulated themselves on their sophistication while finding it personally and politically comfortable to evade moral judgments about Communism.

The five years immediately prior to 1950 had been witness to a horrendous fact: 600 million new victims had fallen under Communist dictatorship. Stalin was still in power and, shielded by the silence of the world intellectual culture, held millions in forced labor in his concentration camps – the Gulags that Aleksandr Solzhenitsyn told us about years later after he himself had served several years in them. These facts are essential to an adequate perspective of Senator McCarthy's crusade. It is important, too, that we recognize something that I have never seen commented upon: that the terrible years of the New Left, which were soon to follow, demonstrated the enormous power of Leftist subversion in the United States. From all these things, we can conclude that, whatever we may think about Joseph R. McCarthy's gentility, he was vastly superior to his detractors both in insight and moral sensibility.

This is especially true in light of the hypocrisy of such a man as

Michael Straight, who during the entire McCarthy episode was the editor of *The New Republic*. During those years in which his journal poured venom on McCarthy for allegedly "smearing" liberals with a Communist label, Straight knew the secret that didn't become public until 1981 – that Straight had for several years been a member of the Communist espionage ring that included Guy Burgess and Anthony Blunt. Straight's own confession of the relationship came in his 1983 book *After Long Silence*. He said there that his last meeting with Burgess had been in 1949 – long after the Hitler-Stalin Pact and just months before McCarthy began his attacks on Communism. His book is full of self-serving rationalization, but he saw his way clear to make one statement that is directly pertinent to our consideration of the McCarthy era. He wrote that "my fear and sense of guilt were secret, shared by no one. At the same time, as editor of *The New Republic*, I had to share my thoughts and my feelings week after week on the allegations of espionage that were surfacing and on the larger issues they raised."[17]

• Fourth, that it is impossible to credit the notion that McCarthy was an insincere, self-serving demagogue. The only way that we can interpret his actions as fundamentally self-serving is if we presume that he was pathologically masochistic. Although he knew that he had the support of many Americans, he also knew that everything he said or did would bring down upon him an avalanche of vituperation. In any discussion of his personal characteristics, he should be credited with enormous courage and a willingness to subject himself to unremitting attack. It will serve as a litmus test for the detachment and courage of future historians to see what they say about his character.

3. *McCarthy's defeat was a major victory for the Left and marked the silencing of articulate anti-Communism.*

When Senator McCarthy was effectively discredited all possibility of an articulate anti-Communism was crushed with him. The silencing of anti-Communism was the American Left's greatest victory. For thirty years after the mid-1950's, anyone who saw Communism as a moral issue was *per se* considered a bigot, not just by the intellectual culture but by the society at large. The result was that public figures were not willing to cast the issues in that light. This is why Presidents Johnson and Nixon didn't articulate an anti-Communist rationale for the Vietnam War. It is why Jane Fonda remained a popular actress in the United States despite her trip to Hanoi while American soldiers were dying on the battlefield and incarcerated in the "Hanoi Hilton." It is why the liberation of Grenada had to be justified on other grounds than anti-Communism, even by the Reagan administration.

Not only was anti-Communism silenced as a conscious force; the attack upon it, which was waged for several decades and which came to a head in the crushing of Senator McCarthy, served yet another vitally important function for American liberalism. It obliterated American consciousness of the intimate connection that had existed between the liberal intellectual culture and Soviet Communism during the three decades prior to 1947, a connection that, if it had been fully comprehended in the context of the Cold War following World War II, would have been thoroughly discreditable to liberalism.

Liberal authors had for many years charged that conservatives raised the issue of Communism to taint liberalism with it. TRB expressed a common theme in 1939 when he wrote that "the danger in the tactics of the Red hunt remains, as always, that the smear will be spread to anyone with the least progressive or liberal leanings."[18]

Significantly, there is more to this than meets the eye: In the first place, the charge that conservatives sought to smear liberals with a Communist taint imputes something to conservatives that was far from their actual intent. Most of the time, conservatives bent over backwards to qualify what they said. They took great pains precisely to distinguish between Communism and liberalism. They did this both because they were aware of what they themselves thought was a vital difference and because they knew that they would be severely criticized if they did not make the distinction.

The second aspect is somewhat startling. It is that, in light of the record of the liberal intellectual culture between 1917 and 1947, conservatives *would have been more accurate if*, instead of avoiding the imputation of a connection between Communism and liberal thought, they had spoken quite candidly about just how great and widespread the infatuation had been. "Liberalism" as a domestic agenda in American politics had clearly been distinguishable from Communism, but the attitudes of the liberal intellectual culture had not been.

Conservatives' own anxiety not to overstep acceptable bounds caused them for the most part to join in a vitally significant obfuscation of ideological reality. One of the illusions the American people have lived under for many years has been a failure to have any conscious, articulated understanding of just how far left the liberal intellectual culture has been. That culture was pro-Communist before 1947, and was, as we have seen, only slightly to the right of Soviet Communism during the four decades thereafter. It has been a fact of the utmost significance that on a great many foreign policy issues there has been something of a perpetual "fifth column" within the United States. This has caused a seriously divided public opinion and half-paralyzed the United States' response to Communist expansion. And yet, as true as these conclusions are, they have been "off limits" in our political discourse. The result, as in so many other areas, is a failure to grasp reality.

4. *Anti-anti-Communism reflected the liberal critique of American culture.*

As seen by the liberal intellectual culture, anti-Communism manifested the very same "petty bourgeois" social characteristics that liberal social critics had so long deplored as coming from "ignoramuses" and "Babbitts." To understand this fully, we need to recall the earlier chapter on "Liberalism and American Culture."

The continuing attack upon anti-Communists and eventually on "McCarthyism" was an extension of the attack upon American culture that had been waged in the generation of Harold Stearns and Randolph Bourne. This stood out clearly in TRB's comment in May 1950 that "'McCarthyism' really represents the revolt of the 'frustrated primitives' against the 'intellectuals' in the complexities of foreign affairs...."[19]

5. *The continuation of the anti-anti-Communist posture since 1954.*

Since the defeat of Senator McCarthy, there was much less articulate anti-Communism. But the pressure against any active anti-Communism remained the same in the few instances that arose:

• In 1956, *The New Republic*'s Gerald W. Johnson praised Arthur Miller for having "refused to betray his friends" by identifying who had attended Communist meetings with him in 1947. It is significant that this had to do with meetings *in 1947*. That was a decade after the Soviet purges and eight years after the Hitler-Stalin Pact. Only the really "hard" people retained a direct affiliation with Communism after the late 1930's. In the passage just quoted, Johnson was treating Communist meetings in 1947 as though they were interchangeable with what liberalism has generally argued was the "excusable naivete and idealism of the pre-purge and pre-Pact period." Thus, he showed a readiness to defend the Communist Left even when there was no such "excuse."[20]

• In August 1957, a *New Republic* editorial observed the thirtieth anniversary of the executions of Sacco and Vanzetti. It said that "almost no one believes any more that Sacco and Vanzetti were guilty... they were victims in part of the anti-radical hysteria after World War I."[21]

• In 1961, TRB wrote that "the witch-hunters are riding again: Eastland's Internal Security Committee demands the names of all members of the 'Fair Play for Cuba Committee.'" [Two years later, Lee

Harvey Oswald, active in the Fair Play for Cuba Committee, assassinated John F. Kennedy.]22
• In 1966, TRB wrote that "the House Un-American Activities Committee is out to smear the whole [New Leftist] protest movement with a red brush. Philip Abbot Luce...is the Golden Boy of change-coats."23

### 6. *A double standard about investigations*

Liberal writing has condemned all Congressional and state legislative investigations of Communism over a span of many decades. This stands in contrast to the support liberals have given to Congressional investigations into the Teapot Dome scandal, the munitions industry in 1935, the use of labor spies, the utility industry, Watergate and Iran-Contra.

We have seen how in 1930 Congressman Hamilton Fish was called a "Redmonger" for investigating Communist activity in Los Angeles. In January 1931, *The New Republic* accused his committee of "witch hunting activities." In 1934, an editorial charged that "California is engaging in an anti-Red campaign worthy of the worst days of Palmerism just after the great war." We have seen, too, how the Dies Committee was attacked in the late 1930's for its "Red-baiting" and for "slandering all sorts of innocent citizens without the slightest respect for truth or the ordinary amenities." Then in the late 1940's the House Committee on Un-American Activities was attacked for its "intimidating tactics" and for "depriving men of their good names." In 1948, a *New Republic* editorial referred to "the Hiss-Chambers circus," which it considered "gaudy." This was followed in the early 1950's by the hostility poured onto Senator McCarthy. Later, TRB called Senator James Eastland a "witch-hunter" for inquiring into the Fair Play for Cuba Committee. And in 1966, TRB charged that "HUAC is out to smear the whole protest movement...."24

All of this should be compared with *The New Republic*'s attitude about investigations into other subjects. An unsigned article in 1924 about the Teapot Dome investigation said that "the most shocking aspect...is the attitude displayed toward the revelations by a large part of the press. All their indignation is saved for the mistakes and frailties of the investigators...." An editorial a month later said that "we wish Judge Gary or anyone else would give us the name of a single honest man whose reputation has been ruined by any of the current investigations...We admit that the work of the Senate Committee has not been in all points perfect; Washington is not the place in which to expect either perfection or an utter absence of political partisanship."25

In early 1935, *The New Republic* declared that "no Senatorial committee has ever performed a more useful public work than the one investigating the munitions business." In 1937, an editorial attacked those who opposed a Congressional investigation into the use of labor spies.[26]

Arthur Schlesinger, Jr., has told about Senator (later Justice) Black's investigation of utility companies in 1936. "The methods employed by Black...underwent much criticism then and later. Certainly his was no model of fair and impartial investigation. He was criticized most for his use of subpoenas *duces tecum* – dragnet subpoenas...In response, Black contended persuasively that he was 'proceeding in exactly the same line of policy and under the same type of proceedings' that had characterized every investigating committee since 1792...Nor did Black often permit his witnesses to amplify their answers when they deemed 'yes' or 'no' inadequate or misleading." Schlesinger defended Black, arguing that an important distinction is that he inquired into actions, not "opinions."[27]

## 7. *Liberal intellectuals who repudiated the far Left.*

A large number of prominent intellectuals who during the 1920's and 1930's were deeply infatuated with the Soviet Union moved rightward, becoming staunchly anti-Communist. Many of these eventually became the intellectual core of the group that, led by William F. Buckley, Jr. (who of course had himself never been on the Left), founded *National Review* magazine. In the next section, we will see that liberal writing severely attacked the great majority of those who repudiated Communism and who then articulated an anti-Communist position.

• *John Dos Passos*. In 1931, Granville Hicks wrote that "Dos Passos is a radical" and referred to "his communistic theories." Dos Passos enjoyed a close association with *The New Republic* until 1934. He told of his later repudiation of Communism in his book *The Fourteenth Chronicle*. A major factor in his change was the Communists' execution of a friend during the Spanish Civil War.[28]

• *J. B. Matthews*. Arthur Schlesinger, Jr., tells us that Matthews was the first chairman of the American League against War and Fascism, which Schlesinger calls "probably the most successful of the Communist fronts." Matthews wrote in his book *Odyssey of a Fellow Traveler* that he was introduced to radicalism through the Social Gospel and became a member of the Socialist Party before becoming a full-fledged "fellow traveler" in 1932 after returning from his fifth visit to the Soviet Union. In the mid-1930's, however, he moved sharply away from Communism. Matthews became a prolific anti-Communist writer, and served also as an investigator for the House Committee on Un-American Activities.[29]

• *William Henry Chamberlin*. Chamberlin's father was a socialist, and he himself grew up favoring a "mild anarchism." He lived in Soviet Russia for twelve years, where he served as the Moscow correspondent for the *Christian Science Monitor* and married a Russian girl. He was assistant book editor under Heywood Broun, and wrote under the pseudonym "A. C. Freeman." While he was in Soviet Russia, his opinions gradually evolved from pro- to anti- Soviet. They reached a breaking point with "the horrors of the First Five Year Plan." In 1937, he was the author of a book *Collectivism: A False Utopia*. Chamberlin eventually embraced Burkean conservative thinking.

• *Eliseo Vivas*. An advertisement in *The New Republic* in 1937 for *The Marxist Quarterly* listed an article by Vivas on "The Class Nature of Science." Vivas later became a leader within conservatism.

• *Eugene Lyons*. Lyons grew up in extreme poverty on the east side of New York City. He was the editor of the *Soviet Russia Pictorial* and worked for the Soviet news agency TASS for four years. After his break with Communism, he wrote *The Red Decade* and throughout the rest of his life was a leader among anti-Communist intellectuals.

• *Max Eastman*. Eastman was editor of *The Masses* and *The Liberator* between 1913 and 1922. He then went to Europe for five years. During a trip to Soviet Russia, he became a follower of Leon Trotsky. He later wrote that "it was in 1933 that my resolute faith in the Soviet system began really to break down." In 1941, he even repudiated socialism. He authored *Reflections on the Failure of Socialism* and was an important member of the *National Review* group.

• *James Burnham*. Burnham was active as a radical from 1932 to 1940. In 1939, he was a signer of the League for Cultural Freedom and Socialism's statement calling on people not to abandon revolutionary socialism. At one time he was the editor of *The New International*, the chief theoretical journal of the Trotskyists. His break with Marxism came in 1940. Until 1953, he was on the board of editors of *The Partisan Review*. He resigned from that journal in 1953 to defend Senator Joseph McCarthy. Burnham then wrote for *National Review* for twenty years.

• *Freda Utley*. In 1940, Richard Rovere wrote that Utley "is a British economist who during the twenties became a Communist and, with her Russian husband, went to live in Moscow. She lost her dream...when she found life there a nightmare and the Soviet economy a planned chaos. She left Russia in 1936, when the OGPU jailed her husband for a wisecrack made in Japan years earlier." Utley wrote *The Dream We Lost*, in which she denounced Stalinism, and *The China Story* about the fall of China to Mao.[30]

• *Frank Meyer*. After being a Communist organizer at Oxford and at the University of Chicago, Meyer began to lose his Communist faith after reading Friedrich Hayek's *The Road to Serfdom*. Meyer became a prominent member of the *National Review* circle, and is known for his advocacy of the "fusionist" position that would bring Burkean conservatism and classical liberalism together.

* *Willmoore Kendall.* Kendall was a Trotskyist in the early 1930's, and sided with the Trotskyists in the Spanish Civil War, at which time he was the UPI correspondent in Madrid. His thinking evolved from a strong anti-Stalinism to anti-Communism. He continued on the Left until at least 1946, but in 1955 became an editor of *National Review*.
* *Whittaker Chambers.* His conversion from Communism is described in his book *Witness*, where he says that the culmination of a long process of breaking from Communism came when he "heard screams in Moscow." Chambers left the party in early 1938. He was later the principal witness against Alger Hiss, developed strong religious convictions, and became an important member of the *National Review* circle.
* *William S. Schlamm.* Born in Austria, Schlamm was a Communist as a teenager, but became anti-Stalinist when he was 25. During the 1930's, he considered himself a "non-Marxian socialist." He was an early editor of *National Review*.
* *Irving Kristol.* At one time a Trotskyist, Kristol became a co-founder of *Encounter*, a liberal anti-Communist journal. He has been a leading member of the neo-conservative movement since the 1970's, and is the author of *Two Cheers for Capitalism*.
* *Will Herberg.* Norman Podhoretz says that Herberg was at one time a Lovestoneite (i.e., a follower of a splinter Communist group after its ouster from the Communist Party). Herberg, too, eventually became a prominent member of the *National Review* circle.
* *Louis Fischer.* Fischer was during the 1930's one of *The New Republic*'s and *The Nation*'s most prolific apologists for Soviet Russia. He resided in Moscow between 1922 and 1938. In a book in 1935, he told how he traveled through the Ukraine in October 1932, witnessing the famine; but he argued that the famine was the peasants' fault and that Stalin was justified in taking as much as sixty percent of their crop to make urban industrialization possible. Fischer was the author of a 1957 book, however, called *Russia Revisited: A New Look at Russia and Her Satellites* in which he concluded that "Communism has failed."[31]
* *Philip Abbott Luce.* Luce was a leader in the Progressive Labor Party faction of the New Left until early 1965, when he broke with it after finding that it crushed the individuality of its members. His book *The New Left* is an excellent insider's account of radicalism in the late 1950's

and first half of the 1960's.

It is pertinent to our analysis of liberalism, although not to our present discussion of liberalism's relation to former Communists, to point out that several other thinkers who became prominent within American conservatism had at one time been on the liberal side. Among those who my notes show moved to the right in varying degrees, but without having been involved with Communism, were Henry Hazlitt, Al Smith, Walter Lippmann, Amos Pinchot, John T. Flynn, and Richard Weaver.

*8. The reaction of the liberal intellectual culture to those who repudiated the far Left.*

Consistently with the liberal intellectual culture's far-left orientation and its attitude toward anti-Communism generally, liberal thought looked upon the great majority of those who abandoned Communism with suspicion and contempt. The attitude was expressed in 1946 by Max Lerner when he spoke of "the paranoid anti-Russian hysteria of former Communist believers grown disillusioned...." In 1953, Reinhold Niebuhr favorably compared those who left Communism but who did not speak up about it with those who became articulate anti-Communists: "It is ironic that men who extricated themselves with the least hurt to their spirit are now declared suspect by our vigilantes because they have not proved their repentance by adhesion to some dogma of the Right or by imitating its hysteria." Hannah Arendt made a distinction between "former Communists" and "ex-Communists." She said that the "former Communists" were those that did not have a "neurotic compulsion."[32]

These attitudes have been reflected in bitter commentary about the specific individuals who became openly anti-Communist:

About Eugene Lyons, a *New Republic* editorial in late 1939 (*after* the Hitler-Stalin Pact and the joint attack by Germany and the Soviet Union on Poland) sneered that "Lyons...has served up another dish of Red-bait." Two years later, Bruce Bliven wrote a review of Lyons' *The Red Decade* in which Bliven attacked Lyons for "heavy-handed ruthlessness" and "fanaticism."[33] About Willy Schlamm, a 1945 article by Richard Watts, Jr., who for several years was *The New Republic*'s main author in support of the Chinese Communists, said that Schlamm "was one of the leftist of the left-wing boys until he saw the light and went in for the usual violent flight from Moscow."[34]

About Louis Fischer, Harvey J. Bresler wrote in 1946 that "Fischer's detailed indictment of Russia [is] but old wine in a new bottle." Richard Watts, Jr., spoke in 1947 of Fischer's "violent revulsion from Moscow."[35]

About James Burnham, George Soule wrote in 1947 that "he may be regarded as a sample of those who, having been too close for comfort to extreme left factions, have swung violently...[to] the fanatical anti-Communist line."[36]

About Lee Pressman, a *New Republic* editorial in 1950 said that he is the latest to renounce Communism, this time over Korea; somehow we can never get very enthusiastic over these repentant sinners."[37] About Philip Abbott Luce, TRB argued in 1966 that "Luce...is the Golden Boy of changecoats."[38]

About Whittaker Chambers, John Kenneth Galbraith wrote in 1970 that "when I came to accept Hiss's guilt,...I never got around to forgiving Whittaker Chambers...Hiss hadn't made it to the Establishment but Chambers was all the way in as a patriot." Galbraith said, however, that he later grew to respect Chambers. The passage I have quoted is valuable in demonstrating how much the intellectuals' alienation from the mainstream of America contributed to their unwillingness to accept those who repudiated Communism.[39]

9. *Alienation and "the loyalty issue."*

Until in the mid-1950's liberalism succeeded in its drive to silence anti-Communism, one of the most heatedly debated public questions in the United States was the "loyalty issue." Conservatives were profoundly suspicious of the loyalty of those on the Left, and sought, among other things, to prevent the employment of those who were of doubtful loyalty by the United States government.

In light of all we've covered, it should be apparent that this issue reflected something quite different from the "paranoia" to which liberal writing has generally ascribed it. The problem of disloyalty originated in two associated phenomena: the intense alienation of the liberal intellectual culture from the predominant American culture; and the equally intense affinity that a great many within the intellectual culture felt toward the Soviet Union over a span of three decades.

The relationship of the loyalty issue to alienation appeared clearly in a 1917 essay by Randolph Bourne. The essay described a fictional young intellectual who was in many ways similar to the character Benjamin in the 1960's movie "The Graduate." Bourne described him as in "a rather constant mood of futility." Note the following passage, which relates directly to the attitudes that have been the root cause of the "loyalty issue": "With his groping philosophy of life, patriotism has merely died as a concept of significance for him. It is to him merely the emotion that fills the herd when it imagines itself engaged in massed defence or massed attack. Having no such images, he has no feeling of patriotism."[40]

Another passage, this time by Edmund Wilson, also illustrates the relationships. Looking back in 1952, Wilson told how "the writers and artists of my generation" had reacted to the Great Depression:

> The next month the slump began, and...a darkness seemed to descend. Yet, to the writers and artists of my generation who had grown up in the Big Business era and had always resented its barbarism, its crowding-out of everything they cared about, these years were not depressing but stimulating. One couldn't help being exhilerated at the sudden unexpected collapse of that stupid gigantic fraud. It gave us a new sense of freedom; and it gave us a new sense of power to find ourselves still carrying on while the bankers, for a change, were taking a beating...[W]e wondered about the survival of republican American institutions; and we became more and more impressed by the achievements of the Soviet Union, which could boast that its industrial and financial problems were carefully studied by the government, and that it was able to avert such crises.[41]

No quote could be more appropriate to come near the end of this series of books in which I have analyzed the modern predicament. It captures the essence of the alienation of the intellectual and of the enormous consequences that have flowed from it.

# NOTES

[1] New Republic, Feb. 22, 1928, pp. 2, 3; New Republic, Nov. 20, 1929, p. 360.
[2] New Republic, May 14, 1930, p. 336; New Republic, Nov. 12, 1930, p. 346.
[3] New Republic, March 8, 1933, p. 112.
[4] New Republic, January 30, 1935, p. 315; New Republic, June 19, 1935, p. 158; New Republic, August 14, 1935, p. 6.
[5] New Republic, April 7, 1937, p. 251; New Republic, Jan. 26, 1938, p. 324.
[6] New Republic, May 10, 1939, p. 4.
[7] New Republic, Dec. 13, 1939, p. 215; New Republic, July 15, 1940, p. 69.
[8] New Republic, October 6, 1941, p. 433.
[9] New Republic, September 7, 1942, p. 268.
[10] New Republic, March 27, 1944, p. 397.
[11] New Republic, May 22, 1944, p. 695.
[12] New Republic, Feb. 26, 1945, p. 309; New Republic, Aug. 20, 1945, p. 228.
[13] New Republic, May 6, 1946, p. 667.
[14] New Republic, July 14, 1947, p. 8; New Republic, November 3, 1947, p. 19; New Republic, December 29, 1947, p. 11.
[15] New Republic, September 1, 1947, p. 14.
[16] New Republic, May 31, 1948, p. 17; New Republic, June 7, 1948, p. 5; New Republic, July 12, 1948, p. 8.

[17] Michael Straight, *After Long Silence* (New York: W. W. Norton Company, 1983), p. 231.
[18] New Republic, December 6, 1939, p. 189.
[19] New Republic, May 22, 1950, p. 4.
[20] New Republic, Aug. 6, 1956, p. 10; see also New Republic, May 27, 1957, p. 8.
[21] New Republic, August 27, 1957, p. 7.
[22] New Republic, May 22, 1961, p. 2.
[23] New Republic, August 27, 1966, p. 4.
[24] New Republic, November 12, 1930, p. 346; New Republic, January 28, 1931, p. 283; New Republic, August 1, 1934, p. 305; New Republic, December 14, 1938, p. 160; New Republic, September 1, 1947, p. 14; New Republic, December 8, 1947, p. 10; New Republic, December 13, 1948, p. 5; New Republic, May 22, 1961, p. 2; New Republic, August 27, 1966, p. 4.
[25] New Republic, April 2, 1924, p. 134; New Republic, May 7, 1924, p. 269.
[26] New Republic, Jan. 16, 1935, p. 259; New Republic, Feb. 10, 1937, p. 2.
[27] Arthur M. Schlesinger, Jr., *The Politics of Upheaval* (Boston: Houghton Mifflin Company, 1960), pp. 320-321, 323.
[28] New Republic, June 24, 1931, p. 157.
[29] Schlesinger, *Politics of Upheaval*, pp. 199, 198.
[30] New Republic, September 23, 1940, p. 424.
[31] Louis Fischer, *Soviet Journey* (Westport: Greenwood Press, 1973), first published in 1935.
[32] New Republic, September 16, 1946, p. 324; New Republic, October 12, 1953, p. 14; New Republic, November 9, 1953, p. 16.
[33] New Republic, Dec. 20, 1939, p. 219; New Republic, Oct. 6, 1941, p. 433.
[34] New Republic, December 3, 1945, p. 742.
[35] New Republic, September 30, 1946, p. 419; New Republic, December 29, 1947, p. 29.
[36] New Republic, March 24, 1947, p. 32.
[37] New Republic, September 11, 1950, p. 4.
[38] New Republic, August 27, 1966, p. 4.
[39] New Republic, March 28, 1970, p. 17.
[40] Quoted in Henry May (ed.), *The Discontent of the Intellectuals: A Problem of the Twenties* (Chicago: Rand McNally & Company, 1963), at p. 17.
[41] Edmund Wilson, *The Shores of Light* (New York: Farrar, Straus, 1952), pp. 498-499.

# CHAPTER EIGHTEEN
## Multiculturalism: Liberalism's Latest and Most Threatening Assault

For almost a century and three-quarters, the world Left, including twentieth century American liberalism, has sought an alliance between the alienated intelligentsia and any unassimilated, disaffected group. In the absence of such an alliance, the intellectual culture has little political power and hence little ability to act in pursuit of its alienation.

This seeking of an alliance was the very essence of Marxism. In the twentieth century, however, the alliance with labor (Marx's "proletariat") has fizzled. Accordingly, the intellectual culture has felt its socialist aspirations blocked. This has led it into a funk similar to that experienced by American liberal intellectuals in the 1920's. Indeed, since World War II American liberals, writing in their in-house literature, have basically despaired of socializing the American economy.

The thing that has kept modern liberalism going since World War II has been the moral appeal of egalitarianism as applied to race and ethnicity (and, with the feminist movement, to gender). Even though the methods of legislated fraternity have left much to be desired from a conservative's point of view, this egalitarianism has been well-nigh irresistible to the American people, who have accepted its moral premises. The struggle for racial and then sexual equality has long given a moribund liberalism a much-needed boost.

This seems to me to have been, at first, a diversion. It amounted to a substitution of goals for the intellectual culture, which had earlier been so focused on socialism. The egalitarianism has in large measure amounted to an insistence on making everyone a participant in the successful middle class. When we realize how alienated the intellectual culture has been against precisely that middle class for well over a century and a half, the struggle to bring everyone into it is really an anomaly.

In recent years, however, "multiculturalism" (enhanced by all the vogue-making mechanisms that the academic and media cultures can muster) has come along to raise the stress on ethnicity to a much higher level. This has become the rage within academic and media circles, and has come to be enforced by irascible taboos that insist on a "politically correct" sensitivity to the needs of the members of "victimized" minorities. This gives us yet another example, on top of the tendencies of the 1930's and late '60's, of just how open the American Left really is to totalitarianism when it feels it has the power (which it does today in important pockets of our society).

A whole new potential has opened up for the Left. It now senses the possibility of multiplying indefinitely the potential ethnic allies that are to be enlisted. A few years ago it seemed that American liberalism would destroy its own appeal by becoming more and more tied into a limited assortment of strident fringe elements. But new vistas have opened up with the multiculturalist vision. Ethnic allies can arise from immigration, the growth of the minority populations that are already here, and an intensified self-awareness on the part of each minority (a self-consciousness that the intellectual culture is working hard to create). The members of each group are encouraged to see themselves as the "victims" of "Eurocentric" society (a recently coined term, as is the term "victimology"). Thus, to the extent the effort succeeds, they are imbued with the intellectuals' own alienation. The multiculturalism picks up on every ethnic nuance in the United States so long as it is not of European origin. The ideal of assimilation is dropped and "cultural pride and identity" are elevated. This portends an eventual Balkanization within American society.

This amounts, in effect, to an attempted alliance of the alienated intellectual culture with the Third World, imported into the United States. (A similar process is occurring in Europe.) The point I would have us realize is that this offers endless potential to those who so desperately hate our predominant culture.

What it does is to open up the prospect of demographic swamping. There are said to be 5.4 billion people in the world today. With enough immigration and population growth among America's minorities, it is projected that Caucasians will themselves become a minority in this country by the middle of the twenty-first century, if not sooner. The alienated intellectual culture can hardly restrain itself for glee.

The irony of it all is that most of the alienated intellectuals' allies eventually go their own way. They have no love for being on the intellectuals' lead-strings. They become "ungrateful" and "obtuse" (as blacks did in the Civil Rights Movement when under Stokely Carmichael they ousted the "white liberals," whom they didn't trust). So there is no assurance that an ethnic swamping-out of mainstream American culture will produce the sort of society the intellectuals want. Will an America patterned after the Third World idolize the intelligentsia, giving it power and social status while holding in check competitors for that same power and status? The question virtually answers itself.

Nor is it clear that all of the "ethnics" will even support the attack on American culture during the interim. Most of the people who come to America want to be part of it. One of the great sources of frustration to the alienated intellectual is that, like Old Man River, the so-called "bourgeoisie" "just keeps rollin' along." People want the good life, which means becoming "middle class."

So the future, as always, is problematical. The issue as framed for the future becomes one of whether Europe and America will continue to lead or even to exist as such. In part this is a question of whether the majority within the West has become so effete and so immobilized by the existence of the alienated intellectual culture within it that it is prepared to see itself displaced and its influence seep away. From all appearances, the current American majority, which rarely asserts its own prerogatives in either ideology or politics, is willing to acquiesce in this transformation.

Stated another way, the new struggle that today's "multiculturalism" poses will be about whether America and Europe are to dissolve into the Third World, or whether all of mankind will rise to a new level under the leadership of positive forces that will include, as one of their primary ingredients, the heritage of the West. There will be very little "heritage of the West" involved in it if the alienated intellectual culture – the driving force behind "liberalism in contemporary America" – has its way.

# INDEX

Abolitionism, 31
"Abstract advocacy" of violence, 140
Acheson, Dean, 268
Adams, Henry, 9, 32-3
Adams, James Ring, 92
"Affirmative Action" programs, 93, 191, 276
Affluence and the welfare state, 24
Agrarian movements, 33, 36
Alinsky, Saul, 215, 226, 231
Allende, Salvador, 249, 250, 272-3
Alliance, intellectuals and have-nots, 125
Alperovitz, Gar, 85
Alsop, Joseph and Stewart, 241
American Charter, 1943, 66
American culture, liberalism and, 119-128, 290
American Federation of Labor, 49, 92
Americans for Democratic Action, 69, 78, 218, 238, 260
American Youth Congress, 285
Amlie, Thomas R., 114
Anderson, Craig, 218-9
Andreski, Stanislav, 194
Anderson, Sherwood, 128
Anthony, Richard, 224
Anti-Communism, liberalism and, 281-301
Anti-trust policy, 54
Apartheid, 248
Arendt, Hannah, 295
Arnold, Thurman, 54, 115
Baldwin, Roger, 65
Balogh, Thomas, 85
Banfield, Edward, 25, 85, 97, 143, 145, 182, 193
Barmine, Alexander, 285
Barnes, Harry Elmer, 153
Barnes, Peter, 175
Barrow, William, 229
Batista, Fulgencio, 268
Bay of Pigs invasion, 269
Beaney, William M., 162
Beard, Charles, 53, 115, 156
Beatniks; Beat Generation, 208-210
Becker, Howard, 206-7
Behavioral sciences, 186
Bell, David, 98
Bellamy, Edward, 33, 36, 40, 165, 176
Benda, Julien, 197
Benson, Lee, 192
Bentley, Eric, 241
Berkeley, radicalism at, 215, 227, 232
Berle, Adolf, 53, 168, 177
"Berle-Means thesis," 168-172
Berman, Ronald, 84, 99, 117, 118, 128, 221, 226
Bernard, Jessie and L. L., 193
Bernstein, Barton, 54
Bestor, Arthur, 130
Black, Hugo, 292
"Black power" ideology, 212
"Black revolution," 22, 224
Blair, John M., 175
Blanshard, Paul, 174
Bliven, Bruce, 50, 58, 60, 108, 114, 180, 285, 295
Blunt, Anthony, 109, 288

Bonjean, Charles M., 72, 193
Bourne, Randolph, 35, 46, 119, 132, 290, 296
Boynton, Percy H., 180
Brailsford, H. N., 47, 51, 263
Brandeis, Louis, 40-1, 44, 54, 174
Branfman, Fred, 272
Brannan Plan, 68
Brazil, Nazi threat to, 243
Brecht, Bertolt, 241
Bresler, Harvey J., 285, 295
Bridges, Harry, 200
Briggs, Walter, 261
Brogam, D. W., 232
Brooks, Peter, 218
Brooks, Tom, 90
Broun, Haywood, 117, 293
Brown, Norman O., 210
Bruce, Lenny, 227
Brustein, Robert, 210, 215, 222, 229-230
Brzezinski, Zbigniew, 244
Buckley, William F., 292
Buenker, John D., 44, 70
Burgess, Anthony, 210
Burgess, Guy, 111, 288
Burnham, James, 293, 295
Burns, James MacGregor, 80, 90, 192
Burroughs, William S., 208
Buttinger, Joseph, 270
Care, Norman S., 80
Carlyle, Thomas, 121
Carmichael, Stokely, 220, 300
Carolene Products decision, 139, 161-2
Carr, E. H., 241
Carter Administration, 88-9, 249, 274
Carter, Pres. Jimmy, 16, 79, 96, 123, 240
Castro, Fidel, 213, 268-9
Chafee, Zechariah, 157
Chamberlain, John, 40, 58, 62, 130, 263
Chamberlain, William Henry, 61, 241, 285, 292-3
Chambers, Whittaker, 294, 296
Chase, Edward, 185
Chase, Stuart, 59
Chavez, Cesar, 142
Chessman, Caryl, 200
Chicago confrontation, 1968, 199, 219-20
Child, Frank C., 270
Chile, 248, 250, 272-3
China, 257, 262, 265-6
Christian, Shirley, 275
Church, Frank, 239
Churchill, Winston, 66, 251
"Civil Liberties," 138-140
Civil Rights, conservative view on, 142
Civil Rights movement, 18-21, 67, 75, 84, 95
Civil War, post-, period, 9, 32-6
Clark, Blair, 107
Clark, Tom, 286
Clarke, Gerald, 90
Class consciousness, 141-2
Classical economics, 6
Classical liberalism, 1, 3, 5-7, 20, 26, 28, 120, 140,

# Index

146-51, 171, 176, 189
Classical liberal legal philosophy, 146-51
Cleaver, Eldridge, 126, 237
Cleghorn, Reese, 215
Cloward, Richard A., 91
Coalescence into ideological consensus, 9-12, 34-6
Coalition, liberal or Democratic, 18, 19, 57-8, 75, 91-6
Coalition, search for a new, 95-6
Coalition, splits in, 91-5
Co-determination, principle of, 167, 177
Cohen, Benjamin, 54
Cohen, Morris, 119, 132
Cohn-Bendit, Daniel and Gabriel, 213
Cole, G. D. H., 67, 169, 177
Collective bargaining, 51
Collins, Thomas P., 194
Columbia University revolt, 218-9, 231
Commager, Henry Steele, 145
Commons, J. R., 170
Communism, liberal attitudes toward, 240-1
Concurrent powers doctrine, 160
Conkin, Paul K., 70
Conservatism, 1, 5
Conservative Congressional coalition, 16, 58
Consumer protection movement, 86
Cook, Bruce, 225
Corcoran, Thomas, 54
Cornell University revolt, 219, 234
Cornforth, Maurice, 176
Corporations, liberalism and, 164-77
Corso, Gregory, 208
Coser, Lewis A., 44, 207
Counter-culture, 39. 46, 197, 203-5, 208-11
Coutts-Smith, Kenneth, 237
Cowley, Malcolm, 39, 46, 53, 64, 125, 128, 199, 205, 207, 237, 265
Crawford, Kenneth, 110
Croly, Herbert, 11-2, 40, 42, 44, 45, 108, 112, 116, 118, 132, 145, 165, 169, 176, 184, 189
Cronin, Morton, 115
Crunden, Robert M., 38
Cuba, 262, 268-9
Curry, Lauchlin, 54
Curtis, Charles, 154
Dadaistic method, 120, 125-6, 227-231
Dam, Hari N., 245, 254
Davis, Jerome, 47, 252
Davis, Wayne, 216
Deakin, James, 90
Dean, Vera Micheles, 61
De Bell, Garrett, 216, 226
Decker, Clarence, 266
DeConcini Reservation re Panama Canal, 248
Dee, Ivan R., 179
Dellinger, David, 200-1, 229-230
De-privatization: see Politicization, 178-95
Dewey, John, 14, 48, 64, 92, 112-3, 120, 131-2, 134, 135-38, 145, 180, 184
Dickstein, Morris, 185
Diem, Ngo Dinh, 270
Dies, Congressman Martin, 282, 285
diPrima, Diane, 208
"Direct action" methods, 20, 140-4, 229-230
"Disengagement," proposal for, 245
Dissimulation, 11, 112-18, 167, 168-9

Dix, Dorothea Lynde, 179
Dolbeare, Kenneth and Patricia, 211
Dominican Republic, 248, 270
"Domino theory," attitudes toward, 250-1, 260-1
Dos Passos, John, 15, 64, 120, 125, 292
Double standards, liberal, 156, 240-2, 249, 291-2
Douglas, Paul H., 52, 174-5
Douglas, William O., 54
Dreiser, Theodore, 119, 123, 128
Duberman, Martin, 185-6
Dunn, Robert, 47
Durand, Walter, 51, 168
Duranty, Walter, 63-4, 96
Dutschke, Rudi, 213, 223
Eastman, Max, 293
Eccles, Marriner, 54, 57
Ecology movement, 87, 216
Educational theory, John Dewey's, 135-38
Eisele, Albert A., 231
Eisenhower Adminstration, 81-2
Ekirch, Jr., Arthur A., 162
Elitism, 42, 124, 188
El Salvador, 275-6
Emerson, Ralph Waldo, 8, 12, 29, 32, 180
"Encounter," 294
Enlightenment, the, 5, 7, 8
Environmentalism, 87
Epstein, Abraham, 49
Ernst, Morris, 140
Ethiopia, 263
Eulau, Heinz H. F., 77, 252
Europe, Western, 264
Evanier, David, 214
Ezorsky, Gertrude, 131
Fabian method, 51, 114
Fads, role of, 235
"Fair Deal," 67-70
"Fair Play for Cuba Committee," 290-1
Fairlie, Henry, 80, 90, 120, 191, 193
Fanon, Frantz, 213
Farley, James, 58
Featherstone, Joseph, 39
Federal Trade Commission Act, 191
Federalism, 189-190
Feiffer, Jules, 219
Fein, Leonard, 276
Feminism, 88, 221
Ferguson, Thomas, 96
Field, Justice Stephen J., 150
Filene, Peter G., 43
Fischer, Louis, 64, 104-5, 297-8, 301
Fish, Congressman Hamilton, 284, 291
Flaubert, Gustave, 126, 228
Flynn, John T., 53, 58, 59, 116, 295
Fonda, Jane, 288
"Footnote Four," 161-2
Forcey, Charles, 83, 99, 132, 145, 194
Ford Administration, 82
"Foreign Affairs" journal, 238
Formosa, 266
Fortas, Abe, 144-5, 158
Fox, Jeff, 85
France, 264
France, Anatole, 104-5
Frank, Jerome, 53, 157, 162, 170, 177

Frank, Waldo, 60, 65, 134
Frankfurter, Felix, 54, 153, 155, 162, 192
Freeman, A. C., 293
Free Speech Movement, 227
Friedenberg, Daniel N., 78, 268-9
Fromm, Erich, 106, 202
Fuller, Harold deWolf, 104
Gabriel, Henry, 44
Galbraith, John Kenneth, 4, 77, 78, 82, 87, 112-3, 168, 176, 182, 296
Gans, Curtis, 79
Garrett, Garet, 68, 78, 251, 255
Garrison, Lloyd, 162
Garrison, Wendell Phillips, 101, 104
Genet, Jean, 209
German Historical School, 9-10, 34-6, 104, 135
German Youth Movement, 206
Geyer, Georgie Anne, 273
Gide, Andre, 60
Gillmor, Daniel, 109, 286
Ginsberg, Allen 208-9
Ginsburg, Benjamin, 115, 184
Girvetz, Harry A., 67
Glasser, Ira, 193
Glazer, Nathan, 84-5, 97, 99-100
Godkin, Edwin Lawrence, 101
Goldberg, Harvey, 117-8
Goldman, Eric, 28, 44, 70, 77, 135, 145, 162, 194
Gompers, Samuel, 92
Good, Robert C., 269
Goodman, Paul, 117-9, 200, 210, 225
Goodwin, Doris Kearns, 88
Goodwyn, Lawrence, 44
Gordon, David, 98, 107
Gould, Lewis L., 44, 72
Graham, David L., 268
Graham, Jr., L. Otis, 44, 222, 226
Great Society, the, 16, 82
Greece, 264-5
Greeley, Andrew, 224
Green, Mark, 89, 99, 176-7
Green, Philip, 212
Green, William, 66
Greene, Graham, 242
Greenstein, Robert, 218, 223
Greenwich Village, 39, 203-4
Grenada, 248, 277-8
Griffin, C. S., 44
Guatemala, 268
Guevara, Che, 218, 246, 268
Guild Socialism, 11-2, 41, 104, 129
Guinea, 269-70
Hale, William Harlan, 46, 204
Haley, Alex, 194
Halle, Louis J., 240
Halperin, Ernst, 245
Hamilton, Richard F., 107
Hamiltonian neo-Mercantilism, 23
Hansen, Alvin, 175
Harlan, John Marshall, 151, 158
Harrington, Michael, 4, 76, 83, 88, 106-7, 113, 117, 199, 219, 232
Harris, Sen. Fred, 96, 175
Harrison, Gilbert A., 89, 110
Hart, Sen. Philip, 175

Hartz, Louis, 5
Harvard Esthetes, 126
Harvard University revolt, 219, 233
Hauser, Philip M., 183
Hayden, Tom, 215, 224, 230, 237
Hayes, Gordon, 56
Hayek, Friedrich, 148, 294
Hazlitt, Henry 295
Hedonism, 234-5
Heilbroner, Robert, 77
Heller, Joseph, 210
Heller, Walter W., 189, 194
Hemingway, Ernest, 46
Henderson, Leon, 54, 57
Hentoff, Nat, 143, 145, 219
Herberg, Will, 294
Hicks, Granville, 65, 292
Higley, Martha, 121
Hill, Joe, 229
Hindus, Maurice, 62-3, 66
Hiss, Alger, 294, 296
Hitler, Adolf, 121
Hitler-Stalin Pact, 15, 64-5
Hoffman, Abbie, 210
Holmes, John Clellon, 208
Holmes, Jr., Oliver Wendell, 150-1, 154-5, 158, 230
Homosexual Rights movement, 86
Hook, Sidney, 77, 282
Hopkins, Harry, 57
Hotham, David, 270-1
Howard, Anthony, 89
Howe, Irving, 4, 77, 199, 202, 207, 225, 235, 237
Hughes, Charles Evans, 154
Hugins, Walter, 44
"Humanistic" Marxism, 202, 212
"Human Rights" campaign, 249
Humphrey, Hubert, 90, 178, 193, 231, 283
Huthmacher, Joseph, 118, 163
Huxley, Julian, 180
Hypocrisy, charge of, 121-2
Ickes, Harold L., 249
Illusions, role of, 242, 276, 278, 289-90
Immaturity of mankind, 26-7
Immigration, 26, 38
"Industrial Democracy," 11, 98, 104, 141, 151, 167
"Industrial Policy," 97
Input-Output analysis, 183
"Instrumentalism," 132
Intellectual culture, liberal, 58-9, 69, 76-7
"Interest-group liberalism," 26, 75
International affairs, liberalism and, 238-255
Iran, 248
Jackson, Sen. Henry, 96, 238, 283
Jacksonian tradition, 28, 191
Jaffe, Adrian, 270
James, William, 131
Jeffersonian tradition, 24, 28, 148
Jencks, Christopher, 4, 77, 114, 219
Jews, as part of coalition, 93-5
Johnson, Gerald W., 269, 290
Johnson, Hugh, 53
Johnson, Lyndon Baines, 83, 90, 123, 242, 271-4
Josephson, Matthew, 65, 115, 241
Judicial activism, 159-1
Judicial restraint, 159-1

## Index

Jugow, A., 65
Jurisprudence, 146-63
Kai-shek, Chiang, 256, 265
Kalb, Barry, 221, 223
Kallen, H. M., 46-7, 204
Karnow, Stanley, 240
Kauffmann, Stanley, 209, 228, 232
Kaus, Robert M., 97
Kaysen, Carl, 78
Kefauver, Estes, 175
Kendall, Willmoore, 294
Kennan, George, 69, 238, 245
Kennedy, Sen. Edward, 91, 175, 181, 190, 193
Kennedy, Pres. John F., 76, 83, 89-90, 245, 258, 269
Kennedy, Stetson, 140
Kent, Frank, 110
Kerouac, Jack, 208
Kent State incident, 227
Kerr, Charles, 222
Kesey, Ken, 210
Kerr-Mills Act of 1960, 189
Keynes, John Maynard, 56, 170
Keynesianism, 56-7, 68, 85
Keyserling, Leon, 58, 82, 84-5
King, Jr., Martin Luther, 95, 142-4, 217, 220, 223
King, Merle, 185
Kinsley, Michael, 96
Kirchwey, Freda, 105-6, 265
Kirk, Russell, 5
Kirkendall, Richard S., 71
Kirkpatrick, Jeane, 99, 247
Kirkup, Thomas, 169-170, 177
Kohler, Heinz, 194
Kondracke, Morton, 87, 97, 175, 275
Konrad, George, 125
Kopkind, Andrew, 84, 200, 214-6, 220, 223
Korea, 266-8
Kravchenko, Victor, 285
Krim, Seymour, 208
Kristol, Irving, 77, 81, 97, 98-9, 113, 117, 194, 294
Krushchev, Nikita, 202
Kulaks, starvation of, 14, 61-3
Kumm, Bjorn, 246
Kunitz, Joshua, 61, 139
Kuttner, Alfred, 119
Kuttner, Bob, 98
Labor movement, American, 91-2, 238
LaFollette, Sr., Robert, 115, 194
Lahey, Edwin A., 89
Lamont, Corliss, 62
Lamont, Hammond, 104
Landis, James, 54
Lange, Victor, 79, 210
Laqueur, Walter, 206-7, 245
Lasch, Christopher, 77, 106, 212, 225
Laski, Harold, 114
Lassalle, Ferdinand, 181
Lattimore, Owen, 253, 267
Lauck, W. Jett, 59
Lazarus, Simon, 220
League for Industrial Democracy, 214
Leary, Timothy, 211
Legal philosophy, 146-163
Lekachman, Robert, 77, 79
Lens, Sidney, 98

Lerner, Max, 41, 65, 105, 113, 151, 185, 295
Levy, Bernard-Henri, 249
Lewis, Sinclair, 122
"Liberal agenda," 82
"Liberal" as a term, 1, 2
Liberal uncertainty and loss of vision, 17-8, 74, 78-81, 88, 192-3
"Liberation," journal, 201, 214
"Liberator, The," journal, 293
Linear programming, 183
Link, Arthur S., 44
Lippmann, Walter, 55, 239, 245, 271, 295
Lloyd, Henry Demarest, 103
Locke, John, 148, 171
Lockwood, Lee, 237
Loeb, Jr., James, 58
London, Jack, 200, 209
Long, Huey, 228
Long, William R., 273
Loss of vision, liberal, 16, 77-80
"Lost Generation," 12, 46, 204
Loury, Glenn C., 98
Lovett, Robert Morss, 65, 141, 285
Lowi, Theodore, 106
Loyalty issue, 296-7
Luce, Phillip Abbott, 212, 217, 225-6, 291, 294, 296
Lumumba, Patrice, 242
Luttwak, E. N., 88
Lynd, Staughton, 185, 199
Lyons, Eugene, 62, 72, 285, 293, 295
Lysenko Affair, 180
MacDonald, Dwight, 199
Machines, big-city political, 92
Mailer, Norman, 210, 219
Majority rule, views about, 124
Malcolm X, 194, 213
Manly, Chesly, 267, 279
Marcuse, Herbert, 138, 213-4, 225, 229, 237
Marquis, Don, 216
Marshall, Gen. George, 266, 285
Marshall, Robert, 173
Martin, James J., 243
Marx, Karl, 164, 176
Marx, Paul, 84, 232
Marxism, 10, 186, 218
Marxism, academic, 75, 186
"Marxist Quarterly, The," 293
Mason, Alpheus Thomas, 162
"Masses, The," 293
Matthews, Herbert, 268
Matthews, J. B., 286, 292
May, Dean L., 70
May, Henry, 127, 298
Mayberry, George, 78
Mayers, Lewis, 153-4
McCarthy, Charles, 44
McCarthy, Sen. Joseph R., 287-9, 293
McCormick, Richard L., 44
McCullers, Carson, 123
McGovern, Sen. George, 96, 175
McWilliams, Carey, 106
Means, Gardiner, 53, 168, 177
Media, the, 94
Mexico, 248
Meyer, Frank, 293

Middle-class ethic, views about, 119-23, 125-7
Middle-class intellectual failure, 21-2, 75, 121
"Middle way," 4
Midgley, John, 111
Miles, Michael, 206, 217, 223
Mill, John Stuart, 7
Miller, Arthur, 290
Miller, Henry, 205
Miller, Justice Samuel F., 150
Mills, C. Wright, 181, 185, 200, 202, 211-3
Minh, Ho Chi, 262, 271-2
Minh, Ho Thong, 270
Minorities, 93
Mises, Ludwig von, 207
Mississippi Freedom Democrats, 215
Mitchell, Broadus, 174
Mitchell, Jonathan, 49, 54, 110
Moley, Raymond, 53
Mondale, Sen. Walter, 181
Mooney-Billings case, 46
Moral equivalency, concept of, 247-8
More, Paul Elmer, 104
Morganthau, Hans J., 80, 244
Morganthau, Jr., Henry F., 56
Morris, David, 268
Moutoux, John T., 49
Moynihan, Daniel Patrick, 85, 97, 182
Muckraker period, 39-40, 103, 157
Mugabe, Robert, 274
Muggeridge, Malcolm, 63
Multiculturalism, 22-3, 299-301
Mumford, Lewis, 55, 117, 134
Munitions industry, investigation of, 292
Murray, Sen. James, 175
Myrdal, Gunnar, 4, 76, 84
"Nation, The," 60, 66, 98, 101-7
National Recovery Administration (NRA), 51-2
"National Review" magazine, 292-4
Nationalization of industry, 173-4
Natural Rights theory, 6
Navasky, Victor, 107
Neo-conservatism, 18, 75, 97, 144
Neo-liberalism, 75, 99-8
Neutralism, attitudes toward, 244-6
"New Class" analyses, 172
New coalition, calls for a, 18, 95-6
New Deal, 13, 48-59
New Deal coalition, 58
New Deal, phases of, 55
New Freedom, 40-1, 54-5, 174-6
"New International, The," 293
New Left, 17, 75, 87, 185-7, 196-237
New Left, collapse of, 221-4
New Left, liberalism's relationship to, 231-3
"New Left Reader," 213
"New Masses, The," 285
New Nationalism, 13, 40-1, 52-4, 164-68
New Politics Convention (1967), 217
"New Politics," 95
"New Populism," 96
"New Republic" magazine, 42, 58-9, 65, 98, 107-11, 232-3, 244, 245, 247-8, 252, 263-6, 268-71, 274-5, 278, 284, 290-2
"New York Compass," 267
Newfield, Jack, 207, 225

Newton, Huey, 213
Nicaragua, 262, 274-5
Niebuhr, Reinhold, 82, 295
Ninth Amendment, 149
Nixon, Pres. Richard, 160
Nixon Administration, 82
"Non-intervention," principle of, 247-9
Non-socialist factors influencing liberalism, 3
Non-socialist factors reenforcing liberalism, 23-7
"Non-violence," see "Direct action"
Norris, Sen. George, 49
North, Oliver, 275
North, Robert C., 262, 266
Nossiter, Bernard D., 175
Novack, George E., 185
Occupational Safety and Health Act (OSHA), 182
Oglesby, Carl, 207
O'Neill, William L., 268, 279
"Openness in government" issue, 87
Oppenheimer, Harry, 276
Ortega y Gasset, Jose, 133, 231
Orton, William, 114, 189
Oser, Jacob, 194
Overview, interpretive, 1-27
Oxford Oath, 200
Page, Joseph A., 273
Palmer, David Richard, 280
Panama Canal treaty, 248
"Partisan Review, the," 293
Patten, Simon, 83
Patton, James G., 84
Paull, Mary, 77
"Peace" movement, 200, 242-3
"Peasant pressure," 24
Peirce, Charles, 131
Pennock, J. Roland, 99
Peretz, Martin, 110
Phillips, Thomas R., 265
Pinchot, Amos, 118, 295
Piven, Frances Fox, 91
"Planning," concept of, 59, 190-1
Plumb Plan, 173
"Pluralistic Communism," attitudes toward, 244-5
Podhoretz, Norman, 97, 294
Politicians, liberal animus toward their own, 3, 69, 83, 88-1, 107
Politicization, 178-95
Pop-liberalism, 94
Populism, 36-7
Port Huron Statement, 214
Porter, Gareth, 272
Poverty, 24-5
Pragmatism, 55, 130-5
Presidency, 192
Pressman, Lee, 296
Progressive Citizens of America (PCA), 260
Progressive Labor Party, 296
Progressivism, 37-43
Prohme, William, 265
"Psychedelic Review, the," 214
Psychology of the intellectual, 45
Public works, 51
Purges, Stalin's, 63-4
Quinn, T. K., 167-8
Rader, Dotson, 218-9

# Index

Radosh, Ronald, 275
"Ramparts" journal, 233
Rand, Ayn, 247
Raskin, Marcus, 233
Rauch, Basil, 55
Rauschenbusch, Walter, 38
Rawls, John, 4, 77
Reagan Administration, 275
"Realist" journal, 211, 214
Reapportionment, 159
"Red Decade," the, 60-6
Reform Darwinism, 135
Regulatory agencies, attitudes toward, 80-1
Reich, Charles, 210, 225
Relativism, 34-5, 130-5, 257-8
Religion, role of, 30, 38
Revolution, liberalism and a world in, 256-80
Rexroth, Kenneth, 208
Rhodesia, 274
Richberg, Donald, 53, 55
Ridgeway, James, 95, 215, 217, 219
Riesman, David, 115
Ripley, William Z., 50
Robertson, Ian, 249
Robinson, William I., 284
Rogers, Joel, 96
Romanticism, 7, 30-1, 186, 203
Roosevelt, Eleanor, 159
Roosevelt, Pres. Franklin D., 13, 159, 175, 252
Roosevelt, Theodore, 40, 102, 115, 192
Ross, Leonard, 96
Rostov, Eugene V., 245
Rostow, W. W., 253, 255
Roszak, Theodore, 106, 194, 203-4, 207, 210
Rovere, Richard, 293
Rubin, Jerry, 120, 128, 194, 226, 237
Rudd, Mark, 202, 213, 218
Ruskin, John, 203
Russia, 263
Sacco-Vanzetti case, 46-7, 290
San Francisco radicalism, 200
Sanford, David, 227
Sartre, Jean Paul, 209
Savary, Louis M., 194
Savio, Mario, 221
Scammon, Richard E., 96
Schiller, F. C. S., 131
Schlamm, William S., 294-5
Schlesinger, Jr., Arthur M., 45, 55, 70, 118, 158, 162, 198, 298
Schuman, Frederick L., 65, 211, 285
Scopes trial, 123
Securities regulation, 49-50
Seiler, Conrad, 284
Seligman, Ben, 67
Semas, Phil, 224
Sentimentality, role of, 30
Shapiro, Samuel, 261, 269
Shaw, George Bernard, 122
Sheean, Vincent, 62, 65, 199
Sheed, Wilfrid, 90
Sherman, Alfred, 245
Sherman, George, 262
Shuman, Howard, 175
Siegfried, Andre, 122

Silver, Kalman, 79
Simpson, Herman, 61
Sit-down strike, the, 141
Skinner, B. F., 126, 180
Smedley, Agnes, 265
Smith, Al, 57, 295
Smith, Bernard, 113
Smith, Ian, 274
Smith, J. Allen, 156
Snow, Edgar, 265-6
Snyder, Gary, 208-9
Social change, emphasis of, 129-45
Social democracy, 2, 74, 78, 258
Social Gospel, 38, 292
"Social responsibility of business," 87, 167-8
Social science, 10, 183-7
Social Security Act, 50
Socialism, relationship of liberalism to, 2-5, 76-7
Socialist International, the, 174
Solid South, 91
Solomon, Stephen, 231
Solzhenitsyn, Aleksandr I., 251-2, 255, 287
Sombart, Werner, 10, 17
Soule, George, 46, 56, 59, 184, 205, 222, 295
South Africa, 249, 262-3, 276-7
South Korea, 266-8
Soviet Russia, infatuation with, 47, 60-6
"Soviet Russia Pictorial," 293
Spanish Civil War, 15, 263-4
Spencer, Herbert, 80
Statistics, discipline of, 182, 187
Stearns, Harold, 119, 128, 290
Steffens, Lincoln, 117
Stegner, Wallace, 228
Stein, Gertrude, 45-6
Stein, Leo, 203
Steinem, Gloria, 138, 145
Sterne, Richard Clark, 105, 111
Sternsher, Bernard, 70
Stevenson, Adlai, 89, 283
Stewart, Maxwell, 61, 65
Stolberg, Benjamin, 187
Stone, Harlan Fiske, 155, 158, 161
Stone, I. F., 65
Straight, Michael, 67, 69, 89, 108-111, 244, 288, 297
Straight, Willard and Dorothy, 110
Strong, Anna Louise, 61, 66, 105, 139
Strout, Richard, 110
Student Non-Violent Coordinating Committee (SNCC), 215
Students for a Democratic Society (SDS), 201, 215, 217-8, 223-4
"Studies on the Left," journal, 212, 214
Sumner, William Graham, 130
Swope, Gerard, 52
Szelenyi, Ivan, 125
Taber, Robert, 269
Taft, Sen. Robert A., 253, 255, 267, 279
Taney, C.J. Roger Brooke, 149
Tawney, R. H., 166
Taylor, Milton C., 270
Taxation, policy toward, 192
Teapot Dome scandal, investigation into, 291
Tennessee Valley Authority (TVA), 48-9
Thayer, H. S., 131

Theobald, Robert, 237
Thomas, Norman, 13
Thoreau, Henry David, 32, 119, 127, 230
Thornbury, Ethel, 284
Thurber, James, 65
Thurow, Lester, 175
Tiedeman, Christopher G., 150
Tolstoy, Nikolai, 251
Tonelson, Alan, 79
Trade cycle, 26
"T.R.B.," 48, 49, 52-4, 56-7, 68, 69, 78, 80, 82-3, 89-90, 92, 108, 112, 119-4, 153, 167, 173, 191, 193, 240, 244, 247-8, 257, 259, 266, 270, 272, 289-291, 296
Trotsky, Leon, 15, 264, 293
Truman Administration, 266, 286
Truman Doctrine, 71, 265
Truman, Pres. Harry S., 49, 66, 173
Tsongas, Sen. Paul, 97
Tucker, Robert W., 275
Tugwell, Rexford, 49, 53, 59, 152, 162, 255
Tyler, Alice Felt, 29, 44
Tyler, Gus, 180
Ulam, Adam B., 63
Ulmer, Melville J., 51, 82, 168
Unemployment insurance, 50
United Front, 58
Unseem, Michael, 221, 226
Utley, Freda, 267, 279, 293
Utopian absolutes, 144, 181-2
Utopian socialist communities, 32, 204
Valley authorities, 48-49, 66-8
Veblen, Thorstein, 112-3, 170
"Venture," SDS journal, 214
Victimology, concept of, 181
Vietnam, South, 257-8
"Vietnam Summer" project, 217
Vietnam War, 239, 259, 270-2
Vietnam War, opposition to, 234
Villard, Oswald Garrison, 60, 104-5
Viorst, Milton, 274
Vivas, Eliseo, 293
Vlasov, General, 252
Voting Rights Act of 1965, 91, 224
Wagner, Sen. Robert, 114
Wallace, Henry, 15, 58, 66, 68-9, 106, 108, 173, 199, 264, 286
War on Poverty, 76, 84, 232
War, role of, 25-6
Ward, Lester, 34, 170, 173, 177, 193
Warner, Denis, 245, 270
Warren Court, 140, 158-160
Warren, C.J. Earl, 158
Warren II, Frank A., 63, 72
Watts, Jr., Richard, 265, 295
Weaver, Richard, 295
Weber, Max, 183
Wechsler, James A., 69, 73, 99
Wedemeyer, Gen. Albert C., 267
Welfare State, 67-8
Werner, M. R., 60
Werth, Alexander, 106
West, Rebecca, 188
Weyl, Walter, 83, 132
White, Morton, 136, 145
White, Theodore H., 82, 91, 99-100

Whitemore, Reed, 186, 223
Whitten, Phillip, 249
Wieck, Paul R., 95
Williams, Albert Rhys, 47
Williams, Tennessee, 123
Williams, William Appleman, 117
Williams, William Carlos, 208
Wilson, Edmund, 59-60, 64, 117, 126, 209, 228, 296, 298
Wilson, Pres. Woodrow, 41, 174
Winocur, Jack, 109
"Wisconsin Idea," 35
Wittner, Lawrence S., 206
Wobblies, the, 228
Worker control, 41, 176
World War II, political aftermath of, 251-3
World War II, strategy during, 66, 70
Wulff, Erich, 270
Yablonsky, Lewis, 188
Yardstick firms, 51, 168
Yates decision, 140
Young, Kimball, 180
Zinn, Howard, 72, 145, 194
Zolo, Daniel, 218
Zurcher, Jr., Louis A., 72, 193